SpringBoard®
English
Language Arts

STUDENT EDITION   ENGLISH II

About The College Board

The College Board is a mission-driven not-for-profit organization that connects students to college success and opportunity. Founded in 1900, the College Board was created to expand access to higher education. Today, the membership association is made up of over 6,000 of the world's leading educational institutions and is dedicated to promoting excellence and equity in education. Each year, the College Board helps more than seven million students prepare for a successful transition to college through programs and services in college readiness and college success—including the SAT® and the Advanced Placement Program®. The organization also serves the education community through research and advocacy on behalf of students, educators, and schools. For further information, visit collegeboard.org.

ISBN: 978-1-4573-1296-0

1 2 3 4 5 6 7 8   20 21 22 23 24 25 26

Printed in the United States of America

Acknowledgements

The College Board gratefully acknowledges the outstanding work of the classroom teachers who have been integral to the development of this program. The end product is testimony to their expertise, understanding of student learning needs, and dedication to rigorous and accessible English Language Arts instruction.

Lance Balla
Everett School District
Everett, Washington

Carisa Barnes
San Diego Unified School
District
San Diego, California

Leia Bell
Hillsborough County Public
Schools
Tampa, Florida

Alysa Broussard
Lafayette Parish School
System
Lafayette, Louisiana

Robert J. Caughey
San Dieguito Union High
School District
San Diego, California

Susie Challancin
Bellevue School District 405
Bellevue, Washington

Doug Cole
Cherry Creek School District
Greenwood Village, Colorado

Cari Davis
Rio Rancho Public School
District
Rio Rancho, New Mexico

Paul De Maret
Poudre School District
Fort Collins, Colorado

Sylvia Ellison
Hillsborough County Public
Schools
Hillsborough, Florida

Karen Fullam
Hillsborough County Public
Schools
Tampa, Florida

Michael Gragert
Plano Independent School
District
Plano, Texas

Nancy Gray
Brevard County Schools
Viera, Florida

Charise Hallberg
Bellevue School District 405
Bellevue, Washington

T.J. Hanify
Bellevue School District 405
Bellevue, Washington

Jessi Hupper
Peninsula School District
Gig Harbor, Washington

Nimat Jones
ICEF Public Schools, Los
Angeles, California

Karen Kampschmidt
Fort Thomas Independent
School District
Fort Thomas, Kentucky

Karen Kennedy
Peninsula School District
Peninsula, Washington

LeAnn Klepzig
Bradley County Schools
Cleveland, Tennessee

Susie Lowry
Volusia County School
District
Deland, Florida

Michelle Lewis
Spokane Public School
Spokane, Washington

John Marshall
Mead School District
Mead, Washington

Cassandra Mattison
Hillsborough County Public
Schools
Tampa, Florida

Glenn Morgan
San Diego Unified School
District
San Diego, California

John Murray
Garland Independent School
District
Sachse, Texas

Kristen J. Ohaver
Charlotte-Mecklenburg
Schools
Charlotte, North Carolina

Amanda Olinger
Harrisburg School District
Harrisburg, South Dakota

Julie Pennabaker
Quakertown Community
School District
Quakertown, Pennsylvania

Bryan Sandala
School District of Palm Beach
County
West Palm Beach, Florida

Angela Seiler
Rio Rancho Public School
District
Rio Rancho, New Mexico

Amanda Shackelford
Lafayette Parish School
System
Lafayette, Louisiana

Kimberlyn Slagle
Lafayette Parish School
System
Lafayette, Louisiana

Sarah Smith Arceneaux
Lafayette Parish School
System
Lafayette, Louisiana

Holly Talley
Hillsborough County Public
Schools
Ruskin, Florida

Derek Thomas
Hillsborough County Public
Schools
Tampa, Florida

Maria Torres-Crosby
Hillsborough County Public
Schools
Tampa, Florida

Susan Van Doren
South Lake Tahoe, California

JoEllen Victoreen
San José Unified School
District
San José, California

Rebecca Wenrich
Peninsula School District
Gig Harbor, Washington

Research and Planning Advisors

We also wish to thank the members of our SpringBoard Advisory Council and the many educators who gave generously of their time and their ideas as we conducted research for both the print and online programs. Your suggestions and reactions to ideas helped immeasurably as we created this edition. We gratefully acknowledge the teachers and administrators in the following districts.

ABC Unified School District
Cerritos, California

Allen Independent School District
Allen, Texas

Bellevue, School District 405
Bellevue, Washington

Burnet Consolidated Independent School District
Burnet, Texas

Community Unit School District 308
Oswego, Illinois

Fresno Unified School District
Fresno, California

Frisco Independent School District
Frisco, Texas

Garland Independent School District
Garland, Texas

Grapevine-Colleyville Independent School District
Grapevine, Texas

Hamilton County Schools
Chattanooga, Tennessee

Hesperia Unified School District
Hesperia, California

Hillsborough County Public Schools
Tampa, Florida

ICEF Public Schools
Los Angeles, California

IDEA Public Schools
Weslaco, Texas

Irving Independent School District
Irving, Texas

Keller Independent School District
Keller, Texas

KIPP Houston
Houston, Texas

Lafayette Parish Schools
Lafayette Parish, Louisiana

Los Angeles Unified School District
Los Angeles, California

Lubbock Independent School District
Lubbock, Texas

Mansfield Independent School District
Mansfield, Texas

Midland Independent School District
Midland, Texas

Milwaukee Public Schools
Milwaukee, Wisconsin

New Haven School District
New Haven, Connecticut

Ogden School District
Ogden, Utah

Rio Rancho Public Schools
Rio Rancho, New Mexico

San José Unified School District
San José, California

Scottsdale Unified School District
Scottsdale, Arizona

Spokane Public Schools
Spokane, Washington

Tacoma Public Schools
Tacoma, Washington

SpringBoard English Language Arts

Lori O'Dea
Executive Director
Content Development

Natasha Vasavada
Executive Director
Pre-AP & SpringBoard

Doug Waugh
VP, SpringBoard &
Pre-AP Programs

Sarah Balistreri
Senior Director
ELA Content Development

Florencia Duran Wald
Senior Director
ELA Content Development

Julie Manley
Senior Director
Professional Learning

Joely Negedly
Senior Director
Pre-AP Humanities

Jessica Brockman
Product Manager
English Language Arts

Suzie Doss
Director
SpringBoard Implementation

Jennifer Duva
Director
English Language Arts

Spencer Gonçalves
Director
Digital Content Development

Rebecca Grudzina
Senior Editor
English Language Arts

Georgia Scurletis
Senior Instructional Writer
Pre-AP English Language Arts

Abigail Johnson
Editor
English Language Arts

Casseia Lewis
Assistant Editor
English Language Arts

Natalie Hansford
Editorial Assistant
English Language Arts

Table of Contents

CONTENTS

ACTIVITY Unit 3: Voice in Synthesis

CONTENTS

Resources

Texts not included in these materials.

Introduction to SpringBoard English Language Arts

About SpringBoard ELA

SpringBoard was built around a simple belief: if you give students and teachers the best materials, engaging methods, and ongoing support, then student success will surely follow. Developed by teachers, SpringBoard brings your classroom to life with materials that help you practice the skills and learn the knowledge you need to excel in high school and beyond. Read on to find out how SpringBoard will support your learning.

Instructional Materials

SpringBoard English Language Arts supplies a Student Edition and Teacher Edition, in print and digital form, for grades 6–12. In addition to using the English Language Arts curriculum, you can sharpen your reading, writing, and language skills with materials including Language Workshop, Close Reading Workshop, and Writing Workshop.

Design that Begins with the End in Mind

- Based on the Understanding by Design model, SpringBoard teaches the skills and knowledge that matter most to meet AP and college and career readiness standards.

- You will start each unit by unpacking the assessment so that you know where you're heading and why the skills you're developing matter.

- Each activity starts with clear, standards-aligned learning targets.

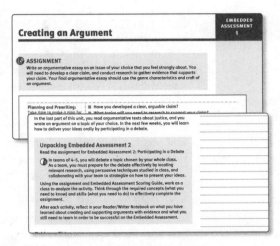

Creating an Argument

EMBEDDED ASSESSMENT 1

ASSIGNMENT

Write an argumentative essay on an issue of your choice that you feel strongly about. You will need to develop a clear claim, and conduct research to gather evidence that supports your claim. Your final argumentative essay should use the genre characteristics and craft of an argument.

Planning and Prewriting: ▪ Have you developed a clear, arguable claim?
Take time to make a plan for   ▪ What topics will you need to research to support your claim?

In the last part of this unit, you read argumentative texts about justice, and you wrote an argument on a topic of your choice. In the next few weeks, you will learn how to deliver your ideas orally by participating in a debate.

Unpacking Embedded Assessment 2

Read the assignment for Embedded Assessment 2: Participating in a Debate.

In teams of 4–5, you will prepare for the debate effectively by locating relevant research, using persuasive techniques studied in class, and collaborating with your team to strategize on how to present your ideas.

Using the assignment and Embedded Assessment Scoring Guide, work as a class to analyze the activity. Think through the required concepts (what you need to know) and skills (what you need to do) to effectively complete the assignment.

After each activity, reflect in your Reader/Writer Notebook on what you have learned about creating and supporting arguments with evidence and what you still need to learn in order to be successful on the Embedded Assessment.

U N I T 4

VISUAL PROMPT
Examine Kehinde Wiley's painting, *Princess Victoire of Saxe-Coburg-Gotha*. What emotions do you feel as you look at the figure in this painting? What details in the painting make you feel this way?

PRAISE, MOCK, MOURN

O ray of sunlight,
most beautiful that ever shone
on Thebes, city of the seven gates,
you've appeared at last . . . .

–from *Antigone*, by Sophocles

A Living System of Learning

- SpringBoard puts you and your classmates in charge of your learning to create a more dynamic classroom experience.

- With a flexible design and rich library of tools and resources, SpringBoard helps your teacher personalize instruction for your class.

The Practice of Reading Closely

- SpringBoard puts a special focus on close reading, giving you strategies and structure for developing this key skill.

- You will encounter compelling texts—fiction, nonfiction, poetry, drama, visuals, and film.

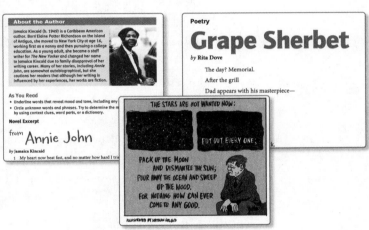

About the Author

Jamaica Kincaid (b. 1949) is a Caribbean American author. Born Elaine Potter Richardson on the island of Antigua, she moved to New York City at age 16, working first as a nanny and then pursuing a college education. As a young adult, she became a staff writer for *The New Yorker* and changed her name to Jamaica Kincaid due to family disapproval of her writing career. Many of her stories, including *Annie John*, are somewhat autobiographical, but she cautions her readers that although her writing is influenced by her experiences, her works is fiction.

As You Read

- Underline words that reveal mood and tone, including any
- Circle unknown words and phrases. Try to determine the m by using context clues, word parts, or a dictionary.

Novel Excerpt

from **Annie John**

by Jamaica Kincaid

1   My heart now beat fast, and no matter how hard I trie

Poetry

Grape Sherbet

by **Rita Dove**

The day? Memorial.

After the grill

Dad appears with his masterpiece—

THE STARS ARE NOT WANTED NOW;

PUT OUT EVERY ONE;

PACK UP THE MOON
AND DISMANTLE THE SUN;
POUR AWAY THE OCEAN AND SWEEP
UP THE WOOD,
FOR NOTHING NOW CAN EVER
COME TO ANY GOOD.

ILLUSTRATED BY NATHAN GELGUD

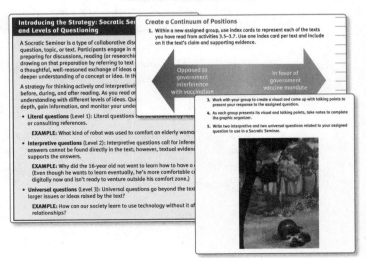

Introducing the Strategy: Socratic Sem... and Levels of Questioning

A Socratic Seminar is a type of collaborative disc... question, topic, or text. Participants engage in m... preparing for discussions, reading (or researchin... drawing on that preparation by referring to text ... a thoughtful, well-reasoned exchange of ideas a... deeper understanding of a concept or idea. In th...

A strategy for thinking actively and interpretively... before, during, and after reading. As you read an... understanding with different levels of ideas. Ques... depth, gain information, and monitor your underst...

- **Literal questions** (Level 1): Literal questions can be answered by refer... or consulting references.

  EXAMPLE: What kind of robot was used to comfort an elderly woma...

- **Interpretive questions** (Level 2): Interpretive questions call for inferen... answers cannot be found directly in the text; however, textual eviden... supports the answers.

  EXAMPLE: Why did the 16-year old not want to learn how to have a ... (Even though he wants to learn eventually, he's more comfortable c... digitally now and isn't ready to venture outside his comfort zone.)

- **Universal questions** (Level 3): Universal questions go beyond the text... larger issues or ideas raised by the text?

  EXAMPLE: How can our society learn to use technology without it af... relationships?

Create a Continuum of Positions

1. Within a new assigned group, use index cards to represent each of the texts you have read from activities 3.5–3.7. Use one index card per text and include on it the text's claim and supporting evidence.

Opposed to government interference with vaccination ⟷ In favor of government vaccine mandate

3. Work with your group to create a visual and come up with talking points to present your response to the assigned question.

4. As each group presents its visual and talking points, take notes to complete the graphic organizer.

5. Write two interpretive and two universal question related to your assigned question to use in a Socratic Seminar.

Bringing the Classroom to Life

When you enter a SpringBoard classroom you don't hear a teacher talking in the front of the room. You hear a buzz of excitement, with students working together and taking charge of how they learn. That's what the teachers who designed SpringBoard wanted for their classrooms, so they created a curriculum and materials that are focused on real classroom needs, encouraging teacher and student involvement.

SpringBoard translates the expectations of state standards into engaging daily lessons. We believe that reading, writing, speaking, and listening should all be learned together. You'll see examples of our integrated approach throughout our materials. And we put a special focus on close reading, giving you strategies and structure for developing this key skill.

Our Approach to Reading

In SpringBoard ELA, we move right into compelling texts—fiction, nonfiction, poetry, drama, visuals, and film—and offer the tools, supports, and approaches that will help you get the most out of every reading.

The Practice of Reading Closely

Texts take center stage in the SpringBoard ELA classroom, where you will prepare for close, critical reading of a wide range of materials. With guidance from your teacher, you will develop the habits of close reading that will serve you for a lifetime.

- **As You Read:** You prepare to read and annotate the text for notable elements like genre characteristics, important use of words, and text structures.

- **First Reading:** You read on your own, with a partner, in a group, or with the class. You annotate the text as you begin to uncover its meaning.

- **Making Observations:** Your teacher guides you to pause during or right after the first reading to observe the small details within a text in order to arrive at a deeper understanding of the whole.

- **Returning to the Text:** You continue to deepen your understanding of the text by responding to a series of text-dependent questions. You will use text evidence, speak with new vocabulary words, reflect on your classmates' ideas, and make connections among texts, ideas, and experiences.

- **Working from the Text:** You use the text as a source as you move from reading and analysis to productive work, including academic discussion and writing.

Reading Independently

As a SpringBoard student, you'll practice good reading habits in class so that you can read challenging texts in other classes and on your own. Independent reading is an integral part of every SpringBoard English Language Arts unit. At the beginning of the year, you will learn how to make a plan for independent reading. **Independent Reading Lists** for each unit give you a jump-start on selecting texts by offering a list of suggested titles, including a number of Spanish-language titles, that connect to the themes, genres, and concepts of the SpringBoard unit.

While you work your way through each unit, you will respond to **Independent Reading Links** that lead you to make connections between the reading you're doing on your own and the skills and knowledge you're developing in class. Twice per unit, **Independent Reading Checkpoints** give you a chance to reflect on and synthesize your independent reading in an informal writing assignment or discussion.

Reading to Build Knowledge

SpringBoard units are designed so that you can delve deeply into an overarching topic, theme, or idea. Each unit will pose essential questions that relate to the ideas and texts within the unit, and you will return to these questions again and again, each time refining your responses with new understanding and new evidence to support your point of view. You will also deepen your knowledge of key topics by conducting both on-the-spot and extended research, asking and answering questions, evaluating multiple sources, and synthesizing your findings.

Twice a unit, you will go on a **Knowledge Quest**. Each Knowledge Quest begins with a Knowledge Question and supporting questions to focus your reading. After reading several texts that explore a topic, theme, or idea, you will get to return to the Knowledge Question and show your growing understanding of the topic by responding to a writing prompt or engaging in a discussion.

At the end of a Knowledge Quest, you will be encouraged to continue building your knowledge of the topic by going to **Zinc Reading Labs** and finding related texts to read. Zinc Reading Labs offers a variety of informational and literary texts that you can choose based on your interests. Vocabulary sets for each text let you learn new words and practice using them.

Your independent reading can also enhance your understanding of the topics you are studying in class if you want it to. SpringBoard's **Independent Reading Lists** include suggested books that relate to the topics and themes from each unit. By choosing those books you can see a different side of the topic, learn new words, and find other topics you want to learn more about.

Reading to Gain Perspectives

Gaining Perspectives features use a text as a jumping off point for examining an issue relevant to you. You will be asked to consider the perspectives of others and to empathize with others who have different points of view. You will also be asked to think about social and ethical norms and to recognize the family, school, and community resources available to you. Each Gaining Perspectives feature concludes with a writing task in which you will summarize the discussion you have with your classmates.

Our Approach to Writing

SpringBoard English Language Arts provides you with the support you need to write in all the major modes, emphasizing argumentative, informational, and narrative. You will write often, and you will learn to become a critical reviewer of your own and your peers' work through frequent opportunities for revision and editing. You will learn to plan with purpose, audience, topic, and context in mind; develop drafts with engaging ideas, examples, facts and commentary; revise for clarity, development, organization, style, and diction; and edit using the conventions of the English language.

The Craft of Writing

As you read texts by skilled authors, you will observe the many choices those authors make. You'll tune in to the ways authors purposefully use words, sentences, and structures to convey meaning. After analyzing and critiquing others' work, you will learn to apply your understanding of author's craft to your own writing. A few SpringBoard features help you do just that:

- **Writing prompts** lead up to the Embedded Assessments and give you practice with writing texts in multiple genres, including personal narratives, argumentative essays, letters, research papers, and more. Writing to Sources writing prompts drive you back to texts you have read or viewed to mine for evidence.

- **Focus on the Sentence** tasks help you process content while also practicing the craft of writing powerful sentences.

- **Grammar & Usage** features highlight interesting grammar or usage concepts that appear in a text, both to improve your reading comprehension and to help you attend to these concepts as you craft your own texts.

- **Language & Writer's Craft** features address topics in writing such as style, word choice, and sentence construction.

- **Language Checkpoints** offer in-depth practice with standard English conventions and guide you to develop an editor's checklist to use as a reference each time you check your own or a peer's written work.

Modes of Writing

SpringBoard helps you become a better academic writer by giving you authentic prompts that require you to use sources, and showing you how to work through the writing process. Over the course of the year you will have the chance to write narratives, arguments, and informational texts, and you will develop a wide range of writing skills:

- Consider task, audience, and purpose when structuring and organizing your writing.

- Incorporate details, reasons, and textual evidence to support your ideas.

- Generate research questions, evaluate sources, gather relevant evidence, and report and cite your findings accurately.

- Use research-based strategies that will guide you through the writing process.

Writing with a Focus on the Sentence

SpringBoard English Language Arts leverages sentence writing strategies that were developed by The Writing Revolution. These evidence-based strategies are part of the Hochman Method, the Writing Revolution's system for helping students learn to write across all content areas and grades. The Writing Revolution emphasizes the importance of embedding writing and grammar instruction into content. That's why SpringBoard's Focus on the Sentence tasks integrate sentence-level writing into the curriculum. These tasks not only help you learn and practice important grammar concepts and sentence forms, but they also provide a chance for you to process and demonstrate your understanding of texts, images, class discussions, and other content.

Our Approach to Vocabulary

Vocabulary is threaded throughout each unit and developed over the course of the SpringBoard English Language Arts year. You will have ample opportunities to read and hear new words, explore their meanings, origins, and connotations, and use them in written and oral responses.

- Important academic and literary terms that you will need to actively participate in classroom discussions are called out in your book.
- Challenging vocabulary terms found in reading passages are glossed at the point of use.
- Periodic Word Connections boxes guide you through the process of exploring a word with multiple meanings and nuances, an interesting etymology, a telling root or affix, a helpful Spanish cognate, a relationship to another word, or a connection to another content area.

Zinc Reading Labs

Zinc Reading Labs combines the best features of a typical vocabulary program with those of a typical reading program and makes reading and learning new words a game. Zinc offers a variety of nonfiction and fiction texts that you can choose from based on individual needs and interest. Each article has a corresponding vocabulary set that pre-teaches challenging words through spaced repetition to help you genuinely learn and internalize the vocabulary. Additional vocabulary games focus on SAT/ACT power words and foundational words for English language learners.

Pre-AP Connections

SpringBoard shares Pre-AP's core principles and encourages you to build skills that you will use in high school and beyond. These principles are evident in every SpringBoard activity.

Close Observation and Analysis
... to notice and consider

When reading, your teacher will guide you to pause to make observations and notice details in the text before analyzing or explaining. Only after you have noticed and enjoyed elements of the text do you then return to the text for deeper analysis and inferential thinking. This close reading sequence helps you interact and engage with the text in increasingly meaningful ways.

Evidence-Based Writing
... with a focus on the sentence

SpringBoard offers varied and frequent writing opportunities, with specific attention to developing complex and precise sentences as the building block to sophisticated paragraph and essay length writing. Instead of being isolated from reading, sentence-level grammar and writing exercises are integrated into the curriculum to enhance your comprehension and your ability to compose a variety of texts.

Higher-Order Questioning
... to spark productive lingering

Each unit opens with two essential questions that relate to the topics, themes, and texts within that unit. You return to these questions throughout the unit and refine your answers as new evidence is presented. SpringBoard also encourages you to craft your own questions and to dig deeply into the texts you read. After each reading passage, you evaluate the meaning of the text and examine the choices that the author made when writing it.

Academic Conversations
... to support peer-to-peer dialogue

SpringBoard classrooms are places where students like you engage in collaborative learning. You will participate in discussion groups, writing groups, debates, Socratic seminars, literature circles, and oral interpretations and performances. These activities create an environment where you can share, compare, critique, debate, and build on others' ideas to advance your learning.

PSAT/SAT Connections

We want you to be rewarded for the hard work you do in your English Language Arts courses, including when you sit down to take important assessments. Therefore, SpringBoard English Language Arts focuses on the same essential knowledge and skills that are the center of the Evidence-Based Reading and Writing sections of the SAT Suite of Assessments (SAT, PSAT/NMSQT, PSAT™ 10, and PSAT™ 8/9). To make our alignment transparent, we conducted a research study, the results of which showed strong to exemplary alignment between the SpringBoard ELA courses and the corresponding SAT Suite tests. This means that you are getting ready for the SAT, PSAT/NMSQT, PSAT™ 10, and PSAT™ 8/9 in the classroom every day.

Tools and Supports

SpringBoard Digital

SpringBoard puts you in charge of what you learn and gives students and teachers the flexibility and support they need. SpringBoard Digital is an interactive program that provides always-available online content that's accessible from any device—desktop computer, laptop, tablet, or interactive whiteboard. The student edition allows you to interact with the text, respond to prompts, take assessments, and engage with a suite of tools, all in the digital space. Teachers get access to a correlations viewer that embeds correlations at point of use, a lesson planner, progress reports, grading, messaging, and more.

Zinc Reading Labs

All SpringBoard users have access to Zinc Reading Labs, where you can find a huge library of reading material chosen specifically to align with the SpringBoard English Language Arts curriculum.

Zinc offers:

- Fresh and engaging nonfiction and fiction content for independent reading.
- Interactive games, quizzes, and tasks that build skills and confidence.
- Freedom of choice: Zinc's massive and ever-growing library means that all students should find texts they want to read.

Turnitin Revision Assistant

When you develop drafts of an available Embedded Assessment through SpringBoard Digital, you can use a tool called Turnitin Revision Assistant. This online tool gives instant feedback to students as they write so they can polish their drafts and practice their revision skills. The feedback model Revision Assistant uses is based on scoring by SpringBoard teachers, and it's trained to assess the same rubric areas that they assess.

Revision Assistant offers:

- A template to help you create an outline.
- Actionable, instant feedback in specific areas such as structure, use of language, and ideas.
- Identification of strengths and weakness in your writing.

A Letter to the Student

Dear Student,

Welcome to the SpringBoard program! We created this program with you in mind: it puts you and your classmates at the center of your learning and equips you with the skills and knowledge you need to excel in high school and beyond.

The energy and excitement you bring to class helps you and your classmates learn. You will explore compelling themes through readings, classroom discussions, and projects. You will dive into fascinating texts—some of which you'll choose on your own—from different genres including myths, poems, biographies, plays, and films. You will engage in lively discussions, debates, and performances so that you become confident sharing and presenting your ideas. You will write frequently to sharpen your ability to craft effective sentences, paragraphs, and longer texts. And you'll start each unit with a clear understanding of where you're headed by unpacking the skills and knowledge you'll need to do well on the assessment at the end.

SpringBoard helps you make connections between the concepts you're reading and writing about in class and the real world. Instead of just memorizing how to do things, you'll draw on your own and your classmates' experiences and knowledge to come to new and deeper understandings. When questions arise from the materials you're studying in class, you'll learn how to do both quick and longer-term research to find answers. Plus, you'll have access to tools and resources that are built right into the program, including powerful learning strategies, independent reading lists to help you select texts to read outside of class, and digital tools that you can access any time from any device—desktop computer, laptop, or tablet.

We want students to be rewarded for the hard work they do in their English Language Arts course. That's why the SpringBoard program focuses on the essential knowledge and skills that will prepare you for the challenging work you'll do in your high school classes, in AP courses, and in college.

Students from around the country are talking about how much they like the SpringBoard approach to learning. We hope you enjoy learning with SpringBoard, too.

Sincerely,

The SpringBoard Team

VISUAL PROMPT
How can words have
power? How can you
express yourself in a way
that persuades others?

THE POWER OF ARGUMENT

There may be times when we are powerless to prevent injustice, but there must never be a time when we fail to protest. ... We may be powerless to open all the jails and free all prisoners, but by declaring our solidarity with one prisoner, we indict all jailers. None of us is in a position to eliminate war, but it is our obligation to denounce it and expose it in all its hideousness.

—from "Hope, Despair, and Memory" by Elie Wiesel

CONTENTS

Texts not included in these materials.

My Independent Reading List

Learning Strategies

Note-taking
Previewing
Skimming-Scanning

My Notes

Learning Targets

- Preview the essential questions for the unit.
- Create a plan for reading independently.

Preview

In this activity, you will explore the essential questions and tasks of the unit and make plans for your independent reading.

About the Unit

One person has the power to influence fellow human beings to take action or change their thinking. To persuade an audience, writers, speakers, and artists work to craft well-organized, well-supported, vivid, and engaging arguments with clear statements of opinion. In this unit, you will study the power of argument. You will begin by analyzing a variety of argumentative texts including an essay, an op-ed, a cartoon, and a spoken word poem.

Essential Questions

Based on your current thinking, how would you answer these questions?

1. How should we interact with the world around us?

2. To what extent are we responsible for our fellow humans?

3. How do we use evidence to create a persuasive argument?

🎁 Planning Independent Reading

The focus of this unit is the power of argument, and you'll have the opportunity to read, watch, and listen to a wide variety of arguments in class. In your Independent Reading, you'll have a chance to investigate persuasive and informative writing on topics that interest you. You might select argumentative books, op-eds, biographies, or historical fiction to explore debatable topics related to defining reality and justice. Consider the following questions to help identify a text for Independent Reading.

- What have you enjoyed reading in the past? What is your favorite book or favorite type of book? Who is your favorite author?

- When you select a potential book, preview it. What do the front and back covers show you? What type of visual is shown? What types of fonts and colors are used? Are there awards or brags that tell you about the book?

- Read the first few pages. Are they interesting? How does the author try to hook you to keep reading? What can you tell about the characters and setting so far? Does this text seem too hard, too easy, or just right?

Reading Discussion Groups

Follow your teacher's oral guidance through a book pass and group discussion. Practice previewing each book by looking at the cover and reading the first few pages.

4. In your Reader/Writer Notebook, record each book's title and author, something that stood out to you as you previewed it, and your rating of the book.

5. After previewing each book and thinking about the goals of this unit, do you want to continue reading the book you brought to the group or choose something else?

6. Create an Independent Reading Plan to help you set personal reading goals. Keep this plan in your Reader/Writer Notebook.

   I have chosen to read _____

   _____

   by (author) _____

   because (reason from previewing) _____

   _____

   I will set aside time to read at (time, place) _____

   _____

   I should finish this text by (date) _____

7. Record your daily reading pace in your Independent Reading Log. Write a brief daily report in your log responding to what you have read. Include in your report questions or predictions about what you have read.

8. Respond to the Independent Reading Links you encounter throughout the unit.

Escape from Reality

My Notes

Learning Targets

- Determine the claims of two texts, and analyze how the authors expand these claims and support them with evidence.
- Draw inferences about a multimedia text.

Preview

In this activity, you will read a cartoon and an argumentative text, and then determine the claims and evidence presented by the authors.

Observations and Inferences

1. Look at the following cartoon by Mike Twohy. What details do you notice?

©Mike Twohy.

M2Ecomics@aol.com

"Wanna toss the ol' virtual pigskin?"

2. Reading a text for meaning includes a close examination of all available clues, including literal meaning (what is stated directly) and figurative meaning (what can be inferred). Any text can be read in this way, including images. Use the following graphic organizer to record your observations about the cartoon. Then, use your observations to make inferences about the subject of the cartoon.

Observations	Inferences
The boy is looking at his computer while typing.	The boy is engaged in what he is doing on his computer.

VOCABULARY

ACADEMIC

Literal meaning is the exact meaning of the text, while a figurative meaning is something that is represented through the text, as in a metaphor. For example, if someone tells you that they are so hungry they could eat a horse, you can either interpret their meaning literally (they actually want to eat a horse) or figuratively (they are very hungry).

An inference, or a conclusion about something that is not directly stated, can be induced or inferred from known information.

My Notes

Claims and Evidence

All successful arguments contain a claim and evidence. The claim presents a position on an issue or topic. For a claim to be debatable, people should be able to hold differing opinions about it. If your claim is something that is generally agreed upon or accepted as fact, then there is no reason to try to convince people.

Evidence is information that supports the claim.

3. What is Twohy arguing?

4. What evidence does Twohy include to support his argument?

As You Read

- Underline the central claim of this excerpt. Put stars next to McGonigal's supporting statements.
- Circle unknown words and phrases. Try to determine the meaning of the words by using context clues, word parts, or a dictionary.

My Notes

About the Author

Jane McGonigal, (b. 1977) is a game designer and author with a PhD in performance studies. She is the Director of Game Research and Development at the Institute for the Future. In 2009, while recovering from a concussion, McGonigal developed a game called *SuperBetter* that helps players tackle health challenges.

Argument

From Reality Is Broken: Why Games Make Us Better and How They Can Change the World (Part One)

by **Jane McGonigal, PhD**

1   Gamers have had enough of reality.

2   They are abandoning it in droves—a few hours here, an entire weekend there, sometimes every spare minute of every day for stretches at a time—in favor of simulated environments and online games. Maybe you are one of these gamers. If not, then you definitely know some of them.

3   Who are they? They are the nine-to-fivers who come home and apply all of the smarts and talents that are underutilized at work to plan and coordinate complex raids and quests in massively multiplayer online games like *Final Fantasy XI* and the *Lineage* worlds. They're the music lovers who have invested hundreds of dollars on plastic *Rock Band* and *Guitar Hero* instruments and spent night after night rehearsing, in order to become virtuosos of video game performance.

4   They're the *World of Warcraft* fans who are so intent on mastering the challenges of their favorite game that, collectively, they've written a quarter of a million wiki articles about the fictional universe—creating a wiki1 resource nearly one-tenth the size of the entire Wikipedia. They're the *Brain Age* and *Mario Kart* players who take handheld game consoles everywhere they go, sneaking in short puzzles, races, and minigames as often as possible, and as a result nearly eliminating mental downtime from their lives.

5   They're the United States troops stationed overseas who dedicate so many hours a week to burnishing their *Halo 3* in-game service record that earning virtual combat medals is widely known as the most popular activity for off-duty soldiers. They're the young adults in China who have spent so much play money or "QQ coins," on magical swords and other powerful game objects that the People's Bank of China intervened to prevent the **devaluation** of the yuan, China's real-world currency.

devaluation: decline in value

---

[1] A *wiki* is an online site that collects information that visitors can contribute to and edit.

6   Most of all, they're kids and teenagers worldwide who would rather spend hours in front of any computer game or video game than do anything else.

7   These gamers aren't rejecting reality entirely. They have jobs, goals, schoolwork, families, commitments, and real lives that they care about. But as they devote more and more of their free time to game worlds, the *real* world increasingly feels like it's missing something.

8   Gamers want to know: Where, in the real world, is that gamer sense of being fully alive, focused, and engaged in every moment? Where is the gamer feeling of power, heroic purpose, and community? Where are the bursts of expanding thrill of success and team victory? While gamers may experience these pleasures occasionally in their real lives, they experience them almost constantly when they're playing their favorite games.

9   The real world just doesn't offer up as easily the carefully designed pleasures, the thrilling challenges, and the powerful social bonding afforded by virtual environments. Reality doesn't motivate us effectively. Reality isn't engineered to maximize our potential. Reality wasn't designed from the bottom up to make us happy.

10   And so, there is a growing perception in the gaming community:

11   Reality, compared to games, is broken.

12   In fact, it is more than a perception. It's a phenomenon. Economist Edward Castronova calls it a "mass **exodus**" to game spaces, and you can see it already happening in the numbers. Hundreds of millions of people worldwide are opting out of reality for larger and larger chunks of time. In the United States alone, there are 183 million *active gamers* (individuals, who in surveys, report that they play the computer or video games "regularly"—on average, thirteen hours a week). Globally, the online gamer community—including

exodus: group departure

WORD CONNECTIONS

Multiple-Meaning Word
The word silo originally refers to a large storage tower used to store grain on a farm, or to an underground structure where a military might store a missile. The word silo is also used metaphorically as a verb to mean to isolate. For instance, a workplace where employees don't share information with each other can be described as a siloed work environment.

My Notes

console, PC, and mobile home gaming—counts more than 4 million gamers in the Middle East, 10 million in Russia, 105 million in India, 10 million in Vietnam, 10 million in Mexico, 13 million in Central and South America, 15 million in Australia, 17 million in South Korea, 100 million in Europe, and 200 million in China.

13 Although a typical gamer plays for just an hour or two a day, there are now more than 6 million people in China who spend at least twenty-two hours a week gaming, the equivalent of a part-time job. More than 10 million "hard-core" gamers in the United Kingdom, France, and Germany spend at least twenty hours a week playing. And at the leading edge of this growth curve, more than 5 million "extreme" gamers in the United States play on the average of forty-five hours a week.

14 With all of this play, we have turned digital games—for our computers, for our mobile phones, and for our home entertainment systems—into what is expected to be a $68 billion industry annually by the year 2012. And we are creating a massive virtual silo of cognitive effort, emotional energy, and collective attention lavished on game worlds instead of the real world.

Making Observations
* Look back at the claim you underlined. Do you agree with this claim?
* Review the statements you starred. Which stand out to you and why?

Returning to the Text

- Reread the argument to answer these text-dependent questions.
- Write any additional questions you have about the text in your Reader/Writer Notebook.

5. In paragraphs 2 and 3, who does the word *they* refer to? What does the word *it* refer to? How do you know?

_____

_____

_____

_____

6. What claim is presented in paragraphs 1–3?

_____

_____

_____

_____

7. How is the word *abandoning* different in tone than its near synonym *leaving*? Why might McGonigal have chosen to use the term *abandoning* in paragraph 2?

_____

_____

_____

_____

8. Based on its context, what do you think the phrase *in droves* means in paragraph 2? How does that term help convey the author's message and intended tone?

_____

_____

_____

_____

9. Which part of the initial claim is best supported by paragraph 3?

_____

_____

_____

_____

10. How does McGonigal use evidence and reasoning to support her claim in paragraph 3?

_____

_____

_____

_____

11. McGonigal opens paragraph 3 by asking a question. What effect does this opening have on the reader?

_____

_____

_____

_____

12. How is the rest of paragraph 3 structured? Do you see any similarities between the second and third sentences? What effect do you think that structure is intended to have on the reader?

_____

_____

_____

_____

13. Do you notice anything about sound patterns in paragraph 3? What effect do you think these sound patterns are intended to have on the reader?

_____

_____

_____

_____

14. Which part of the initial claim is best supported by paragraphs 4 and 5? (Refer to specific words and phrases in the opening claim as you answer this question.)

_____

_____

_____

_____

15. How are evidence and reasoning used to effectively reinforce the claim in paragraphs 4 and 5?

_____

_____

_____

_____

Working from the Text

16. Collaborative Conversation: How does McGonigal use claims, evidence, and reasoning together to produce an argument?

17. Both images and texts can present arguments, but they communicate their messages in different ways. How might McGonigal's claim be presented in a visual text? If Twohy were writing his argument instead of drawing it, what types of evidence might he include?

18. Both the cartoon and the excerpt from Reality Is Broken contrast life within virtual environments and life in reality. Would McGonigal most likely agree or disagree with the claim that Twohy makes in his cartoon? What evidence from McGonigal's excerpt supports your response?

19. How does McGonigal use diction to strengthen her argument? Revisit your answers to questions 6, 7, and 12.

✎ Writing Prompt: Informational

Read paragraphs 12–14 individually, and write a paragraph explaining how McGonigal expands her initial claim in this section. What evidence has she provided so far to support this newly expanded version of the claim? Be sure to:

- Organize your ideas using a logical structure.
- Identify the author's claim.
- Evaluate the author's various types of evidence.

It's All a Part of the Game: Countering Opposing Claims

Learning Strategies

Drafting
Marking the Text
Predicting
Previewing

Learning Targets

- Analyze the author's treatment of counterarguments, concessions, and rebuttals.
- Write an analysis of how an author strengthens an argument.

Preview

In this activity, you will finish reading the excerpt from *Reality Is Broken* and examine how the author uses counterarguments. Then, you will write an analysis of her argument.

My Notes

✍ Opening Writing Prompt

Read the following excerpt from *Reality Is Broken*:

In the opening book of *The Histories*, Herodotus writes:

When Atys was king of Lydia in Asia Minor some three thousand years ago, a great scarcity threatened his realm. For a while people accepted their lot without complaining, in the hope that times of plenty would return. But when things failed to get better, the Lydians devised a strange remedy for their problem. The plan adopted against the famine was to engage in games one day so entirely as not to feel any craving for food ... and the next day to eat and abstain from games. In this way they passed eighteen years, and along the way they invented the dice, knuckle-bones, the ball, and all the games which are common.

Why might Jane McGonigal have included this excerpt in her argument? In your Reader/Writer Notebook, make a prediction and explain why you think McGonigal would include this in her argument.

As You Read

- Place stars next to the author's historical supporting evidence. Then sum up the claim in a few words.
- Circle unknown words and phrases. Try to determine the meaning of the words by using context clues, word parts, or a dictionary.

Argument

From Reality Is Broken: Why Games Make Us Better and How They Can Change the World (Part Two)

by **Jane McGonigal, PhD**

15   The ever-skyrocketing amounts of time and money spent on games are being observed with alarm by some—concerned parents, teachers, and politicians—and eagerness by others—the many technology industries that

expect to profit greatly from the game boom. Meanwhile, they are met with bewilderment and disdain by more than a few nongamers, who still make up nearly half of the U.S. population, although their numbers are rapidly decreasing. Many of them deem gaming a clear waste of time.

16 As we make these value judgments, hold moral debates over the addictive quality of games, and simultaneously rush to achieve massive industry expansion, a vital point is being missed. The fact that so many people of all ages, all over the world, are choosing to spend so much time in game worlds is a sign of something important, a truth that we urgently need to recognize.

17 The truth is this: in today's society, computer and video games are fulfilling *genuine human needs* that the real world is currently unable to satisfy. Games are providing rewards that reality is not. They are teaching and inspiring and engaging us in ways that reality is not. They are bringing us together in ways that reality is not.

18 And unless something dramatic happens to reverse the resulting exodus, we're fast on our way to becoming a society in which a substantial portion of our population devotes its greatest efforts to playing games, creates its best memories in game environments, and experiences its biggest successes in game worlds.

19 Maybe this sounds hard to believe. To a nongamer, this forecast might seem surreal, or like science fiction. Are huge swaths of civilization really disappearing into game worlds? Are we really rushing headlong into a future where the majority of us use games to satisfy many of our most important needs?

20 If so, it will not be the first time that such a mass exodus from reality to games has occurred. Indeed, the very first written history of human gameplay, Herodotus' Histories, the ancient Greek account of the Persian Wars—dating back more than three thousand years—describes a nearly identical scenario. While the oldest known game is the ancient counting game Mancala—evidence shows it was played during Egypt's age of empires, or the fifteenth to the eleventh centuries BC—it was not until Herodotus that anyone thought to record the origins or cultural functions of these games. And from his ancient text, we can learn a great deal about what's happening today—and what's almost certainly coming next.

21 It's a bit counterintuitive to think about the future in terms of the past. But as a research director at the Institute for the Future—a nonprofit think tank in Palo Alto, California, and the world's oldest future-forecasting organization—I've learned an important trick: to develop foresight, you need to practice hindsight. Technologies, cultures, and climates change, but our basic human needs and desires—to survive, to care for our families, and to lead happy, purposeful lives—remain the same. So at IFTF we like to say, "To understand the future, you have to look back at least twice as far as you're looking ahead." Fortunately, when it comes to games, we can look even farther back than that. Games have been a fundamental part of human civilization for thousands of years.

22 In the opening book of *The Histories*, Herodotus writes:

23 When Atys was king of Lydia in Asia Minor some three thousand years ago, a great scarcity threatened his realm. For a while people accepted their lot without complaining, in the hope that times of plenty would return. But when things failed to get better, the Lydians devised a strange remedy for their problem. The plan adopted against the famine was to engage in games one day so entirely as not to feel any craving for food . . . and the next day to eat and abstain from games. In this way they passed eighteen years, and along the way they invented the dice, knuckle-bones, the ball, and all the games which are common.

This set of dice from Ancient Rome was made from animal bones.

24 What do ancient dice made from sheep's knuckles have to do with the future of computer and video games? More than you might expect.

25 Herodotus invented history as we know it, and he has described the goal of history as uncovering moral problems and moral truths in the concrete data of experience. Whether Herodotus' story of an eighteen-year famine survived through gameplay is true or, as some modern historians believe, apocryphal, its moral truths reveal something important about the essence of games.

26 We often think of immersive gameplay as "escapist," a kind of passive retreat from reality. But through the lens of Herodotus' history, we can see how games could be a *purposeful* escape, a thoughtful and active escape, and most importantly an extremely helpful escape. For the Lydians, playing together as a nearly full-time activity would have been a behavior highly adaptive to difficult conditions. Games made life bearable. Games gave a starving population a feeling of power in a powerless situation, a sense of structure in a chaotic environment. Games gave them a better way to live when their circumstances were otherwise completely unsupportive and uninhabitable.

My Notes

apocryphal: fictitious, untrue
uninhabitable: not fit to live in

27 Make no mistake: we are no different from the ancient Lydians. Today, many of us are suffering from a vast and primal hunger. But it is not a hunger for food—it is a hunger for more and better engagement from the world around us.

28 Like the ancient Lydians, many gamers have already figured out how to use the immersive power of play to distract themselves from their hunger: a hunger for more satisfying work, for a stronger sense of community, and for a more engaging and meaningful life.

29 Collectively, the planet is now spending more than 3 billion hours a week gaming.

30 We are starving, and our games are feeding us.

This pot dates back to 540–530 BCE, and depicts the Greek heroes Achilles and Ajax playing dice.

Making Observations

- What facts surprised you in this argument?
- Are you persuaded by McGonigal's argument?

☑ Focus on the Sentence

Use the conjunctions *because*, *but*, and *so* to complete this sentence. Be sure to use correct capitalization and punctuation.

The Lydians experienced hunger because _____

_____

The Lydians experienced hunger, so _____

_____

The Lydians experienced hunger, but _____

_____

Returning to the Text

- Reread paragraphs 15–30 from *Reality Is Broken* to answer these text-dependent questions.
- Write any additional questions you have about the text in your Reader/Writer Notebook.

1. McGonigal chooses to use the phrase *engage in games* instead of *play games*. How does each phrase communicate a different tone? Why might McGonigal have chosen the phrase *engage in games*?

_____

_____

_____

_____

2. McGonigal chooses to use the words *scarcity*, *famine*, and *abstain*. What do these words have in common, and why might McGonigal have selected them? Use context clues or a dictionary for help, if needed.

_____

_____

_____

_____

3. Whom is McGonigal trying to convince? What evidence supports your answer?

_____

_____

_____

_____

4. As part of McGonigal's counterargument, which groups does she identify as the opponents of her claim?

_____

_____

_____

_____

5. To strengthen her counterargument, which negative emotions does McGonigal associate with these groups?

_____

_____

_____

_____

VOCABULARY

ACADEMIC

A **counterargument** is a set of reasons or evidence put forward to oppose an idea or theory developed in another argument. A counterargument often contains a **concession**, where the author allows that some of what the opposing argument is claiming is true. Then, in the **rebuttal**, the author refutes the rest of the opposing argument.

INDEPENDENT READING LINK

Read and Respond

What claim(s) do you see asserted in the text that you are reading independently? How does the author present evidence in support of each claim? What specific counterarguments, rebuttals, or concessions have you noted? Record your responses in your Reader/Writer Notebook.

Working from the Text

A strong argument does not shy away from opposition. In fact, it tackles the opposition directly by presenting a **counterargument**. A counterargument is a counterclaim that might be made by the opposing party. The argument offers a **rebuttal** to the counterargument. The rebuttal provides evidence and reasoning that disproves or highlights the shortcomings of the counterclaim.

Because it is often difficult to persuade an opponent to change a stance by dismissing a counterargument entirely, an effective rhetorician knows the power of **concession**—the practice of acknowledging the validity of part of a counterclaim. Conceding some things while still rebutting the overall counterclaim can make the argument stronger by making the writer or speaker seem balanced and reasonable.

6. According to McGonigal, how do these opposing parties view gaming? How does the acknowledgment of these opposing parties strengthen McGonigal's argument?

7. Choose one of the opposing perspectives that McGonigal identifies in paragraphs 15–21 and write a paragraph or two voicing your concerns about gaming from that point of view. Your paragraph(s) should present a brief argument, asserting a claim and supplying evidence and reasoning to support that claim. Your word choice should reflect the emotional tone that McGonigal ascribes to your perspective (e.g., if you are expressing bewilderment, you might use a word like *mystified*).

8. **Collaborative Conversation:** Return to the essential question: How should we interact with the world around us? How do you think McGonigal would answer this question? How might Twohy answer the question? What is your answer?

✍ Writing Prompt: Informational

In the excerpt from *Reality Is Broken*, Jane McGonigal makes the claim that gamers are rejecting reality in favor of playing games that offer superior experiences and rewards. Select two of the ways McGonigal strengthens her argument, and write to explain how and why they serve to strengthen the argument and support the claim. Be sure to:

- Use textual evidence in your response.
- Employ reasoning.
- Provide a historical example.
- Include a counterargument.
- Use rhetorical features such as powerful language and repetition.

Technology and Communication

Learning Strategies

Graphic Organizer
Marking the Text
Questioning the Text
Socratic Seminar

Learning Targets

- Determine the claim of an argumentative text and analyze how the author supports the claim with various types of evidence.
- Analyze how an author's choice of words informs and shapes the reader's perception.

Preview

In this activity, you will watch a performance and read an argumentative text to consider the ways in which the authors make and support their claims.

LITERARY

The term **diction** refers to an author's choice of words for the purposes of accuracy, clarity, and effectiveness. Authors can use diction to create contribute to the mood, voice, and tone of a text.

VOCABULARY

Examining Diction

1. Take notes as your teacher shows you the video performance of "Touchscreen" by Marshall Davis Jones.

In poetry, an author achieves much of a poem's meaning through **diction** or his choice of words. As you listen to "Touchscreen," note the ways in which the author creates word play through the use of multiple-meaning words and homophones. Homophones are words that share a pronunciation but have different spellings and meanings. Jones achieves contrast by using words that have both a general meaning and a meaning specifically related to technology. Use the following graphic organizer to record your observations regarding Jones's word choice.

Tech-related Word (and Meaning)	Word (and Non-tech-related Meaning)
click (as in mouse click)	clique (as in social group)
Facebook (the social media site)	face (as in the noun and as in the verb, "to face")

My Notes

Claims and Evidence

Although Jones has chosen to present his ideas in the form of a spoken word poem, it is possible to interpret his text as an argument with an implied claim that is supported through evidence in the form of word play. An implied claim is suggested through details rather than directly stated.

2. If you consider "Touchscreen" as an argument with an implied claim, how would you summarize that claim?

3. What is one example of diction Jones uses to support his claim?

As You Read

• Look for the claim of the text and underline it, then place stars next to statements that support it.
• Circle unknown words and phrases. Try to determine the meaning of the words by using context clues, word parts, or a dictionary.

About the Author

Sherry Turkle, PhD (b. 1948), a graduate of Harvard, is a professor at the Massachusetts Institute of Technology (MIT). She is a licensed clinical psychologist and has a joint doctorate in sociology and psychology. Professor Turkle is interested in the relationships between people and technology.

Op-Ed

The Flight from Conversation

by **Sherry Turkle, PhD**

1   We live in a technological universe in which we are always communicating. And yet we have sacrificed conversation for mere connection.

2   At home, families sit together, texting and reading e-mail. At work executives text during board meetings. We text (and shop and go on Facebook) during classes and when we're on dates. My students tell me about an important new skill: it involves maintaining eye contact with someone while you text someone else; it's hard, but it can be done.

3   Over the past 15 years, I've studied technologies of mobile connection and talked to hundreds of people of all ages and circumstances about their

My Notes

plugged-in lives. I've learned that the little devices most of us carry around are so powerful that they change not only what we do, but also who we are.

4   We've become accustomed to a new way of being "alone together." Technology-enabled, we are able to be with one another, and also elsewhere, connected to wherever we want to be. We want to customize our lives. We want to move in and out of where we are because the thing we value most is control over where we focus our attention. We have gotten used to the idea of being in a tribe of one, loyal to our own party.

5   Our colleagues want to go to that board meeting but pay attention only to what interests them. To some this seems like a good idea, but we can end up hiding from one another, even as we are constantly connected to one another.

6   A businessman laments that he no longer has colleagues at work. He doesn't stop by to talk; he doesn't call. He says that he doesn't want to interrupt them. He says they're "too busy on their e-mail." But then he pauses and corrects himself. "I'm not telling the truth. I'm the one who doesn't want to be interrupted. I think I should. But I'd rather just do things on my BlackBerry."[1]

7   A 16-year-old boy who relies on texting for almost everything says almost wistfully, "Someday, someday, but certainly not now, I'd like to learn how to have a conversation."

8   In today's workplace, young people who have grown up fearing conversation show up on the job wearing earphones. Walking through a college library or the campus of a high-tech start-up, one sees the same thing: we are together, but each of us is in our own bubble, furiously connected to keyboards and tiny touch screens. A senior partner at a Boston law firm describes a scene in his office. Young associates lay out their suite of technologies: laptops, iPods

---

[1] A *Blackberry* was a wireless, handheld, communication device released in the early 2000s.

and multiple phones. And then they put their earphones on. "Big ones. Like pilots. They turn their desks into cockpits." With the young lawyers in their cockpits, the office is quiet, a quiet that does not ask to be broken.

9   In the silence of connection, people are comforted by being in touch with a lot of people—carefully kept at bay. We can't get enough of one another if we can use technology to keep one another at distances we can control: not too close, not too far, just right. I think of it as a Goldilocks effect.

10   Texting and e-mail and posting let us present the self we want to be. This means we can edit. And if we wish to, we can delete. Or retouch: the voice, the flesh, the face, the body. Not too much, not too little—just right.

11   Human relationships are rich; they're messy and demanding. We have learned the habit of cleaning them up with technology. And the move from conversation to connection is part of this. But it's a process in which we shortchange ourselves. Worse, it seems that over time we stop caring, we forget that there is a difference.

12   We are tempted to think that our little "sips" of online connection add up to a big gulp of real conversation. But they don't. E-mail, Twitter, Facebook, all of these have their places—in politics, commerce, romance, and friendship. But no matter how valuable, they do not substitute for conversation.

13   Connecting in sips may work for gathering discrete bits of information or for saying, "I am thinking about you." Or even for saying, "I love you." But connecting in sips doesn't work as well when it comes to understanding and knowing one another. In conversation we tend to one another. (The word itself is **kinetic**; it's derived from words that mean to move, together.) We can attend to tone and **nuance**. In conversation, we are called upon to see things from another's point of view.

14   Face-to-face conversation unfolds slowly. It teaches patience. When we communicate on our digital devices, we learn different habits. As we ramp up the volume and **velocity** of online connections, we start to expect faster answers. To get these, we ask one another simpler questions; we dumb down our communications, even on the most important matters. It is as though we have all put ourselves on cable news. Shakespeare might have said, "We are consum'd with that which we were nourish'd by."

15   And we use conversation with others to learn to converse with ourselves. So our flight from conversation can mean diminished chances to learn skills of self-reflection. These days, social media continually asks us what's "on our mind," but we have little motivation to say something truly self-reflective. Self-reflection in conversation requires trust. It's hard to do anything with 3,000 Facebook friends except connect.

16   As we get used to being shortchanged on conversation and to getting by with less, we seem almost willing to dispense with people altogether. Serious people muse about the future of computer programs as psychiatrists. A high school sophomore confides to me that he wishes he could talk to an artificial

GRAMMAR & USAGE

Semicolon

Writers use a semicolon to join independent clauses when two or more clauses are of equal importance. In paragraph 11, notice the sentence "Human relationships are rich; they're messy and demanding." In this sentence, the two independent clauses are about two aspects of human relationships.

kinetic: active
nuance: subtle distinction
velocity: speed

intelligence program instead of his dad about dating; he says the A.I. would have so much more in its database. Indeed, many people tell me they hope that as Siri, the digital assistant on Apple's iPhone, becomes more advanced, "she" will be more and more like a best friend—one who will listen when others won't.

17   During the years I have spent researching people and their relationships with technology, I have often heard the sentiment "No one is listening to me." I believe this feeling helps explain why it is so appealing to have a Facebook page or a Twitter feed—each provides so many automatic listeners. And it helps explain why—against all reason—so many of us are willing to talk to machines that seem to care about us. Researchers around the world are busy inventing sociable robots, designed to be companions to the elderly, to children, to all of us.

18   One of the most haunting experiences during my research came when I brought one of these robots, designed in the shape of a baby seal, to an elder-care facility, and an older woman began to talk to it about the loss of her child. The robot seemed to be looking into her eyes. It seemed to be following the conversation. The woman was comforted.

19   And so many people found this amazing. Like the sophomore who wants advice about dating from artificial intelligence and those who look forward to computer psychiatry, this enthusiasm speaks to how much we have confused conversation with connection and collectively seem to have embraced a new kind of delusion that accepts the simulation of compassion as sufficient unto the day. And why would we want to talk about love and loss with a machine that has no experience of the arc of human life? Have we so lost confidence that we will be there for one another?

20   We expect more from technology and less from one another and seem increasingly drawn to technologies that provide the illusion of companionship without the demands of relationship. Always-on/always-on-you devices provide three powerful fantasies: that we will always be heard; that we can put our attention wherever we want it to be; and that we never have to be alone. Indeed our new devices have turned being alone into a problem that can be solved.

21   When people are alone, even for a few moments, they fidget and reach for a device. Here connection works like a symptom, not a cure, and our constant, reflexive impulse to connect shapes a new way of being.

22   Think of it as "I share, therefore I am." We use technology to define ourselves by sharing our thoughts and feelings as we're having them. We used to think, "I have a feeling; I want to make a call." Now our impulse is, "I want to have a feeling; I need to send a text."

23   So, in order to feel more, and to feel more like ourselves, we connect. But in our rush to connect, we flee from solitude, our ability to be separate and gather ourselves. Lacking the capacity for solitude, we turn to other people but

My Notes

don't experience them as they are. It is as though we use them, need them as spare parts to support our increasingly fragile selves.

24   We think constant connection will make us feel less lonely. The opposite is true. If we are unable to be alone, we are far more likely to be lonely. If we don't teach our children to be alone, they will know only how to be lonely.

25   I am a partisan for conversation. To make room for it, I see some first, deliberate steps. At home, we can create sacred spaces: the kitchen, the dining room. We can make our cars "device-free zones." We can demonstrate the value of conversation to our children. And we can do the same thing at work. There we are so busy communicating that we often don't have time to talk to one another about what really matters. Employees asked for casual Fridays; perhaps managers should introduce conversational Thursdays. Most of all, we need to remember—in between texts and e-mails and Facebook posts—to listen to one another, even to the boring bits, because it is often in unedited moments, moments in which we hesitate and stutter and go silent, that we reveal ourselves to one another.

26   I spend the summers at a cottage on Cape Cod, and for decades I walked the same dunes that Thoreau[2] once walked. Not too long ago, people walked with their heads up, looking at the water, the sky, the sand and at one another, talking. Now they often walk with their heads down, typing. Even when they are with friends, partners, children, everyone is on their own devices.

27   So I say, look up, look at one another, and let's start the conversation.

Making Observations

- Review the claim you underlined. Do you find yourself agreeing with this claim?
- Which starred supporting evidence stands out to you and why?

---

[2] *Henry David Thoreau* (1817–62) was an American writer and philosopher credited with helping to develop Transcendentalism—a system of thought that valued nature, experience, and intuition above religion, science, and reason.

Returning to the Text

- Reread the op-ed to answer these text-dependent questions.
- Write any additional questions you have about the text in your Reader/Writer Notebook.

4. In paragraph 4, Turkle uses an oxymoron (contradictory words): *alone together*. What does Turkle mean by this phrase? As Turkle elaborates on this phrase throughout the paragraph, how does it influence the op-ed as a whole?

_____

_____

_____

_____

5. In paragraph 9, Turkle makes an allusion (reference to another author, character, or work) to Goldilocks. What do you think Turkle's purpose is in using this allusion?

_____

_____

_____

_____

6. Turkle suggests people use technology to edit themselves to "present the self [they] want to be" in paragraph 10. How does Turkle view this practice?

_____

_____

_____

_____

7. In paragraph 12, Turkle begins an extended metaphor: little "sips" of online connection. What does Turkle's metaphor describe?

_____

_____

_____

_____

WORD CONNECTIONS

Etymology

The word **oxymoron** comes from the Greek *oxys*, meaning *sharp*, and *moros* meaning *stupid*. An oxymoron, therefore, is a rhetorical device where two contradictory terms are used together. For example, *open secret* and *deafening silence* are commonly used phrases that are oxymorons.

My Notes

8. In paragraph 19, Turkle poses a set of rhetorical questions (queries not meant to be answered directly). Find an example. What effect does Turkle create with these questions?

_____

_____

_____

_____

9. In paragraph 22, the author says that our impuse has become to think, "I want to have a feeling; I need to send a text." How do the independent clauses in this sentence relate to each other?

_____

_____

_____

_____

10. In paragraph 25, Turkle uses the phrase "partisan for conversation" to describe herself. Why does Turkle choose the word *partisan*?

_____

_____

_____

_____

☑ Focus on the Sentence

Complete the following sentence.

Turkle calls herself a "partisan for conversation" because _____.

_____

_____

Now, rewrite the sentence as two independent clauses joined by a semicolon.

Turkle calls herself a "partisan for conversation"; she _____.

_____

_____

Introducing the Strategy: Socratic Seminar and Levels of Questioning

A Socratic Seminar is a type of collaborative discussion designed to explore a complex question, topic, or text. Participants engage in meaningful and respectful discourse by preparing for discussions, reading (or researching) required material, and then explicitly drawing on that preparation by referring to text evidence. The goal is for participants to have a thoughtful, well-reasoned exchange of ideas and, by the end of the discussion, arrive at a deeper understanding of a concept or idea. In this way, a Socratic Seminar is not a debate.

A strategy for thinking actively and interpretively about your reading is to ask questions before, during, and after reading. As you read any text, you can ask questions that aid your understanding with different levels of ideas. Questioning helps you experience a text in depth, gain information, and monitor your understanding.

- **Literal questions** (Level 1): Literal questions can be answered by referring back to the text or consulting references.

  EXAMPLE: What kind of robot was used to comfort an elderly woman? (seal)

- **Interpretive questions** (Level 2): Interpretive questions call for inferences because the answers cannot be found directly in the text; however, textual evidence points to and supports the answers.

  EXAMPLE: Why did the 16-year old not want to learn how to have a conversation now? (Even though he wants to learn eventually, he's more comfortable communicating digitally now and isn't ready to venture outside his comfort zone.)

- **Universal questions** (Level 3): Universal questions go beyond the text. What are the larger issues or ideas raised by the text?

  EXAMPLE: How can our society learn to use technology without it affecting our personal relationships?

Working from the Text

11. **Preparing for a Socratic Seminar:** Consider this overarching question: *To what extent does technology assist or impair our ability to communicate with one another?* In response, annotate the Turkle article to prepare for a Socratic Seminar by using varying colors of highlighters to identify the claim and show specific supporting evidence and rhetorical devices (for example, allusions, anecdotes, diction, figurative interviews, language, metaphors, oxymorons, parallelism, rhetorical questions, and tone).

12. **Generating Questions about Text:** During a Socratic Seminar, it is your responsibility to pose original questions about the text under discussion. To prepare, generate a minimum of three higher-order questions about the text that address different ways of thinking.

    - **Interpretive Questions:** These types of questions require readers to come to an understanding regarding the author's intended purpose or meaning.

      Example: *Why does Turkle begin the article using a first-person point of view?*

    - **Inferential Questions:** These types of questions require readers to combine text evidence with prior knowledge and experience.

      Example: In paragraph 22, why does Turkle alter the famous quotation from French philosopher René Descartes, "I think, therefore I am"?

My Notes

- **Evaluative Questions:** These types of questions require readers to make judgments regarding the author's ideas, argument, or the effectiveness of the text.

  Example: *In what ways is the author's example regarding the robotic baby seal effective or ineffective in supporting her claim?*

13. **Engaging in Discourse:** Using your best judgment, mark each participant guideline for a Socratic Seminar as true or false:

    _____ Bring your annotated article and your responses to the text-dependent questions to the seminar.

    _____ As you ask and answer questions, there is no need to refer to the text.

    _____ Back up opinions with textual evidence.

    _____ Make references to your classmates' comments as you respond.

    _____ Key vocabulary is not an important element of your questions and responses.

    _____ Maintain eye contact with students in the circle.

    _____ Be polite when interrupting other speakers.

    _____ Try to win the debate.

14. **Reflecting on the Socratic Seminar:** After participating in the seminar, respond to the following questions in writing:

    - What is the most interesting point that was raised in the seminar that you had not yet considered before it was raised?
    - Reflecting on your own participation, what do you wish you would have said that you neglected to say? Or what do you wish you could restate more clearly?
    - Did any of your opinions or insights about the article change throughout the course of the seminar? If so, which one(s) and how?
    - When preparing for another Socratic Seminar, what personal goals will you set?

Analyzing an Argument

Learning Targets

- Analyze the author's use of language and rhetorical devices.
- Write an explanatory essay with a clear thesis, relevant supporting evidence, and pertinent examples to support your explanation regarding how the author builds a persuasive argument.
- Use the writing process to plan, draft, and revise your essay.

Preview

In this activity, you will continue to analyze Sherry Turkle's op-ed, and write an original essay explaining how Turkle builds her argument in "The Flight from Conversation."

My Notes

Examining a Multiple-Meaning Word

Return to the opening of Sherry Turkle's article "The Flight from Conversation":

We live in a technological universe in which we are always communicating. And yet we have sacrificed conversation for mere connection.

When constructing a claim, an author chooses her diction carefully. For example, Turkle's use of the word *mere* before *connection* reiterates the idea that she believes connection is worth less than conversation. In addition, *connection* is a multiple-meaning word that adds nuance to her claim. Use the following graphic organizer to explain the difference between two definitions of *connection* and *universe*.

1.

Definition	What Turkle Might Say About This Type of Connection
Connection: a relationship between two people	
Connection: a means of communication, as in a telephone connection	
Universe: all existing matter	
Universe: a space of activity, interest, or experience	

Developing the Claim

Turkle follows protocol by stating her claim in a sentence or two near the beginning of her article. In the remainder of the article, she works to further her ideas regarding this claim.

INDEPENDENT READING LINK

Read and Connect

In what ways does your Independent Reading text compare and contrast with the arguments you have been reading in class? Focus on the presentation of evidence. What types of evidence do you find in each text? In what order is evidence generally presented? Which evidence is most effective or least effective and why? Record your responses in your Reader/Writer Notebook.

2. What does Turkle see as the most important distinction between face-to-face conversation and communication on digital devices?

3. What does Turkle see as the relationship between the use of tech devices, spending time alone, and the feeling of loneliness?

Explain How an Author Builds an Argument

In Sherry Turkle's article "The Flight from Conversation," she makes the claim that we are allowing technology to have a negative effect on our personal lives and relationships. Write an explanatory essay analyzing how Turkle supports this claim. Consider her diction, rhetorical devices, and other persuasive strategies. You will use the steps that follow this prompt to plan and draft your essay. Be sure to:

- Plan your explanatory essay using a range of strategies such as brainstorming and reading.
- Choose an organizational structure for your essay appropriate to purpose, audience, topic, and context.
- Develop the essay with specific details, examples, and commentary.
- Review your draft to improve the clarity, organization, and diction.

Gather Ideas

4. Revisit the article, your annotations, and your notes to make a list here of the specific elements (minimum of two or three) of Turkle's argument you wish to consider in your essay. You may want to address anecdotes, interviews, allusions, figurative language, or diction, for example.

Write a Thesis

A thesis is usually one or two sentences that appear near the end of an introduction and act as a roadmap for the rest of the essay. In the case of your essay, it will act as a roadmap that provides the reader with a way to navigate or understand Turkle's argument through a specific lens. Your thesis should go beyond a vague assertion and instead make a clear, convincing claim.

5. Revise the following vague assertion into a thesis by replacing the phrase "a variety of strategies" with some specific strategies Turkle uses and the word "claim" with Turkle's belief regarding the effect of technology on human relationships:

In "The Flight from Conversation," Turkle uses a variety of strategies to support her claim.

6. Now, use these sentence frames to get started on your own thesis. Then, consult your teacher for help in selecting the best thesis for your essay. Your teacher may suggest some revisions before allowing you to move on.

Turkle uses _____, _____, and _____

to argue that _____

_____

Turkle makes use of rhetorical devices such as _____, _____,

and _____ to illustrate _____

Turkle supports her claim that _____

through evidence such as _____, _____,

and _____

Craft the Introduction

7. An introduction generally includes three parts (ANT): (A) attention getter; (N) necessary information such as the author, title, genre, situation, or context; and (T) a thesis. Use brackets to label the ANT elements of the following introduction.

People often assume that connection enables communication. However, Sherry Turkle argues that connection makes it hard to communicate. In her article "The Flight from Conversation," Turkle claims that although technology enables people to connect on superficial levels, it is also causing people to lose their abilities to have meaningful conversations. Turkle uses figurative language, allusions, and personal anecdotes to illustrate how tech connections are continuously allowing people to hide from one another behind their devices. By the end of her argument, this combination of strategies convinces the reader that people need to become more aware of their isolation and try to do something about it.

My Notes

8. Now, note some attention-getting ideas for your essay here, such as describing a scene where someone is distracted from social interaction due to technology.

Compose Body Paragraphs and Incorporate Quotations

The body paragraphs (minimum of two to three) should each focus on a separate persuasive strategy of Turkle's and its intended effect on the reader. For example, if you've named three strategies in your thesis, each strategy should get its own body paragraph.

9. Embed direct quotations from Turkle's article into each body paragraph. Remember to sandwich each quotation between your own points. Each quotation should be introduced, stated, and then analyzed. List some quotations (three to four) you plan to use here along with your reasons for choosing them.

LANGUAGE & WRITER'S CRAFT: Embedding Quotations

When writers quote directly from other sources, they must surround the borrowed words with quotation marks. This signals to readers that the words are from another writer. For example, you could quote an important line from the argument you are analyzing:

> Sherry Turkle states, "Texting and e-mail and posting let us present the self we want to be."

Sometimes, however, a quotation includes words quoted from a different source or words already in quotation marks. You still use double quotation marks around the entire quote, but the quotation marks inside the quote become single quotation marks:

> Turkle asserts that our addiction to technology has caused us to lower our expectations for communication and that "Shakespeare might have said, 'We are consum'd with that which we were nourish'd by.'"

PRACTICE Using these guidelines, use the following quotations from Sherry Turkle's "The Flight from Conversation" in sentences, paying attention to proper punctuation:

- A 16-year-old boy who relies on texting for almost everything says almost wistfully, "Someday, someday, but certainly not now, I'd like to learn how to have a conversation."

- Human relationships are rich; they're messy and demanding.

Write the Conclusion

10. The conclusion should echo the ideas introduced earlier without repeating them directly. Also, the conclusion should answer the question, "So what?" It's a chance to comment on the significance of Turkle's argument and how she crafted it. You might consider the question *What does the text want readers to believe, feel, or do, and how successfully does it accomplish this purpose?* Note some ideas for your conclusion here.

Self-Review and Peer Feedback

11. Use the following checklist to review your own work. Then, swap essays with a partner and review their essay using the same checklist.

Does the essay

- include a strong claim?
- evaluate Turkle's use of evidence, reasoning, and persuasive elements?
- include relevant text evidence that supports the claim?
- include an introduction and a conclusion?
- follow standard English conventions, with few to no spelling and grammatical errors?

Finalize Your Essay and Reflect

12. Look over the feedback you received from your peer, and decide what changes you would like to make to your essay. When you have finished incorporating these changes and finalized your essay, take a moment to reflect on the process you have just completed.

Consider the following questions:

- What aspects of your essay are you most proud of?
- What do you think makes them strong?
- What things did you have trouble with that you feel you can learn from?
- What areas do you think you need to focus on in the future in order to improve your writing?

13. Look back at your essay. Did you use correct punctuation when incorporating quotations? Revise your writing as needed.

Joining the Conversation

Learning Strategies

Close Reading
Graphic Organizer
Marking the Text
Note-taking
Think-Pair-Share

Learning Targets

- Analyze details and fallacies in an argument.
- Explain how an author builds an argument.

Preview

In this activity, you will read a text about communication and analyze the evidence the author uses to support her argument.

My Notes

Making Connections

In the first part of the unit, you analyzed a variety of argumentative texts. In this section, you will continue to read argumentative texts across genres, and learn how to craft your own. You will explore the topic of justice before researching an issue of your own choice.

Unpacking the Embedded Assessment

Read the assignment for Embedded Assessment 1: Creating an Argument.

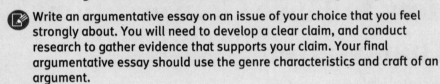 Write an argumentative essay on an issue of your choice that you feel strongly about. You will need to develop a clear claim, and conduct research to gather evidence that supports your claim. Your final argumentative essay should use the genre characteristics and craft of an argument.

Using the assignment and the Scoring Guide, work with your class to analyze the prompt and outline the tasks needed to complete your argument. Then create a preliminary outline of your essay's organizational structure. Copy the task list and outline into your Reader/Writer Notebook. After each of the following activities, revisit the Scoring Guide to identify potential areas of improvement to ensure success on the Embedded Assessment.

Evidence and Appeals

When presenting an argument, writers use evidence to support their positions. Of the types of evidence—empirical, logical, and anecdotal—anecdotal is the least reliable because it may be based on a personal account rather than fact or research.

When presenting their support for a particular point of view, writers use persuasive language to make their cases. A powerful argument is crafted using emotional, logical, and ethical appeals to those who have the power to take action on an issue.

As You Read

- Look for evidence presented to support the arguments. Mark each text with specific marks, such as underlining or circling, to identify each type of evidence.
- Circle unknown words and phrases. Try to determine the meaning of the words by using context clues, word parts, or a dictionary.

VOCABULARY

ACADEMIC

Evidence is information that supports a position in an argument. Empirical evidence is based on experiences and direct observation through research. Logical evidence is based on facts and a clear rationale. Anecdotal evidence is based on personal accounts of incidents.

Strong authors often make **appeals** to their readers' emotions, ethics, and logic in order to persuade their audience, known as *pathos*, *ethos*, and *logos*, respectively.

About the Author

Celeste Headlee (b. 1969) is an award-winning journalist, speaker, and author who has appeared on a variety of radio and television networks, including NPR, CNN, and BBC, as both a host and correspondent. Headlee also anchored the presidential election broadcast for PBS World in 2012. In addition to her day job as a journalist, Headlee is a professional opera singer, performing with opera companies across the country. She also lectures about her grandfather William Grant Still, who is considered the "dean" of African American composers, and edited a book about his illustrious career.

Argument

From We Need to Talk: How to Have Conversations That Matter

by **Celeste Headlee**

1   On January 13, 1982, a tragedy occurred just outside Washington, DC. More than six inches of snow fell at Ronald Reagan International. The airport was closed for most of the morning and reopened at noon. Air Florida Flight 90 had already been severely delayed when the captain had to make a choice about whether or not to take off. He could wait a little longer and have the plane de-iced one more time, or he could depart immediately and try to get his passengers back on schedule. It had been forty-nine minutes since the plane was de-iced. He chose to take off.

2   We know from the plane's voice recorder that soon after takeoff, the first officer tried to warn the captain that something was wrong.

3   FIRST OFFICER: Look how the ice is just hanging on his back there, see that? See all those icicles on the back there and everything?

CAPTAIN: Yeah.

FIRST OFFICER: Boy, this is a losing battle here on trying to de-ice those things; it gives you a false feeling of security, that's all it does.

[Some minutes go by]

FIRST OFFICER: God, look at that thing, that don't seem right, does it? *[3-second pause]* Ah, that's not right. Well—

CAPTAIN: Yes, it is, there's 80. [Referring to the airspeed]

FIRST OFFICER: Naw, I don't think that's right. *[7-second pause]* Ah, maybe it is… I don't know.

4 What neither pilot realized was that the readings in the cockpit weren't reliable because the instruments were clogged with ice. Also, the captain never turned on the heater in the plane's engines. About thirty-five seconds after the plane left the ground, we have this exchange from the cockpit:

5 FIRST OFFICER: Larry, we're going down, Larry.

CAPTAIN: I know it.

6 The plane slammed into the Fourteenth Street Bridge and then plunged into the Potomac River. Seventy-eight people died; only five ultimately survived. The crash of Air Florida Flight 90 is seen as a **pivotal** moment in the development of airline safety standards; it prompted the Federal Aviation Administration (FAA) to study how often a plane should be de-iced, how to create longer-lasting de-icing chemicals, and how airplane instruments are affected by cold temperatures. Experts also spent a lot of time studying that exchange in the cockpit, captured by the black box.

7 Twenty years later, I read about this incident while researching a story and it made me rethink my entire philosophy on conversation. Most communication experts who listened to the black box recording concluded that copilots should be trained to be more direct with their captains. But my first thought when I read the **transcript** was that we need to train pilots to listen better. I'd never before considered that improving conversational techniques could be a survival skill.

8 It may seem that the stakes will never be that high for most of us—that lives will never hang in the balance of our conversations. But let me ask you this: have you ever been admitted to a hospital? Oftentimes, lives *are* at stake. Communication failures led to 1,744 deaths in American hospitals between 2009 and 2013, and that includes only the cases that were tracked because a malpractice suit was filed. "Communication failures" is a fairly broad term used to describe everything from a night nurse failing to relay vital information to the nurse working the next shift to a doctor prescribing treatment without reviewing a patient's chart. It also includes breakdowns in communication with patients and their family members, who often arrive at the hospital anxious and confused.

9 Imagine for a moment how important it is to get these conversations exactly right. The need for **brevity** and efficiency must be balanced with careful listening. There are any number of emotional factors (physical pain, stress, confusion, anger) that could derail such a conversation and an equal number make it vital that the exchange be clear and comprehensive.

10 Personally, I'm grateful lives don't hang in the balance when I converse on the radio every day. But important, life-changing events are influenced and affected by the words we choose to say or leave unspoken.

My Notes

---

pivotal: crucially important
transcript: written or printed version
brevity: being brief and concise

My Notes

11 Take a moment to consider how many opportunities you may have missed, how many outcomes in your life may have been altered because of poor communication. Could you have landed that dream job if you'd nailed the interview? Saved a relationship if you'd been more open about certain issues? What about that political conversation at Thanksgiving dinner that got out of hand; was there a different way to defend your principles so that your cousin didn't storm away from the table (and still won't return your text messages)?

12 After I read the cockpit transcripts from Flight 90, I spent a lot of time reflecting on how many times I've failed to get my point across in a conversation and how often I've misunderstood what someone else was trying to tell me. I've also realized that saying the wrong thing in a conversation is a universal experience. We've all lost something because of what we heard and misunderstood. So we can all benefit from learning a better way.

13 Some of my greatest insights have come about as the result of failures. And one of my most valuable lessons in listening resulted from my failure to listen. Two days after the massive earthquake in Haiti in 2010, I spoke on air with a woman in Michigan named Mallery Thurlow. She had been trying for two days to reach her fiancé in Port-au-Prince and had been unsuccessful. She was desperate to reach him or anyone else who might be able to tell her if her loved ones were alive or dead.

14 Our production staff worked tirelessly to track down her fiancé, France Neptune, and we brought them both onto the air. Mallery and France heard each other's voices for the first time since the earthquake and my cohost and I listened as the couple spoke with each other, relief and gratitude audible in every syllable. It was moving for all of us. Up to that point, we were listening to a powerful conversation, but I should have stopped congratulating myself over a well-planned segment and really listened to where the discussion was headed.

15 We weren't expecting France to inform Mallery on live radio that her young godchild had died in the collapse of a school building. Mallery, not surprisingly, began to cry. I wasn't sure what to say. It was an uncomfortable moment for me and I can only imagine it was painful for the thousands of listeners who felt they were intruding on a highly personal and agonizing conversation. Our station later received a number of complaints.

16 Even if you set aside the humanity involved, that a person has just learned of the death of a loved one while thousands of people listened in, her tears don't make for a good broadcast. Hearing someone cry on the radio is painful, not powerful. Most people, understandably, want to console the person and can't. They want me, the host, to console the guest and often I don't have the words or time to do so. If I had been listening more carefully, I would have heard the turn in the conversation. I could have ended the segment and allowed Mallery and France their privacy. I didn't, and it still bothers me. I was too caught up in my own story to pay attention to theirs.

17 In my private life, I've lost contact with family members and I've seen friendships die in silence when I failed to say what was really on my mind.

WORD CONNECTIONS

Etymology

The word **fiancé** is a French term that first appeared in 1844 and means "a man engaged to be married." Originally, the word comes from the Latin verb *fidare*, meaning "to trust." Later, the word was adapted into Old French as *fiancier*, meaning "promise or trust."

audible: able to be heard

I've suffered in my career as well because I couldn't seem to make myself understood during important conversations with recruiters or managers.

18 I now believe that conversation may be one of the most fundamental skills we can learn and improve upon. So much hinges on what may seem like trivial chats.

...

19 It's hard to overestimate the power of conversation. It's hard to say too much about the gaps it can bridge and the wounds it can heal. At its best, conversation is a **potent** force for good. But when it goes wrong, that force can be equally damaging, equally harmful.

20 What I've seen in my own country and around the globe is what happens when conversation goes wrong or doesn't happen at all. And the irony is, we talk *about* conversation all the time. How many calls have there been in the United States for a "national conversation" on drugs, race, law enforcement, education, or immigration? Over and over we say we need to talk about issues, and then we proceed to shout out our own opinions with no regard to what the other side is saying. That's not a conversation!

21 Our world has become so fractured by politics and distracted by technology that having a meaningful conversation about anything has become a challenge. As Wesley Morris wrote in the *New York Times*, "We used to talk, and people would listen… People still gathered for the evening news. Mass culture was experienced *en masse*. A national conversation involved a large portion of the public talking about both important and **frivolous** stuff more or less at the same time."

22 It may be that conversations that matter most won't be held on a national stage at all, but rather in office cubicles or grocery store aisles. It might be that authentic conversations can't happen online but only in living rooms and lunchrooms and airports and restaurants.

23 No matter how much you like to think of yourself as a private person, your actions affect those around you in real, **tangible** ways. Like the famous flutter of Edward Lorenz's butterfly that eventually causes a hurricane, what you do has implications for the wider world around you. We must learn how to talk to one another and, more important, listen to one other. We must learn to talk to people we disagree with, because you can't unfriend everyone in real life.

Making Observations

- What argument is the author making about talking—and about listening?
- What details in the text caught your attention?

potent: powerful or influential
frivolous: unimportant
tangible: identifiable

Returning to the Text

- Reread the argument to answer these text-dependent questions.
- Write any additional questions you have about the text in your Reader/Writer Notebook.

1. What does the author suggest caused the tragedy of Air Florida Flight 90? How does she come to this conclusion?

2. What is the key idea of this passage, and how does Headlee support it?

3. What was one of Headlee's most valuable lessons in listening? What kind of appeal does she make?

4. The author writes, "In my private life, I've lost contact with family members and I've seen friendships die in silence when I failed to say what was really on my mind. " What is the author's purpose for including this reflection?

5. What do you think was Headlee's purpose in beginning with the story of Air Florida Flight 90? How does the story work with her argument throughout the text?

☑ Focus on the Sentence

Use information from *We Need to Talk* to write sentences using the words provided, as illustrated in the example.

Example: because/fractured

Because our world has become fractured by politics, it is more important than ever

that we learn how to have a conversation.

since/Mallery Thurlow

Even though/talk about conversation

Working from the Text

6. Return to the text and locate examples of evidence that you marked and identify whether they are empirical, logical, or anecdotal. With your group, discuss the impact of the evidence on the text and the reader, using examples from the text to support your answers.

Logical Fallacies

When you read an argumentative text, it's important to make sure you are examining the author's reasoning. Sometimes, writers may make statements that are not fully supported by logic or evidence.

A logical fallacy is a common error in reasoning that undermines the logic of an argument. Fallacies may be based on irrelevant points and are often identified because they lack evidence to support their claim. Some common fallacies are given in the following chart.

LITERARY

A logical fallacy is a mistaken belief or a false or misleading statement based on unsound evidence. Fallacious reasoning is illogical because it relies on a fallacy.

VOCABULARY

Examples of Common Fallacies

Hasty Generalization	A conclusion that is based on insufficient or biased evidence; in other words, rushing to a conclusion before all relevant facts are available.	**Example:** I asked two people if they like ice cream and they both said yes. If 100% of the people I asked like ice cream, then I can assume that all people like ice cream.
Either/Or	A conclusion that oversimplifies the argument by reducing it to only two sides or choices.	**Example:** You're either a cat person or a dog person.
Ad Populum	An argument that concludes that a fact, position, or proposition must be true because many people believe in it.	**Example:** Most people disagree with this new law; therefore, it is a bad idea.
Moral Equivalence	A comparison of minor misdeeds with major atrocities.	**Example:** Anyone who harms an animal is worse than Hitler.
Red Herring	A diversionary tactic that avoids the key issues, often by avoiding opposing arguments rather than addressing them.	**Example:** I know I'm late to school, but I did well on my last test.

7. With a partner, reread the excerpt from *We Need to Talk* and look for evidence of fallacious reasoning. Provide evidence for why you think the reasoning is fallacious and discuss how the writer could have changed her text to avoid these problems.

✅ Check Your Understanding

What other fallacies are commonly used in arguments? With a partner, discuss the ways in which anecdotal evidence could be an example of false or fallacious reasoning.

LANGUAGE & WRITER'S CRAFT: Colons and Semicolons

Colons and semicolons are used to help organize information in sentences.

The **colon** is used to introduce a list or quotation.

- Students can bring four items to take the test: calculator, protractor, pencil, and study guide.
- The welcome mat told her everything she needed to know: "Beware of Dog."

PRACTICE Write two sentences, one that uses a colon before a list and one that uses a colon to introduce a quotation.

The **semicolon** is used to join two closely related independent clauses.

- On went her old brown jacket; on went her old brown hat.
- Jaime's favorite food is spaghetti; his father's is a juicy burger.

Similar to the word *but*, **semicolons** can be used with the word *however* as a transitional phrase.

- Jaime's favorite food is spaghetti; however, his father can't stand it.

PRACTICE Write two sentences, one that uses a semicolon to link closely related independent clauses and one that uses a semicolon before the word *however*.

🖉 Explain How an Author Builds an Argument

Evaluate the claim Celeste Headlee makes about the importance of communication. Then assess the evidence she cites to support the claim and identify any logical fallacies or faulty reasoning she uses in her argument. Be sure to:

- Identify the author's main claim.
- Evaluate the various types of evidence the author provides to support the claim, including counterarguments, concessions, and rebuttals.
- Identify any logical fallacies or faulty reasoning, such as hasty generalization or either-or reasoning.
- Use semicolons and colons correctly and effectively.

Learning Strategies

Discussion Groups
Marking the Text
Think-Pair-Share

My Notes

Learning Targets

- Analyze a persuasive speech and identify the speaker's purpose.
- Analyze and evaluate text structure.
- Evaluate rhetorical devices and their effectiveness in an argument.

Preview

In this activity, you will read a speech about civil disobedience and analyze how the author builds his argument.

As You Read

- Put a star next to Gandhi's central claim, and underline the most important evidence that supports Gandhi's claim.
- Circle unknown words and phrases. Try to determine the meaning of the words by using context clues, word parts, or a dictionary.

About the Author

Mohandas Karamchand Gandhi (1869–1948) was a great believer in the power of using civil disobedience against governments that oppressed the poor and the disenfranchised. He spent seven years in South Africa leading and defending Indians born and living there without legal rights. It was there that he began practicing *satyagraha*, or passive resistance. Later, he returned to his homeland of India where he helped the country gain its independence from the British in 1947. He became known there as Mahatma, or "Great Soul." India, though free from Britain, suffered from internal turmoil as religious factions fought for power. Gandhi was assassinated by a fanatic.

Speech

From On Civil Disobedience

by **Mohandas K. Gandhi**

1   There are two ways of countering injustice. One way is to smash the head of the man who perpetrates injustice and to get your own head smashed in the process. All strong people in the world adopt this course. Everywhere wars are fought and millions of people are killed. The consequence is not the progress of a nation but its decline .... No country has ever become, or will ever become, happy through victory in war. A nation does not rise that way; it only falls further. In fact, what comes to it is defeat, not victory. And if, perchance, either our act or our purpose was ill-conceived, it brings disaster to both belligerents.

ill-conceived: poorly thought out

belligerents: participants in a war

My Notes

2   But through the other method of combating injustice, we alone suffer the consequences of our mistakes, and the other side is wholly spared. This other method is satyagraha.[1] One who resorts to it does not have to break another's head; he may merely have his own head broken. He has to be prepared to die himself suffering all the pain. In opposing the atrocious laws of the Government of South Africa, it was this method that we adopted. We made it clear to the said Government that we would never bow to its outrageous laws. No clapping is possible without two hands to do it, and no quarrel without two persons to make it. Similarly, no State is possible without two entities, the rulers and the ruled. You are our **sovereign**, our Government, only so long as we consider ourselves your subjects. When we are not subjects, you are not the sovereign either. So long as it is your endeavour to control us with justice and love, we will let you to do so. But if you wish to strike at us from behind, we cannot permit it. Whatever you do in other matters, you will have to ask our opinion about the laws that concern us. If you make laws to keep us **suppressed** in a wrongful manner and without taking us into confidence, these laws will merely adorn the statute books. We will never obey them. Award us for it what punishment you like; we will put up with it. Send us to prison and we will live there as in a paradise. Ask us to mount the **scaffold** and we will do so laughing. Shower what sufferings you like upon us; we will calmly endure all and not hurt a hair of your body. We will gladly die and will not so much as touch you. But so long as there is yet life in these our bones, we will never comply with your **arbitrary** laws.

In 1930, Gandhi led the Salt March, a nonviolent demonstration protesting British restrictions on salt production in Dandi, India.

Making Observations

- Which part of the text makes the strongest impression on you? Why?
- Based on the text you highlighted, what questions does this text raise for you about violent and nonviolent responses to injustice?

sovereign: supreme power
suppressed: put down by force
scaffold: platform on which people are executed by hanging
arbitrary: random and illogical

[1] Gandhi uses the term *satyagraha* (Sanskrit, meaning "insistence on truth") to describe his policy of seeking reform by means of nonviolent resistance.

INDEPENDENT READING LINK

Read and Recommend

Review the notes you have been taking in your Reader/Writer Notebook about your independent reading. In what ways does the selection address the issues of justice or civil disobedience? Write a one-paragraph review that explains how the work addresses these issues. Be specific. Include one or more reasons why the work might be helpful for peers to read as they consider arguments about justice or civil disobedience.

My Notes

Returning to the Text

- Reread the speech to answer these text-dependent questions.
- Write any additional questions you have about the text in your Reader/Writer Notebook.

1. What are the strongest pieces of evidence Gandhi gives to support his claim?

2. What kind of language does Gandhi use to appeal to his listeners when he states that unjust laws oppress people? What effect do his choices have?

3. What can you infer about how Gandhi feels about passive resistance? Cite text evidence to support your response.

4. According to Gandhi, what are the effects of a person resisting the law peacefully?

Working from the Text

5. Explain the following statement: "No clapping is possible without two hands to do it, and no quarrel without two persons to make it." What do you think Gandhi's purpose is in using these images?

My Notes

6. Look at how the author transitions from idea to idea. How does Gandhi use cause and effect to organize his speech? Create a graphic organizer in your Reader/Writer Notebook that shows the cause-and-effect patterns you identify in the speech.

7. **Collaborative Conversation:** Return to the essential question, "To what extent are we responsible for our fellow humans?" How do you think Gandhi would answer this question? How would you answer this question?

LANGUAGE & WRITER'S CRAFT: Organizing an Argument

Transition words and **phrases** can help the writer of an argument guide a reader from one idea to the next. In this sentence from "On Civil Disobedience," Gandhi uses the transition phrase *in fact* to emphasize a key point: "A nation does not rise that way; it only falls further. In fact, what comes to it is defeat, not victory." Other transitions that can be used to emphasize key points include *clearly* and *of course*.

Words that show contrast: *but, however, on the other hand*

Words that emphasize key points: *clearly, in fact, of course*

Words that introduce additional support: *additionally, also, furthermore, in addition*

Words that summarize an argument: *finally, in conclusion, to summarize*

Transitions can alter a sentence's meaning. Read the following examples, and then choose one more transition word to use and describe how it changes the meaning of the sentence.

Sentence	Implied Meaning
On the other hand, Gandhi gained respect in the West.	This contrast hints that elsewhere Gandhi may not have had respect.
Furthermore, Gandhi gained respect in the West.	This addition indicates that Gandhi was achieving many positive things, including gaining respect in the West.
_____, Gandhi gained respect in the West.	

PRACTICE Look back at your answers to the text-dependent questions. Find two places where you might use transitions to clarify and strengthen your ideas. Rewrite your responses using those transitions.

Parallelism

Writers use a variety of rhetorical devices to make the claims and evidence of their arguments clear to their audiences. One of these devices is parallelism.

Parallelism occurs when words or phrases are repeated to create a rhythmical pattern within a sentence or passage. Parallelism often contrasts images or ideas to highlight differences, or it connects similar ideas to show association. Parallelism is an effective rhetorical device because it makes statements memorable and powerful.

Review these examples of rhetorical parallelism with a partner. Identify the parallelism and then discuss the ways in which the parallelism makes the statement memorable and powerful.

"Ask not what your country can do for you; ask what you can do for your country."
—John F. Kennedy

"We make a living by what we get, we make a life by what we give."
—Winston Churchill

"If you want others to be happy, practice compassion. If you want to be happy, practice compassion." —Dalai Lama

8. What are some examples of parallelism Gandhi uses in his speech? What effect do they have on the reader?

📝 Explain How an Author Builds an Argument

Write an essay in which you explain how Gandhi builds an argument to persuade his audience that civil disobedience is more effective than violence. In your essay, analyze Gandhi's claim and how he uses parallelism to strengthen the logic and persuasiveness of his argument. Be sure to:

- Identify the author's claim.
- Evaluate various type of evidence, such as facts or examples, that support the claim.
- Analyze rhetorical devices such as appeals to emotion or parallelism.
- Use transition words and phrases, including common punctuation for transitions, such as a semicolon.

Taking a Stand on Legal Issues

As You Read

- Look for evidence presented to support the arguments. Note in the margin whether each type of evidence appeals to the readers' pathos, ethos, or logos.
- Circle unknown words and phrases. Try to determine the meaning of the words by using context clues, word parts, or a dictionary.

About the Author

Chief Joseph (1840–1904) was the leader of a band of the Nez Percé people, originally living in the Wallowa Valley in what is now Oregon. During years of struggle against whites who wanted their lands and broken promises from the federal government, Chief Joseph led his people in many battles to preserve their lands. On a desperate retreat toward Canada, Chief Joseph and his band were fighting the Army and the weather, and he finally surrendered in the Bear Paw Mountains of Montana.

Speech

On Surrender at Bear Paw Mountains, 1877

by **Chief Joseph**

1   Tell General Howard that I know his heart. What he told me before I have in my heart. I am tired of fighting. Our chiefs are killed. Looking Glass is dead, Tu-hul-hil-sote is dead. The old men are all dead. It is the young men who now say yes or no. He who led the young men [Joseph's brother Alikut] is dead. It is cold and we have no blankets. The little children are freezing to death. My people—some of them have run away to the hills and have no blankets and no food. No one knows where they are—perhaps freezing to death. I want to have time to look for my children and see how many of them

chiefs: rulers of a group of people

My Notes

I can find. Maybe I shall find them among the dead. Hear me, my chiefs, my heart is sick and sad. From where the sun now stands I will fight no more forever.

Making Observations
- What questions do you have about why Chief Joseph wanted to speak?
- What emotions did you have as you read the speech?

Returning to the Text
- Reread the speech to answer these text-dependent questions.
- Write any additional questions you have about the text in your Reader/Writer Notebook.

1. Which rhetorical appeal does Chief Joseph primarily use to appeal to his listeners: ethos, pathos, or logos? Give examples and explain their appeal.

2. What tone does Chief Joseph use in this speech? Provide examples and explain how they work to create the tone.

As You Read

- Look for evidence presented to support the arguments. Note each type of evidence in the margin or with sticky notes.
- Circle unknown words and phrases. Try to determine the meaning of the words by using context clues, word parts, or a dictionary.

About the Author

Susan B. Anthony (1820–1905) became a prominent leader for women's suffrage, giving speeches in both the United States and Europe. With Elizabeth Cady Stanton, she created and produced The Revolution, a weekly publication that lobbied for women's rights. The newspaper's motto was "Men their rights, and nothing more; women their rights, and nothing less." After lobbying for the right to vote for many years, in 1872 Anthony took matters into her own hands and voted illegally in the presidential election. Anthony was arrested and unsuccessfully fought the charges. She was fined $100, which she never paid. Anthony delivered this address to explain her own civil disobedience.

Speech

On Women's Right to Vote

by Susan B. Anthony

Philadelphia **1872**

1   Friends and fellow citizens: I stand before you tonight under indictment for the alleged crime of having voted at the last presidential election, without having a lawful right to vote. It shall be my work this evening to prove to you that in thus voting, I not only committed no crime, but, instead, simply exercised my citizen's rights, guaranteed to me and all United States citizens by the National Constitution, beyond the power of any state to deny.

2   The preamble of the Federal Constitution says:

3   We, the people of the United States, in order to form a more perfect union, establish justice, insure domestic tranquillity, provide for the common defense, promote the general welfare, and secure the blessings of liberty to ourselves and our posterity, do ordain and establish this Constitution for the United States of America.

domestic: related to the United States

posterity: all future generations

My Notes

4   It was we, the people; not we, the white male citizens; nor yet we, the male citizens; but we, the whole people, who formed the Union. And we formed it, not to give the blessings of liberty, but to secure them; not to the half of ourselves and the half of our posterity, but to the whole people—women as well as men. And it is a downright mockery to talk to women of their enjoyment of the blessings of liberty while they are denied the use of the only means of securing them provided by this democratic-republican government—the ballot.

5   For any state to make sex a qualification that must ever result in the disfranchisement of one entire half of the people, is to pass a bill of attainder, or, an ex post facto law, and is therefore a violation of the supreme law of the land. By it the blessings of liberty are forever withheld from women and their female posterity.

6   To them this government has no just powers derived from the consent of the governed. To them this government is not a democracy. It is not a republic. It is an odious aristocracy; a hateful oligarchy of sex; the most hateful aristocracy ever established on the face of the globe; an oligarchy of wealth, where the rich govern the poor. An oligarchy of learning, where the educated govern the ignorant, or even an oligarchy of race, where the Saxon rules the African, might be endured; but this oligarchy of sex, which makes father, brothers, husband, sons, the oligarchs over the mother and sisters, the wife and daughters, of every household—which ordains all men sovereigns, all women subjects, carries dissension, discord, and rebellion into every home of the nation. Webster, Worcester, and Bouvier[1] all define a citizen to be a person in the United States, entitled to vote and hold office.

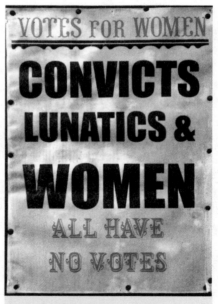

A sign used during the women's suffrage movement

disfranchisement: deprivation of the right to vote; modern spelling is *disenfranchisement*

bill of attainer: a law that punishes a person or people for a crime, often without a trial

ex post facto: after the fact

oligarchy: a small group that runs a government

dissension: disagreement

---

[1] Webster, Worcester, and Bouvier were all authors of dictionaries.

7 The only question left to be settled now is: Are women persons? And I hardly believe any of our opponents will have the hardihood to say they are not. Being persons, then, women are citizens; and no state has a right to make any law, or to enforce any old law, that shall abridge their privileges or immunities. Hence, every discrimination against women in the constitutions and laws of the several states is today null and void, precisely as is every one against Negroes.

Making Observations
- What is your first reaction to the speech?
- Which words or phrases jump out at you?

Returning to the Text

- Reread the speech to answer these text-dependent questions.
- Write any additional questions you have about the text in your Reader/Writer Notebook.

3. What evidence does Anthony use to support her claim that she committed no crime when she voted?

_____

_____

_____

_____

4. What rhetorical appeal does Anthony primarily use in this speech? What secondary appeal does she use? Give examples.

_____

_____

_____

_____

Working from the Text

5. Explain which rhetorical appeal—pathos, ethos, or logos—used in "On Women's Right to Vote" is the most effective.

📝 Writing Prompt: Informational

Compare and contrast how the author of each historic speech uses argument to take a stand on a legal issue. Identify the issue in each speech and the claim made by each speaker. Which type of rhetorical appeals are used, and what are the similarities and differences in how the authors use them? Be sure to:

- Identify the title, author, and issue presented in each speech.
- Begin with a thesis statement that provides your main idea about how each author uses rhetorical appeals.
- Establish and maintain a formal style and objective tone, staying true to conventions of the discipline in which you are writing.
- Link main points with effective transitions to clearly identify similarities and differences in the way the speeches build an argument.
- Provide a concluding section that supports your main point.

Taking a Stand Against Hunger

Learning Strategies

Brainstorming
Discussion Groups
Marking the Text
Note-taking
Paraphrasing
Think-Pair-Share

Learning Targets

- Identify an author's purpose and analyze the argument presented.
- Synthesize information from print and multimedia sources.
- Conduct research and present findings in an argumentative text.
- Integrate ideas from multiple texts to build knowledge and vocabulary about advocacy.

Preview

In this activity, you will read two texts and analyze the evidence the authors use to support their arguments.

As You Read

- As you read the text and the graph, circle the claims, and underline and label the various types of evidence that support the claims.
- Circle unknown words and phrases. Try to determine the meaning of the words by using context clues, word parts, or a dictionary.

About the Document

The following document is a proclamation issued by the United Nations on November 20, 1959. The United Nations is an international organization made up of representatives from countries around the world that promotes justice on issues that transcend individual cultures and societies. The United Nations maintains peace and security among nations, and aids in the development of countries around the world. This proclamation was issued in order to promote the rights of children around the world.

Proclamation

Declaration of the Rights of the Child

PROCLAIMED BY GENERAL ASSEMBLY RESOLUTION 1386(XIV) OF 20 NOVEMBER 1959

1   *Whereas* the peoples of the United Nations have, in the Charter, reaffirmed their faith in fundamental human rights and in the dignity and worth of the human person, and have determined to promote social progress and better standards of life in larger freedom,

2   *Whereas* the United Nations has, in the Universal Declaration of Human Rights, proclaimed that everyone is entitled to all the rights and freedoms set forth therein, without distinction of any kind, such as race, color, sex, language, religion, political or other opinion, national or social origin, property, birth or other status,

My Notes

KNOWLEDGE QUEST

Knowledge Question:
Why might someone feel compelled to advocate for others?
In Activity 1.9, you will read two texts about the fundamental rights of children. While you read and build knowledge about the topic, think about your answer to the Knowledge Question.

whereas: because it is true that

GRAMMAR & USAGE

Verb Tenses

Verbs have active and passive voice in all six tenses. A passive-voice verb always contains a form of *be* followed by the past participle of the verb. The voice of a verb (active or passive) indicates whether the subject performs (active) or receives (passive) the action.

Active voice, future tense: "The child shall enjoy all the rights. ..."

Passive voice, future tense: "Every child shall be entitled. ..."

Generally, it is preferable to use the active voice in your writing. The active voice is more direct and concise. Sometimes, however, the passive voice is more appropriate when the doer of the action is unknown or is less important than the person receiving the action. In a formal document such as this proclamation, why is the use of passive voice appropriate?

My Notes

3   *Whereas* the child, by reason of his physical and mental immaturity, needs special safeguards and care, including appropriate legal protection, before as well as after birth,

4   *Whereas* the need for such special safeguards has been stated in the Geneva Declaration of the Rights of the Child of 1924, and recognized in the Universal Declaration of Human Rights and in the statutes of specialized agencies and international organizations concerned with the welfare of children,

5   *Whereas* mankind owes to the child the best it has to give,

6   *Now therefore,*

7   *The General Assembly*

8   *Proclaims* this Declaration of the Rights of the Child to the end that he may have a happy childhood and enjoy for his own good and for the good of society the rights and freedoms herein set forth, and calls upon parents, upon men and women as individuals, and upon voluntary organizations, local authorities and national Governments to recognize these rights and strive for their observance by legislative and other measures progressively taken in accordance with the following principles:

Principle 1

9   The child shall enjoy all the rights set forth in this Declaration. Every child, without any exception whatsoever, shall be entitled to these rights, without distinction or discrimination on account of race, color, sex, language, religion, political or other opinion, national or social origin, property, birth or other status, whether of himself or of his family.

Principle 2

10   The child shall enjoy special protection, and shall be given opportunities and facilities, by law and by other means, to enable him to develop physically, mentally, morally, spiritually and socially in a healthy and normal manner and in conditions of freedom and dignity. In the enactment of laws for this purpose, the best interests of the child shall be the paramount consideration.

Principle 3

11   The child shall be entitled from his birth to a name and a nationality.

Principle 4

12   The child shall enjoy the benefits of social security. He shall be entitled to grow and develop in health; to this end, special care and protection shall be provided both to him and to his mother, including adequate pre-natal and post-natal care. The child shall have the right to adequate nutrition, housing, recreation and medical services.

Principle 5

13   The child who is physically, mentally or socially handicapped shall be given the special treatment, education and care required by his particular condition.

Principle 6

14 The child, for the full and harmonious development of his personality, needs love and understanding. He shall, wherever possible, grow up in the care and under the responsibility of his parents, and, in any case, in an atmosphere of affection and of moral and material security; a child of tender years shall not, save in exceptional circumstances, be separated from his mother. Society and the public authorities shall have the duty to extend particular care to children without a family and to those without adequate means of support. Payment of State and other assistance towards the maintenance of children of large families is desirable.

Principle 7

15 The child is entitled to receive education, which shall be free and compulsory, at least in the elementary stages. He shall be given an education which will promote his general culture and enable him, on a basis of equal opportunity, to develop his abilities, his individual judgement, and his sense of moral and social responsibility, and to become a useful member of society.

16 The best interests of the child shall be the guiding principle of those responsible for his education and guidance; that responsibility lies in the first place with his parents.

17 The child shall have full opportunity for play and recreation, which should be directed to the same purposes as education; society and the public authorities shall endeavour to promote the enjoyment of this right.

Principle 8

18 The child shall in all circumstances be among the first to receive protection and relief.

Principle 9

19 The child shall be protected against all forms of neglect, cruelty and exploitation. He shall not be the subject of traffic, in any form.

20 The child shall not be admitted to employment before an appropriate minimum age; he shall in no case be caused or permitted to engage in any occupation or employment which would prejudice his health or education, or interfere with his physical, mental or moral development.

Principle 10

21 The child shall be protected from practices which may foster racial, religious and any other form of discrimination. He shall be brought up in a spirit of understanding, tolerance, friendship among peoples, peace and universal brotherhood, and in full consciousness that his energy and talents should be devoted to the service of his fellow men.

Knowledge Quest

- What about this proclamation surprises you?
- What questions do you have about advocating for children after reading this proclamation?

My Notes

WORD CONNECTIONS

Multiple Meaning Word
Traffic means both "vehicles driving on a road" and "illegal activity."

compulsory: enforced
exploitation: use for someone else's benefit

Returning to the Text

- Reread the informational text to answer these text-dependent questions.
- Write any additional questions you have about the text in your Reader/Writer Notebook.

1. Reread the statements at the beginning of the proclamation starting with "Whereas." How do these statements serve to set up the principles that follow?

_____

_____

_____

_____

2. KQ According to this declaration, why do children need someone to advocate for them?

_____

_____

_____

_____

3. KQ What does the word *welfare* mean in paragraph 4? Use a dictionary and the word's context to help you decide. Then use the declaration's principles to help you infer what the General Assembly believes are possible threats to a child's welfare.

_____

_____

_____

_____

4. How does this document advocate for the rights of children? Why is this important to understand?

_____

_____

_____

_____

Data and Statistics from the World Health Organization

Read the following pie chart, and then discuss the statistics on world hunger from the World Health Organization.

KNOWLEDGE QUEST

Knowledge Question:
Why might someone feel compelled to advocate for others?

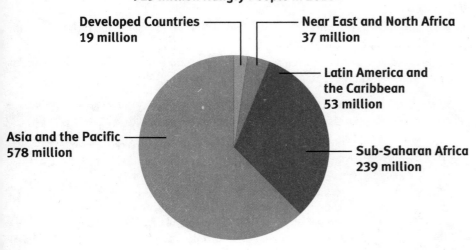

Number of Hungry People in the World
925 Million Hungry People in 2010

Developed Countries
19 million

Near East and North Africa
37 million

Latin America and
the Caribbean
53 million

Asia and the Pacific
578 million

Sub-Saharan Africa
239 million

My Notes

Statistic 1

"In round numbers there are 7 billion people in the world. Thus, with an estimated 925 million hungry people in the world, 13.1 percent, or almost 1 in 7 people are hungry."

Statistic 2

"Children are the most visible victims of undernutrition. Children who are poorly nourished suffer up to 160 days of illness each year. Poor nutrition plays a role in at least half of the 10.9 million child deaths each year—5 million deaths. Undernutrition magnifies the effect of every disease, including measles and malaria."

Working from the Text

5. Look back at the "Declaration of the Rights of the Child," Principle 4. Considering the World Health Organization data, how is the world upholding the promises of the declaration?

6. Compare the data in the chart with Statistic 1. What does the chart show you that the statistic does not? What does the statistic tell you that the chart does not show?

My Notes

☑ **Check Your Understanding**

Are any of these statistics surprising? Are there any that you would like to investigate further? Discuss your ideas with a partner. As you move through this activity, you will have the opportunity to conduct research on the issue of hunger or other issues of interest to you.

As You Read

- Put a star next to the author's claim, and underline the evidence that the author provides to support the claim.
- Circle unknown words and phrases. Try to determine the meaning of the words by using context clues, word parts, or a dictionary.

About the Author

Billy Shore is the founder and executive chairman of Share our Strength, a nonprofit organization working to end childhood hunger in the United States. Since its founding in 1984, the organization has raised more than $600 million in the battle against hunger. Shore is also the chair of Community Wealth Partners, a group that strives to solve social problems in communities. In 2014, Congress appointed Shore to the National Commission on Hunger, a bipartisan group designed to find new ways to end hunger in the United States.

⊘ **KNOWLEDGE QUEST**

Knowledge Question:
Why might someone feel compelled to advocate for others?

Editorial

The Summer Hunger Crisis

by **Billy Shore**

1 From the city streets of Baltimore to the wide open spaces of Kansas and the suburban cul-de-sacs of Fort Worth, kids will struggle to eat this summer. Summer vacation will be a time of anxiety and stress for low-income families forced to decide between buying a bag of groceries and paying the electric bill.

2 It doesn't have to be this way. Summer meals are available to help millions of children get the nutrition they need. These meals could be a **catalyst** for improving the overall well-being of children across the nation.

3 One in five kids in the United States lives in a "food insecure" family, a family that struggles to consistently put enough food on the table for everyone. During the school year, free and reduced-price meals at school are a lifeline, ensuring that children get reliable access to nutrition. When schools close for the summer, however, these meals disappear. In one recent survey, low-income families say grocery bills can rise as much as $300 a month during the summer, putting incredible pressure on already-strained budgets.

catalyst: cause for change

4 The national summer meals program was created 40 years ago to help students get enough nutrition when school is out of session. When the program works well, it's an essential aid. No Kid Hungry works with local organizations around the nation to find new, effective, **innovative** ways to connect kids to the program and provide healthy meals during the summer months.

5 Today, however, the program just doesn't reach a majority of kids in need. Of the 22 million kids who receive a free or reduced-price school lunch, only 4 million are getting a summer meal.

6 There is a variety of barriers that block kids from accessing meals. Excessive red tape discourages many organizations from becoming meal sites. Kids are required to eat their meals at the sites, but with many parents at work and with school buses out of service for the summer, transportation can be impossible. In rural areas and the suburbs, kids can live miles away from meal sites. Summer storms and extreme heat close sites. As a result, for every kid who eats regularly at a summer meals site, there are five more who miss out. That adds up to millions of hungry kids.

7 This has major **ramifications**. A summer meals program that doesn't reach kids **exacerbates** the struggles faced by many children growing up in poverty. Studies show that students from low-income families experience a greater "summer slide" in academics than their peers, returning to school two months behind in reading. The effect is cumulative, and by the end of fifth grade, low-income students are nearly three grade equivalents behind their peers in reading.

8 Students who do not get enough nutrition over the summer months are more likely to experience long-term health consequences than their more affluent peers. Hunger makes children more **susceptible** to **chronic** diseases, like iron deficiency, anemia, asthma, type 2 diabetes, and heart disease. It also leads to a higher rate of pediatric hospitalizations.

9 These problems are costly and avoidable. Consistent access to nutritious meals during the summer can act as a vaccine that ensures that kids are healthier, smarter, and stronger.

10 We need to spur our federal lawmakers into action. Congress is currently considering improvements to the summer meals program through child nutrition reauthorization, but the process has been slow moving and plagued by inaction.

11 We must continue to urge our lawmakers to stand up for kids and pass a strong bill that supports and strengthens existing summer meals sites. We also need policies to make it easier for states to reach low-income children in hard-to-reach places, such as rural communities or areas currently ineligible to host summer sites.

12 For example, when accessing a summer meal site is difficult or impossible for children, states should have the option of delivering meals or allowing children to leave a site with a meal for later. And where it makes sense, states should have the option of providing low-income families with a grocery store credit during the summer months to purchase nutritious foods, a model that has been proven to reduce the most severe forms of childhood hunger by up to one-third.

My Notes

innovative: new
ramifications: consequences
exacerbates: makes more severe
susceptible: at risk
chronic: long-term

13   We can't let our foot off the gas. Kids can't push pause on their growling stomachs until we figure this out—this is happening in real time.

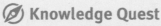

Knowledge Quest
- Which words or phrases show that the author is advocating on behalf of children?
- How do you feel after reading this editorial?

Returning to the Text
- Reread the editorial to answer these text-dependent questions.
- Write any additional questions you have about the text in your Reader/Writer Notebook.

7. How does the author use emotional appeal to set up his claim about a summer hunger crisis? What effect is the author trying to achieve? What words and phrases does he use to appeal to emotion?

_____

_____

_____

_____

8. **KQ** In paragraph 6, it says that red tape is a barrier to children getting proper nutrition. What does *red tape* mean? Use a dictionary and context clues to help you decide. Then tell why children are made especially vulnerable by the red tape for meal sites.

_____

_____

_____

_____

9. **KQ** What evidence does the author provide to support his claim that a lack of meals can have significant consequences for kids during the summer?

_____

_____

_____

_____

10. What is the author's purpose in writing this essay? Provide details from the text to support your argument.

_____

_____

_____

_____

_____

11. **KQ** Why is proper nutrition a fundamental right of children? How does a lack of nutrition over the summer become a long-term problem later on?

_____

_____

_____

_____

Ⓞ Knowledge Quest

After reading two texts about fundamental child rights, talk with a partner about why a person might feel compelled to advocate for others. Discuss why it is important for children to have a written declaration of rights.

🔲 INDEPENDENT READING LINK

You can continue to build your knowledge about advocacy by reading other articles at ZINC Reading Labs. Search for keywords such as *fundamental rights* or *advocacy*.

🍃 | Z I N C

Working from the Text

12. In a small group, critique the effect of the author's argument. Share examples of the author's evidence (logical, empirical, anecdotal) and discuss the effectiveness of the evidence presented. Can you identify whether the author uses fallacious reasoning and, if so, where?

My Notes

13. **On-the-Spot Research:** Is hunger a problem in your community? Conduct research on the issue of hunger in your community. Connect your research findings to the text in an effort to defend or challenge Shore's claims.

   - First, create a question you would like to answer through your research. Then, use available resources to find answers to your question, creating new questions or revising your questions as needed based on your findings.
   - Organize your evidence by form (empirical, logical, anecdotal). Be sure to include at least two pieces of empirical evidence.
   - Finally, synthesize your findings and supporting evidence and present them to a small group of peers. Be sure to present information clearly and concisely. Also, focus on presenting in a logical way so that listeners can easily follow your line of reasoning.

Gaining Perspectives

Childhood hunger is a health problem that affects most communities across the United States. Imagine that you have been selected by your school to participate in a summer program that provides meals to students enrolled in district schools. How would you begin to spread the news about the program to students in your community? What steps would you take to ensure students' privacy? How would you continue to promote wellness throughout the summer? Discuss the potential challenges and benefits with a partner. Then explain your decision-making process for each question, and write it in your Reader/Writer Notebook.

Writing Prompt: Argumentative

After researching the issue of hunger in your community, write an essay that elaborates on the problem of hunger, how we can solve it, and why we are responsible to help. Support your position with evidence from your research. Be sure to:

- Establish a clear, arguable claim.
- Use various types of relevant supporting evidence and pertinent examples to support your claim.
- Use rhetorical devices such as appeals or parallelism.

INDEPENDENT READING LINK

Read and Connect
Review the notes you have been taking in your Reader/Writer Notebook about your independent reading. In what ways does your selection address the issue of poverty or hunger or another social issue? Collaborate with your peers to discuss the elements of argumentative texts that address social issues. Remember to listen actively during the discussion and respond appropriately and respectfully.

Taking a Stand on Truth and Responsibility

Learning Strategies

Close Reading
Guided Reading
Marking the Text
Metacognitive Markers
Note-taking
Socratic Seminar

Learning Targets

- Analyze language in two speeches by Nobel Prize winners.
- Synthesize textual evidence by participating actively in a Socratic Seminar.
- Emulate the model speeches by drafting an argumentative speech.

Preview

In this activity, you will read two speeches on the topic of truth and responsibility in the face of adversity and then participate in a Socratic Seminar.

Introducing the Strategy: Metacognitive Markers

Metacognition refers to the thinking you do about your own learning. Using metacognitive markers involves marking the text with symbols to reflect the thinking you are doing as you read. After reading, you can scan the text and use your metacognitive markers to quickly find evidence when you are talking or writing about a text.

Here are the markers:

? Use a question mark for questions you have about the text.

! Use an exclamation point for a reaction to what you are reading.

* Use an asterisk for a comment about the text.

_ Use an underline to identify a key idea or detail in the text.

As You Read

- Highlight text that suggests what Annan believes it means to speak truth in the face of adversity.
- Circle unknown words and phrases. Try to determine the meaning of the words by using context clues, word parts, or a dictionary.

About the Author

Kofi Annan (1938–2018) was a Ghanaian diplomat who served as secretary-general of the United Nations from January 1997 until December 2006. Born into an aristocratic family in Ghana, Annan studied in Ghana, the United States, and Switzerland before joining the United Nations as an international civil servant in 1962. As the secretary-general, Annan urged corporations to follow environmental standards and respect human rights and issued a "Call to Action" to combat the global HIV/AIDS pandemic. He also focused on ending poverty and violence, promoting equality, and protecting the environment. In December 2001, Annan and the United Nations were awarded the Nobel Peace Prize.

My Notes

Speech

Nobel Lecture

by **Kofi Annan**

Oslo, **December 10, 2001**

1   Your Majesties, Your Royal Highnesses, Excellencies, Members of the Norwegian Nobel Committee, Ladies and Gentlemen,

2   Today, in Afghanistan, a girl will be born. Her mother will hold her and feed her, comfort her and care for her—just as any mother would anywhere in the world. In these most basic acts of human nature, humanity knows no divisions. But to be born a girl in today's Afghanistan is to begin life centuries away from the prosperity that one small part of humanity has achieved. It is to live under conditions that many of us in this hall would consider inhuman.

3   I speak of a girl in Afghanistan, but I might equally well have mentioned a baby boy or girl in Sierra Leone. No one today is unaware of this divide between the world's rich and poor. No one today can claim ignorance of the cost that this divide imposes on the poor and **dispossessed** who are no less deserving of human dignity, fundamental freedoms, security, food and education than any of us. The cost, however, is not borne by them alone. Ultimately, it is borne by all of us—North and South, rich and poor, men and women of all races and religions.

4   Today's real borders are not between nations, but between powerful and powerless, free and **fettered**, privileged and humiliated. Today, no walls can separate humanitarian or human rights crises in one part of the world from national security crises in another.

5   Scientists tell us that the world of nature is so small and interdependent that a butterfly flapping its wings in the Amazon rainforest can generate a violent storm on the other side of the earth. This principle is known as the "Butterfly Effect." Today, we realize, perhaps more than ever, that the world of human activity also has its own "Butterfly Effect"—for better or for worse.

6   Ladies and Gentlemen,

7   We have entered the third **millennium** through a gate of fire. If today, after the horror of 11 September, we see better, and we see further—we will realize that humanity is indivisible. New threats make no distinction between races, nations or regions. A new insecurity has entered every mind, regardless of wealth or status. A deeper awareness of the bonds that bind us all – in pain as in prosperity—has gripped young and old.

8   In the early beginnings of the 21st century—a century already violently **disabused** of any hopes that progress towards global peace and prosperity is inevitable—this new reality can no longer be ignored. It must be confronted.

dispossessed: those who are deprived of homes, possessions, or safety
fettered: restrained
millennium: thousand years
disabused: freed from error or misunderstanding

My Notes

9 The 20th century was perhaps the deadliest in human history, devastated by innumerable conflicts, untold suffering, and unimaginable crimes. Time after time, a group or a nation inflicted extreme violence on another, often driven by irrational hatred and suspicion, or unbounded arrogance and thirst for power and resources. In response to these cataclysms, the leaders of the world came together at mid-century to unite the nations as never before.

10 A forum was created—the United Nations—where all nations could join forces to affirm the dignity and worth of every person, and to secure peace and development for all peoples. Here States could unite to strengthen the rule of law, recognize and address the needs of the poor, restrain man's brutality and greed, conserve the resources and beauty of nature, sustain the equal rights of men *and* women, and provide for the safety of future generations.

11 We thus inherit from the 20th century the political, as well as the scientific and technological power, which—if only we have the will to use them—give us the chance to vanquish poverty, ignorance and disease.

12 In the 21st Century I believe the mission of the United Nations will be defined by a new, more profound, awareness of the sanctity and dignity of every human life, regardless of race or religion. This will require us to look beyond the framework of States, and beneath the surface of nations or communities. We must focus, as never before, on improving the conditions of the individual men and women who give the state or nation its richness and character. We must begin with the young Afghan girl, recognizing that saving that one life is to save humanity itself.

Making Observations
- What images did you see in your mind as you read this speech?
- Are there any words or phrases in this speech that stand out to you?

cataclysms: violent events
forum: place where ideas can be exchanged

Returning to the Text

- Reread the speech to answer these text-dependent questions.
- Write any additional questions you have about the text in your Reader/Writer Notebook.

1. Who is Kofi Annan addressing in this speech? What clues in the text help identify that he is speaking not only to the people in the room, but to the world?

2. What words and phrases does Annan use to describe the horrors of the twentieth century? How does this help shape the perception of readers?

3. What conclusion does Annan draw about the future of the United Nations? What argument does he make about how the United Nations should change?

As You Read

- Mark the text for evidence of Elle Wiesel's claim, counterarguments, evidence, and examples.
- Circle unknown words and phrases. Try to determine the meaning of the words by using context clues, word parts, or a dictionary.

About the Author

Elie Wiesel (1928–2016) was born in the town of Sighet, now part of Romania. During World War II, he and his family were deported to the German concentration and extermination camps. His parents and little sister perished, while Wiesel and his two older sisters survived. Liberated from Buchenwald in 1945 by Allied troops, Wiesel went to Paris, where he studied at the Sorbonne and worked as a journalist. In 1958, he published his first book, *La Nuit* (*Night*), a memoir of his experiences in the concentration camps. He authored nearly thirty books, some of which use these events as their basic material. In his many lectures, Wiesel concerned himself with the situation of the Jews and other groups who have suffered persecution and death because of their religion, race, or national origin. Wiesel made his home in New York City and became a United States citizen. He was awarded the Nobel Peace Prize in 1986.

Speech

From

Hope, Despair, and Memory

by **Elie Wiesel**

December 11, 1986

1 Just as man cannot live without dreams, he cannot live without hope. If dreams reflect the past, hope summons the future. Does this mean that our future can be built on a rejection of the past? Surely such a choice is not necessary. The two are **incompatible**. The opposite of the past is not the future but the absence of future; the opposite of the future is not the past but the absence of past. The loss of one is equivalent to the sacrifice of the other.

2 A recollection. The time: After the war. The place: Paris. A young man struggles to readjust to life. His mother, his father, his small sister are gone. He is alone. On the verge of despair. And yet he does not give up. On the contrary, he strives to find a place among the living. He acquires a new language. He

> **incompatible:** unable to be used together

My Notes

makes a few friends who, like himself, believe that the memory of evil will serve as a shield against evil; that the memory of death will serve as a shield against death.

3   This he must believe in order to go on. For he has just returned from a universe where God, betrayed by His creatures, covered His face in order not to see. Mankind, jewel of his creation, had succeeded in building an inverted Tower of Babel[1], reaching not toward heaven but toward an anti-heaven, there to create a parallel society, a new "creation" with its own princes and gods, laws and principles, jailers and prisoners. A world where the past no longer counted—no longer meant anything.

4   Stripped of possessions, all human ties severed, the prisoners found themselves in a social and cultural void. "Forget," they were told. "Forget where you came from; forget who you were. Only the present matters." But the present was only a blink of the Lord's eye. The Almighty himself was a slaughterer: it was He who decided who would live and who would die; who would be tortured, and who would be rewarded. Night after night, seemingly endless processions vanished into the flames, lighting up the sky. Fear dominated the universe. Indeed this was another universe; the very laws of nature had been transformed. Children looked like old men, old men whimpered like children. Men and women from every corner of Europe were suddenly reduced to nameless and faceless creatures desperate for the same ration of bread or soup, dreading the same end. Even their silence was the same for it resounded with the memory of those who were gone. Life in this accursed universe was so distorted, so unnatural that a new species had evolved. Waking among the dead, one wondered if one were still alive. …

5   Of course, we could try to forget the past. Why not? Is it not natural for a human being to repress what causes him pain, what causes him shame? Like the body, memory protects its wounds. When day breaks after a sleepless night, one's ghosts must withdraw; the dead are ordered back to their graves. But for the first time in history, we could not bury our dead. We bear their graves within ourselves.

6   For us, forgetting was never an option. …

7   And yet it is surely human to forget, even to want to forget. The Ancients saw it as a divine gift. Indeed the memory helps us to survive, forgetting allows us to go on living. How could we go on with our daily lives, if we remained constantly aware of the dangers and ghosts surrounding us? The Talmud[2] tells us that without the ability to forget, man would soon cease to learn. Without the ability to forget, man would live in a permanent, paralyzing fear of death. Only God and God alone can and must remember everything.

8   How are we to reconcile our supreme duty towards memory with the need to forget that is essential to life? No generation has had to confront this

---

[1] In the Bible, the building of the *Tower of Babel* caused God to divide humanity into speakers of different languages.

[2] The *Talmud* is an important scholarly text in the Jewish religion.

My Notes

paradox with such urgency. The survivors wanted to communicate everything to the living: the victim's solitude and sorrow, the tears of mothers driven to madness, the prayers of the doomed beneath a fiery sky.

9   They needed to tell of the child who, in hiding with his mother, asked softly, very softly: "Can I cry now?" They needed to tell of the sick beggar who, in a sealed cattlecar, began to sing as an offering to his companions. And of the little girl who, hugging her grandmother, whispered: "Don't be afraid, don't be sorry to die … I'm not." She was seven, that little girl who went to her death without fear, without regret.

10   Each one of us felt compelled to record every story, every encounter. Each one of us felt compelled to bear witness. Such were the wishes of the dying, the **testament** of the dead. Since the so-called civilized world had no use for their lives, then let it be inhabited by their deaths. …

11   After the war we reassured ourselves that it would be enough to relate a single night in Treblinka, to tell of her cruelty, the senselessness of murder, and the outrage born of indifference: it would be enough to find the right word and the **propitious** moment to say it, to shake humanity out of its indifference and keep the torturer from torturing ever again. We thought it would be enough to read the world a poem written by a child in the Theresienstadt ghetto to ensure that no child anywhere would ever again have to endure hunger or fear. It would be enough to describe a death-camp "Selection," to prevent the human right to dignity from ever being violated again.

12   We thought it would be enough to tell of the tidal wave of hatred which broke over the Jewish people for men everywhere to decide once and for all to put an end to hatred of anyone who is "different"—whether black or white, Jew or Arab, Christian or Moslem[3]—anyone whose orientation differs politically, philosophically, sexually. A naive undertaking? Of course. But not without a certain logic.

13   We tried. It was not easy. At first, because of the language; language failed us. We would have to invent a new vocabulary, for our own words were inadequate, **anemic**. And then too, the people around us refused to listen; and even those who listened refused to believe; and even those who believed could not comprehend. Of course they could not. Nobody could. The experience of the camps defies comprehension. …

14   I remember the killers, I remember the victims, even as I struggle to invent a thousand and one reasons to hope.

---

paradox: situation in which two opposite things are true
testament: proof
propitious: most advantageous
anemic: weak

[3] *Moslem* is an older spelling for *Muslim*, a follower of Islam.

My Notes

15 There may be times when we are powerless to prevent injustice, but there must never be a time when we fail to protest. The Talmud tells us that by saving a single human being, man can save the world. We may be powerless to open all the jails and free all prisoners, but by declaring our solidarity with one prisoner, we indict all jailers. None of us is in a position to eliminate war, but it is our obligation to denounce it and expose it in all its hideousness. War leaves no victors, only victims. . . . Mankind needs peace more than ever, for our entire planet, threatened by nuclear war, is in danger of total destruction. A destruction only man can provoke, only man can prevent.

16 Mankind must remember that peace is not God's gift to his creatures, it is our gift to each other.

Making Observations

- What image or details stand out to you?
- Based on the text you highlighted, what questions do you have for the author?

Returning to the Text

- Reread the speech to answer these text-dependent questions.
- Write any additional questions you have about the text in your Reader/Writer Notebook.

4. What is the meaning of the comparison the author makes in paragraph 5 with the simile "Like the body, memory protects its wounds"?

5. What experience is Wiesel describing in paragraphs 2–4? Which narrative techniques does he use? How does this contribute to his argument?

6. Why do you think both Wiesel and Annan speak of the importance of truth and personal responsibility?

☑ Focus on the Sentence

Cite information from the speeches to write a sentence beginning with the subordinating conjunction provided.

until

after

since

when

My Notes

_____
_____
_____
_____
_____
_____
_____
_____
_____
_____
_____
_____
_____
_____
_____
_____
_____
_____
_____
_____
_____
_____
_____
_____
_____
_____
_____
_____
_____
_____
_____
_____
_____
_____
_____
_____
_____
_____
_____
_____

Working from the Text

7. Provide one example of parallelism in Kofi Annan's "Nobel Lecture" and one example from "Hope, Despair, and Memory" and describe their effects.

8. Review your notes and prepare for a **Socratic Seminar** about the responsibility of speaking the truth in the face of adversity and upholding significant memories. Socratic Seminars work best when all participants come to the discussion prepared with textual evidence and possible questions. Make sure you have three or four Level 2 or 3 questions, as well as evidence to support your thoughts on this issue, when you participate in the Socratic Seminar.

Pre-Seminar Questions:

- To what extent are we responsible for our fellow humans?
- What is the importance of speaking the truth in the face of adversity?

Participating in the Socratic Seminar

A successful seminar depends on the participants and their willingness to engage in the conversation. The following are things to keep in mind as you participate in a Socratic Seminar:

- Talk to the participants and not the teacher or seminar leader.
- Refer to the texts to support your thinking or to challenge an idea.
- Paraphrase what other students say to make sure that you understand their points before challenging their opinions and evidence.

Post-Seminar Reflection

Reflect on your experience during the seminar and your learning by reviewing your responses to the pre-seminar questions.

- Do you think that you have a better understanding of the texts?
- What questions do you still have about the texts?
- How would you rate your participation in the seminar? What would you do differently in your next seminar?

My Notes

✐ Writing Prompt: Argumentative

Write an argumentative speech supporting a deeply held belief of your own. Support your argument by including some narrative elements. Be sure to:

- Establish a clear, arguable claim.
- Use various types of supporting evidence and pertinent examples to support your claim. Include counterarguments, as well as concessions and rebuttals, in your argument.
- Identify the audience of your argumentative text.
- Persuade your readers using rhetorical devices such as word choice and parallelism.

9. Read your speech to a small group of your peers. Ask them to evaluate it for the elements of an argument. Remember that asking for feedback on your writing will help you determine how to revise your work so that it provides the best message for your specific purpose and audience.

Language Checkpoint:
Using Parallel Structure

- State equal and closely related ideas in parallel constructions.
- Revise writing to check for non-parallel structures.

Preview

In this activity, you will write using parallel structures.

Parallel Structure

In Activity 1.7 you identified examples of parallelism in Gandhi's speech, "On Civil Disobedience." Parallelism is a rhetorical device in which words or phrases are repeated in a rhythmic way. In this Language Checkpoint, you will examine parallel structure, a convention used to order items in a series.

Sentences have parallel structure when two or more elements create a series. Each element in the series is of equal rank or importance, and all elements are expressed in a similar way. Words, phrases, and clauses can all be parallel.

Words

Lists of words in a series should maintain a parallel structure.

1. Label the three parallel and equal parts of the following sentences with a 1, 2, and 3.

   a. The 20th century was perhaps the deadliest in human history, devastated by innumerable conflicts, untold suffering, and unimaginable crimes.

   b. New threats make no distinction between races, nations or regions

2. With a partner, write an observation about what it is that makes each of the parts parallel.

3. Revise the following sentence to show word parallel structure.

   Kofi Annan argues that the United Nations has the power to eliminate poverty, getting rid of ignorance, and diseases can also be eliminated.

Clauses

A clause is a word group that contains both a subject and its verb. It may or may not express a complete thought. Notice the parallel structure in this sentence.

Here States could unite to strengthen the rule of law, address the needs of the poor, restrain man's brutality and greed, conserve the resources and beauty of nature, sustain the equal rights of men *and* women, and provide for the safety of future generations.

4. Label the first word of each of the six parallel and equal parts of the sentence with a 1, 2, 3, 4, 5, and 6.

5. With a partner, write an observation about what it is that make each of the parts parallel.

6. Revise the following sentence to show clausal parallel structure.

Kofi Annan argues that the United Nations has the power to eliminate poverty, getting rid of ignorance, and diseases can also be eliminated.

Phrases

A **phrase** is a word group that functions as a specific part of speech but does not contain both a subject and its verb.

---

7. Label the two parallel parts of the sentence with a 1 and 2.

Today, we realize, perhaps more than ever, that the world of human activity also has its own "Butterfly Effect"—for better or for worse.

---

8. With a partner, write an observation about what it is that makes each of the parts parallel.

---

9. Revise the following sentence to show phrasal parallel structure.

Kofi Annan argues that the United Nations has the power to eliminate poverty, getting rid of ignorance, and diseases can also be eliminated.

Revising

Read the following paragraph taken from a student's essay about Annan's speech. Work with a partner to check the draft for parallel structure. Note any mistakes, and then mark the text to show how you would correct the mistakes.

Kofi Annan begins his speech by discussing the birth of a girl in Afghanistan. He describes how the mother will hold the daughter, that she will feed her, and also care for her. However, he also mentions how the girl will be born in circumstances that many people would consider cruel. Annan claims that the real borders are between the rich and poor and the strong and weak, as well as those who are fortunate and unfortunate.

Later in the speech, Annan explains that the United Nations was created to make the world a safe place and to help people. Yet Annan believes the focus of the United Nations must change in the twenty-first century. In a call to action, he declares that people must look beyond nations, and different states, and past borders. The United Nations must focus on improving the lives of individuals.

☑ Check Your Understanding

Imagine you are editing a classmate's writing, and you notice these sentences:

- Annan states that the twentieth century contained some of the worst atrocities in human history, including wars, pain and suffering, and other wrongdoings.
- Despite these hardships, he believes that the United Nations should call on nations to concentrate on the needs of all people, including men as well as women, rich and poor people, and also people of all races and creeds.

In your own words, write an explanation so that your classmate understands the mistakes in parallel structure and how to revise them. Begin an Editor's Checklist in your Reader/Writer Notebook to help you remember to check for parallel structure when revising your writing.

Practice

Revisit a piece of your writing from this unit, and revise it to include parallel structure.

Learning Strategies

Close Reading
Graphic Organizer
Marking the Text

Learning Targets

- Analyze the text structure of an argument and how the author uses it to achieve a purpose.
- Write an essay that explains how an author builds an argument using evidence to persuade an audience.

Preview

In this activity, you will read an editorial and analyze the author's argument and use of persuasive techniques.

As You Read

- Put a star next to the main claim the author makes, and underline supporting evidence.
- Circle unknown words and phrases. Try to determine the meaning of the words by using context clues, word parts, or a dictionary.

My Notes

sustainable: able to be maintained

About the Author

Kathleen Kingsbury (b. 1979) edits the "Ideas" section for the *Boston Globe*. After graduating from the Columbia School of Journalism, she worked at CNN and then at *Time* magazine as a reporter and a business correspondent based in Asia. She won the Walker Stone Award for Editorial Writing and the Pulitzer Prize in 2015 for a series of stories on the low wages of restaurant workers called "Service Not Included," which ran in *The Boston Globe*. The following editorial is from that series.

Editorial

Diners should pay attention to workers, not just the food

by **Kathleen Kingsbury**

December **29, 2014**

1   Americans have started to care deeply about how their food came to be. At restaurants, we ask probing questions: Are the greens organic? Were the cows grass-fed? We fret over whether our chicken could run around the farmyard. We take comfort in knowing that the pickles were prepared in-house, and that the cucumbers came from just an hour away. In short, we've come to demand high quality and **sustainable** sourcing in every part of a restaurant's operation.

2   Well, except in how the employees who work there are treated.

3   In a series of editorials over the past year, the Globe has detailed the challenges that food service workers routinely face: wages too low to live on, minimal job security, few organizing rights, the risk of wage theft, and even human trafficking.

4   These are all indecencies that, **theoretically**, should fall to lawmakers to address. But political will in Washington to raise the minimum wage has stalled, and labor enforcement, at both the federal and state levels, has been ineffectual.

5   No, more humane working conditions in restaurants aren't likely to arrive until patrons start demanding them as part of their dining experience, too.

6   Contrary to the protests of industry bigwigs and some politicians, there is room in restaurant economics for higher pay and benefits—if customers are willing to pay a little bit more.

7   Ask top executives at Chipotle Mexican Grill. The burrito chain has achieved record margins and robust sales in recent years as Americans (and Europeans and Canadians) embrace its "Food with Integrity" motto. The company does offer its employees some luxuries rare in its industry—quick advancement, health insurance, regular full-time shifts, for instance—but its average wage for non-managers works out to be just slightly above $9 per hour (including bonuses).

8   Yet, in discussing proposals for a $10 minimum wage, Chipotle's chief financial officer, Jack Hartung, shrugged it off . "A move to $10 would have an effect, but not too significant," Hartung told analysts last January. In other words, an extra buck an hour isn't a major threat to Chipotle's bottom line, but the chain is also in no hurry to get there. For the Chipotle "crew member" trying to support a child, a raise to $10 represents an 11 percent pay hike and can mean the difference between making rent and being evicted, paying the gas bill, even putting enough food on the table.

9   Already, plenty of eateries and smaller chains in the Boston area ... have committed to **compensating** hourly employees more than the bare minimum: Shake Shack, Boloco, the Salty Pig, and Coda in the South End, Canary Square in Jamaica Plain, Porters Bar and Grill near North Station, Haley House Bakery Café in Roxbury.

10   In addition to a minimum wage of $10, Boloco offers employees at its burrito joints other perks, including 401(k) matching, transportation **subsidies**, and English-language courses. Virtue isn't the only reward: "There are **quantifiable** savings in terms of lower turnover and training costs," said CEO Patrick Renna. "Happier employees mean better service and higher customer satisfaction."

theoretically: in theory
compensating: paying
subsidies: financial help
quantifiable: measurable

INDEPENDENT READING LINK

Read and Research

Review the notes you have been taking in your Reader/Writer Notebook regarding your independent reading. Is there a topic such as exploitation that you would like to learn more about? Choose a topic and generate questions for an informal inquiry into the subject. Locate relevant sources, including newspapers, magazines, and other periodicals, and check the sources for bias and faulty reasoning. Then share your findings with the class in the form of a brief and informal oral report.

My Notes

11 But customers shouldn't wait for other restaurant owners to figure that out on their own. The dining public must show that it wants better treatment for workers. Here's how:

- Demand intelligence. Unlike health code violations, an eatery's bad labor practices aren't regularly catalogued in any city-run online databases.

- Patronize the good guys … Pay attention to online reviews that mention good labor practices. Tell owners that's why you are there. Tell your friends, too.

- Tip in cash. Servers who make the tipped minimum wage ($3 in Massachusetts as of Jan. 1) often must rely on generous tippers to make up most of their take-home pay. And, as backwards as it sounds in an electronic age, wait staff report that leaving cash is the best guarantee your tip will end up in the right pocket.

- Push for higher wages and workers' rights. The Fight for $15 campaign continues. Polls suggest most Americans support an increased minimum wage, so be vocal about it.

12 Being a more conscientious consumer will pay off in unexpected ways. Restaurants today lie at the heart of 21st-century American life. These employers aren't headed overseas; for the foreseeable future, millions of Americans will wait tables, cook food, or wash dishes for their livelihoods.

13 Meanwhile, an ever-more-frazzled public eats out instead of cooking at home. Neighborhood development and redevelopment plans increasingly hinge on attracting new restaurants. Having that local eatery on the corner, or a perhaps short drive away, has become an intrinsic part of what makes a community feel livable.

14 That's all the more reason for customers to make sure their friends, neighbors, and family members who work in these vital businesses earn enough to live on. And when restaurateurs, from small chef-owners to fast-food giants, see customers paying closer attention to equity in their industry, they'll know what to do.

Making Observations

- What questions do you have for the author of this text?
- What information did you find most surprising?

Returning to the Text

- Reread the editorial to answer these text-dependent questions.
- Write any additional questions you have about the text in your Reader/Writer Notebook.

1. What claim does Kingsbury introduce in paragraph 1? Following that introduction, what is the effect of paragraph 2 on the reader?

_____

_____

_____

_____

2. Review paragraphs 3 and 4. How does the use of the word *indecencies* affect the tone of the article? What kind of appeal is the author using with this word choice?

_____

_____

_____

_____

3. What is the author's purpose in paragraph 8, where she describes the impact of a higher minimum wage on Chipotle's bottom line and on restaurant workers?

_____

_____

_____

_____

4. What element of an argument is displayed in the section with the bulleted list? What rhetorical appeal is used? Cite text evidence.

_____

_____

_____

_____

Working from the Text

5. Taking an editorial apart and looking at its details can help you determine how the author builds his or her argument. With a partner, use this frame to create an outline of the main argument and details of the passage. Be careful to use your own words to paraphrase or summarize each section of the editorial, and check to make sure that your summary is accurate.

My Notes

Claim or main idea: _____

Reason 1: _____

Details given as evidence:

- _____
- _____
- _____

Reason 2: _____

Details given as evidence:

- _____
- _____
- _____

Reason 3: _____

Details given as evidence:

- _____
- _____
- _____

☑ Check Your Understanding

Review your outline. Choose the evidence you think is most important to the author's argument and explain to your group what makes it so important.

📝 Explain How an Author Builds an Argument

Write an essay in which you explain how Kathleen Kingsbury builds an argument using evidence to persuade her audience to support her claim regarding better treatment for restaurant workers. Your essay should not explain whether you agree with Kingsbury's claim, but rather should explain how the author builds an argument to persuade her audience.
Be sure to:

- Identify the author's clear, arguable claim.
- Include various types of evidence, such as examples and details from the text, combined with your commentary.
- Address an identifiable audience.
- Analyze the author's use of text structure.

Creating an Argument

ASSIGNMENT

Write an argumentative essay on an issue of your choice that you feel strongly about. You will need to develop a clear claim, and conduct research to gather evidence that supports your claim. Your final argumentative essay should use the genre characteristics and craft of an argument.

Planning and Prewriting: Take time to make a plan for your essay.	■ Have you developed a clear, arguable claim? ■ What topics will you need to research to support your claim? ■ Have you found various types of evidence to support your claim? ■ Who is your audience, and what are their concerns that must be addressed as counterclaims?
Drafting: Determine the best organizational structure for your essay.	■ How will you organize your ideas in a way that is appropriate to purpose, audience, topic, and context? ■ What transitions will you use to connect evidence as you support your claim? ■ What counterclaims will you acknowledge, and what evidence do you have to refute them? ■ How will you avoid faulty reasoning?
Revising: Make changes to your essay to better meet the expectations of the Scoring Guide.	■ In what way can the claim be revised to make it clearer and more arguable? ■ Where can you add various types of evidence to support your claim, including a discussion of counterarguments? ■ In what ways can the organization be revised to show a clear relationship among claim, counterclaim, reasons, and evidence? ■ In what ways can your conclusion be improved to follow logically from and support your argument? ■ In what places have you broken from formal style? How can you revise these examples? ■ Where can you vary your sentence structure to increase reader interest while maintaining complete sentences?
Editing for Publication: Check that your essay is free of errors and ready for publication.	■ Where can you add transitional words, phrases, and clauses to clarify and connect ideas? ■ Which style guides have you consulted to ensure that you are citing evidence correctly? ■ Where have you made errors in punctuation that need to be corrected? ■ Which words need to be checked for correct spelling?

Reflection

After completing this Embedded Assessment, think about the relationship between crafting an argument and persuading an audience.

- What have you learned about the importance of audience in determining the way an argument is developed?
- How are logic and reasoning important parts of creating an argument?

SCORING GUIDE

Scoring Criteria	Exemplary	Proficient	Emerging	Incomplete
Ideas	The argument • skillfully presents a claim and provides background and a clear explanation of the issue. • synthesizes evidence from a variety of sources that strongly support the claim. • summarizes and refutes counterclaims with relevant reasoning and clear evidence. • concludes by clearly summarizing the main points and reinforcing the claim.	The argument • supports a claim that is clearly presented with appropriate background details. • synthesizes evidence from multiple sources that support the claim. • develops claims and counterclaims fairly and uses valid reasoning, relevant and sufficient evidence, and a variety of rhetorical appeals. • concludes by revisiting the main points and reinforcing the claim.	The argument • states a claim but does not adequately explain the issue or provide background details. • attempts to synthesize evidence from several sources that support the claim. • develops some counterclaims, but reasoning may not be completely relevant or sufficient for the evidence cited. • concludes by listing the main points of the thesis.	The argument • states a vague or unclear claim and does not explain the issue or provide background details. • contains no synthesis of evidence from different sources to support the claim. • may or may not develop counterclaims, and reasoning may not be relevant or sufficient for the evidence cited. • concludes without restating the main points of the claim.
Structure	The argument • follows a logical progression of ideas that establish relationships between the essential elements of hook, claim, evidence, counterclaims, and conclusion. • links main points with effective transitions that establish coherence.	The argument • establishes clear relationships between the essential elements of hook, claim, evidence, counterclaims, and conclusion. • uses transitions to link the major sections of the essay and create coherence.	The argument • demonstrates an awkward progression of ideas, but the reader can understand them. • uses some elements of hook, claim, evidence, and conclusion. • spends too much time on some irrelevant details and uses few transitions.	The argument • does not follow a logical organization. • includes some details and elements of an argument, but the writing lacks clear direction and uses no transitions to help readers follow the line of thought.
Use of Language	The argument • uses a formal style and tone appropriate to the audience and purpose. • smoothly integrates textual evidence from multiple sources, with correct citations. • shows excellent command of standard English capitalization, punctuation, spelling, grammar, and usage.	The argument • uses a formal style and tone appropriate to the audience and purpose. • correctly cites textual evidence from at least three sources. • follows conventions of standard English capitalization, punctuation, spelling, grammar, and usage.	The argument • mixes informal and formal writing styles. • cites some textual evidence, but citations may be missing or inaccurate. • includes some incorrect capitalization, punctuation, spelling, grammar, or usage that interfere with meaning.	The argument • uses mostly informal writing style. • uses some textual evidence but does not include citations. • includes incorrect capitalization, punctuation, spelling, grammar, or usage that interfere with meaning.

Searching for Evidence

Learning Targets

- Synthesize more than one argument from a variety of modes to gain greater understanding of a topic.
- Analyze the structural elements of informational texts to discover how they support a thesis.
- Use evidence and examples from a text to support a position.
- Integrate ideas from multiple texts to build knowledge and vocabulary about video games and brain development.

Preview

In this activity, you will unpack the requirements of the second Embedded Assessment and use multiple texts to gain greater understanding of a topic, including how each author supports a position with evidence.

My Notes

Making Connections

In the last part of this unit, you read argumentative texts about justice, and you wrote an argument on a topic of your choice. In the next few weeks, you will learn how to deliver your ideas orally by participating in a debate.

Unpacking Embedded Assessment 2

Read the assignment for Embedded Assessment 2: Participating in a Debate

In teams of 4–5, you will debate a topic chosen by your whole class. As a team, you must prepare for the debate effectively by locating relevant research, using persuasive techniques studied in class, and collaborating with your team to strategize on how to present your ideas.

Using the assignment and Embedded Assessment Scoring Guide, work as a class to analyze the activity. Think through the required concepts (what you need to know) and skills (what you need to do) to effectively complete the assignment.

After each activity, reflect in your Reader/Writer Notebook on what you have learned about creating and supporting arguments with evidence and what you still need to learn in order to be successful on the Embedded Assessment.

Taking a Side

In the next two activities you will explore the topic, "Do video games make you smarter?"

In this activity, your teacher will assign half of the students in your class to be for the motion (arguing that video games *do* make you smarter), and the other half will be against the motion (arguing that video games *do not* make you smarter) By being randomly assigned to a position rather than choosing for yourself, you will gain understanding and practice in developing a claim and using text evidence to support your position. In the next activity, you will be able to choose the side that you agree with to argue.

KNOWLEDGE QUEST

Knowledge Question:
How do video games affect the brain and behavior? Across Activity 1.12, you will read three texts and view an infographic about how video games shape and change the brain. While you read and build knowledge about the topic, think about your answer to the Knowledge Question.

My Notes

_____
_____
_____
_____
_____
_____
_____
_____
_____
_____
_____
_____
_____
_____
_____
_____
_____
_____
_____
_____
_____

consensus: agreement

As You Read
- Highlight ways that video gaming allows people to interact with the world around them or keeps them from it.
- Circle unknown words and phrases. Try to determine the meaning of the words by using context clues, word parts, or a dictionary.

Article

How video games affect the brain

by **Hannah Nichols**

Monday, 10 July 2017

From Medical News Today

1   Video gaming is clearly a popular form of entertainment, with video gamers collectively spending 3 billion hours per week in front of their screens. Due to their widespread use, scientists have researched how video games affect the brain and behavior. Are these effects positive or negative? We examine the evidence.

2   At a glance, more than 150 million people in the United States play video games regularly, or for at least 3 hours per week. The average American gamer is a 35-year-old adult, with 72 percent of gamers aged 18 or older. For video game use by children, most parents—71 percent—indicate that video games have a positive influence on their child's life.

3   Video game sales continue to increase year on year. In 2016, the video game industry sold more than 24.5 billion games—up from 23.2 billion in 2015, and 21.4 billion in 2014.

4   The top three best-selling video games of 2016 were Call of Duty: Infinite Warfare, Battlefield 1, and Grand Theft Auto V. These games fall into the first-person shooter or action-adventure genres—the top two genres, accounting for 27.5 percent and 22.5 percent of sales, respectively. First-person shooter and action genres often stand accused of stirring aggression and causing violence and addiction.

5   Decades of research examining video gaming and violence have failed to reach **consensus** among scientists. Scientists have been unable to find a causal link between playing video games and acts of violence in the real world.

Video games and brain changes

6   A growing body of evidence, however, shows that video gaming can affect the brain and, furthermore, cause changes in many regions of the brain.

My Notes

7 Scientists have recently collected and summarized results from 116 scientific studies to determine how video games can influence our brains and behaviors. The findings of their review were published in *Frontiers in Human Neuroscience*.

8 "Games have sometimes been praised or **demonized**, often without real data backing up those claims. Moreover, gaming is a popular activity, so everyone seems to have strong opinions on the topic," says Marc Palaus, first author of the review.

9 By looking at all research to date, Palaus and team aimed to observe whether any trends had emerged with regard to how video games impact the structure and activity of the brain. A total of 22 of the reviewed studies explored structural changes in the brain and 100 studies analyzed changes in brain functionality and behavior.

10 Results of the studies indicate that playing video games not only changes how our brains perform but also their structure.

11 For example, video game use is known to affect attention. The studies included in the review show that video game players display improvements in several types of attention, including sustained attention and selective attention. Furthermore, the regions of the brain that play a role in attention are more efficient in gamers compared with non-gamers, and they require less activation to stay focused on demanding tasks.

12 Evidence also demonstrates that playing video games increases the size and competence of parts of the brain responsible for visuospatial skills—a person's ability to identify visual and spatial relationships among objects. In long-term gamers and individuals who had volunteered to follow a video game training plan, the right **hippocampus** was enlarged.

13 Researchers have discovered that video gaming can be addictive—a phenomenon known as "Internet gaming disorder."

14 In gaming addicts, there are functional and structural alterations in the neural reward system—a group of structures associated with feeling pleasure, learning, and motivation. Exposing video game addicts to game-related cues that cause cravings, and monitoring their brain responses, highlighted these changes—changes that are also seen in other addictive disorders.

15 "We focused on how the brain reacts to video game exposure, but these effects do not always translate to real-life changes," notes Palaus. The research into the effects of video gaming is still in its infancy and scientists are still **scrutinizing** what aspects of gaming impact what brain regions and how.

16 "It's likely that video games have both positive (on attention, visual and motor skills) and negative aspects (risk of addiction), and it is essential we embrace this complexity," Palaus continues.

Are brain-training games beneficial?

17 A team of researchers from the Florida State University has stated that people should be skeptical of **adverts** that promote an increase in the

demonized: portrayed as bad
hippocampus: portion of the brain controlling emotion, memory, and the nervous system
scrutinizing: analyzing
adverts: advertisements

performance of the brain that results from brain training games. They have said that science does not support these claims.

18   "Our findings and previous studies confirm there's very little evidence these types of games can improve your life in a meaningful way," says Wally Boot, associate professor of psychology, an expert on age-related cognitive decline.

19   People are increasingly under the impression that brain-training apps will safeguard them against memory loss or cognitive disorders.

20   Researchers tested whether playing brain-training games enhanced the working memory of players and thus improved other cognitive abilities, including reasoning, memory, and processing speed—a process scientists call "far transfer." However, this was not the case.

21   "It's possible to train people to become very good at tasks that you would normally consider general working memory tasks: memorizing 70, 80, even 100 digits," explains Neil Charness, professor of psychology and a leading authority on aging and cognition.

22   "But these skills tend to be very specific and not show a lot of transfer. The thing that seniors, in particular, should be concerned about is, if I can get very good at crossword puzzles, is that going to help me remember where my keys are? And the answer is probably no," he adds.

23   Charness points out that if your goal is to improve cognitive function, then aerobic exercise may help. Some research has found that aerobic activity rather than mental activity enhances the brain.

Video Games Boost Memory

24   In contrast, a study published in *Nature* found that through the use of a specially designed 3-D video game, cognitive performance could be improved in older adults and some of the adverse effects on the brain associated with aging, reversed.

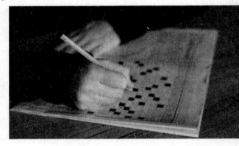

25   Scientists at the University of California, San Francisco (UCSF) clarify that this provides a measure of scientific support in the brain fitness arena—criticized for lacking evidence—that brain training can stimulate meaningful and lasting changes.

26   After 12 hours of training over the period of a month, study participants aged between 60 to 85 years improved performance on the game that surpassed that of individuals in their 20s playing the game for the first time. Moreover, two other significant cognitive areas were improved: working memory and sustained attention. These skills were maintained 6 months after completion of their training.

27   "The finding is a powerful example of how plastic the older brain is," says Dr. Adam Gazzaley, Ph.D., UCSF associate professor of neurology, physiology

adverse: undesirable

and psychiatry and director of the Neuroscience Imaging Center. Dr. Gazzaley notes that it is encouraging that even a little brain training can reverse some of the brain decline that occurs with age.

28 A recent study conducted by neurobiologists at the University of California, Irvine (UCI) found that playing 3-D video games could also boost the formation of memories. Participants were **allocated** to either a group that played video games with a 2-D environment or a 3-D environment. After playing the games for 30 minutes per day for 2 weeks, the students were given memory tests that engaged the brain's hippocampus.

29 The participants in the 3-D group significantly improved their memory test scores compared with the 2-D group. The 3-D group's memory performance increased by 12 percent—the same amount that memory performance usually declines by between 45 and 70 years of age.

30 "First, the 3-D games have a few things the 2-D ones do not," says Craig Stark, of UCI's Center for the Neurobiology of Learning & Memory. "They've got a lot more spatial information in there to explore. Second, they're much more complex, with a lot more information to learn. Either way, we know this kind of learning and memory not only stimulates but requires the hippocampus."

31 Strategy video games, in particular, have shown promise in improving brain function among older adults and may provide protection against dementia and Alzheimer's disease.

32 "If the target is to improve older adults' cognitive control, reasoning, and higher-order cognitive skills, and **stave** off dementia and Alzheimer's disease as long as possible, then maybe strategy games are the way to go," informs Chandramallika Basak, assistant professor at the Center for Vital Longevity and School of Behavioral and Brain Sciences at the University of Texas at Dallas.

33 Basak, like Charness, agrees that cognitive training should come second to physical activity programs when it comes to improving cognitive function. Physical fitness programs have been linked with positive effects on cognition and brain function and structure.

34 There is evidence to suggest that video games may be a **viable** treatment for depression and improve memory and mood in adults with mild cognitive impairment.

35 The effect of video games on the brain is a new area of research that will continue to be explored. We may just be scraping the surface of the potential that video games could present in enhancing cognitive ability and preventing cognitive disorders.

Ø Knowledge Quest

- What surprises you most about the ways that video games can change the brain?
- What thoughts do you have about the potential benefits of video games?

allocated: assigned
stave: fend
viable: workable

Returning to the Text

- Reread the article to answer these text-dependent questions.
- Write any additional questions you have about the text in your Reader/Writer Notebook.

1. What is a key idea of the section titled "Video Games and Brain Changes"?

_____

_____

_____

_____

2. KQ What does the word *trends* mean within the context of paragraph 9, and what does the study of trends have to do with the time-consuming nature of brain research?

_____

_____

_____

_____

3. What is the thesis of the section titled "Are Brain-Training Games Beneficial?" and what evidence does the author use to support it?

_____

_____

_____

_____

4. What evidence does the author provide that video games have a positive impact on brain activity?

_____

_____

_____

_____

5. KQ Make an inference about why researchers need time to determine how video games affect the brain.

_____

_____

_____

_____

Article

Video Games Are Good for Your Brain

by **Kevin Anderton**

1   In 2015 at the University of California, Irvine, a study was made to test the effects of playing video games on a part of our brains called the hippocampus, which is part of the **limbic system** and helps spatial memory and the transition of information from short-term memory to long-term memory. The results were interesting, to say the least.

2   Previously it had been shown that an **enriched** environment had a positive effect on memory in animals. What does this mean for human beings? Well to answer that very question a few experiments were done using video games as a way of enriching a person's environment. If successful the subjects would be able to score higher on certain tests that show hippocampal stimulation.

3   In the first experiment, a group of gamers was given a questionnaire to find out more about their gaming habits. They were asked how often they played, what games they played, and many more game-related questions. They were then given a few tests including an **enumeration** test and a **mnemonic** similarity test. These test results were then compared to the test results of a group of non-gamers to see if there was any difference. In addition, a group of competitive gamers from the 2015 Winter Game Fest were also tested to see if a gamer's skill level provided any additional benefit.

4   The results were pretty interesting. The experiment did, in fact, show that those who were playing video games had better hippocampal-related memory but not all of them. It was only the gamers who were playing 3D games. Players who were playing 2D games had close to the same results as non-gamers. In addition, competitive level gaming skills showed no additional benefit.

5   A second experiment was done to see if asking a person to play 3D games would result in higher hippocampal-related memory. Participants were broken down into three groups. The first group would not play any video games during the testing period, the second group would play only Angry Birds (a 2D game), and the third group that would play only Super Mario 3D. If the theory was correct then the third group should show an increase in hippocampal-related memory.

6   The results of all the experiments are in the following infographic.

KNOWLEDGE QUEST
Knowledge Question:
How do video games affect the brain and behavior?

My Notes

limbic system: system of the brain that deals with emotions, memories, and stimulation
enriched: enhanced
enumeration: recall of words, phrases, numbers, or symbols
mnemonic: pattern of letters or ideas

My Notes

VIDEO GAMES
ARE GOOD FOR YOUR BRAIN

Environmental enrichment has been known to have positive effects on the hippocampus in animal studies. These experiments show that video games can provide environmental enrichment for humans and have similar effects on the brain.

Hippocampus
Part of the limbic system, helps spatial memory that enables navigation, and helps to transition information from short-term memory to long-term.

Experiment 1A
Participants:

Gamers:
15 male
24 female

Non-Gamers:
8 male
21 female

Procedure:

Testing whether or not video game exposure leads to an alteration of hippocampal function. Participants were given a questionnaire to discover information on the types of games that they played. They were also given an enumeration test and mnemonic similarity test.

Results:

There was no effect of previous game experience on enumeration but gamers did show better mnemonic discrimination than non-gamers. In short playing video games did lead to improved hippocampal-associated memory.

Experiment 1B
Participants:

Gamers were pulled from the 2015 Winter Game Fest at UCSD:

Super Smash Bro
13 players

League of Legends
19 players

Procedure:

Competitive gamers were given the same mnemonic similarity test from experiment 1A.

Results:

Competitive gamers showed the same results as gamers from experiment 1A. Being a competitive level gamer made no difference.

Experiment 2
Participants:

69 players total, Ages 18–22 years old
Non-Gamer Control Group:
8 male   16 female

2D Active Control Group:

Angry Birds
8 male
14 female

3D Experimental Group:

Super Mario 3D Worlds
6 male   17 female

Procedure:

The idea was to test whether or not playing a 3D game can improve hippocampal-associated memory rather than proving that people who played 3D games already had improved hippocampal-associated memory.

Each group went through a schedule of testing, followed by 2 weeks of playing their game of choice for 30 minutes daily, followed by testing, followed by two weeks of not playing, and followed by a final round of testing. Non-Gamers had two periods of not playing any games.

Results:

3D gaming did, in fact, improve hippocampal-associated memory.

Knowledge Quest

- What information about time does the infographic show?
- What is one new detail you learned about how video games affect the brain?

Returning to the Text

- Reread the article and the infographic to answer these text-dependent questions.
- Write any additional questions you have about the text in your Reader/Writer Notebook.

6. How is the term *hippocampus* related to brain research? Use context clues to find out. Then tell what the hippocampus has to do with an experiment described in the article.

_____

_____

_____

_____

7. KQ What claim do both the author of this article and the author of the previous article, "How video games affect the brain," agree on?

_____

_____

_____

_____

8. KQ Based on the article and infographic, how does research support the claim that video games are good for the brain?

_____

_____

_____

_____

9. What does the infographic reveal about the results of Experiment 2, as discussed in the article? How does this information support or refute Experiment 1?

_____

_____

_____

_____

KNOWLEDGE QUEST

Knowledge Question:
How do video games affect the brain and behavior?

My Notes

Article

Brain training apps don't seem to do much of anything

But figuring out whether or not they work is almost as tough as creating them.
by **Claire Maldarelli**

July 12, 2017

1   Video games are pretty fun, but most of us don't expect much more than that from entertainment media. But what if a fun video game also, conveniently, helped you succeed more in school and in life? That's the idea behind the **plethora** of "brain training" apps on the market today. But just as quickly as they've hit the virtual shelves of iTunes and the like, the validity of their claims has been called into question. A new study out this week in the *Journal of Neuroscience* found that one popular app, Lumosity, doesn't do anything for your brain—other than helping you get better at playing the game itself.

2   While one study on a single app can't be used to make any sweeping conclusions on the benefits (or lack thereof) of brain training games as a whole, it does highlight an important point: It's difficult not only to create the right type of brain training exercise for a specific behavior or condition, but also to figure out if that training actually *works*.

3   The logic behind these brain training apps is based on the idea that certain brain **circuits** are involved in a type of cognitive performance called delayed discounting, which is your preference for choosing immediate, smaller rewards versus waiting for a bigger reward, as well as one called risk sensitivity—whether you choose reliable or risky rewards. Scientists have found that choosing immediate and risky rewards is associated with unhealthy behavior like smoking, drinking, eating poorly, and generally being more **prone** to addiction. Apps like Lumosity work these same brain circuits—supposedly strengthening them—to help people focus more and avoid rash, unhealthy decisions.

4   But here's the problem: There's still a lot we don't know about neuroscience and brain circuitry. The thing about Lumosity (and other brain training games and apps), says Joaquin Anguera, an assistant professor of neurology at the University of San Francisco School of Medicine who was not involved in the study, is that there are a number of different **modules** and games to choose from—and all of them work different neural networks in the brain. It could be that one app on the market does help improve one certain type of brain behavior, but we just haven't pinned those results down yet. Scientists still need to do more research to figure out which circuits are actually associated with different behaviors, and it will take even more research to figure out whether certain exercises can help.

plethora: abundance
circuits: connections made up of bundles of neurons
prone: likely to suffer from
modules: components or parts

5   In this specific study, the researchers split up a group of 128 young adults into two sets. One group received 10 weeks of training with Lumosity. The other, the control group, played video games for 10 weeks. Before and after the 10-week period, the researchers gave them a series of cognitive tests to see how well each group would do. Both of them did indeed improve by the end of the study, but their improvements were, on average, exactly the same. Neither improved more than the other. In fact, the researchers also gave a third group—who didn't receive any training at all—the same cognitive tests, and those participants improved about as much as the game players. The more you play Mario Kart, the better you are going to be at it. But the fact that you can kick Mario's butt doesn't mean you are going to do better in school or kick your smoking habit.

6   "There's vast literature on decision making and neuroimaging to figure out what are the key brain areas involved and how do they all interact. But I've never seen a study that says, 'If you play these games in this cocktail effect you are going to improve decision-making processes,'" Anguera says.

7   That's what this study tried to accomplish, he says, but it still left a lot of questions unanswered. First, it was done in a very specific group: young, healthy people without any pre-existing conditions that might affect their memory. Joseph Kable, a psychologist at the University of Pennsylvania and lead author of the study, says that with a group this narrow, it's possible that the participants were already functioning at such a high level that they couldn't get much benefit out of the brain training. However, all three groups—including the video game group and the control—improved in much the same way. So according to Kable and his colleagues, there clearly was some room for improvement.

8   Anguera says the other problem could be that the training was not specific enough to cause a change. The key, he says, is that the game needs to target the right cognitive processes—in the right population—to help with specific deficits. "It's just like medicine or a pill. It needs to be directed toward a specific group of people with a specific condition." Doing that, he says, requires effort not just on the part of research scientists, but also on the companies themselves. And we aren't completely lost when it comes to the brain, Anguera adds—we just need to figure out how to effectively target the areas of the brain that we know are important.

9   Based on this study and ones like it, these brain training exercises don't currently have any solid evidence to back them up. The good news is that playing these games isn't bad for you; it doesn't decrease your cognitive abilities. But Lumosity doesn't seem to improve them any more than playing video games, or even simply taking the same cognitive test multiple times. When it comes to neural circuitry and the manner in which our noggins are wired, there's still a lot left to figure out. And if companies plan to market these games as a way to improve cognitive functioning, they need to work with scientists to develop specific trials to back them up.

deficits: shortfalls

My Notes

10　For now, if you are debating between engaging in a brain training exercise or your favorite video game, maybe go with the game. Or skip the game altogether and exercise your brain the good old fashioned way—by doing whatever work you're trying to avoid.

Knowledge Quest

- What is brain training?
- What is one detail about brain development from the article you noticed that someone else might have missed?

Returning to the Text

- Reread the editorial to answer these text-dependent questions.
- Write any additional questions you have about the text in your Reader/Writer Notebook.

10. What can the reader infer as a possible reason for the increase in scores on the cognitive test described in the article? What evidence backs up this inference?

11. KQ What evidence would you apply to challenge the author's claim that brain training doesn't do anything as it applies to the research study discussed?

_____

_____

_____

_____

12. KQ According to the article, what is a brain-training app supposed to do? Also, what is _neural circuitry_? Use context clues and a dictionary to find out. Then tell what neural circuity has to do with why it is difficult to figure out if brain-training apps work as intended.

_____

_____

_____

_____

13. What is the end goal of a brain-training exercise? Why might time only tell if the exercises work?

_____

_____

_____

_____

🧭 Knowledge Quest

After reading the three texts and viewing the infographic about brain development and video game usage, write about how video games affect the brain and behavior. Then work with a partner to discuss whether you think time spent studying the effects of video games on the brain has value. Support your point of view with reasons and evidence from the texts you read, and listen openly to your partner's point of view. Then work with your partner to write a summary of your discussion that highlights points of agreement and disagreement and tells how you and your partner justified your points of view.

INDEPENDENT READING LINK

You can continue to build your knowledge about how video games affect the brain by reading other articles at ZINC Reading Labs. Search for keywords such as _screen time_ or _neuroscience_.

 ZINC

Working from the Text

14. Look back at your marked-up text and the notes in the My Notes section for each text. Think back to the position that you were assigned for the topic, "Do video games make you smarter?" In the graphic organizer that follows, write the position that you were assigned in the form of a claim. Next, write down evidence and examples provided in the text that support your claim in the appropriate columns. Finally, write a sentence for each that explains your reasoning—why the evidence or example supports the claim.

Claim	Evidence	Example	Reasoning

15. Form groups of 4–5 people all assigned the same position. Discuss the question: How does each author support the claim through evidence and examples? How and why does each piece of evidence or example support the claim? Compare and contrast charts with group members. Place a check mark next to each piece of evidence or example that is confirmed by the group. Add any evidence or examples you are missing to complete your chart.

☑ Focus on the Sentence

Use your graphic organizer to complete the following sentences. If you were assigned to support the motion, complete the sentences without including the words in the parentheses. If you were assigned to negate the motion, complete the sentences using the words in the parentheses:

Video games (do not) make people smarter because _____

_____

Video games (do not) make people smarter, but _____

_____

Video games (do not) make people smarter, so _____

_____

16. **Quickwrite:** Take a moment to reflect. What kinds of evidence were you able to find in these articles? How could you use them to support your claim? Are there any kinds of evidence you wish you had?

Taking Sides

Learning Targets

- Learn how to structure an argument for debate that includes a clear thesis and valid evidence based on reliable sources.
- Analyze and evaluate characteristics and structural elements of oral arguments.
- Define the audience and purpose for oral arguments.

Preview

In this activity, you will participate in a Four Corners debate on the topic "Do video games make you smarter?" and evaluate a video debate on the same topic. You will collaborate with peers to set rules for discussions and set clear goals for the activity.

INDEPENDENT READING LINK

Read and Discuss

Think about claims that are made or positions that are taken in the text you are reading independently in light of what you have learned in this activity. Identify one way the author could strengthen his or her argument. Discuss your ideas with a partner.

Four Corners Debate

Your teacher will label each corner of the room "Strongly Agree," "Agree," "Disagree," or "Strongly Disagree." Now consider the claim: "Video games make you smarter." Move to the corner that most accurately describes your position on this claim.

Within the group gathered in the corner you chose, discuss the claim. Answer the question: Why did you choose the response you did?

1. Take notes on the graphic organizer based on your group's discussion.

My group's claim:		
Reason 1:	Reason 2:	Reason 3:
Evidence to support reason 1:	Evidence to support reason 2:	Evidence to support reason 3:

2. Each of the four groups should choose a representative to share the main points of the group's discussion and notes on the subject, concentrating on the evidence that backs up the position on the claim. Then write your answers to these questions.

- What new information did you learn from the other groups?

- Were you persuaded to change your position based on the evidence presented by other groups? Why or why not?

- What evidence presented by other groups was most compelling or persuasive and why?

Evaluating Oral Argument

3. Take notes as your teacher shows the video "Video Games Will Make Us Smarter." As you watch, use the graphic organizer to organize your thoughts about how the speaker draws on text evidence to build an argument.

Thesis	Evidence	Structure	Speaking Skills
Is the thesis clear to the viewer?	Why is the evidence presented valid or invalid?	Is there a logical progression of ideas?	Evaluate the following as exemplary, proficient, or beginner by writing E, P, or B next to each speaking skill: _____ Preparation _____ Eye contact
What evidence supports your answer?	Why is the evidence relevant or irrelevant?	Explain why or why not.	_____ Speaking rate _____ Volume _____ Enunciation _____ Gestures _____ Conventions of language

4. In your Four Corners groups, discuss the video and your notes. Share your thinking in a Think-Pair-Share. Continue to fill in information in your graphic organizer that you learn from your group members.

5. As directed by your teacher, discuss with the whole class the successful techniques you saw in the video that you should replicate in a speech or debate. In what ways are these techniques related to audience and purpose? What did you see that you should avoid?

☑ Check Your Understanding

How do the characteristics and structural elements of oral or visual arguments impact their effectiveness? Think specifically about characteristics that don't necessarily occur in written arguments, such as speaking skills or images.

Team Research

Learning Targets

- Work collaboratively to develop and revise a plan for research and presentation.
- Research a topic by organizing information from a variety of relevant sources.
- Cite and evaluate sources for validity, reliability, and proper reasoning.

Preview

In this activity, you will brainstorm and discuss a list of topics for a debate and then research the chosen topic to support a position. In your research, you will collaborate with group members to share ideas and evaluate the sources you locate.

Selecting a Debate Topic

Your teacher will display a list of potential debate topics. As a class, view the topics and brainstorm additional topics that might be interesting to research and debate. Working as a collaborative group, write these topic suggestions on the board or in a chart. and discuss each. Your goal is to come to a consensus—agreement—about the topic your class will debate. Consensus requires give-and-take along with the sharing of ideas and information. Here are some ground rules for selecting your debate topic.

- Allow everyone the chance to be heard.
- Participate. Everyone's ideas are needed for consensus.
- Discuss ideas, not stances—you will get to research and explore a stance for the debate itself.
- Support your ideas with reasoning and rationale.
- Combine and clarify suggestions to streamline similar ideas.
- Be candid but respectful.

After discussing the topics as a class, nominate your favorites. Be sure to give reasons to support your choices. Vote on the topics nominated for the debate to select the final debate topic.

Research

Your teacher will form groups of 4–5 students and will assign a position to each group. Begin the research process by considering the questions in the following chart.

Learning Strategies

Note-taking

VOCABULARY

ACADEMIC
A group comes to consensus when they reach a general agreement that all group members are comfortable with. Consensus is different from a popular vote where the idea that gets the most votes wins. In a consensus, not everyone will get their first choice, but the result is something that everyone is comfortable with.

INDEPENDENT READING LINK

Read and Respond
Think about your independent reading and analyze the author's claim. Is it reliable and valid? How do you know? Write down the most compelling evidence or example the text provides. Then write one way the author could strengthen his or her reasoning.

Research Considerations

Planning	• What research will support your assigned position?
	• What research will help you identify and address counterarguments—claims the opposing side might make?
Audience	• Who is your audience?
	• In what ways will this particular audience drive your research?
Organization	• How will you organize your notes?
Evaluation	• In what ways does each source answer the research question?
	• How does each source relate to other sources?
	• What is the date of publication? Is it recent and up to date?
	• In what ways does the source show appropriate credibility and reasoning?
	• Is the source free of bias, omission, faulty reasoning, incorrect premises, hasty generalizations, and either-or thinking?
Collaboration	• How will your group work together to listen actively and respond appropriately to each other?
	• How will your group work together to perform tasks, answer questions, and solve problems?
	• How will your group work together to share ideas, build consensus, and make decisions?

Take notes on the research log for relevant sources that support your position. Use these notes to ensure the ethical use of source materials and to avoid plagiarism.

Research Log

Research Question (your research topic written as a question):

Position/Claim (a statement of your assigned stance on the topic):

Research Log continued

Source 1

Academic Citation (author/title/year published/source type):

Paraphrased ideas from the text:

Quotations from the text:

Evidence or examples that support the claim:

Evaluation of source
- In what ways is the source credible/reliable?

- How does it relate to other sources?

Source 2

Academic Citation:

Paraphrased ideas from the text:

Quotations from the text:

Evidence or examples that support the claim:

Evaluation of source
- In what ways is the source credible/reliable?

- How does it relate to other sources?

Research Log continued

Source 3

Academic Citation:

Paraphrased ideas from the text:

Quotations from the text:

Evidence or examples that support the claim:

Evaluation of source
- In what ways is the source credible/reliable?

- How does it relate to other sources?

Source 4

Academic Citation:

Paraphrased ideas from the text:

Quotations from the text:

Evidence or examples that support the claim:

Evaluation of source
- In what ways is the source credible/reliable?

- How does it relate to other sources?

Next find sources that address the counterclaim. Try to think about the arguments those debating the opposite stance might use, and find sources with evidence to rebut, or disprove, them.

Research Log continued

Source 5

Academic Citation:

Paraphrased ideas from the text:

Quotations from the text:

Evidence or examples that support rebuttal of the counterclaim:

Evaluation of source
- In what ways is the source credible/reliable?

- How does it relate to other sources?

Source 6

Academic Citation:

Paraphrased ideas from the text:

Quotations from the text:

Evidence or examples that support rebuttal of the counterclaim:

Evaluation of source
- In what ways is the source credible/reliable?

- How does it relate to other sources?

Preparing for the Debate

My Notes

Learning Targets

- Organize information from research to plan oral responses, returning to a variety of sources to revise as needed.
- Practice a formal oral presentation within a collaborative group, providing feedback on presentation skills.

Preview

In this activity, you will learn about the structure of a formal debate and your group will plan and practice oral responses based on the position assigned and research you did in Activity 1.13.

Introducing the Debate

A debate is a structured argument that examines both sides of a topic or issue. During a debate, the participants follow a specific speaking sequence within a designated amount of time. Often, different members of a team have different jobs in a debate. Participants must communicate their position on the issue using evidence from research. They should employ good speaking habits such as eye contact and appropriate rate, volume, enunciation, and conventions of language.

Preparing to Debate

A debate provides an opportunity to argue a perspective on a given topic based on reason and evidence. Your goal is to convince the audience that your point of view is correct. Your debate will follow this sequence.

STEP 1A **First Affirmative Constructive Statement** (3–5 minutes): *The first speaker from the affirmative team ("pro" or for the resolution) makes their statement with evidence.*	**STEP 1B** **First Negative Constructive Statement** (3–5 minutes): *The first speaker from the negative team ("con" or against the resolution) makes their statement with evidence.*
STEP 2A **Second Affirmative Constructive Statement** (3–5 minutes): *The second speaker from the affirmative team presents further supporting arguments and answers any questions raised by the negative constructive statement.*	**STEP 2B** **Second Negative Constructive Statement** (3–5 minutes): *The second speaker from the negative team presents further supporting arguments and answers any questions raised by the affirmative constructive statement.*
STEP 3 **Recess for each team to plan rebuttals**	
STEP 4A **First Negative Rebuttal** (2–3 minutes): *A speaker from the negative team defends the team's arguments and attempts to discredit the affirmative team's evidence.*	**STEP 4B** **First Affirmative Rebuttal** (2–3 minutes): *A speaker from the affirmative team defends the team's arguments and attempts to discredit the negative team's evidence.*

STEP 5A
Second Negative Rebuttal (2–3 minutes):
A speaker from the negative team further defends their position and attempts to discredit the affirmative team's evidence.

STEP 5B
Second Affirmative Rebuttal (2–3 minutes):
A speaker from the affirmative team further defends their position and attempts to discredit the negative team's evidence.

STEP 6A
Closing Statement (Negative Team) (2–3 minutes): *A speaker from the negative team makes concluding remarks, restating their claim and offering the clearest evidence in support of their position.*

STEP 6B
Closing Statement (Affirmative Team) (2–3 minutes): *A speaker from the affirmative team makes concluding remarks, restating their claim and offering the clearest evidence in support of their position. The affirmative team has the last opportunity to speak.*

1. Decide which members of your group will take each speaking role.

Speaking Role	Student
First Constructive Statement	
Second Constructive Statement	
First Rebuttal	
Second Rebuttal	
Closing Statement	

2. Collaborate on how each speaker will present relevant information. Use the following outline to synthesize and organize the evidence from your research. Develop a plan to support the claim with reasons, evidence from your research, and rhetorical appeals.

First Constructive Statement			
Claim:	Reasons:	Evidence:	Appeals:

Second Constructive Statement

Claim:	Reasons:	Evidence:	Appeals:

First Rebuttal

Anticipated counterclaim:	Reasons for rebuttal:	Evidence:	Appeals:

Second Rebuttal

Anticipated counterclaim:	Reasons for rebuttal:	Evidence:	Appeals:

Closing Statement			
Claim:	Reasons:	Evidence:	Appeals:

3. After planning your debate responses, critique your evidence to determine whether you need additional information. Return to your research log and source notes, as needed.

Practice for the Debate

4. Practice as a team. Each speaker should practice presenting his or her portion of the debate. Evaluate each speaker with the following informal rubric and provide feedback on each participant's delivery to strengthen your team's debate for the Embedded Assessment.

Feedback Rubric

	Excellent	Above Average	Average	Below Average	Weak
Claim is clearly expressed.					
Reasoning is supported by evidence.					
Presentation follows a logical progression.					
Statements are effective and convincing.					

	Excellent	Above Average	Average	Below Average	Weak
Response to opposing view is well supported.					
Speaker uses appropriate speaking skills to communicate effectively.					

Notes for the Speaker:

One thing you did well was (circle one: present a clear thesis or valid evidence; make appropriate eye contact; use an appropriate speaking rate; use appropriate volume, enunciation, gestures, or conventions of language; or _____) because ...

_____

_____

One thing you can improve on is (circle one: presentation of a clear thesis or valid evidence; making appropriate eye contact; using an appropriate speaking rate; using appropriate volume, enunciation, gestures, or conventions of language; or _____) because ...

_____

_____

Independent Reading Checkpoint

Review your independent reading and analyze how the author uses evidence to support a claim. Compare and contrast the way this is done in your reading with the sources your group has collected during research. Take notes about how the audience and purpose for an argumentative text contribute to the structural presentation and support of claims.

Participating in a Debate

 ASSIGNMENT

In teams of 4–5, you will debate a topic chosen by your whole class. As a team, you must prepare for the debate effectively, assign speaking roles, and participate in the debate.

Planning: As a debate team, work collaboratively to prepare your claim and evidence.	■ What further research do you need to do to support your claim? ■ Who is the audience and what is the purpose for the debate? ■ Review the Scoring Guide. Are you meeting the criteria?
Drafting and Scripting: As a debate team, identify possible counterarguments and plan to rebut them.	■ How will you use your source notes and outline from previous activities to draft your assigned statement? ■ Have you stated your claim precisely and identified counterclaims?
Debate: Each team gets two opportunities to speak constructively, two opportunities to rebut the opposing team, and one opportunity to present a concluding remark.	■ How will you argue your claim using evidence, reasoning, and appeals that follow a logical sequence? ■ How will you use appropriate eye contact, speaking rate, volume, enunciation, gestures, and conventions of language? ■ What are some sentence frames you might use in your debate?
Evaluation: During or after the debate, listen actively to reflect on the ideas shared by your team and other teams arguing both viewpoints. Identify examples of effective and ineffective evidence and appeals.	■ What will you do when other members of the class are debating? ■ How will you evaluate the arguments of your peers?

Reflection

What have you learned about the importance of the quality and strength of evidence when it comes to defending a claim? How is the way you present yourself and your ideas in a formal presentation important to the outcome of a debate?

SCORING GUIDE

Scoring Criteria	Exemplary	Proficient	Emerging	Incomplete
Ideas	The debate • includes a clear claim with a wide variety of supporting evidence. • skillfully addresses counterclaims, with both a concession and a rebuttal. • skillfully uses rhetorical devices, including appeals.	The debate • includes a clear claim and a variety of evidence that supports the claim. • addresses counterarguments and includes a rebuttal. • uses rhetorical devices, including appeals.	The debate • includes a claim, with some supporting evidence. • acknowledges counterarguments but without addressing them effectively.	The debate • includes a claim that may not be clearly defined, with evidence that does not necessarily support the claim. • does not acknowledge counterarguments.
Structure	The debate • presents a logical and easy-to-follow progression of ideas supported by thorough and valid evidence. • models meaningful and respectful discourse through thoughtful, appropriate, and relevant responses that skillfully build on others' ideas. • includes a compelling conclusion.	The debate • presents a logical progression of ideas supported by valid evidence. • demonstrates meaningful and respectful discourse through appropriate, relevant responses that build on others' ideas. • includes a convincing conclusion.	The debate • presents a mostly logical progression of ideas with some invalid evidence. • demonstrates respectful discourse through generally appropriate responses that may be disconnected from others' ideas. • includes a conclusion.	The debate • presents an illogical progression of ideas with invalid evidence. • does not demonstrate respectful discourse due to inappropriate, irrelevant, or disconnected responses. • lacks a conclusion.
Use of Language	The debate • employs compelling use of eye contact, speaking rate, volume, enunciation, and gestures. • consistently follows language conventions to communicate ideas convincingly for the audience and purpose.	The debate • employs effective use of eye contact, speaking rate, volume, enunciation, and gestures. • follows language conventions to communicate ideas effectively for the audience and purpose.	The debate • inconsistently employs effective eye contact, speaking rate, volume, enunciation, and gestures. • sometimes breaks from language conventions, resulting in occasionally ineffective communication of ideas.	The debate • lacks effective eye contact, speaking rate, volume, enunciation, and gestures. • frequently breaks from language conventions, resulting in ineffective communication of ideas.

PERSUASION IN LITERATURE

The sky was overcast with heavy black clouds and a high wind began to blow, filling the air with dust and dry leaves. It was one of those rare occasions when even Nature takes a hand in a human fight.

—Chinua Achebe, "Marriage Is a Private Affair"

ACTIVITY	CONTENTS	

*Texts not included in these materials.

My Independent Reading List

Learning Strategies

Previewing
QHT
Skimming/Scanning

My Notes

Learning Targets

- Preview the Essential Questions for the unit and unpack Embedded Assessment 1.
- Create a plan for reading independently.

Preview

In this activity, you will explore the essential questions and tasks of the unit and make plans for your own independent reading.

About the Unit

In the previous unit, you examined the ways writers, speakers, and artists use their craft to persuade audiences. In this unit, you will look at the ways story characters persuade each other and how authors use story elements and language to influence their readers. In the first part of this unit, you will read Chinua Achebe's novel *Things Fall Apart* and explore how Achebe develops character, plot, and theme. Then you will write a literary analysis of the novel.

Essential Questions

Based on your current knowledge, respond to the following Essential Questions.

1. What can a character's use of persuasion reveal to a reader?

2. How can a work of literature reflect a cultural perspective?

3. What is the value of making connections between characters from different texts, time periods, or cultures?

Unpacking Embedded Assessment 1

Read the assignment for Embedded Assessment 1: Writing a Literary Analysis

Write an analytical essay about *Things Fall Apart* in which you examine how the cultural and historical settings of the novel influence the development of one character. How does this character react to the cultural collision between Western ideas and Ibo culture, and how does this reaction affect the plot?

Using the assignment and Embedded Assessment Scoring Guide, work as a class to analyze the activity. Think through the required concepts (what you need to know) and skills (what you need to do) to effectively complete the assignment.

INDEPENDENT READING LINK

Read and Research

As you preview your self-selected text, make notes in your Reader/Writer Notebook about key historical people and events. Conduct quick research online or at your school's library to learn more about these people and events. Use a reporter's questions—who, what, when, where, why, and how—to organize your notes. As you read, consider how this context informs the development of characters or ideas in the text.

Planning Independent Reading

The primary focus of this unit is the Nigerian novel *Things Fall Apart*, which chronicles cultural conflict among white missionaries, a colonial government, and the Ibo (or Igbo) people. During independent reading, you will have the opportunity to explore a variety of cultural and historical settings within different genres. You might choose to read a collection of short stories, a novel, a memoir, or a biography set in a cultural and historical context you are interested in learning more about.

Love and Marriage

Learning Strategies

Graphic Organizer
Marking the Text
Note-taking

Learning Targets

- Analyze how a character uses persuasion in a short story.
- Analyze how an author creates complex characters and uses diction to express their relationships.

Preview

In this activity, you will use your understanding of persuasion to analyze a short story and write a possible ending for it.

My Notes

About the Author

Chinua Achebe (1930–2013), the son of a Christian minister, was one of Nigeria's most celebrated novelists. Born in Ogidi, Nigeria, Achebe was educated in English. Achebe taught English at the university level at colleges in Africa and the United States. His first and best-known novel, *Things Fall Apart*, was published in 1958. Achebe wrote several novels, short story collections, and books of essays. Achebe was born into the Ibo nation and later worked in Lagos—the two settings in the following short story, "Marriage Is a Private Affair."

As You Read

- Underline the theme of this excerpt. Put stars where you would like to learn about something mentioned.
- Circle unknown words and phrases. Try to determine the meaning of the words by using context clues, word parts, or a dictionary.

Short Story

Marriage Is a Private Affair (Part One)

by **Chinua Achebe**

1   "Have you written to your dad yet?" asked Nene one afternoon as she sat with Nnaemeka in her room at 16 Kasanga Street, Lagos[1].

2   "No. I've been thinking about it. I think it's better to tell him when I get home on leave!"

---

[1] Lagos is the largest city in Nigeria.

3 "But why? Your leave is such a long way off yet—six whole weeks. He should be let into our happiness now."

4 Nnaemeka was silent for a while, and then began very slowly as if he groped for his words: "I wish I were sure it would be happiness to him."

5 "Of course it must," replied Nene, a little surprised. "Why shouldn't it?"

6 "You have lived in Lagos all your life, and you know very little about people in remote parts of the country."

7 "That's what you always say. But I don't believe anybody will be so unlike other people that they will be unhappy when their sons are engaged to marry."

8 "Yes. They are most unhappy if the engagement is not arranged by them. In our case it's worse—you are not even an Ibo[2]."

9 This was said so seriously and so bluntly that Nene could not find speech immediately. In the **cosmopolitan** atmosphere of the city it had always seemed to her something of a joke that a person's tribe could determine whom he married.

10 At last she said, "You don't really mean that he will object to your marrying me simply on that account? I had always thought you Ibos were kindly **disposed** to other people."

11 "So we are. But when it comes to marriage, well, it's not quite so simple. And this," he added, "is not peculiar to the Ibos. If your father were alive and lived in the heart of Ibibio-land he would be exactly like my father."

12 "I don't know. But anyway, as your father is so fond of you, I'm sure he will forgive you soon enough. Come on then, be a good boy and send him a nice lovely letter . . ."

13 "It would not be wise to break the news to him by writing. A letter will bring it upon him with a shock. I'm quite sure about that."

14 "All right, honey, suit yourself. You know your father."

Making Observations
- What is your first impression of each character?
- What do you notice about the relationship between Nene and Nnaemeka?

cosmopolitan: worldly or sophisticated
disposed: inclined

---

[2] The Ibo are a tribe in southeast Nigeria.

Returning to the Text

- Reread the short story to answer these text-dependent questions.
- Write any additional questions you have about the text in your Reader/Writer Notebook.

1. What is implied by Nene's use of the word *yet* in the first paragraph? What can we infer about the characters' relationship?

_____

_____

_____

_____

2. What might have been Achebe's purpose in naming such a specific address in paragraph 1?

_____

_____

_____

_____

3. What cultural differences exist between Nene and Nnaemeka? How do these differences influence the perspective of each character? Review your starred text.

_____

_____

_____

_____

4. What attitude does Nene display toward Nnaemeka's cultural upbringing? What words reveal this attitude?

_____

_____

_____

_____

Working from the Text

5. In the story, Nene doesn't seem to understand the cultural traditions of Nnaemeka's tribe. Return to the text and find three details that reveal her misconceptions.

My Notes

6. At this point in the reading, you might feel as confused as Nene if you, too, lack background knowledge. Return to the text and note any starred places as starting points for your research. Use print or digital resources to conduct research to build your background knowledge and gain information about the setting of the story. Record your notes in your Reader/Writer Notebook.

7. Reread the excerpt with your new information in mind. How does it increase your understanding of the conflicts in this piece? Discuss your ideas with a partner.

As You Read

- Underline the theme of this part of the short story. Write a note in the margin that compares the themes from Part One and Part Two.
- Circle unknown words and phrases. Try to determine the meaning of the words by using context clues, word parts, or a dictionary.

Short Story

Marriage Is a Private Affair (Part Two)

by **Chinua Achebe**

15   As Nnaemeka walked home that evening he turned over in his mind different ways of overcoming his father's opposition, especially now that he had gone and found a girl for him. He had thought of showing his letter to Nene but decided on second thoughts not to, at least for the moment. He read it again when he got home and couldn't help smiling to himself. He remembered Ugoye quite well, an Amazon of a girl who used to beat up all the boys, himself included, on the way to the stream, a complete dunce at school.

16   *I have found a girl who will suit you admirably—Ugoye Nweke, the eldest daughter of our neighbor, Jacob Nweke. She has a proper Christian upbringing. When she stopped schooling some years ago her father (a man of sound judgment) sent her to live in the house of a pastor where she has received all the training a wife could need. Her Sunday school teacher has told me that she reads her Bible very fluently. I hope we shall begin negotiations when you come home in December.*

17   On the second evening of his return from Lagos, Nnaemeka sat with his father under a cassia tree. This was the old man's retreat where he went to read his Bible when the parching December sun had set and a fresh, reviving wind blew on the leaves.

18   "Father," began Nnaemeka suddenly, "I have come to ask for forgiveness."

19   "Forgiveness? For what, my son?" he asked in amazement.

20   "It's about this marriage question."

21   "Which marriage question?"

My Notes

22 "I can't—we must—I mean it is impossible for me to marry Nweke's daughter."

23 "Impossible? Why?" asked his father.

24 "I don't love her."

25 "Nobody said you did. Why should you?" he asked.

26 "Marriage today is different . . ."

27 "Look here, my son," interrupted his father, "nothing is different. What one looks for in a wife are a good character and a Christian background."

28 Nnaemeka saw there was no hope along the present line of argument.

29 "Moreover," he said, "I am engaged to marry another girl who has all of Ugoye's good qualities, and who . . ."

30 His father did not believe his ears. "What did you say?" he asked slowly and **disconcertingly**.

31 "She is a good Christian," his son went on, "and a teacher in a girls' school in Lagos."

32 "Teacher, did you say? If you consider that a qualification for a good wife I should like to point out to you, Emeka, that no Christian woman should teach. St. Paul in his letter to the Corinthians says that women should keep silence." He rose slowly from his seat and paced forward and backward. This was his pet subject, and he condemned **vehemently** those church leaders who encouraged women to teach in their schools. After he had spent his emotion on a long **homily** he at last came back to his son's engagement, in a seemingly milder tone.

33 "Whose daughter is she, anyway?"

34 "She is Nene Atang."

35 "What!" All the mildness was gone again. "Did you say Neneataga, what does that mean?"

36 "Nene Atang from Calabar. She is the only girl I can marry." This was a very rash reply and Nnaemeka expected the storm to burst. But it did not. His father merely walked away into his room. This was most unexpected and perplexed Nnaemeka. His father's silence was infinitely more menacing than a flood of threatening speech. That night the old man did not eat.

37 When he sent for Nnaemeka a day later he applied all possible ways of **dissuasion**. But the young man's heart was hardened, and his father eventually gave him up as lost.

38 "I owe it to you, my son, as a duty to show you what is right and what is wrong. Whoever put this idea into your head might as well have cut your throat. It is Satan's work." He waved his son away.

39 "You will change your mind, Father, when you know Nene."

disconcertingly: with confusion or disturbance
vehemently: forcefully
homily: sermon or lecture
dissuasion: advising against something

My Notes

40 "I shall never see her," was the reply. From that night the father scarcely spoke to his son. He did not, however, cease hoping that he would realize how serious was the danger he was heading for. Day and night he put him in his prayers.

The Betrothed (Os Noivos) by Candido Portinari, 1947

Making Observations

- What happens in this part of the story?
- What do you notice about the relationship between father and son?

Returning to the Text

Reread the short story to answer these text-dependent questions.

• Write any additional questions you have about the short story in your Reader/Writer Notebook.

8. How is Nnaemeka's father introduced in the story? What is the effect of this on the reader?

_____

_____

_____

_____

9. What is the significance of the cassia tree as a setting for the discussion between father and son?

_____

_____

_____

_____

10. What is Nnaemeka's argument about marriage? What points does Nnaemeka's father make to counter his son's argument?

_____

_____

_____

_____

Working from the Text

11. Reread the discussion between father and son. In what ways are the characters making statements about culture? Analyze their arguments by filling in details in the graphic organizer

Character	Rhetorical Technique Used	How the Argument Is Crafted	What We Learn About the Character
Son	Appeals to father's emotions	He asks forgiveness and explains that he doesn't love the girl his father has arranged for him to marry.	Nnaemeka is respectful of his father. He tries to obtain his father's blessing.
Son			
Father			
Father			

12. Reflect on the essential question: What can a character's use of persuasion reveal to a reader

☑ Focus on the Sentence

Use subordinating conjunctions and your understanding of the beginning of "Marriage Is a Private Affair" to write two sentences about the beginning of the story.

Although/not in love with her

_____

_____

Since/proper upbringing

_____

_____

As You Read

- Compare and contrast Parts One, Two, and Three by circling similarities and underlining differences.
- Circle unknown words and phrases. Try to determine the meaning of the words by using context clues, word parts, or a dictionary.

Short Story

Marriage Is a Private Affair (Part Three)

by **Chinua Achebe**

41   Nnaemeka, for his own part, was very deeply affected by his father's grief. But he kept hoping that it would pass away. If it had occurred to him that never in the history of his people had a man married a woman who spoke a different tongue, he might have been less optimistic. "It has never been heard," was the verdict of an old man speaking a few weeks later. In that short sentence he spoke for all of his people. This man had come with others to **commiserate** with Okeke when news went round about his son's behavior. By that time the son had gone back to Lagos.

42   "It has never been heard," said the old man again with a sad shake of his head.

43   "What did Our Lord say?" asked another gentleman. "Sons shall rise against their Fathers; it is there in the Holy Book."

44   "It is the beginning of the end," said another.

45   The discussion thus tending to become **theological**, Madubogwu, a highly practical man, brought it down once more to the ordinary level.

46   "Have you thought of consulting a native doctor about your son?" he asked Nnaemeka's father.

47   "He isn't sick," was the reply.

48   "What is he then? The boy's mind is diseased and only a good herbalist can bring him back to his right senses. The medicine he requires is Amalile, the same that women apply with success to recapture their husbands' straying affection."

49   "Madubogwu is right," said another gentleman. "This thing calls for medicine."

50   "I shall not call in a native doctor." Nnaemeka's father was known to be **obstinately** ahead of his more superstitious neighbors in these matters. "I will not be another Mrs. Ochuba. If my son wants to kill himself let him do it with his own hands. It is not for me to help him."

My Notes

commiserate: express or feel sympathy
theological: religious
obstinately: stubbornly

My Notes

51 "But it was her fault," said Madubogwu. "She ought to have gone to an honest herbalist. She was a clever woman, nevertheless."

52 "She was a wicked murderess," said Jonathan, who rarely argued with his neighbors because, he often said, they were incapable of reasoning. "The medicine was prepared for her husband, it was his name they called in its preparation, and I am sure it would have been perfectly beneficial to him. It was wicked to put it into the herbalist's food, and say you were only trying it out."

53 Six months later, Nnaemeka was showing his young wife a short letter from his father:

54 *It amazes me that you could be so unfeeling as to send me your wedding picture. I would have sent it back. But on further thought I decided just to cut off your wife and send it back to you because I have nothing to do with her. How I wish that I had nothing to do with you either.*

55 When Nene read through this letter and looked at the **mutilated** picture her eyes filled with tears, and she began to sob.

56 "Don't cry, my darling," said her husband. "He is essentially good-natured and will one day look more kindly on our marriage."

57 But years passed and that one day did not come.

58 For eight years, Okeke would have nothing to do with his son, Nnaemeka. Only three times (when Nnaemeka asked to come home and spend his leave) did he write to him.

59 "I can't have you in my house," he replied on one occasion. "It can be of no interest to me where or how you spend your leave—or your life, for that matter."

60 The prejudice against Nnaemeka's marriage was not confined to his little village. In Lagos, especially among his people who worked there, it showed itself in a different way. Their women, when they met at their village meeting, were not hostile to Nene. Rather, they paid her such excessive **deference** as to make her feel she was not one of them. But as time went on, Nene gradually broke through some of this prejudice and even began to make friends among them. Slowly and grudgingly they began to admit that she kept her home much better than most of them.

61 The story eventually got to the little village in the heart of the Ibo country that Nnaemeka and his young wife were a most happy couple. But his father was one of the few people in the village who knew nothing about this. He always displayed so much temper whenever his son's name was mentioned that everyone avoided it in his presence. By a tremendous effort of will he had succeeded in pushing his son to the back of his mind. The strain had nearly killed him but he had persevered, and won.

62 Then one day he received a letter from Nene, and in spite of himself he began to glance through it perfunctorily until all of a sudden the expression on his face changed and he began to read more carefully.

mutilated: cut up or destroyed
deference: regard for another's
wants

My Notes

63 . . . *Our two sons, from the day they learnt that they have a grandfather, have insisted on being taken to him. I find it impossible to tell them that you will not see them. I implore you to allow Nnaemeka to bring them home for a short time during his leave next month. I shall remain here in Lagos . . .*

64 The old man at once felt the resolution he had built up over so many years falling in. He was telling himself that he must not give in. He tried to steel his heart against all emotional appeals. It was a reenactment of that other struggle. He leaned against a window and looked out. The sky was overcast with heavy black clouds and a high wind began to blow, filling the air with dust and dry leaves. It was one of those rare occasions when even Nature takes a hand in a human fight. Very soon it began to rain, the first rain in the year. It came down in large sharp drops and was accompanied by the lightning and thunder which mark a change of season. Okeke was trying hard not to think of his two grandsons. But he knew he was now fighting a losing battle. He tried to hum a favorite hymn but the pattering of large raindrops on the roof broke up the tune. His mind immediately returned to the children. How could he shut his door against them? By a curious mental process he imagined them standing, sad and forsaken, under the harsh angry weather—shut out from his house.

65 That night he hardly slept, from remorse—and a vague fear that he might die without making it up to them.

Making Observations
- What changes do you notice in Nnaemeka's father?
- What details do you notice in this passage that someone else might have missed?

Returning to the Text

- Reread the short story to answer these text-dependent questions.
- Write any additional questions you have about the short story in your Reader/Writer Notebook.

13. Why might Achebe have included the story of Mrs. Ochuba? What does it reveal about the father?

_____

_____

_____

_____

14. In the end, who wins the argument—father or son? Explain your choice.

_____

_____

_____

_____

15. What might the weather at the end of the story symbolize?

_____

_____

_____

_____

Working from the Text

16. Study the title and explain its irony. In what ways does the text contradict your expectations based on the title?

17. How do cultural traditions influence Okeke's relationship with his son?

18. Return to the text and highlight examples of cultural conflicts or places where the individual clashes with a community's traditions or expectations. Put an asterisk next to the example you think best typifies this struggle.

19. Work in small groups to compare and contrast the marked excerpts of text. Discuss each of your choices to begin building a statement of theme for the text. What is the author saying about social tradition and the individual in this story? Use your responses to the previous three questions to provide evidence.

☑ Check Your Understanding

Based on your group discussion, what is a possible theme for the story?

Gaining Perspectives

In "Marriage Is a Private Affair," Okeke's neighbors mention native doctors and herbalists. What the native doctors and herbalists practice is what we in the United States call *alternative medicine*, or a way of treating and healing people that is outside traditional Western medicinal practices. Though the text suggests it is a superstitious aspect of the Ibo tribe, alternative medicine from different cultures is growing in popularity in the United States. However, not many people are familiar with its practices and effectiveness. How would you begin learning about alternative medicine practices? What types of information would you need to gather to justify a practice as valid and beneficial to a person's health? Discuss the risks and benefits with a partner. Then share your thoughts with the class, providing visuals to support your presentation.

✏️ Writing Prompt: Literary

The story has an ambiguous ending that leaves the outcome up to the reader's imagination. Based on your understanding of the characters, as well as your knowledge of plot and setting, write a continuation of the story that tells what you think will happen after Okeke's revelation. Be sure to:

- Maintain consistency with how the characters are portrayed in the original story.
- Keep your story grounded in its historical and cultural context.
- Write a conclusion that effectively ends the story.

My Notes

🔓 INDEPENDENT READING LINK

Read and Discuss

Consider the use of persuasion in your independent reading. Choose a persuasive passage and mark it for claim, evidence, counterarguments, and rhetorical strategies. Discuss your marked passage with a partner. Address whether or not you are convinced of the argument and why. Then, allow your partner to do the same with his or her passage. What similarities and differences between the two passages do you note?

VOCABULARY

ACADEMIC
A proverb is a short saying about a general truth.

LITERARY
A folktale is a story without a known author that has been preserved through oral retellings.

Learning Targets

- Analyze and make personal connections to proverbs and folktales.
- Examine how an author's use of proverbs and folktales influences the characterization of a people.

Preview

In this activity, you will prepare to read the novel *Things Fall Apart* by analyzing the proverbs and folktales of the Ibo and broader African culture.

Proverbs and Folktales

Proverbs and folktales are one part of a culture's oral tradition. People share proverbs and folktales in order to express important stories, ideas, and beliefs about their culture.

1. As you read the novel *Things Fall Apart*, you will encounter many proverbs and folktales that illustrate the beliefs of the Ibo people. One memorable Ibo proverb is "Proverbs are the palm oil with which words are eaten." Explain what you think this proverb means. How does the proverb help the reader's understanding?

My Notes

2. In small groups, read and discuss the following proverbs from the novel. Then explain each one in the graphic organizer.

Proverb	Explanation
If a child washes his hands, he could eat with kings.	
Since men have learned to shoot without missing, [the bird] has learned to fly without perching.	
The clan was like a lizard. If it lost its tail it soon grew another.	
I cannot live on the bank of a river and wash my hands with spittle.	
A man who pays respect to the great paves the way for his own greatness.	

☑ Check Your Understanding

What general truth believed by the Ibo culture is revealed through the proverb "If one finger brought oil it soiled the others"?

3. In addition to proverbs, you will also encounter a number of folktales in the novel. Use the following graphic organizer to record details about the folktales discussed in class. Be sure to summarize and paraphrase the information using your own words. Then, copy this organizer or create your own to record details about the folktales you find in *Things Fall Apart*, especially in Chapters 7, 9, 11, and 15.

Folktales	
Title	
Characters	
Setting	
Plot Summary	
Symbols and Archetypes	
Meaning of the Folktale	
Significance (reason for its retelling across generations and its inclusion in the novel)	

LITERARY

An **archetype** is a pattern, a symbol, an image, or an idea that recurs in literature. It can also be a character, a theme, or a setting. Archetypes can represent ideas in a specific culture or in the entire human race. For example, as a hero archetype, Beowulf is a Scandinavian character who exemplifies courage and honor by fighting monsters and attempting to restore peace and order to the world.

VOCABULARY

My Notes

☑ Check Your Understanding

- What connections can you make between the proverbs and the folktales?
- How can proverbs and folktales provide insight into a culture?
- How and why might an author use proverbs and folktales in a novel?

📝 Writing Prompt: Informational

Explain how the proverbs and folktales you analyzed in this activity provide insight into the values of the cultures from which they come. Be sure to:

- Begin with a thesis summarizing your understanding of how the themes of proverbs and folktales can tell readers about a culture's values.
- Develop the topic, making sure to include specific relevant details from proverbs and folktales that tell readers about the culture.
- Include transitions among major sections and complex ideas throughout the explanation.
- Use precise language and domain-specific vocabulary, as appropriate.
- Maintain a formal style of writing throughout the explanation, including any precise language and vocabulary that add complexity to the topic.
- Annotate the text and cite direct quotations and specific examples from the text. Introduce and punctuate all quotations correctly.
- Include a strong conclusion that supports and summarizes your main points or leaves the reader with something to ponder.

Father and Son

Learning Targets

- Compare and contrast two characters from the novel.
- Analyze specific chapters and their contributions to the plot.

Preview

In this activity, you will begin reading the novel *Things Fall Apart* and compare and contrast the characters of Unoka and Okonkwo. Then you will write a literary analysis examining their differences and similarities.

Reading *Things Fall Apart*, Chapters 1–4

Copy the following names and pronunciations onto a blank bookmark supplied by your teacher. *Things Fall Apart* focuses on a culture that may be unfamiliar to you. Even though the novel is written in English, the author uses words and phrases from his native Ibo language. Review the glossary at the back of the novel. Create your own glossary in your Reader/Writer Notebook where you record words that are new to you and their definitions. Look up the meanings of these words in the glossary at the back of the novel, and if they are not there, then consult a print or digital dictionary.

Achebe (Ah-chay-bay)	Nwoye (Nuh-woh-yeh)
Chinua (Chin-oo-ah)	Ojiubo (Oh-jee-ooh-boh)
Ekwefi (Eh-kweh-fee)	Okonkwo (Oh-kawn-kwoh)
Ezinma (Eh-zeen-mah)	Umuofia (Oo-moo-oh-fee-ah)
Ikemefuna (Ee-keh-meh-foo-nah)	Unoka (Ooh-no-kah)
Obierika (Oh-bee-air-ee-kah)	

Comparing and Contrasting Characters

1. As you read, use the following graphic organizer or create one of your own to compare and contrast Okonkwo and his father. Record facts and details about each.

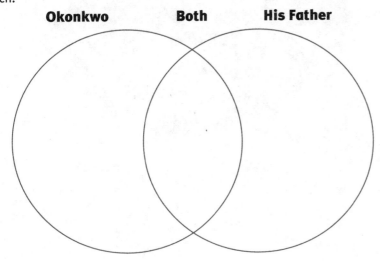

Okonkwo   **Both**   **His Father**

LITERARY

A **motif** is a recurring image, symbol, theme, character type, or subject that becomes a unifying element in an artistic work. A **foil** is a character whose traits contrast with and therefore highlight the traits of another.

My Notes

2. **Collaborative Conversation:** Authors use a **motif** for many reasons, including to establish themes and moods. Achebe uses the motif of tension between fathers and sons in his novel. Review the facts and details about Okonkwo and his father that you recorded. How do these similarities and differences create tension between the two? Discuss how Okonkwo's father serves as a **foil** to his son.

3. **Collaborative Conversation:** When he learns he is going to receive the Idemili title, Okoye visits Okonkwo's father, Unoka, to collect on his debts, using persuasive techniques to get to his point. How does Okoye feel about asking Unoka about the debt? What devices does Okoye use to try to persuade Unoka to repay his debt? How does Unoka react to the request, and what does this reveal about Unoka?

4. **Collaborative Conversation:** In a later scene, Okonkwo visits Nwakibie to ask for seed yams. This time it is his turn to use persuasive techniques to try to get his point across. How does Okonkwo try to persuade Nwakibie to help him? What do you learn about Okonkwo? How does Nwakibie react to Okonkwo? And what does the difference between these two scenes tell us?

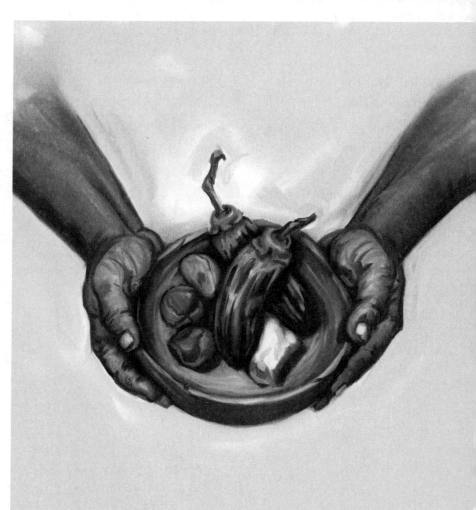

LANGUAGE & WRITER'S CRAFT:
Active and Passive Voice

Sentences can be in active or passive voice. Active voice occurs when the subject of a sentence performs the action, so it emphasizes the person or thing that does the action. For example, in the following sentence, Okonkwo performs the action of throwing: "In the end, Okonkwo threw the Cat." Most of the time, you should use the active voice in your writing to enhance clarity and avoid wordiness. In other words, use active voice unless there is a compelling reason to use passive voice.

Passive voice occurs when the subject of the sentence receives the action; passive voice always uses a form of *to be* with the past participle of the verb. For example, the following sentence uses a form of *to be (was)* and the past participle of *throw (thrown)*: "The Cat was thrown by Okonkwo." Only use passive voice when you want to emphasize the receiver of the action, either because the receiver of the action is more important than the doer, or because the person or thing that does the action is unknown.

PRACTICE Read the following sentences. Identify the ones that use passive voice and rewrite them so that they use active voice.

- *Things Fall Apart* was written by Chinua Achebe.
- Chinua Achebe included many proverbs in his novel.
- Showing Nigerians in stereotypical ways was avoided by Achebe.

📝 Writing Prompt: Literary Analysis

Explain how the two persuasive scenes you analyzed in steps 3 and 4 reveal the differences and similarities between Unoka and Okonkwo. Be sure to:

- Include a topic sentence that compares or contrasts the two characters.
- Use specific details and quotations from the novel as support.
- Use active voice.

WORD CONNECTIONS

Roots and Affixes

Dominated contains the root *dom*, from the Latin words *domus*, meaning "house," and *dominus*, meaning "master (of the house)." This root also appears in *dominant*, *predominant*, *domineer*, *dominion*, *domestic*, and *domicile*.

My Notes

Independent Practice: Create a Double-Entry Journal

5. Look for examples of Okonkwo's feelings and fears, the reasons for those fears, and the effect they have on his actions. Also look for a motif or foil.

- Include textual evidence from each chapter in the left-hand column.
- Write your personal response or interpretation in the right-hand column.
- As you read Chapters 1–4, continue the chart on a separate sheet of paper.

Passages from the Text: Feelings and Fears	Personal Responses or Interpretations
Example: "But his whole life was dominated by fear, the fear of failure and of weakness." (Ch. 2)	I wonder why Okonkwo is so afraid. How could he be a successful wrestler if he is dominated by fear?

☑ Check Your Understanding

Review the notes in your Double-Entry Journal and respond to the following questions:

- How do Okonkwo's fears influence his actions?
- What are the reasons for his fears?

Visualizing a Character in Conflict

Learning Targets

- Develop a visual interpretation that supports mental images and deepens understanding of a text.
- Analyze how the author develops complex yet believable characters.

Preview

In this activity, you will revisit Chapters 1–4 and make connections to the text by discussing the dual nature of Okonkwo, including his positive and negative traits. Then you will write an argument analyzing the flawed character of such a powerful leader.

My Notes

Visual Interpretations

1. With your group, discuss the first four chapters of *Things Fall Apart*. In those chapters, Achebe presents Okonkwo as a man of high status in his village despite some of his less admirable traits.

   Fill in the following chart with details from Chapters 1–4 to explore the conflicting sides of Okonkwo's character.

Okonkwo's Achievements and Status	Negative Traits and Actions

2. With your group, plan a presentation using digital media that illustrates Okonkwo's dual nature. You can use a digital drawing tool like Microsoft Paint or assemble clip art in a PowerPoint to create your visual interpretation. Make strategic use of digital media to enhance your interpretation and to add interest to your presentation. If digital media is not available, create illustrations to enhance the presentation.

3. Present your visual interpretation to another group. Be sure to:

   - Assign talking points to all members of your group.
   - Make eye contact with your audience when speaking, and use an appropriate speaking rate that includes a suitable volume and pauses for effect.
   - Refer to specific details in your visual and cite textual evidence, then build on the ideas of others when they contribute relevant information. Adjust your communication, as needed, to meet your purpose and the needs of your audience.

My Notes

4. In preparation for completing an argumentative text, work with your group to reflect on the following writing prompt. Use a Round Table Discussion graphic organizer to take notes from your discussion.

> ### 📝 Writing Prompt: Argumentative
>
> Take a position on the question: *Is it common for powerful leaders to have flawed characters? Why? How might this affect the community?* Write an argumentative essay to support your position and explain how it relates to Okonkwo's character. Be sure to:
>
> - State your claim in the beginning sentence.
> - Use relevant evidence from the text and valid reasoning to support your claim.
> - Provide a concluding statement that supports the claim you have presented.

Family Ties

Learning Targets

- Analyze how themes are developed through characterization.
- Write a literary analysis using genre characteristics about a character in the story.

Preview

In this activity, you will read Chapters 5–6 and analyze the relationships between characters in the novel, as well as what the relationships teach you about the characters. Then you will write a literary analysis discussing how Okonkwo's family relationships make him a sympathetic or an unsympathetic character.

Characterization

Writers use characterization to create vivid images of characters in the reader's mind.

1. Compare and contrast Okonkwo's relationships in the chapters you have read so far. What do all of his relationships with family members have in common? How are some different from others? What themes emerge from these relationships? Choose a compare/contrast structure, such as a Venn diagram or other graphic organizer that you create.

2. Work with a partner or group to note the names and relationships of characters from the novel. Pay special attention to Okonkwo's family. Include quotes from the novel to support your ideas. Add rows as needed to the following graphic organizer, or use your Reader/Writer Notebook.

VOCABULARY

LITERARY

Characterization refers to the methods a writer uses to develop characters, including descriptions of what they say, what they do, how they act, what they think, and what others say about them.

Character	Relationship to Okonkwo and others in the family	What do you learn about the character?	What is your reaction to the character?

INDEPENDENT READING LINK

Read and Connect

Review the notes you have been taking in your Reader/ Writer Notebook about your independent reading. In what ways does your text include familial relationships? Choose an excerpt and draw connections between the in-class text and the independent reading text. For example, compare and contrast how characters interact with other members of their families in the two texts, as well as what these relationships teach you about the characters.

LANGUAGE & WRITER'S CRAFT: Compare/Contrast

In this unit, you have been comparing and contrasting characters in *Things Fall Apart*. In a compare/contrast essay, the way you organize ideas is an important part of communicating similarities and differences.

Recall that a thesis is a statement of your perspective on a topic. A compare/contrast thesis, therefore, must introduce your ideas about how the subjects of your essay are similar and different. Many compare/contrast thesis statements begin with words like *although*, *whereas*, *even though*, or *while*. These words signal that a contrast is to follow. Here is an example:

- Although Okonkwo and Unoka are both tall men, Unoka walks with a stoop, suggesting that he is burdened by the expectations of his tribe.

Another way to write a compare/contrast thesis statement is to focus on differences and similarities. For example, consider this thesis:

- A similarity between Okonkwo and Unoka is that both are tall men. Their differences, though, are more pronounced than their similarities.

The organization of your body paragraphs also helps you present your ideas logically. Two possible ways to organize your writing are:

- Subject by Subject: You may choose to use a subject-by-subject outline, where you discuss one subject thoroughly in one paragraph and then turn to the other subject in the next paragraph, pointing out its similarities and differences. This structure is a good choice when the first subject is more familiar or provides a lens through which to view the other subject.

- Point by Point: Alternatively, you may use a point-by-point outline, where you discuss one point of comparison at a time, explaining how the subjects compare on that point before turning to another point of comparison. In this type of organization, each point of comparison is usually discussed in its own paragraph.

PRACTICE On a separate sheet of paper, draw a graphic organizer such as a Venn diagram to use as a prewriting tool to help you compare and contrast two of Okonkwo's family relationships in response to the following writing prompt. Using your graphic organizer, decide if you will use a subject-by-subject or a point-by-point organizational structure. Explain your choice in your Reader/Writer Notebook.

Writing Prompt: Literary Analysis

Write a literary analysis paragraph explaining how Okonkwo's family relationships make him a sympathetic or an unsympathetic character. Be sure to:

- Write a thesis statement that compares and contrasts at least two relationships and explores their effect on characterization.
- Include supporting details and quotations from the novel.
- Use an effective organizational structure with transition words and phrases.

Sacrificial Son

Learning Strategies

Discussion Groups
Drafting
Graphic Organizer
Note-taking
Questioning the Text
Sharing and Responding
Socratic Seminar

Learning Targets

- Engage in a meaningful discourse by participating actively in a Socratic Seminar.
- Analyze the use of foreshadowing in a novel.

Preview

In this activity, you will read Chapters 7–8 and prepare for and participate in a Socratic Seminar.

Foreshadowing

1. Consider how Achebe uses **foreshadowing** in the last two sentences of Chapter 1. Why do you think he tells the reader so early on that Ikemefuna is "doomed" and "ill-fated"?

Preparing for a Socratic Seminar

2. Skim/scan Chapters 7 and 8, annotating pages and taking notes to answer at least one assigned question from the following graphic organizer. Include details and page numbers from the text.

3. Work with your group to create a visual and come up with talking points to present your response to the assigned question.

4. As each group presents its visual and talking points, take notes to complete the graphic organizer.

5. Write two interpretive and two universal questions related to your assigned question to use in a Socratic Seminar.

LITERARY

Foreshadowing refers to the use of hints or clues in a narrative to suggest future action. Foreshadowing is used to create suspense and hook the reader to continue reading.

VOCABULARY

My Notes

Socratic Seminar Norms

Socratic Seminar discussions follow the norms of effective discussions, such as:

- Come to discussions prepared by having read the material and collected needed evidence.
- Engage in meaningful discourse by setting ground rules for the discussion, listening actively, and responding appropriately.
- Answer questions or solve problems to keep the discussion moving.
- Employ eye contact and appropriate speaking rate that includes pauses for effect, volume, enunciation, purposeful gesture, and proper language conventions.
- Participate collaboratively and build on the ideas of others, contributing relevant information at appropriate times, and verify ideas while also adjusting conclusions based on evidence.

Question	Page	Response and Support
How has Nwoye changed, and what has caused the changes?		
Describe the arrival of the locusts. What is the reaction of the people of Umuofia?		
Do you think that Ikemefuna suspects that he is going to be killed? Why or why not?		
How does Okonkwo feel about Ikemefuna's death? How does Nwoye feel?		
Genesis 22:1–19 of the Bible presents the story of Abraham and Isaac. What similarities and differences are there in the sacrifices of Isaac and Ikemefuna? How does this incident illustrate the novel's father/son motif?		
How do you think the death of Ikemefuna will affect the relationship between Okonkwo and Nwoye?		
Okonkwo does not heed the advice of the old man, Ogbuefi Ezeudu. What consequences do you think there may be for his part in the death of Ikemefuna?		

LANGUAGE & WRITER'S CRAFT: Academic Voice

Literary analysis is typically written in academic voice, which uses a straightforward, formal style and avoids a conversational tone. Academic writing focuses readers on the ideas as presented in the text, rather than on the personality and voice of the author.

Academic voice uses the third-person point of view as well as formal diction, which avoids the use of slang, contractions, and unnecessary words such as *possibly, very, maybe,* and *really*. Academic voice sends a message to readers; it tells them that you take your writing and your readers seriously.

Consider the author's purpose of using formal diction in this passage from *Things Fall Apart*, which helps set a tone of dignity and sorrow:

> As soon as his father walked in, that night, Nwoye knew that Ikemefuna had been killed, and something seemed to give way inside him like the snapping of a tightened bow. He did not cry. He just hung limp. He had had the same feeling not long ago, during the last harvest season.

As a contrast, read this passage from Mark Twain's 1882 "Advice to Youth." Twain's style is informal and conversational, full of the writer's personality and sense of humor:

> Go to bed early, get up early—this is wise. Some authorities say get up with the sun; some say get up with one thing, others with another. But a lark is really the best thing to get up with. It gives you a splendid reputation with everybody to know that you get up with the lark; and if you get the right kind of lark, and work at him right, you can easily train him to get up at half past nine, every time—it's no trick at all.

Note that an informal style is well suited to Twain's purpose, which is to entertain with humor. In the same way, a formal academic voice is suited to the purpose of a literary analysis.

PRACTICE Compare the differences between formal (academic) and informal style and voice in the space that follows.

My Notes

6. Before you begin the following writing prompt, look over your notes, which were probably written in an informal style and voice. When you respond to the prompt, you will want to use a formal style and voice to lend credibility to your academic writing. The previous description of formal diction will help you make the necessary changes.

Writing Prompt: Literary Analysis

Look back at the scene where Ezedu tries to persuade Okonkwo not to participate in the killing of Ikemefuna. How does Ezedu build his case? What does Okonkwo's response reveal about his character? Write a literary analysis explaining your answer. Be sure to:

- Include a clear thesis statement.
- Provide details and quotations from the text with meaningful commentary.
- Use a formal style and voice.

Creating a Character Tableau

Learning Strategies

Drafting
Graphic Organizer
Marking the Text
Rereading
Role Playing

Learning Targets

- Analyze how the introduction of a new character affects the themes and development of the plot.
- Create a tableau of characters from the novel to illustrate your understanding of characterization.

Preview

In this activity, you will read Chapter 9 and analyze how the introduction of the character Ikemefuna affects the themes and development of the plot. Then you will write a short narrative about Ikemefuna's influence on the community.

My Notes

kemefuna

1. With your group, discuss how the events of Chapter 9 are connected to Ikemefuna's death in the previous chapter. What conclusions might Okonkwo's community draw from the juxtaposition of these two events? How does the author develop the theme of death in the story?

2. Consider the character of Ikemefuna. Choose or create an appropriate graphic organizer in which you list details about Ikemefuna. Your organizer may be a chart, a web, or another graphic. Be sure to include details about Ikemefuna's appearance and actions as well as the attitudes other people have toward him.

3. Discuss with a partner or small group Ikemefuna's influence on the community. Be sure to discuss not only how he influences the community but also how specific characters feel about that influence.

4. Analyze ways that Achebe creates a complex yet believable character in Ikemefuna.

☑ Check Your Understanding

Answer the following question in two or three sentences: How do Ikemefuna's arrival, presence, and death affect the community?

Creating an Ibo Tableau

5. Work with your group members to create a tableau (a freeze-frame snapshot) of characters from *Things Fall Apart*.

   - Begin by writing the name of each character on its own index card and giving each group member a character card.

   - Review the basic facts about your character. Write a short statement that your character will give. The statement should begin with "I am ..."; then state your character's name and reveal an interesting fact about that character. Just as the characters' positions in the tableau will explain their relationships with one another, try to let the lines you write and the way you deliver them reveal your character's attitude and personality.

WORD CONNECTIONS

Etymology

Tableau is a French word meaning "a graphic description or representation." Unlike English words that usually form a plural by adding an "s" or "es," the plural of tableau is *tableaux*.

My Notes

- Work with your group to decide where each character should stand, how he or she should pose, and where he or she should be positioned in relation to others. Be prepared to present your tableau to the class. You and fellow characters should strike the pose and then step out of the freeze-frame one at a time to deliver your lines.

☑ Focus on the Sentence

Reflect on your experience creating a tableau by writing two sentences and two questions for your group.

Sentences:

Questions:

INDEPENDENT READING LINK

Read and Connect

In this part of the unit, you will continue reading *Things Fall Apart* with a focus on the ways that Ibo culture changes in the novel. For your independent reading, you might have chosen a collection of short stories, a novel, a memoir, or a biography that reflects historical and cultural settings and events (for example, Southeast Asian, South American, or African nations). Establish whether the text was written during or after colonization. Look for ways in which the characters respond to colonization or to life after colonization and record these observations in your Reader/Writer Notebook.

✍ Writing Prompt: Literary

Consider the impact of Ikemefuna's time in Umuofia. On a separate sheet of paper, write a short narrative from the point of view of either Okonkwo or Nwoye that reveals Ikemefuna's influence on the community (his arrival, presence, death). Be sure to:

- Convey the character's voice and point of view.
- Include and build on specific details from the novel.
- Use precise words and phrases, telling details, and sensory language to convey a vivid picture of the event.
- Reflect on the impact of Ikemefuna on the community.

Ibo Norms and Values

Learning Strategies

Drafting
Graphic Organizer
Marking the Text

Learning Targets

- Develop research questions and conduct research about various aspects of a culture.
- Write an informational paragraph explaining the values and norms of the Ibo culture.

Preview

In this activity, you will research cultural aspects of precolonial and postcolonial Nigeria, as well as read Chapter 10 of Things Fall Apart to gather evidence about the norms and values of the Ibo culture. Then you will write an informational paragraph explaining the values and norms of the Ibo culture.

WORD CONNECTIONS

Multiple-Meaning Words
The root word of **civilization** is *civil*. *Civil* can mean "polite" or "courteous"; it also refers to anything relating to citizens or to ordinary community life.

On the Spot Research

1. Work in a group to choose a topic from the following list, or another topic of your choice. Write research questions to compare and contrast how that cultural aspect of civilization changes from precolonial to postcolonial Nigeria. Note: As you research, you will find "Ibo" can also be spelled "Igbo."

Aspects of Ibo (Igbo) Culture Affected by Colonialism

Music	Language	Justice	Sports
Weddings	Hospitality	Gender Roles	Housing
War	Food	Clothing	Medicine
Festivals/ Holidays	Funeral Rites	Business Dealings	Farming
View of Nature	Status	Family	Religion

Research Questions

My Notes

2. Research information about your topic using print and digital resources. Organize your notes using notecards or a notebook. Write the topic and resource at the top or the card or page, with the information you gained from that resource below. Be sure to summarize or paraphrase the information you gathered using your own words to avoid plagiarism. Finally, organize your list of resources into a bibliography.

3. Share your research information with your group. For example, focus on one aspect of the topic and have group members share the information they gathered. Compile the information using notecards or a notebook.

Norms and Values of the Ibo Culture

4. After you complete a close read of Chapter 10, think about the norms and values of the Ibo culture that are illustrated in the text. Remember that the term *norms* refers to the attitudes and behaviors that are considered normal or typical to a group of people. For instance, think about the discussion norms that were established in your classroom during Unit 1. With your group, revisit Chapters 1–10 and use the following table to record the norms and values that you find evidence for in the text. What is important to the Ibo civilization and how does Achebe show this to the readers of the novel?

Norms and Values of the Ibo	Textual Evidence

5. Work with a partner to write several universal questions on the topic of the norms and values of the Ibo culture. Use them to explore the concept of cultural norms and values in your discussion group.

LANGUAGE & WRITER'S CRAFT:
Using Precise Language and Domain-Specific Vocabulary

When describing another culture, it is especially important to use **precise language** to avoid generalizing, stereotyping, or unintentionally offending your reader.

For example, consider this sentence about the Ibo people:

They honor their elders in a way that we do not.

Framing the Ibo as *they* and the culture of the writer as *we* is a generalization that makes the Ibo seem different or "other."

Here is a better way to write the sentence, replacing the imprecise pronouns *they* and *we* with specific references to the culture or ethnic group under discussion:

The Ibo people honor their elders in a way that may seem unusual to Americans.

Another way to make your writing stronger is to use **domain-specific vocabulary** to describe the subject. Domain-specific vocabulary words are terms associated with a narrow topic or field, rather than general terms you might see more often.

Think about how you could make the following sentence more precise using domain-specific vocabulary:

When Okonkwo visits the clan elder at home, he brings offerings of food and drink to show his respect.

For example, you could revise the sentence this way:

When Okonkwo visits the clan elder in his obi, he brings offerings of kola nut and palm wine to show his respect.

The words *obi, kola nut,* and *palm wine* refer to specific aspects of Ibo culture.

PRACTICE Use precise language and domain-specific vocabulary to improve the following sentences:

The case of Uzowulu is decided in a manner similar to a trial you might see in our country, including a decision made by a jury. After the trial, Uzowulu is told to bring a gift to his wife's parents and ask his wife to come back to him.

My Notes

_____

_____

_____

_____

_____

_____

_____

_____

_____

_____

_____

_____

_____

_____

_____

_____

_____

_____

_____

_____

_____

_____

_____

_____

_____

_____

_____

_____

_____

_____

_____

_____

_____

_____

_____

_____

_____

✏️ **Writing Prompt: Informational**

From your notes, write a paragraph to explain the values and norms of the Ibo culture. Be sure to:

- Include a well-stated topic sentence.
- Include the best details and textual evidence that highlight the values and norms of Ibo culture, using precise or domain-specific vocabulary when possible.
- Use a logical organizational structure, and employ transitions effectively to move from one key point to the next.

After you write your paragraph, share it with a discussion group.

Learning Targets
- Analyze isolated scenes and make inferences about events in the plot.
- Write a narrative using genre characteristics to explore a character's voice.

Preview
In this activity, you will read Chapters 11–12 and use the RAFT strategy to create a narrative in the voice of a character from the novel.

My Notes

Revisiting Folktales in Chapter 11

1. Go back to the graphic organizer that you used to analyze folktales in Activity 2.3. Re-create it in your Reader/Writer Notebook and add notes analyzing Ekwefi's story about the Tortoise at the beginning of Chapter 11. What do you think is the purpose of this folktale in Ibo culture: What moral or lesson does it teach?

2. What do you think Achebe's purpose is in including this story in the novel, and how does this story contribute to the success of the plot as a whole?

3. Why do you think Achebe might have chosen an Ibo folktale rather than alluding to a text by a European author?

Making Inferences in Chapter 12

4. As you reread the first three pages of Chapter 12, take notes in the following chart to record textual evidence showing how Okonkwo, Ekwefi, and Ezinma act in response to the events of the previous evening. What inferences can you make from their thoughts, words, and actions?

My Notes

Okonkwo
Ekwefi
Ezinma

Introducing the Strategy: RAFT

RAFT stands for role, audience, format, and topic. Using this strategy, a writer can create a new text by brainstorming various roles (e.g., self, characters from other texts), audiences (e.g., a different character, a real person), formats (e.g., letter, brochure, essay, travel guide), and topics. Writers may choose a new role, audience, format, and/or topic to create a new text.

Using the RAFT Strategy

5. Discuss your evidence and inferences in a small group. Have each group member choose the role of a different character and use the RAFT strategy to write about Chielo's abduction of Ezinma in Chapter 11. While in the role, each group member should write what his or her character is thinking, using the pronoun "I," from the time Chielo, as Priestess of Agbala, comes for Ezinma until the end of the chapter. (The character's thoughts serve as the topic.)

Role: Okonkwo, Ekwefi, or Ezinma

Audience: Another character, self, a god

Format: Letter, monologue, diary entry, song, prayer

Topic: Character's reaction to the events of Chapter 11

Remember to:

- Write in the first person (*I*, *my*).
- Use diction, imagery, syntax, and tone to convey the character's voice.
- Include specific details from the chapter.

☑ Check Your Understanding

As each member of your group shares his or her writing through oral reading, consider how the voices of each character are similar and different. What elements of voice (diction, imagery, syntax, or tone) are distinct to each character? Discuss your ideas with your group.

📖 INDEPENDENT READING LINK

Read and Connect

Choose two or three characters from your independent reading. Take notes to record how the characters act in response to an important event. How are their responses similar and different? Share your observations with a group.

Tracing Two Themes

Learning Targets

- Analyze how the two themes of violence and gender are developed throughout the novel.
- Discuss how historical and cultural settings influence cultural views on gender

Preview

In this activity, you will revisit Chapters 1–13 and consider Okonkwo's actions and how they develop a theme in Part 1. You will also analyze how the Ibo culture views gender and then continue to find evidence in Chapter 14 to prepare for a group discussion.

Revisiting Part 1: Okonkwo's Actions and Their Consequences

1. While at public gatherings, observances of rites, or festivals, Okonkwo often commits acts of violence that ruin the occasion and generate public disapproval. Review Part 1 and complete the following graphic organizer to identify Okonkwo's violent acts and their consequences.

Violent Acts	Consequences

2. Work with your class to construct a statement on the theme of Okonkwo's violent tendencies and their consequences.

☑ Check Your Understanding

Why do you think Achebe ended Part 1 of the novel with this event? Make a prediction with a partner about what might happen in Part 2.

Revisiting Part 1: Gender Views

You may have noticed that another theme in *Things Fall Apart* is that the characters have clear ideas about how men and women should act or be. For example, in Chapter 2, Okonkwo expresses a fear of appearing to be feminine, a characteristic he equates with weakness and ineffectualness.

Learning Strategies

Drafting
Graphic Organizer
Outlining
Skimming/Scanning

GRAMMAR & USAGE

Subjunctive Mood
A verb written in subjunctive mood indicates speculations, wishes, or indirect requests rather than facts. For example, the phrase "If I were president" expresses a speculation or wish, so it uses *were* rather than *was*. The clause "Mother asks that you be home by dark" expresses an indirect request, so it uses *be* rather than *are*.

Think about how you might use the subjunctive mood in your writing; for example, "If Okonkwo were less violent, his character would develop differently in the novel."

WORD CONNECTIONS

Roots and Affixes
Prediction contains the root *dict* from the Latin word *dicere*, meaning "to tell or say." This root also appears in *contradict*, *dictate*, and *dictionary*. The prefix *pre-* means "before." The suffix *-ion* indicates that the word is a noun.

WORD CONNECTIONS

Roots and Affixes

Resented contains the root *sent*, from the Latin word *sentire*, meaning "to feel." This root also appears in *sentimental, consent,* and *dissent*. The prefix *re-* means "back" or "again."

My Notes

3. Use the following chart to record textual evidence of what it means to be a man or woman in the Ibo culture. Examine the historical and cultural settings and how they influence Okonkwo's views. In the second column, respond to the examples you find. Use additional paper as needed.

Ideas About Gender in Part 1 of *Things Fall Apart*	
Quotation	**My Comments**
"Even as a little boy he [Okonkwo] had resented his father's failure and weakness, and even now he still remembered how he had suffered when a playmate had told him that his father was *agbala*. That was how Okonkwo first came to know that *agbala* was not only another name for a woman, it could also mean a man who had taken no title." (Chapter 2, p. 13)	

Gender Views in Chapter 14

4. Reexamine the historical and cultural settings and how they influence Okonkwo's views. Then, as you reread Chapter 14, look for textual evidence that presents a different view of gender now that Okonkwo has been exiled to live with his mother's kinsmen for seven years.

Ideas About Gender in Chapter 14 of *Things Fall Apart*	
Quotation	**My Comments**

Group Discussion on Violence and Gender

5. Prepare to discuss views on the two themes of violence and gender with a small group.

- Generate questions of your own about how violence is expressed in the novel and the views on gender in the text. You can generate questions about each theme individually, but you should also generate at least one question that connects the two themes. Then share your questions with the group. Take notes during the discussion as you work collaboratively to build on each other's ideas and contribute relevant information to the discussion.

- Be sure to engage in respectful discourse by listening actively, asking and answering any questions you have about the topic, and building on the ideas of others.

INDEPENDENT READING LINK

Read and Connect

Choose one of your independent reading selections. Identify the characters' ideas about gender in the selection. Make a chart like the one you made for the ideas about gender in *Things Fall Apart*. Record your observations about your independent reading selection.

- Discuss the following questions with the group: What motivates Okonkwo to commit the acts of violence? How and why do the views of gender shift from Part 1 of the novel to the first chapter of Part 2? How do you feel about the attitudes toward gender that are expressed in the novel? Do you agree or disagree with them?
- Highlight textual evidence from each chart to support your responses.

☑ Check Your Understanding

How are the ideas of gender expressed in the novel similar to and different from those in your own culture? Discuss your ideas with a partner.

My Notes

Learning Strategies

Drafting
Graphic Organizer

VOCABULARY

LITERARY

A **tragic hero** is a central character who is usually of high or noble birth and demonstrates a "fatal flaw." The tragic hero's fatal flaw is *hamartia*, an ingrained character trait that causes the hero to make decisions leading to his or her death or downfall.

Learning Targets

- Analyze how authors develop archetypes such as the tragic hero.
- Understand and apply the concept of the tragic hero to Okonkwo.
- Write a literary analysis using genre characteristics to explain how Okonkwo fits Aristotle's definition of a tragic hero.

Preview

In this activity, you will reread Chapters 1–15 and apply Aristotle's definition of a tragic hero to Okonkwo.

Tragic Hero

1. One archetype is the **tragic hero**, or a hero who experiences failure due to an internal flaw or external power. Read Aristotle's classical definition of a tragic hero, cited in the first column of the following table. Then provide examples and events from Okonkwo's life to analyze how the author develops him as a believable tragic hero. In addition, provide examples of heroic behavior using the lives of other characters from literature or film.

Aristotle's Definition of a Tragic Hero	Examples of Okonkwo's Heroic Behavior	Examples of Heroic Behavior from Books/Film
He has a mixture of good and bad in his personality.		
He has a fatal flaw, or *hamartia*, which leads to his downfall.		
He usually goes on a journey or participates in a quest.		
He has a large capacity for suffering.		
His downfall is often preceded by self-realization.		

LANGUAGE & WRITER'S CRAFT: Word Patterns

Many words follow specific patterns as they change from one part of speech to another. It is important to use the correct form to make sure your writing is clear and correct. Consider these examples:

Verb: analyze

Noun: analysis

Adjective: analytical

Verb: beautify

Noun: beauty

Adjective: beautiful

Some words do not change form when they are used as different parts of speech. For example:

Verb: address (speak to)

Noun: address (a speech)

Verb: challenge (defy or issue a call to a contest)

Noun: challenge (a dare or invitation to a contest)

PRACTICE Using the verbs *define, advocate, indicate,* and *equate,* form a noun or an adjective for each one.

📝 Writing Prompt: Literary Analysis

To what degree does Okonkwo fit Aristotle's definition of a tragic hero? What flaws lead to his downfall? Be sure to:

- Defines a tragic hero in the introduction.
- Provide supporting details and textual evidence from different chapters.
- Make sure to use the correct forms of nouns, verbs, and adjectives in your writing.

🎁 INDEPENDENT READING LINK

Read and Discuss

Think about your independent reading selections. Do any of the main characters meet the criteria for classification as a tragic hero? Complete a chart in your Reader/Writer Notebook like the one you completed for Okonkwo in this activity. Discuss your ideas with a group.

Learning Strategies

Discussion Groups
Graphic Organizer
Socratic Seminar

Learning Targets

- Analyze how key plot events develop a theme related to cultural conflict.
- Generate questions about key plot events in the text.

Preview

In this activity, you will read Chapters 16–19 and analyze the beginning of the cultural conflict between the Ibo and the Westerners who are newly arrived.

Predicting Cultural Conflicts

1. In Chapter 15, Uchendu says, "The world has no end, and what is good among one people is an abomination with others." Part 2 of *Things Fall Apart* introduces the cultural conflict when white people come into contact with the Ibo. Predict what aspects of each culture might appear as an "abomination" to the other.

Key Events in Chapters 15–19

2. Chapters 15–19 span a number of years in the life of Okonkwo and his village. Record key events and explain their significance on the following chart.

Key Events of Chapter	Why Events Are Important
Chapter 15–second year of exile	
Chapter 16–fourth year of exile	
Chapter 17	
Chapter 18–last year of exile	
Chapter 19	

Socratic Seminar

3. Work with a partner to select three to five key events. List them in the following space. For each event, write an interpretive or universal question that will help you explore the conflicting cultures in Part 2 of Things Fall Apart. As you discuss the events, make sure to listen and respond appropriately to your partner. You will use these questions as you participate in a Socratic Seminar.

Event 1:

Event 2:

Event 3:

Event 4:

Event 5:

✍ Writing Prompt: Informational

After you participate in a Socratic Seminar about cultural conflict in *Things Fall Apart*, choose one of the events discussed and write an informational response in which you explore its significance. You will be timed as you write your response. Be sure to:

• Discuss how the event develops a theme related to cultural conflict.
• Use precise vocabulary and an academic voice.
• Cite textual evidence to support your interpretation.

Cultural Misunderstandings

Learning Strategies

Graphic Organizer
Rereading
Skimming/Scanning

GRAMMAR & USAGE

Complex Sentences
Writers use complex sentences to create interesting styles. A complex sentence contains an independent clause and at least one subordinate clause. Think about how clauses work in these two sentences: "He knew *that he had lost his place* (noun clause) among the nine masked spirits *who administered justice in the clan* (adjective clause)." "How do you think we can fight *when our own brothers have turned against us* (adverb clause)?" What other examples can you find from the text?

Learning Targets

- Discuss how historical and cultural settings contribute to cultural misunderstandings between characters.
- Analyze personal connections or experiences with other cultures.

Preview

In this activity, you will read Chapters 20–22 and make connections to the cultural misunderstandings between the Ibo and the missionaries.

How Things Fall Apart

1. Read the following excerpt from Chapter 20 of *Things Fall Apart*. Underline or highlight statements that illuminate the misunderstandings between the Ibo and the missionaries.

"Does the white man understand our customs about land?"

"How can he when he does not even speak our tongue? But he says that our customs are bad; and our own brothers who have taken up his religion also say that our customs are bad. How do you think we can fight when our own brothers have turned against us? The white man is very clever. He came quietly and peaceably with his religion. We were amused at his foolishness and allowed him to stay. Now he has won our brothers, and our clan can no longer act like one. He has put a knife on the things that held us together and we have fallen apart."

2. With a partner, analyze the persuasive techniques that Okonkwo (the first speaker) and Obierka (the second speaker) use in this excerpt. Then decide whether or not Obierika's assessment of the situation is accurate. Find textual evidence from the novel to support or refute your point of view.

Mr. Brown and Mr. Smith

3. Use the following chart to compare and contrast the two missionaries, Mr. Brown and Mr. Smith. Record what each says and does, along with their attitudes and beliefs. Continue on a separate sheet of paper, if needed.

Mr. Brown	Mr. Smith

Cultural Misunderstandings

4. Think about your own personal connections or experiences with other cultures. Then work with group members to consider why someone from another culture might think the practices or beliefs listed in the following chart are strange. Add at least one more cultural aspect to the organizer along with your response.

Cultural Practice or Belief	Why Someone from Another Culture Might Find the Practice or Belief Strange
In the novel *The Poisonwood Bible*, an African man comes to America and is shocked to find that Americans use bathrooms *in* their homes and not outside, away from the home.	
Many Americans adorn their bodies with different types of tattoos and piercings.	
Many people idolize sports heroes, even to the point of wearing clothing with someone else's name on it.	

5. Identify Ibo beliefs and practices in *Things Fall Apart* that differ from those of modern Americans. Contrast them in the following chart.

Ibo Belief or Practice	Modern American Belief or Practice
Twins are considered evil and abandoned in the Evil Forest.	Twins are usually welcomed and cared for by their families.

☑ Check Your Understanding

- Can one culture be "right" and another culture "wrong"? Explain.
- How did the two missionaries respond differently to cultural misunderstandings?

🎲 INDEPENDENT READING LINK

Read and Respond

From the texts you have read independently, choose one main character and analyze the beliefs and practices of that character's culture. Create a chart like the one you used in this activity. Compare the beliefs or practices of the culture with those of modern Americans. Share your observations with a peer.

Learning Targets

- Make connections between *Things Fall Apart* and the ideas in poetry.
- Examine how the author's use of language in a poem helps inform and shape the perceptions of readers.
- Integrate ideas from multiple texts to build knowledge and vocabulary about cultural conflicts.

Preview

In this activity, you will work with a group to analyze two poems and present a choral reading of one that conveys your interpretation of its meaning.

Reading *Things Fall Apart*, Chapter 22

1. Reread the following excerpt from Chapter 22 of *Things Fall Apart*, in which the clan responds to Enoch tearing the mask from an *egwugwu*. Underline words that have strong negative connotations. What tone is conveyed in this passage? Why do Enoch's actions so horrify the people of Umuofia?

The other *egwugwu* immediately surrounded their desecrated companion to shield him from the profane gaze of women and children, and led him away. Enoch had killed an ancestral spirit, and Umuofia was thrown into confusion.

That night the Mother of the Spirits walked the length and breadth of the clan, weeping for her murdered son. It was a terrible night. Not even the oldest man in Umuofia had ever heard such a strange and fearful sound, and it was never to be heard again. It seemed as if the very soul of the tribe wept for a great evil that was coming—its own death.

As You Read

- Jot notes in the margin about connections you can make between the poem and the novel *Things Fall Apart*.
- Circle words and phrases that reveal the tone of the poem.
- Circle unknown words and phrases. Try to determine the meaning of the words by using context clues, word parts, or a dictionary.

About the Author

Léopold Senghor (1906–2001) was an influential poet, teacher, and politician. Educated in Senegal, a French colony at the time of his birth, and France, Senghor became one of the first black teachers in the French educational system. He cofounded the literary movement Negritude, which validated the artistic expressions of black Africans. He served for more than 20 years as Senegal's first freely elected president.

My Notes

Poetry

Prayer to the Masks

by **Léopold Sédar Senghor**

Masks! Masks!

Black mask red mask, you white-and-black masks

Masks of the four points from which the spirit blows

In silence I salute you!

5   Nor you the least, the Lion-headed Ancestor

You guard this place forbidden to all laughter of women, to all smiles that fade

You **distill** this air of eternity in which I breathe the air of my Fathers.

Masks of unmasked faces, stripped of the marks of illness and the lines of age

You who have **fashioned** this portrait, this my face bent over the altar of white paper

10   In your own **image**, hear me!

The Africa of the empires is dying, see, the agony of a pitiful princess

And Europe too where we are joined by the navel.

Fix your unchanging eyes upon your children, who are given orders

Who give away their lives like the poor their last clothes.

15   Let us report present at the rebirth of the World

Like the yeast which white flour needs.

For who would teach rhythm to a dead world of machines and guns?

Who would give the cry of joy to wake the dead and the **bereaved** at dawn?

Say, who would give back the memory of life to the man whose hopes are smashed?

20   They call us men of coffee cotton oil

They call us men of death.

We are the men of the dance, whose feet draw new strength pounding the hardened earth.

Knowledge Quest

- What questions about conflict does this poem raise for you?
- What emotions do you experience as you read the poem?

---

distill: purify
fashioned: created or shaped
image: visual representation
bereaved: mournful

Returning to the Text

- Reread the poem to answer these text-dependent questions.
- Write any additional questions you have about the poem in your Reader/Writer Notebook.

2. What ideas do the masks represent in the poem? Why do you think the speaker greets the masks in silence?

_____

_____

_____

_____

3. KQ How does the speaker's use of the words *they* and *we* add an adversarial tone to the poem? Who is "they"? Who is "we"?

_____

_____

_____

_____

4. KQ What is the theme of the poem? What details does the speaker use to describe cultural conflicts?

_____

_____

_____

_____

5. KQ The speaker of the poem describes Africa as "the yeast which white flour needs." What does this figure of speech mean, and what does its meaning have to do with rebirth?

_____

_____

_____

_____

As You Read

- Jot notes in the margin about connections you can make between the poem and the novel *Things Fall Apart*.
- Circle unknown words and phrases. Try to determine the meaning of the words by using context clues, word parts, or a dictionary.

About the Author

Winner of the 1923 Nobel Prize for Literature, William Butler Yeats (1865–1939) produced some of the most enduring poems written in English in the twentieth century. Despite living in Ireland during decades of great political and religious upheaval, Yeats's poems are marked by a deep mysticism, specific symbolism, and universal emotions.

Poetry

The Second Coming

by **William Butler Yeats**

Turning and turning in the widening **gyre**
The falcon cannot hear the falconer;
Things fall apart; the center cannot hold;
Mere anarchy is loosed upon the world,
5   The blood-dimmed **tide** is loosed, and everywhere
The ceremony of innocence is drowned;
The best lack all conviction, while the worst
Are full of passionate **intensity**.
Surely some revelation is at hand;
10 Surely the Second Coming is at hand;
The Second Coming! Hardly are those words out
When a vast **image** out of *Spiritus Mundi*[1]
Troubles my sight: somewhere in sands of the desert
A shape with lion body and the head of a man,
15 A gaze blank and pitiless as the sun,
Is moving its slow thighs, while all about it
Reel shadows of the indignant desert birds.
The darkness drops again; but now I know
That twenty centuries of stony sleep
20 Were **vexed** to nightmare by a rocking cradle,
And what rough beast, its hour come round at last,
Slouches towards Bethlehem to be born?

---

[1] Spiritus Mundi, Latin for "world spirit," is a collective, universal soul that contains the memories of all time and inspires poets.

KNOWLEDGE QUEST

Knowledge Question:
In what ways might a cultural conflict begin?

WORD CONNECTIONS

Roots and Affixes
Anarchy contains the root *arch*, from the Greek word *archos*, meaning "leader." This root also appears in *architect*, *patriarch*, *archangel*, and *monarchy*. The prefix *an-* means "not" or "without."

gyre: spiral that expands as it goes up
mere: absolute
anarchy: lawlessness
tide: water-like ebb or flow of something
intensity: extreme feeling
image: visual representation
vexed: worried or concerned

Knowledge Quest

- Which words or phrases stand out to you as they relate to cultural conflicts?
- What imagery can you picture in your mind?

Returning to the Text

- Reread the poem to answer these text-dependent questions.
- Write any additional questions you have about the poem in your Reader/Writer Notebook.

6. **KQ** What images and words does Yeats use to develop the theme that anarchy has overrun the world? Why do you think the poet chooses this language to describe conflicts?

_____

_____

_____

_____

7. The term the "Second Coming" is a biblical allusion to the return of Christ from Heaven as described in the New Testament. In lines 11–17 of the poem, what other allusion does Yeats use? Why do you think he uses it? What is the author's message?

_____

_____

_____

_____

8. **KQ** Why does the author use the word _beast_ to describe what "slouches towards Bethlehem to be born"? How does this add to the feeling of conflict throughout the poem?

_____

_____

_____

_____

9. **KQ** What do Léopold Sédar Senghor and William Butler Yeats say comes out of a cultural conflict? In both poems, what causes the conflict?

_____

_____

_____

_____

Knowledge Quest

After reading "Prayer to the Masks" and "The Second Coming," reflect on the ways cultural conflicts can begin. Also, think about how we tend to describe conflicts. With a partner, make a t-chart with the heads "Positive" and "Negative." Then brainstorm lists of positive and negative words that relate to the idea of conflict. After you have completed your chart, observe which column contains more words and think about why. Discuss: *Why might someone view conflict as a negative thing? When might conflict yield a positive result?*

INDEPENDENT READING LINK

You can continue to build your knowledge about cultural conflict by reading other articles at ZINC Reading Labs. Search for keywords such as *world conflict* or *cultural conflict*.

 ZINC

Working from the Text

10. Work with your group to prepare and present a choral reading and analysis of your assigned poem to a group that worked on the other poem. As you listen to the other group's presentation, take notes to compare and contrast the two poems. Which side of the cultural conflict is represented by each poem? What do they have in common? In what ways do the poems help you think about why Achebe uses the opening of "The Second Coming" as an **epigraph** and references it in his title?

LITERARY

An **epigraph** is a phrase, quotation, or poem that is set at the beginning of a document or component. An epigraph may help direct the reader to the author's purpose or theme.

VOCABULARY

📝 Writing Prompt: Literary Analysis

Refer to your notes to write an essay that determines your understanding of texts and makes connections between the poems you analyzed and the novel *Things Fall Apart*. What similarities in theme or central idea do you notice? Write a literary analysis answering these questions. Be sure to:

- Include quotes or specific details from the poems and the novel to support your claims.
- Explain the authors' use of language and how specific words in the poems and the novel relate to each other.
- Analyze the similarity between themes that are found in both the poems and the novel.
- Use a coherent organizational structure and employ transitions effectively to highlight similarities and differences.

Learning Strategies

Discussion Groups
Drafting

VOCABULARY

LITERARY

Irony is a literary device that exploits a reader's expectations. Irony occurs when what is expected turns out to be quite different from what actually happens.

Learning Targets

- Analyze the use of irony in the novel and its purpose.
- Write about cultural misunderstanding.

Preview

In this activity, you will read Chapters 23–25 and analyze the author's use of irony to achieve a certain purpose.

Irony

Irony is a literary device that exploits a reader's expectations. It is an event or saying that has a different or opposite result from what is expected. For example, one instance of irony is an ambulance getting in an accident on its way to an accident. There are various types of irony used in literature:

- **Dramatic irony** occurs when the reader or audience knows more about the circumstances or future events in a story than the characters do.
- **Verbal irony** occurs when a speaker or narrator says one thing while meaning the opposite.
- **Situational irony** occurs when an event contradicts the expectations of the characters or the reader.

1. Consider the following three summarized events from the novel. What kind of irony does each represent? Explain.

   Event 1: At the end of Chapter 15, Okonkwo tells his good friend Obierka that he doesn't know how to thank him enough for tending his yam crop while Okonkwo is in exile. Obierka tells Okonkwo to kill himself.

   Event 2: Okonkwo's greatest fear is that he will appear weak and feminine. He appears to have little respect for women. Yet his favorite child, the one with whom he has the closest bond and understanding, is his daughter Ezinma.

   Event 3: In Chapter 7, when Ikemefuna thinks he is journeying with the clansmen to the home of his birth, he is worried about whether his mother is alive, but otherwise feels safe. The reader knows that he is actually about to be killed.

My Notes

2. With a partner, review Chapters 23–25, looking for textual evidence of different kinds of irony. List and explain at least two examples:

Example 1:

Example 2:

3. With a partner, analyze what Achebe's purpose might be in using irony in the story.

4. Reread the following two excerpts. Mark the text to show evidence of the District Commissioner's attitude toward the Ibo.

Excerpt from Chapter 23

"We shall not do you any harm," said the District **Commissioner** to them later, "if only you agree to cooperate with us. We have brought a peaceful administration to you and your people so that you may be happy. If any man ill-treats you, we shall come to your rescue. But we will not allow you to ill-treat others. We have a court of law where we judge cases and administer justice just as it is done in my own country under a great queen. I have brought you here because you joined together to molest others, to burn people's houses and their place of worship. That must not happen in the **dominion** of our queen, the most powerful ruler in the world. I have decided that you will pay a fine of two hundred bags of cowries. You will be released as soon as you agree to this and undertake to collect that fine from your people. What do you say to that?"

Excerpt from Chapter 25

In the many years in which he had **toiled** to bring civilization to different parts of Africa he had learned a number of things. One of them was that a District Commissioner must never attend to such undignified details as cutting a hanged man from the tree. Such attention would give the natives a poor opinion of him. In the book which he planned to write he would stress that point. As he walked back to the court he thought about that book. Every day brought him some new material. The story of this man who had killed a messenger and hanged himself would make interesting reading. One could almost write a whole chapter on him. Perhaps not a whole chapter but a reasonable paragraph, at any rate. There was so much else to include, and one must be firm in cutting out details. He had already chosen the title of the book, after much thought: *The Pacification of the Primitive Tribes of the Lower Niger*.

My Notes

commissioner: government official
dominion: territory
toiled: worked long and hard
pacification: forced peace

My Notes

Working from the Text

5. Discuss the types of irony used in the previous excerpts. What do you think the author is trying to emphasize with his use of irony?

Writing Prompt: Letter

Write a letter to the District Commissioner explaining how his attitude toward the Ibo people is based on cultural misunderstanding. Suggest ways he might change to be more accommodating to the culture of the people. Decide whether to write your letter to the District Commissioner using a polite but formal manner or a friendly manner and tone. In addition, include a heading, salutation, closing, and signature in your letter. Be sure to:

- State your purpose for writing in the first sentence.
- Provide textual evidence of the District Commissioner's misunderstanding.
- Suggest ways the District Commissioner can be more accommodating toward the Ibo people.
- Use an appropriate voice and tone in the body of your letter.
- Include a heading, salutation, body, closing, and signature in your letter.

6. After you write your letter, reflect on the essential question: How can a work of literature reflect a cultural perspective?

Language Checkpoint: Using Noun Agreement

- Understand how to create noun agreement in sentences.
- Revise writing to create noun agreement.

Preview

In this activity, you will learn about noun agreement and then revise text for noun agreement.

Using Noun Agreement

Writers have to pay attention to a few types of agreement to ensure that they are communicating their ideas clearly. For example, pronouns need to agree in number and gender with the nouns they are replacing, and present-tense verbs must agree with their subjects.

In some sentences, nouns have to agree with other nouns for the sentence to make sense. Look at this example from *Things Fall Apart* by Chinua Achebe:

> The Commissioner and his men followed, their firearms held at the ready. He had warned Obierika that if he and his men played any monkey tricks they would be shot.

In these sentences, the narrator refers to *the Commissioner and his men*, each of whom has a gun. Because the subject *the Commissioner and his men* is plural, the phrase *their firearms* is also plural. In other words, the nouns agree in number. In longer, more complex sentences where the nouns are far apart, it is especially important to pay attention to nouns to make sure they agree.

1. Look at the following sentences, and identify the nouns that do not agree in number. How would you revise each sentence so that the nouns agree?

Noun Agreement	
Before Revision	**After Revision**
Mr. Brown believed all of the people he encountered deserved to become a follower of his teachings.	Mr. Brown believed all of the people he encountered deserved to become <u>followers</u> of his teachings.
All of the men in the obi had presented Ibe with a horn to fill with the palm drink.	
Both her parents, who had hoped she would find a husband worthy of her beauty, shook their head in disbelief when she rejected the suitor.	
Chinua Achebe and Chimamanda Ngozi Adichie both became well known by worldwide audiences as a Nigerian novelist.	

2. Discuss your revisions with a partner. How did you decide which nouns needed to change?

Revising

3. Read the following student letter, paying close attention to singular and plural nouns. Annotate the letter to show how you would revise it to ensure noun agreement.

Dear District Commissioner,

While I understand your goals of bringing Christianity and a unified government to the peoples of the Niger, <u>this is not a goal</u> you should be pursuing. You may be misunderstanding some key aspects of the Ibo culture. The Ibo people are both civilized and thoughtful, <u>a quality</u> that you seem to overlook. They are not weak people, nor are they savages. Okonkwo and his clan, like Obeirika and Okika, are tribesmen who believe they must use their knowledge and skills as <u>a warrior</u> to protect the tribe, even if it means going against their brothers. They do so as protection. You told them you "have brought a peaceful administration" to their people in order that they "may be happy." However, soldiers pointing <u>a gun</u> at their <u>head</u> is not peaceful.

Your violence brought unhappiness, division, and fear to the people living here. Perhaps if you looked upon them with openness and approached them with kindness, <u>a strategy</u> that you and your men never seem to employ, you would see they have a deep understanding of the land around them. The many rules that they follow, all of which have foundations in their understanding of life in the region, were created for <u>a specific reason</u> and help bring order to their society.

All of the people in this region should let their <u>opinion</u> be heard. The people here have the right to become <u>a participant</u> in their future, not just <u>a passive observer</u> of the changes you are trying to impose. I hope you and your men, many of whom have a sincere interest in making life better for people here, will open your <u>mind</u> to these ideas.

With kind regards,

Mariana Okri

☑ Check Your Understanding

Imagine you were helping the writer of the preceding letter to understand noun agreement. How would you help her identify sentences where nouns need to agree? How would you explain the revisions needed to create noun agreement?

Add an item to your Editor's Checklist reminding yourself to check your writing for noun agreement.

Practice

Reread the letter to the District Commissioner you wrote in Activity 2.16 explaining the misunderstanding with the Ibo people. You have already had to consider tone and voice. Now revise the letter by checking for noun agreement. Be sure to:

- Verify that corresponding nouns match in number when required.
- Look for words such as *all*, *each*, and *both* to make sure that the related nouns agree in number.

The Author's Perspective

Learning Strategies

Discussion Groups
Metacognitive Markers
Note-taking

Learning Targets

- Evaluate details in the text to determine Achebe's purpose for writing *Things Fall Apart*.
- Synthesize information from Achebe's interview and his novel.

Preview

In the following activity, you will read and analyze an interview with Chinua Achebe to determine the author's purpose for writing the novel.

As You Read

- As you read the interview, use metacognitive markers as follows to mark the text:

  ! something that surprises you

  * something you can comment on: an opinion or a connection

  ? something you have a question about or do not understand

- Make adjustments as you read to aid comprehension, such as rereading, using background knowledge, and annotating the text.
- Circle unknown words and phrases. Try to determine the meaning of the words by using context clues, word parts, or a dictionary.

About the Author

Katie Bacon is a writer and editor from Boston, Massachusetts. She is a former editor at *The Atlantic*, where she published "An African Voice" in 2000.

Interview

An African Voice

Chinua Achebe, the author of one of the enduring works of modern African literature, sees postcolonial cultures taking shape story by story.

by **Katie Bacon**

1   Chinua Achebe's emergence as "the founding father of African literature … in the English language," in the words of the Harvard University philosopher K. Anthony Appiah, could very well be traced to his encounter in the early fifties with Joyce Cary's novel *Mister Johnson*, set in Achebe's native Nigeria. Achebe read it while studying at the University College in Idaban during the last years of British colonial rule, and in a curriculum full of Shakespeare, Coleridge, and Wordsworth, *Mister Johnson* stood out as one of the few books about Africa. *Time* magazine had recently declared *Mister Johnson* the "best book ever written about Africa," but Achebe and his classmates had quite a different reaction. The students saw the Nigerian hero

My Notes

emergence: process of becoming known

GRAMMAR & USAGE

Dash

Writers use a dash to indicate a break in their thoughts. The dash may mean "in other words," it may be used to emphasize or clarify ideas, or it may set off parenthetical information. Notice how Bacon uses a dash in this sentence: "Yet he himself has lived in the United States for the past ten years—a reluctant exile." Bacon wants to emphasize that Achebe's choice to live in the United States is not ideal. Now consider this sentence: "[M]uch of Nigeria's wealth—the country has extensive oil fields—went into the pocket of its leader." What function do the dashes perform here?

WORD CONNECTIONS

Etymology
Progenitor is a Latin word meaning "ancestor; the founder of a family." Today, we sometimes use it to describe someone who is the first to think of or do something.

colonization: establishment of colonies, or areas under the control of a distant government
realization: understanding
dispossession: loss of land or property
maintained: continued
resonance: ability to create an emotional response

as an "embarrassing nitwit." *Mister Johnson*, Achebe writes, "open[ed] my eyes to the fact that my home was under attack and that my home was not merely a house or a town but, more importantly, an awakening story."

2   In 1958, Achebe responded with his own novel about Nigeria, *Things Fall Apart*, which was one of the first books to tell the story of European **colonization** from an African perspective. (It has since become a classic, published in fifty languages around the world.) *Things Fall Apart* marked a turning point for African authors, who in the fifties and sixties began to take back the narrative of the so-called "dark continent."

3   Achebe depicts his gradual **realization** that *Mister Johnson* was just one in a long line of books written by Westerners that presented Africans to the world in a way that Africans didn't agree with or recognize, and he examines the "process of 're-storying' peoples who had been knocked silent by all kinds of **dispossession**." He ends with a hope for the twenty-first century—that this "re-storying" will continue and will eventually result in a "balance of stories among the world's peoples."

4   Achebe encourages writers from the Third World to stay where they are and write about their own countries, as a way to help achieve this balance. Yet he himself has lived in the United States for the past ten years—a reluctant exile. In 1990, Achebe was in a car accident in Nigeria, and was paralyzed from the waist down. While recuperating in a London hospital, he received a call from Leon Botstein, the president of Bard College, offering him a teaching job and a house built for his needs. Achebe thought he would be at Bard, a small school in a quiet corner of the Hudson River Valley, for only a year or two, but the political situation in Nigeria kept worsening. During the military dictatorship of General Sani Abacha, who ruled from 1993 to 1998, much of Nigeria's wealth—the country has extensive oil fields—went into the pocket of its leader, and public infrastructure that had been quite good, like hospitals and roads, withered. In 1999, Olusegan Obasanjo became Nigeria's first democratically elected President since 1983, and the situation in Nigeria is improving, albeit slowly and shakily. Achebe is watching from afar, waiting for his country to rebuild itself enough for him to return.

5   Achebe, who is sixty-nine, has written five novels, including Arrow of God (1964) and Anthills of the Savannah (1987), five books of nonfiction, and several collections of short stories and poems. Achebe spoke recently with *Atlantic Unbound*'s Katie Bacon at his home in Annandale-on-Hudson, in New York.

QUESTION 1

6   **You have been called the progenitor of the modern African novel, and** *Things Fall Apart* **has maintained its resonance in the decades since it was written. Have you been surprised by the effect the book has had?**

7   Was I surprised? Yes, at the beginning. There was no African literature as we know it today. And so I had no idea when I was writing *Things Fall Apart* whether it would even be accepted or published. All of this was new—there was nothing by which I could gauge how it was going to be received.

My Notes

8   But, of course, something doesn't continue to surprise you every day. After a while I began to understand why the book had resonance. I began to understand my history even better. It wasn't as if when I wrote it I was an expert in the history of the world. I was a very young man. I knew I had a story, but how it fit into the story of the world—I really had no sense of that. Its meaning for my Igbo people was clear to me, but I didn't know how other people elsewhere would respond to it. Did it have any meaning or resonance for them? I realized that it did when, to give you just one example, the whole class of a girls' college in South Korea wrote to me, and each one expressed an opinion about the book. And then I learned something, which was that they had a history that was similar to the story of *Things Fall Apart*—the history of colonization. This I didn't know before. Their colonizer was Japan. So these people across the waters were able to relate to the story of dispossession in Africa. People from different parts of the world can respond to the same story, if it says something to them about their own history and their own experience.

QUESTION 2

9   **It seems that people from places that haven't experienced colonization in the same way have also responded to the story.**

10   There are different forms of dispossession, many, many ways in which people are deprived or subjected to all kinds of victimization—it doesn't have to be colonization. Once you allow yourself to identify with the people in a story, then you might begin to see yourself in that story even if on the surface it's far removed from your situation. This is what I try to tell my students: this is one great thing that literature can do—it can make us identify with situations and people far away. If it does that, it's a miracle. I tell my students, it's not difficult to identify with somebody like yourself, somebody next door who looks like you. What's more difficult is to identify with someone you don't see, who's very far away, who's a different color, who eats a different kind of food. When you begin to do that then literature is really performing its wonders.

QUESTION 3

11   **A character in *Things Fall Apart* remarks that the white man "has put a knife on the things that held us together, and we have fallen apart." Are those things still severed, or have the wounds begun to heal?**

12   What I was referring to there, or what the speaker in the novel was thinking about, was the upsetting of a society, the disturbing of a social order. The society of Umuofia, the village in *Things Fall Apart,* was totally disrupted by the coming of the European government, missionary Christianity, and so on. That was not a temporary disturbance; it was a once and for all alteration of their society. To give you the example of Nigeria, where the novel is set, the Igbo people had organized themselves in small units, in small towns and villages, each self-governed. With the coming of the British, Igbo land as a whole was incorporated into a totally different polity, to be called Nigeria, with a whole lot of other people with whom the Igbo people had not had direct contact before. The result of that was not something from which you could recover, really. You had to learn a totally new reality, and accommodate yourself

severed: split or separated
incorporated: introduced into as part of the whole
polity: politically organized unit

to the demands of this new reality, which is the state called Nigeria. Various nationalities, each of which had its own independent life, were forced by the British to live with people of different customs and habits and priorities and religions. And then at independence, fifty years later, they were suddenly on their own again. They began all over again to learn the rules of independence. The problems that Nigeria is having today could be seen as resulting from this effort that was initiated by colonial rule to create a new nation. There's nothing to indicate whether it will fail or succeed. It all depends.

13　One might hear someone say, How long will it take these people to get their act together? It's going to take a very, very long time, because it's really been a whole series of interruptions and disturbances, one step forward and two or three back. It has not been easy. One always wishes it had been easier. We've compounded things by our own mistakes, but it doesn't really help to pretend that we've had an easy task.

QUESTION 4

14　In *Home and Exile,* you talk about the negative ways in which British authors such as Joseph Conrad and Joyce Cary portrayed Africans over the centuries. What purpose did that portrayal serve?

15　It was really a straightforward case of setting us up, as it were. The last four or five hundred years of European contact with Africa produced a body of literature that presented Africa in a very bad light and Africans in very lurid terms. The reason for this had to do with the need to justify the slave trade and slavery. The cruelties of this trade gradually began to trouble many people in Europe. Some people began to question it. But it was a profitable business, and so those who were engaged in it began to defend it—a lobby of people supporting it, justifying it, and excusing it. It was difficult to excuse and justify, and so the steps that were taken to justify it were rather extreme. You had

initiated: started or introduced
lurid: sensational or shocking
justify: support or defend
lobby: group that tries to influence people in authority

people saying, for instance, that these people weren't really human, they're not like us. Or, that the slave trade was in fact a good thing for them, because the alternative to it was more brutal by far.

16   And therefore, describing this fate that the Africans would have had back home became the motive for the literature that was created about Africa. Even after the slave trade was abolished, in the nineteenth century, something like this literature continued, to serve the new imperialistic needs of Europe in relation to Africa. This continued until the Africans themselves, in the middle of the twentieth century, took into their own hands the telling of their story.

QUESTION 5

17   **And that's what started with *Things Fall Apart* and other books written by Africans around the 1950s.**

18   Yes, that's what it turned out to be. It was not actually clear to us at the time what we were doing. We were simply writing our story. But the bigger story of how these various accounts tie in, one with the other, is only now becoming clear. We realize and recognize that it's not just colonized people whose stories have been suppressed, but a whole range of people across the globe who have not spoken. It's not because they don't have something to say, it simply has to do with the division of power, because storytelling has to do with power. Those who win tell the story; those who are defeated are not heard. But that has to change. It's in the interest of everybody, including the winners, to know that there's another story. If you only hear one side of the story, you have no understanding at all.

QUESTION 6

19   **Do you see this balance of stories as likely to emerge in this era of globalization and the exporting of American culture?**

20   That's a real problem. The mindless absorption of American ideas, culture, and behavior around the world is not going to help this balance of stories, and it's not going to help the world, either. People are limiting themselves to one view of the world that comes from somewhere else. That's something that we have to battle with as we go along, both as writers and as citizens, because it's not just in the literary or artistic arena that this is going to show itself. I think one can say this limiting isn't going to be very healthy for the societies that abandon themselves.

QUESTION 7

21   **In an *Atlantic Unbound* interview this past winter Nadine Gordimer said, "English is used by my fellow writers, blacks, who have been the most extreme victims of colonialism. They use it even though they have African languages to choose from. I think that once you've mastered a language it's your own. It can be used against you, but you can free yourself and use it as black writers do—you can claim it and use it." Do you agree with her?**

22   Yes, I definitely do. English is something you spend your lifetime acquiring, so it would be foolish not to use it. Also, in the logic of colonization and decolonization it is actually a very powerful weapon in the fight to regain what was

My Notes

---

alternative: other choice
motive: driving purpose
suppressed: kept from being known or published
globalization: worldwide integration and development
absorption: soaking up
extreme: severe
claim: take ownership of

My Notes

yours. English was the language of colonization itself. It is not simply something you use because you have it anyway; it is something which you can actively claim to use as an effective weapon, as a counterargument to colonization.

QUESTION 8

23 **There are those who say that media coverage of Africa is one-sided—that it focuses on the famines, social unrest, and political violence, and leaves out coverage of the organizations and countries that are working. Do you agree? If so, what effect does this skewed coverage have? Is it a continuation of the anti-Africa British literature you talk about in *Home and Exile*?**

24 Yes, I do agree. I think the result has been to create a fatigue, whether it's charity fatigue or fatigue toward being good to people who are less fortunate. I think that's a pity. The reason for this concentration on the failings of Africans is the same as what we've been talking about—this tradition of bad news, or portraying Africa as a place that is different from the rest of the world, a place where humanity is really not recognizable. When people hear the word *Africa*, they have come to expect certain images to follow. If you see a good house in Lagos, Nigeria, it doesn't quite fit the picture you have in your head, because you are looking for the slum—that is what the world expects journalists covering a city in Africa to come back with.

25 Now, if you are covering America, you are not focusing on slums every day of your life. You see a slum once in a while, maybe you talk about it, but the rest of the time you are talking about other things. It is that ability to see the complexity of a place that the world doesn't seem to be able to take to Africa, because of this baggage of centuries of reporting about Africa. The result is the world doesn't really know Africa. If you are an African or you live in Africa, this stands out very clearly to you, you are constantly being bombarded with bad news, and you know that there is good news in many places. This doesn't mean that the bad news doesn't exist, that's not what I'm saying. But it exists alongside other things. Africa is not simple—people want to simplify it. Africa is very complex. Very bad things go on—they should be covered—but there are also some good things.

26 This is something that comes with this imbalance of power that we've been talking about. The people who consume the news that comes back from the rest of the world are probably not really interested in hearing about something that is working. Those who have the ability to send crews out to bring back the news are in a position to determine what the image of the various places should be, because they have the resources to do it. Now, an African country doesn't have a television crew coming to America, for instance, and picking up the disastrous news. So America sends out wonderful images of its success, power, energy, and politics, and the world is bombarded in a very partial way by good news about the powerful and bad news about the less powerful.

QUESTION 9

27 You mentioned that literature was used to justify slavery and imperialism. What is this negative coverage of Africa being used to justify now?

---

skewed: biased; distorted
concentration: focus of attention
complexity: complicated nature
consume: take in and use
partial: biased

28 It's going to be used to justify inaction, which is what this fatigue is all about. Why bother about Africa? Nothing works there, or nothing ever will work. There is a small minority of people who think that way, and they may be pushing this attitude. But even if nobody was pushing it, it would simply happen by itself. This is a case of sheer inertia, something that has been happening for a long time just goes on happening, unless something stops it. It becomes a habit of mind.

QUESTION 10

29 **Has living here changed the way you think about Nigeria?**

30 It must have, but this is not something you can weigh and measure. I've been struck, for instance, by the impressive way that political transition is managed in America. Nobody living here can miss that if you come from a place like Nigeria which is unable so far to manage political **transitions** in peace. I wish Nigeria would learn to do this. There are other things, of course, where you wish Americans would learn from Nigerians: the value of people as people, the almost complete absence of race as a factor in thought, in government. That's something that I really wish for America, because no day passes here without some racial **factor** coming up somewhere, which is a major burden on this country.

QUESTION 11

31 **Could you talk about your dream, expressed in *Home and Exile*, of a "universal civilization"—a civilization that some believe we've achieved and others think we haven't?**

32 What the universal civilization I dream about would be, I really don't know, but I know what it is not. It is not what is being presented today, which is clearly just European and American. A universal civilization is something that we will create. If we accept the **thesis** that it is desirable to do, then we will go and work on it and talk about it. We have not really talked about it. All those who are saying it's there are really suggesting that it's there **by default**— they are saying to us, let's stop at this point and call what we have a universal civilization. I don't think we want to swindle ourselves in that way; I think if we want a universal civilization, we should work to bring it about. And when it appears, I think we will know, because it will be different from anything we have now.

33 There may be cultures that may sadly have to go, because no one is rooting for them, but we should make the effort to prevent this. We have to hold this conversation, which is a conversation of stories, a conversation of languages, and see what happens.

Making Observations

- What is your initial impression of Chinua Achebe?
- What additional questions do you wish you could ask Achebe?

WORD CONNECTIONS

Content Connections
Achebe applies the term **inertia** to society to indicate its unwillingness to change. The term comes from science, where it relates to matter and movement. Inertia is the tendency of an object to resist any change in its state of motion unless acted upon by an outside force. For example, if at rest, an object needs a push in order to move.

My Notes

transitions: changes from one stage to the next
factor: element
thesis: proposition
by default: automatically, as the only choice

Returning to the Text

- Return to the interview as you respond to the following questions. Use text evidence to support your responses.
- Write any additional questions you have about the interview in your Reader/Writer Notebook.

1. What notable contrast does Achebe recognize between *Time* magazine's assessment of Joyce Cary's novel *Mister Johnson* and his own assessment of the work?

   _____

   _____

   _____

   _____

2. Reread paragraph 3 of this interview. What is the author's purpose in discussing the book *Mister Johnson* before discussing Achebe's novel *Things Fall Apart*? How does this help you understand Achebe's purpose for writing his novel?

   _____

   _____

   _____

   _____

3. What details from the answer to Question 1 of the interview explain the key idea of why Achebe's work "fit[s] into the story of the world"?

   _____

   _____

   _____

   _____

4. Achebe states that literature can make us identify with situations and people far away. Based on the evidence and details he cites in his response to Questions 1 and 2, is this claim valid?

   _____

   _____

   _____

   _____

5. How does Achebe feel about the changes to Igbo society? What details in the text support this idea?

_____

_____

_____

_____

6. Achebe claims that the problems of Nigeria today may be traced to "this effort that was initiated by colonial rule to create a new nation." What evidence does he use to support his claim? Cite particular sentences or phrases from the text.

_____

_____

_____

_____

7. According to Achebe, what is the relationship between storytelling and power? How does storytelling contribute to our understanding of the world?

_____

_____

_____

_____

8. What claim does Achebe make about mastering the English language? Do you think that he gives enough evidence to prove this claim is valid?

_____

_____

_____

_____

9. How does Achebe contrast the media coverage of Africa with the coverage of places like America? What conclusion does he draw from the contrast?

_____

_____

_____

_____

10. Achebe states that a "universal civilization" may be possible to achieve. He asserts, "A universal civilization will be something we will create." Do you think that Achebe provides a sufficiently clear definition of "universal civilization" and how it may be achieved to prove his assertion?

_____

_____

_____

_____

Working from the Text

11. Use metacognitive markers as you read your assigned chunk of the interview with your group. Discuss your findings. Work together to complete the following chart. Be sure each person in the group takes notes so that each of you is prepared to present your findings to a new group.

Copy the Interviewer's Question	Summarize Achebe's Response	Add Your Commentary or Questions

12. Present your chunk of the interview to a group of students who read different chunks. Include your notes from the graphic organizer, your metacognitive markers, and your responses to the key questions. Work together with your new group to write a list of additional questions you would like to ask Achebe.

☑ Check Your Understanding

Consider the following proverb:

> "Until the lion has a voice, stories of safaris will always glorify the hunter."

How can you use this proverb to explain Chinua Achebe's purpose in writing the novel *Things Fall Apart?* Do you think he was successful?

✍ Writing Prompt: Informational

Consider the Essential Question for this unit: How can a work of literature reflect a cultural perspective? Write an essay explaining your answer to this question. Be sure to:

- Begin with a clear statement of your idea.
- Use evidence from the novel and from the interview to develop and support your response.
- Use transition words to link your main ideas and clarify the relationships between them.
- Check your essay for noun agreement.

ⓘ INDEPENDENT READING LINK

Read and Respond

Think about your independent reading selection. Imagine you are interviewing the author. Draft questions that you might ask the author, such as "How did you use the characters to make a statement about a real issue?" Then, imagine how the author might respond to your questions. Write your responses in your Reader/Writer Notebook, and discuss your ideas with the class.

Writing a Literary Analysis Essay

 ASSIGNMENT

Write an analytical essay about *Things Fall Apart* in which you examine how the cultural and historical settings of the novel influence the development of one character. How does this character react to the cultural collision between Western ideas and Ibo culture, and how does this reaction affect the plot?

Planning and Prewriting: Take time to make a plan for your essay.	■ Which characters have strong positive or negative responses to the cultural collision in the novel, and which one will you choose to focus on for your analysis?
	■ What is this character's sense of identity before encountering Western influence?
	■ What is this character's response to the new culture? What does he or she do, think, or say? How does he or she interact with others? How does his or her role and/or perspective shift?
	■ What are the consequences of this character's response and his or her willingness or unwillingness to change?
	■ What statement about culture is the author making through this fictional character, and how can you include this in your thesis?
	■ What textual support can you find for your thesis?
	■ How can you use an outline to plan the structure of your essay?
Drafting and Revising: Write your literary analysis essay.	■ How will you introduce your topic, organize your ideas, and provide a thoughtful conclusion?
	■ How will you integrate textual evidence, including direct quotes from the novel?
	■ How will you be sure to use precise language and academic voice?
	■ How can you experiment with syntax and use a variety of sentence structures and transitions?
Editing and Publishing: Prepare a final draft for publication.	■ How will you proofread and edit your essay for proper conventions of standard English capitalization, punctuation, spelling, grammar, and usage?
	■ What tools are available for you to further polish and refine your work, such as a dictionary, thesaurus, spell-check, or grammar check?
	■ How can the Scoring Guide help you evaluate how well you have met the requirements of the assignment?

Reflection

After completing this Embedded Assessment, think about how you went about accomplishing this task, and respond to the following:

- How did your research on pre- and postcolonial Ibo culture help you understand your character's reaction to the cultural collision?

- Why is it important to read literature written from the perspective of a culture other than your own?

SCORING GUIDE

Scoring Criteria	Exemplary	Proficient	Emerging	Incomplete
Ideas	The essay • thoroughly examines a character's response to the cultural collision in the novel • clearly and accurately analyzes characterization, theme, and author's purpose • develops the topic with smooth integration of relevant textual evidence, including details, quotations, and examples.	The essay • examines a character's response to the cultural collision in the novel • adequately analyzes characterization, theme, and author's purpose • develops the topic with sufficient textual evidence, including details, quotations, and examples.	The essay • incompletely examines a character's response to the cultural collision in the novel • provides insufficient analysis of characterization, theme, or author's purpose • provides insufficient textual evidence, including details, quotations, and examples.	The essay • does not examine a character's response to the cultural collision in the novel • lacks analysis of characterization, theme, or author's purpose • provides little or no textual evidence, including details, quotations, and examples.
Structure	The essay • uses an effective organizational strategy that follows a logical progression of ideas • introduces the topic engagingly, links supporting ideas, and provides a thoughtful conclusion • uses appropriate and varied transitions.	The essay • uses an adequate organizational strategy that contains a logical progression of ideas • introduces the topic, links supporting ideas, and provides a conclusion • uses some varied transitions.	The essay • uses an inconsistent or flawed organizational structure • lacks an introduction to the topic, links between supporting ideas, and/or a conclusion • uses weak, repetitive, or insufficient transitions.	The essay • does not use an obvious organizational structure • lacks an introduction to the topic, links between supporting ideas, and/or a conclusion • uses no transitions.
Use of Language	The essay • uses precise language and variety of sentence structures • maintains an academic voice and objective tone • demonstrates consistent command of conventions (grammar, usage, capitalization, punctuation, and spelling).	The essay • uses some precise language and variety of sentence structures • generally maintains an academic voice and objective tone • demonstrates adequate command of conventions; may have some errors in grammar, usage, capitalization, punctuation, or spelling that do not interfere with meaning.	The essay • uses vague or inappropriate language and flawed or simplistic sentence structures • lacks an academic voice and objective tone • demonstrates partial or insufficient command of conventions; errors in grammar, usage, capitalization, punctuation, or spelling interfere with meaning.	The essay • uses inappropriate language and only simple sentences • lacks an academic voice and objective tone • demonstrates little command of conventions; significant errors in grammar, usage, capitalization, punctuation, or spelling interfere with meaning.

Journeys Through Time and Space

Learning Strategies

Discussion Groups
Graphic Organizer

Learning Strategies

Discussion Groups
Graphic Organizer

My Notes

Learning Targets

- Analyze an author's development of characters and setting in a short story.
- Analyze how historical and cultural settings have an impact on the meaning of text.

Preview

In this activity, you will unpack the requirements of the second Embedded Assessment and begin reading a short story, analyzing the author's use of setting and characterization.

Making Connections

In the first part of this unit, you read the novel Things Fall Apart and learned about the historical and cultural context that Achebe wrote the novel in. In the rest of the unit, you will read short stories from different time periods and countries, and write a short story of your own in which you convey a cultural or historical perspective.

Unpacking Embedded Assessment 2

Read the assignment for Embedded Assessment 2: Writing a Short Story

 Write an original short story that conveys a specific cultural perspective or historical moment. Conduct research into the time period and setting that you choose in order to convey the setting accurately.

Using the assignment and Embedded Assessment Scoring Guide, work as a class to analyze the activity. Think through the required concepts (what you need to know) and skills (what you need to do) to effectively complete the assignment.

After each activity, use your Reader/Writer Notebook to reflect on what you have learned about how historical and cultural settings and influences contribute to characterization, plot, and theme in order to be successful on the Embedded Assessment.

About Short Stories

Short stories are works of fiction that include the following elements: characters, plot, conflict, setting, and an overarching theme.

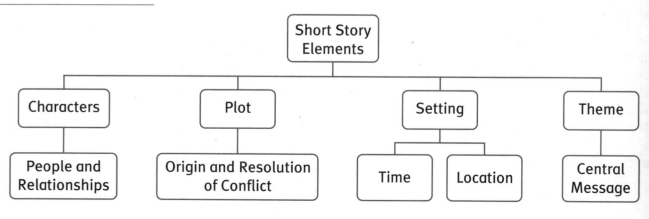

short stories can be anywhere from just a few paragraphs to many pages long, but most can usually be read in one sitting. Unlike novels, they frequently have a limited number of characters, a single setting, and a plot that, though often not as complicated as that of a longer work, still robustly connects the setting and characters.

About the Author

Jhumpa Lahiri (b. 1967) is an award-winning American author of Indian descent. Her works include the *New York Times* best seller *Unaccustomed Earth* and the short story collection *Interpreter of Maladies*, which includes "The Third and Final Continent" as its final entry. Lahiri writes often about being Indian American, drawing from her own experiences and those of her family and friends, forcing her two worlds to, as she states, "mingle on the page."

As You Read

Highlight details about the story's setting, including times, places, and dates.

Circle unknown words and phrases. Try to determine the meaning of the words by using context clues, word parts, or a dictionary.

Short Story

The Third and Final Continent (Part One)

by Jhumpa Lahiri

1   I left India in 1964 with a certificate in commerce and the equivalent, in those days, of ten dollars to my name. For three weeks I sailed on the *SS Roma*, an Italian cargo vessel, in a cabin next to the ship's engine, across the Arabian Sea, the Red Sea, the Mediterranean, and finally to England. I lived in London, in Finsbury Park, in a house occupied entirely by penniless Bengali bachelors like myself, at least a dozen and sometimes more, all struggling to educate and establish ourselves abroad.

2   I attended lectures at LSE[1] and worked at the university library to get by. We lived three or four to a room, shared a single, icy toilet, and took turns cooking pots of egg curry, which we ate with our hands on a table covered with newspapers. Apart from our jobs we had few responsibilities. . . . On weekends we lounged barefoot in drawstring pajamas, drinking tea and smoking Rothmans, or set out to watch cricket at Lord's. Some weekends the house was crammed with still more Bengalis, to whom we had introduced ourselves at the greengrocer, or on the Tube[2], and we made yet more egg curry, and

[1] *LSE* is the London School of Economics and Political Science.
[2] The *Tube* is London's subway.

My Notes

My Notes

INDEPENDENT READING LINK

Read and Recommend

Discuss with your partner which texts you both have enjoyed reading this year. Then thoughtfully recommend a text that you think your partner will like. Give a brief summary, without revealing anything that would spoil the ending. Be sure to give reasons to back up your recommendation to sell the text to your partner.

accommodation: place to live or stay

played Mukesh[3] on a Grundig reel-to-reel[4], and soaked our dirty dishes in the bathtub. Every now and then someone in the house moved out, to live with a woman whom his family back in Calcutta had determined he was to wed. In 1969, when I was thirty-six years old, my own marriage was arranged. Around the same time, I was offered a full-time job in America, in the processing department of a library at MIT. The salary was generous enough to support a wife, and I was honored to be hired by a world-famous university, and so I obtained a sixth-preference green card, and prepared to travel farther still.

3   By then I had enough money to go by plane. I flew first to Calcutta, to attend my wedding, and a week later to Boston, to begin my new job. During the flight I read _The Student Guide to North America_, a paperback volume that I'd bought before leaving London, for seven shillings six pence on Tottenham Court Road, for although I was no longer a student, I was on a budget all the same. I learned that Americans drove on the right side of the road, not the left, and that they called a lift an elevator and an engaged phone busy. "The pace of life in North America is different from Britain, as you will soon discover," the guidebook informed me. "Everybody feels he must get to the top. Don't expect an English cup of tea." As the plane began its descent over Boston Harbor, the pilot announced the weather and the time, and that President Nixon had declared a national holiday: two American men had landed on the moon. Several passengers cheered. "God bless America!" one of them hollered. Across the aisle, I saw a woman praying.

4   I spent my first night at the YMCA in Central Square, Cambridge, an inexpensive **accommodation** recommended by my guidebook. It was walking distance from MIT, and steps from the post office and a supermarket called Purity Supreme. The room contained a cot, a desk, and a small wooden cross on one wall. A sign on the door said that cooking was strictly forbidden. A bare window overlooked Massachusetts Avenue, a major thoroughfare with traffic in both directions. Car horns, shrill and prolonged, blared one after another. Flashing sirens heralded endless emergencies, and a fleet of buses rumbled past, their doors opening and closing with a powerful hiss, throughout the night. The noise was constantly distracting, at times suffocating. I felt it deep in my ribs, just as I had felt the furious drone of the engine on the _SS Roma_. But there was no ship's deck to escape to, no glittering ocean to thrill my soul, no breeze to cool my face, no one to talk to. I was too tired to pace the gloomy corridors of the YMCA in my pajamas. Instead I sat at the desk and stared out the window, at the city hall of Cambridge and a row of small shops. In the morning I reported to my job at the Dewey Library, a beige fortlike building by Memorial Drive. I also opened a bank account, rented a post-office box, and bought a plastic bowl and a spoon at Woolworth's, a store whose name I recognized from London. I went to Purity Supreme, wandering up and down the aisles, converting ounces to grams and comparing prices to things in England. In the end I bought a carton of milk and a box of cornflakes. This was

---

[3] _Mukesh_ is a famed Indian singer.
[4] Reel-to-reel audio tape recordings use magnetic tape to record sound, similar to a cassette tape.

my first meal in America. I ate it at my desk. I preferred it to hamburgers or hot dogs, the only alternative I could afford in the coffee shops on Massachusetts Avenue, and, besides, at the time I had yet to consume any beef. Even the simple chore of buying milk was new to me; in London we'd had bottles delivered each morning to our door.

5   In a week I had adjusted, more or less. I ate cornflakes and milk morning and night, and bought some bananas for variety, slicing them into the bowl with the edge of my spoon. I left my carton of milk on the shaded part of the windowsill, as I had seen other residents at the YMCA do. To pass the time in the evenings I read the *Boston Globe* downstairs, in a spacious room with stained-glass windows. I read every article and advertisement, so that I would grow familiar with things, and when my eyes grew tired I slept. Only I did not sleep well. Each night I had to keep the window wide open; it was the only source of air in the **stifling** room, and the noise was intolerable. I would lie on the cot with my fingers pressed into my ears, but when I drifted off to sleep my hands fell away, and the noise of the traffic would wake me up again. Pigeon feathers drifted onto the windowsill, and one evening, when I poured milk over my cornflakes, I saw that it had soured.

6   Nevertheless I resolved to stay at the YMCA for six weeks, until my wife's passport and green card were ready. Once she arrived I would have to rent a proper apartment, and from time to time I studied the classified section of the newspaper, or stopped in at the housing office at MIT during my lunch break to see what was available in my price range. It was in this manner that I discovered a room for immediate occupancy, in a house on a quiet street, the listing said, for eight dollars per week. I copied the address into my guidebook and dialed the number from a pay telephone, sorting through the coins, with which I was still unfamiliar, smaller and lighter than shillings, heavier and brighter than *paisas*[5].

7   "Who is speaking?" a woman demanded. Her voice was bold and clamorous.

8   "Yes, good afternoon, madame. I am calling about the room for rent."

9   "Harvard or Tech?"

10   "I beg your pardon?"

11   "Are you from Harvard or Tech?" Gathering that Tech referred to the Massachusetts Institute of Technology, I replied, "I work at Dewey Library," adding tentatively, "at Tech."

12   "I only rent rooms to boys from Harvard or Tech!"

13   "Yes, madame."

14   I was given an address and an appointment for seven o'clock that evening. Thirty minutes before the hour I set out, my guidebook in my pocket, my breath fresh with Listerine. I turned down a street shaded with trees,

[5] *Paisas* are Indian coins that are no longer in circulation.

stifling: suffocating

My Notes

perpendicular to Massachusetts Avenue. Stray blades of grass poked between the cracks of the footpath. In spite of the heat I wore a coat and tie, regarding the event as I would any other interview; I had never lived in the home of a person who was not Indian. The house, surrounded by a chain-link fence, was off-white with dark-brown trim. Unlike the stucco row house I'd lived in in London, this house, fully detached, was covered with wooden shingles, with a tangle of forsythia bushes plastered against its front and sides. When I pressed the calling bell, the woman with whom I had spoken on the phone hollered from what seemed to be just the other side of the door, "One minute, please!"

15 Several minutes later the door was opened by a tiny, extremely old woman. A mass of snowy hair was arranged like a small sack on top of her head. As I stepped into the house she sat down on a wooden bench positioned at the bottom of a narrow carpeted staircase. Once she was settled on the bench, in a small pool of light, she peered up at me, giving me her undivided attention. She wore a long black skirt that spread like a stiff tent to the floor, and a starched white shirt edged with ruffles at the throat and cuffs. Her hands, folded together in her lap, had long pallid fingers, with swollen knuckles and tough yellow nails. Age had battered her features so that she almost resembled a man, with sharp, shrunken eyes and prominent creases on either side of her nose. Her lips, chapped and faded, had nearly disappeared, and her eyebrows were missing altogether. Nevertheless she looked fierce.

16 "Lock up!" she commanded. She shouted even though l stood only a few feet away. "Fasten the chain and firmly press that button on the knob! This is the first thing you shall do when you enter, is that clear?"

17 I locked the door as directed and examined the house. Next to the bench was a small round table, its legs fully concealed, much like the woman's, by a skirt of lace. The table held a lamp, a transistor radio, a leather change purse with a silver clasp, and a telephone. A thick wooden cane was propped against one side. There was a parlor to my right, lined with bookcases and filled with shabby claw-footed furniture. In the corner of the parlor I saw a grand piano with its top down, piled with papers. The piano's bench was missing; it seemed to be the one on which the woman was sitting. Somewhere in the house a clock chimed seven times.

18 "You're punctual!" the woman proclaimed. "I expect you shall be so with the rent!"

19 "I have a letter, madame." In my jacket pocket was a letter from MIT confirming my employment, which I had brought along to prove that I was indeed from Tech.

20 She stared at the letter, then handed it back to me carefully, gripping it with her fingers as if it were a plate heaped with food. She did not wear glasses, and I wondered if she'd read a word of it. "The last boy was always late! Still owes me eight dollars! Harvard boys aren't what they used to be! Only Harvard and Tech in this house! How's Tech, boy?"

21 "It is very well."

pallid: pale

22   "You checked the lock?"

23   "Yes, madame."

24   She slapped the space beside her on the bench with one hand, and told me to sit down. For a moment she was silent. Then she intoned, as if she alone possessed this knowledge: "There is an American flag on the moon!"

25   "Yes, madame." Until then I had not thought very much about the moon shot. It was in the newspaper, of course, article upon article. The astronauts had landed on the shores of the Sea of Tranquility[6], I had read, travelling farther than anyone in the history of civilization. For a few hours they explored the moon's surface. They gathered rocks in their pockets, described their surroundings (a magnificent desolation, according to one astronaut), spoke by phone to the President, and planted a flag in lunar soil. The voyage was hailed as man's most awesome achievement.

26   The woman bellowed, "A flag on the moon, boy! I heard it on the radio! Isn't that splendid?"

27   "Yes, madame."

28   But she was not satisfied with my reply. Instead she commanded, "Say splendid!"

29   I was both baffled and somewhat insulted by the request. It reminded me of the way I was taught multiplication tables as a child, repeating after the master, sitting cross-legged on the floor of my one-room Tollygunge school. It also reminded me of my wedding, when I had repeated endless Sanskrit verses after the priest, verses I barely understood, which joined me to my wife. I said nothing.

30   "Say 'splendid!'" the woman bellowed once again.

31   "Splendid," I murmured. I had to repeat the word a second time at the top of my lungs, so she could hear. I am soft-spoken by nature and was especially reluctant to raise my voice to an elderly woman, but she did not appear to be offended. If anything the reply pleased her, because her next command was:

32   "Go see the room!"

33   I rose from the bench and mounted the narrow staircase. There were five doors, two on either side of an equally narrow hallway, and one at the opposite end. Only one door was open. The room contained a twin bed under a sloping ceiling, a brown oval rug, a basin with an exposed pipe, and a chest of drawers. One door led to a closet, another to a toilet and a tub. The window was open; net curtains stirred in the breeze. I lifted them away and inspected the view: a small back yard, with a few fruit trees and an empty clothesline. I was satisfied. From the bottom of the stairs I heard the woman demand, "What is your decision?"

---

6 The *Sea of Tranquility* is the landing site of Apollo 11, the space mission that first put a human on the moon.

34 When I returned to the foyer and told her, she picked up the leather change purse on the table, opened the clasp, fished about with her fingers, and produced a key on a thin wire hoop. She informed me that there was a kitchen at the back of the house, accessible through the parlor. I was welcome to use the stove as long as I left it as I found it. Sheets and towels were provided, but keeping them clean was my own responsibility. The rent was due Friday mornings on the ledge above the piano keys. "And no lady visitors!"

35 "I am a married man, madame." It was the first time I had announced thi fact to anyone.

36 But she had not heard. "No lady visitors!" she insisted. She introduced herself as Mrs. Croft.

37 My wife's name was Mala. The marriage had been arranged by my older brother and his wife. I regarded the proposition with neither objection nor enthusiasm. It was a duty expected of me, as it was expected of every man. She was the daughter of a schoolteacher in Beleghata. I was told that she could cook, knit, embroider, sketch landscapes, and recite poems by Tagore, but these talents could not make up for the fact that she did not possess a fair complexion, and so a string of men had rejected her to her face. She was twenty-seven, an age when her parents had begun to fear that she would never marry, and so they were willing to ship their only child halfway across the world in order to save her from spinsterhood.

38 For five nights we shared a bed. Each of those nights, after applying cold cream and braiding her hair, which she tied up at the end with a black cotton string, she turned from me and wept; she missed her parents. Although I woul be leaving the country in a few days, custom dictated that she was now a part of my household, and for the next six weeks she was to live with my brother and his wife, cooking, cleaning, serving tea and sweets to guests. I did nothing to console her. I lay on my own side of the bed, reading my guidebook by flashlight and anticipating my journey. At times I thought of the tiny room on the other side of the wall which had belonged to my mother. Now the room was practically empty; the wooden pallet on which she'd once slept was piled with trunks and old bedding.

39 The next morning I moved into Mrs. Croft's house. When I unlocked the door I saw that she was sitting on the piano bench, on the same side as the previous evening. She wore the same black skirt, the same starched white blouse, and had her hands folded together the same way in her lap. She looked so much the same that I wondered if she'd spent the whole night on the bench. I put my suitcase upstairs and then headed off to work. That evening when I came home from the university, she was still there.

40 "Sit down, boy!" She slapped the space beside her.

41 I perched on the bench. I had a bag of groceries with me—more milk, mor cornflakes, and more bananas, for my inspection of the kitchen earlier in the day had revealed no spare pots or pans. There were only two saucepans in the refrigerator, both containing some orange broth, and a copper kettle on the stove

42   "Good evening, madame."

43   She asked me if I had checked the lock. I told her I had.

44   For a moment she was silent. Then suddenly she declared, with the equal measures of disbelief and delight as the night before, "There's an American flag on the moon, boy!"

45   "Yes, madame."

46   "A flag on the moon! Isn't that splendid?"

47   I nodded, dreading what I knew was coming. "Yes, madame."

48   "Say 'splendid!'"

49   This time I paused, looking to either side in case anyone was there to overhear me, though I knew perfectly well that the house was empty. I felt like an idiot. But it was a small enough thing to ask. "Splendid!" I cried out.

50   Within days it became our routine. In the mornings when I left for the library Mrs. Croft was either hidden away in her bedroom, on the other side of the staircase, or she was sitting on the bench, oblivious to my presence, listening to the news or classical music on the radio. But each evening when I returned the same thing happened: she slapped the bench, ordered me to sit down, declared that there was a flag on the moon, and declared that it was splendid. I said it was splendid, too, and then we sat in silence. As awkward as it was, and as endless as it felt to me then, the nightly encounter lasted only about ten minutes; inevitably she would drift off to sleep, her head falling abruptly toward her chest, leaving me free to retire to my room. By then, of course, there was no flag standing on the moon. The astronauts, I read in the paper, had seen it fall before they flew back to Earth. But I did not have the heart to tell her.

51   Friday morning, when my first week's rent was due, I went to the piano in the parlor to place my money on the ledge. The piano keys were dull and discolored. When I pressed one, it made no sound at all. I had put eight dollar bills in an envelope and written Mrs. Croft's name on the front of it. I was not in the habit of leaving money unmarked and unattended. From where I stood I could see the profile of her tent-shaped skirt. It seemed unnecessary to make her get up and walk all the way to the piano. I never saw her walking about, and assumed, from the cane propped against the round table at her side, that she did so with difficulty. When I approached the bench she peered up at me and demanded:

52   "What is your business?"

53   "The rent, madame."

54   "On the ledge above the piano keys!"

55   "I have it here." I extended the envelope toward her, but her fingers, folded together in her lap, did not budge. I bowed slightly and lowered the envelope, so that it hovered just above her hands. After a moment she accepted it, and nodded her head.

56 That night when I came home, she did not slap the bench, but out of habit I sat beside her as usual. She asked me if I had checked the lock, but she mentioned nothing about the flag on the moon. Instead she said: "It was very kind of you!"

57 "I beg your pardon, madame?"

58 "Very kind of you!"

59 She was still holding the envelope in her hands.

The Apollo 11 mission landed on July 16, 1969, and Neil Armstrong and Buzz Aldrin became the first men to walk on the moon. Here, astronaut John W. Young salutes the flag during the Apollo 16 Mission in April 1972.

Making Observations
- What do you notice about the setting of this story?
- How would you describe the narrator of this story?

☑ Focus on the Sentence

Read the following sentence. Then expand the sentence by providing more details as prompted by the questions.

The narrator of the story meets her.

Who? _____

When? _____

Where? _____

Why? _____

Expanded Sentence: _____

_____

Returning to the Text

- Reread the short story to answer these short story-dependent questions.
- Write any additional questions you have about the short story in your Reader/Writer Notebook.

1. What do you learn about the narrator at the beginning of the story? How would you describe him?

_____

_____

_____

_____

2. What shifts does the narrator see in his life in his travels from India to London to Boston? What is meant by the line "Don't expect an English cup of tea"?

_____

_____

_____

_____

3. Describe Mrs. Croft. Find text evidence that supports your answer.

_____

_____

_____

_____

4. Describe the narrator's interactions with Mrs. Croft. Are the two characters similar or different?

_____

_____

_____

_____

5. What is the narrator's reaction to his wife's distress after their marriage? What does this reveal about their relationship?

_____

_____

_____

_____

Working from the Text

6. Reread paragraphs 14–15. These two paragraphs describe the narrator meeting Mrs. Croft for the first time. Complete the graphic organizer with your thoughts about the effect of each descriptive detail Lahiri chooses to describe. Then add a few of your own.

Descriptive Details from Paragraphs 14 and 15	
Detail	**Effect**
"my breath fresh with Listerine" (paragraph 14)	The narrator wants to make a good impression; he takes this interview seriously.
"tangle of forsythia bushes" (paragraph 14)	
"skirt that spread like a stiff tent" (paragraph 15)	
"sharp, shrunken eyes" (paragraph 15)	

7. In what ways does Lahiri use sensory or figurative language in this section to create a dramatic moment in the story?

8. Authors use details in a story to reveal characteristics of each of the main characters. Complete this graphic organizer with a partner to reveal the author's characterization. Be sure to use specific evidence from the text.

Details That Reveal Character			
Character	Narrator	Mrs. Croft	Mala
Write at least two adjectives to describe the character.			
What details does the author uses to support her characterization?			
What do the details reveal about the character's perspective at this point in the story?			

9. Consider the setting of the story. What are the three settings and how does each influence the narrator? Complete the graphic organizer with a partner.

	Setting 1:	Setting 2:	Setting 3:
What details does the narrator give about the setting?			
How is the narrator shaped by the setting? Cite evidence from the text.			

☑ Check Your Understanding

In a few sentences in your Reader/Writer Notebook, explain the effects the various settings have on the narrator.

Learning Strategies

Close Reading

My Notes

Learning Targets

- Analyze how the author develops complex yet believable characters.
- Analyze how the author develops a theme through characterization and plot.

Preview

In this activity, you will read the second part of "The Third and Final Continent" and analyze how the author continues to develop character and theme.

As You Read

- Underline descriptive details that help you visualize the story.
- Circle unknown words and phrases. Try to determine the meaning of the words by using context clues, word parts, or a dictionary.

Short Story

The Third and Final Continent (Part Two)

by **Jhumpa Lahiri**

60 On Sunday there was a knock on my door. An elderly woman introduced herself: she was Mrs. Croft's daughter, Helen. She walked into the room and looked at each of the walls as if for signs of change, glancing at the shirts that hung in the closet, the neckties draped over the doorknob, the box of cornflakes on the chest of drawers, the dirty bowl and spoon in the basin. She was short and thick-waisted, with cropped silver hair and bright pink lipstick. She wore a sleeveless summer dress, a necklace of white plastic beads, and spectacles on a chain that hung like a swing against her chest. The backs of her legs were mapped with dark-blue veins, and her upper arms sagged like the flesh of a roasted eggplant. She told me she lived in Arlington, a town farther up Massachusetts Avenue. "I come once a week to bring Mother groceries. Has she sent you packing yet?"

61 "It is very well, madame."

62 "Some of the boys run screaming. But I think she likes you. You're the first boarder she's ever referred to as a gentleman."

63 She looked at me, noticing my bare feet. (I still felt strange wearing shoes indoors, and always removed them before entering my room.)

64 "Are you new to Boston?"

65 "New to America, madame."

66 "From?" She raised her eyebrows.

67 "I am from Calcutta, India."

68 "Is that right? We had a Brazilian fellow, about a year ago. You'll find Cambridge a very international city."

69 I nodded, and began to wonder how long our conversation would last. But at that moment we heard Mrs. Croft's electrifying voice rising up the stairs. When we stepped into the hallway we heard her hollering:

70 "You are to come downstairs immediately!"

71 "What is it?" Helen cried back.

72 "Immediately!"

73 I put on my shoes. Helen sighed.

74 We walked down the staircase. It was too narrow for us to descend side by side, so I followed Helen, who seemed to be in no hurry, and complained at one point that she had a bad knee. "Have you been walking without your cane?" Helen called out. "You know you're not supposed to walk without that cane." She paused, resting her hand on the bannister, and looked back at me. "She slips sometimes."

75 For the first time Mrs. Croft seemed vulnerable. I pictured her on the floor in front of the bench, flat on her back, staring at the ceiling, her feet pointing in opposite directions. But when we reached the bottom of the staircase she was sitting there as usual, her hands folded together in her lap. Two grocery bags were at her feet. She did not slap the bench, or ask us to sit down. She glared.

76 "What is it, Mother?"

77 "It's improper"

78 "What's improper?"

79 "It is improper for a lady and gentleman who are not married to one another to hold a private conversation without a chaperone!"

80 Helen said she was sixty-eight years old, old enough to be my mother, but Mrs. Croft insisted that Helen and I speak to each other downstairs, in the parlor. She added that it was also improper for a lady of Helen's station to reveal her age, and to wear a dress so high above the ankle.

81 "For your information, Mother, it's 1969. What would you do if you actually left the house one day and saw a girl in a miniskirt?"

82 Mrs. Croft sniffed. "I'd have her arrested."

83 Helen shook her head and picked up one of the grocery bags. I picked up the other one, and followed her through the parlor and into the kitchen. The bags were filled with cans of soup, which Helen opened up one by one with a few cranks of a can opener. She tossed the old soup into the sink, rinsed the saucepans under the tap, filled them with soup from the newly opened cans, and put them back in the refrigerator. "A few years ago she could still open the cans herself," Helen said. "She hates that I do it for her now. But the piano killed her hands." She put on her spectacles, glanced at the cupboards, and spotted my tea bags. "Shall we have a cup?"

My Notes

84 I filled the kettle on the stove. "I beg your pardon, madame. The piano?"

85 "She used to give lessons. For forty years. It was how she raised us after my father died." Helen put her hands on her hips, staring at the open refrigerator. She reached into the back, pulled out a wrapped stick of butter, frowned, and tossed it into the garbage. "That ought to do it," she said, and put the unopened cans of soup in the cupboard. I sat at the table and watched as Helen washed the dirty dishes, tied up the garbage bag, and poured boiling water into two cups. She handed one to me without milk, and sat down at the table.

86 "Excuse me, madame, but is it enough?"

87 Helen took a sip of her tea. Her lipstick left a smiling pink stain on the rim of the cup. "Is what enough?"

88 "The soup in the pans. Is it enough food for Mrs. Croft?"

89 "She won't eat anything else. She stopped eating solids after she turned one hundred. That was, let's see, three years ago."

90 I was mortified. I had assumed Mrs. Croft was in her eighties, perhaps as old as ninety. I had never known a person who had lived for over a century. That this person was a widow who lived alone mortified me further still. Widowhood had driven my own mother insane. My father, who worked as a clerk at the General Post Office of Calcutta, died of encephalitis[1] when I was sixteen. My mother refused to adjust to life without him; instead she sank deeper into a world of darkness from which neither I, nor my brother, nor concerned relatives, nor psychiatric clinics on Rash Behari Avenue could save her. What pained me most was to see her so unguarded, to hear her burp after meals or expel gas in front of company without the slightest embarrassment. After my father's death my brother abandoned his schooling and began to work in the jute mill he would eventually manage, in order to keep the household running. And so it was my job to sit by my mother's feet and study for my exams as she counted and recounted the bracelets on her arm as if they were the beads of an abacus. We tried to keep an eye on her. Once she had wandered half naked to the tram depot before we were able to bring her inside again.

91 "I am happy to warm Mrs. Croft's soup in the evenings," I suggested. "It is no trouble."

92 Helen looked at her watch, stood up, and poured the rest of her tea into the sink. "I wouldn't if I were you. That's the sort of thing that would kill her altogether."

93 That evening, when Helen had gone back to Arlington and Mrs. Croft and I were alone again, I began to worry. Now that I knew how very old she was, I worried that something would happen to her in the middle of the night, or when I was out during the day. As vigorous as her voice was, and **imperious** as she seemed, I knew that even a scratch or a cough could kill a person that old; each day she lived, I knew, was something of a miracle. Helen didn't seem concerned. She came and went, bringing soup for Mrs. Croft, one Sunday after the next.

imperious: domineering

[1] *Encephalitis* is an inflammation of the brain.

94 In this manner the six weeks of that summer passed. I came home each evening, after my hours at the library, and spent a few minutes on the piano bench with Mrs. Croft. I gave her a bit of my company, and assured her that I had checked the lock, and told her that the flag on the moon was splendid. Some evenings I sat beside her long after she had drifted off to sleep, still in awe of how many years she had spent on this earth. At times I tried to picture the world she had been born into, in 1866—a world, I imagined, filled with women in long black skirts, and **chaste** conversations in the parlor. Now, when I looked at her hands with their swollen knuckles folded together in her lap, I imagined them smooth and slim, striking the piano keys. At times I came downstairs before going to sleep, to make sure she was sitting upright on the bench, or was safe in her bedroom. On Fridays I made sure to put the rent in her hands. There was nothing I could do for her beyond these simple gestures. I was not her son, and apart from those eight dollars, I owed her nothing.

95 At the end of August, Mala's passport and green card were ready. I received a telegram with her flight information; my brother's house in Calcutta had no telephone. Around that time I also received a letter from her, written only a few days after we had parted. There was no salutation; addressing me by name would have assumed an intimacy we had not yet discovered. It contained only a few lines. "I write in English in preparation for

chaste: virtuous

the journey. Here I am very much lonely. Is it very cold there. Is there snow. Yours, Mala."

96   I was not touched by her words. We had spent only a handful of days in each other's company. And yet we were bound together; for six weeks she had worn an iron bangle on her wrist, and applied **vermillion** powder to the part in her hair, to signify to the world that she was a bride. In those six weeks I regarded her arrival as I would the arrival of a coming month, or season—something inevitable, but meaningless at the time. So little did I know her that while details of her face sometimes rose to my memory, I could not conjure up the whole of it.

97   A few days after receiving the letter, as I was walking to work in the morning, I saw an Indian woman on Massachusetts Avenue, wearing a sari with its free end nearly dragging on the footpath, and pushing a child in a stroller. An American woman with a small black dog on a leash was walking to one side of her. Suddenly the dog began barking. I watched as the Indian woman, startled, stopped in her path, at which point the dog leaped up and seized the end of the sari between its teeth. The American woman scolded the dog, appeared to apologize, and walked quickly away, leaving the Indian woman to fix her sari, and quiet her crying child. She did not see me standing there, and eventually she continued on her way. Such a mishap, I realized that morning, would soon be my concern. It was my duty to take care of Mala, to welcome her and protect her. I would have to buy her first pair of snow boots, her first winter coat. I would have to tell her which streets to avoid, which way the traffic came, tell her to wear her sari so that the free end did not drag on the footpath. A five-mile separation from her parents, I recalled with some irritation, had caused her to weep.

98   Unlike Mala, I was used to it all by then: used to cornflakes and milk, used to Helen's visits, used to sitting on the bench with Mrs. Croft. The only thing I was not used to was Mala. Nevertheless I did what I had to do. I went to the housing office at MIT and found a furnished apartment a few blocks away, with a double bed and a private kitchen and bath, for forty dollars a week. One last Friday I handed Mrs. Croft eight one-dollar bills in an envelope, brought my suitcase downstairs, and informed her that I was moving. She put my key into her change purse. The last thing she asked me to do was hand her the cane propped against the table, so that she could walk to the door and lock it behind me. "Goodbye, then," she said, and retreated back into the house. I did not expect any display of emotion, but I was disappointed all the same. I was only a boarder, a man who paid her a bit of money and passed in and out of her home for six weeks. Compared with a century, it was no time at all.

Making Observations

- Based on your underlined text, what changes do you notice in the narrator's perspective after some time in the United States?
- What new information do you notice about Mrs. Croft in this section?

vermillion: red

Returning to the Text

- Reread the short story to answer these text-dependent questions.
- Write any additional questions you have about the text in your Reader/Writer Notebook.

1. Describe the relationship between Mrs. Croft and her daughter Helen.

_____

_____

_____

_____

2. What does the narrator learn from Helen about Mrs. Croft? How does his perspective change as a result?

_____

_____

_____

_____

3. How does the narrator weave information about his background into the narrative, and what effect does this structure have on the story? Specifically, does the information about the narrator's mother help the reader understand his relationship with Mrs. Croft?

_____

_____

_____

_____

4. How does the narrator portray Mala and how does he respond to her letter? What does this reveal about the narrator's character?

_____

_____

_____

_____

5. What is the narrator's reaction to Mrs. Croft's goodbye? What does this reveal about his development?

_____

_____

_____

_____

Working from the Text

6. Reread this description of Helen:

She was short and thick-waisted, with cropped silver hair and bright pink lipstick. She wore a sleeveless summer dress, a necklace of white plastic beads, and spectacles on a chain that hung like a swing against her chest. The backs of her legs were mapped with dark-blue veins, and her upper arms sagged like the flesh of a roasted eggplant.

What character traits does the author's use of figurative language reveal about Helen? Record your response in your Reader/Writer Notebook.

7. An author often molds a character over the course of a story. Think about how Lahiri molds Mrs. Croft into a more complex character over time in the story. Turn to a partner and discuss how Lahiri accomplishes this characterization. Jot notes about Mrs. Croft's interactions with other characters and what these interactions reveal about her own developing character.

8. Reread paragraphs 76–82 in a small group. What does this scene in the story contribute to the theme of being an outsider? Discuss this question in your small group, record notes, then share with the whole class.

9. Can you relate the "outsider" theme to the narrator in any way? How do Mrs. Croft and the narrator develop as outsiders as the story progresses? Record your response.

10. The characters in this story occupy a different cultural setting and time period from the characters in *Things Fall Apart*. Are there any connections you can draw between the characters in "The Third and Final Continent" and the characters in *Things Fall Apart*? How do the characters reflect the views of their culture? How to they react to new cultures?

☑ Check Your Understanding

What impact does the scene in paragraph 97 have on the development of the plot?

Learning Strategies

Close Reading
Discussion Groups

My Notes

Learning Targets
* Read and analyze the conclusion of the short story.
* Write a literary analysis about how historical and cultural setting influences characterization, plot, and theme.

Preview

In this activity, you will read Part Three of "The Third and Final Continent" and write a literary analysis.

As You Read

* Use a sticky note to mark a section where you notice change in a character or place. Write on the sticky note what you observe.
* Circle unknown words and phrases. Try to determine the meaning of the words by using context clues, word parts, or a dictionary.

Short Story

The Third and Final Continent (Part Three)

by **Jhumpa Lahiri**

99 At the airport I recognized Mala immediately. The free end of her sari did not drag on the floor, but was draped in a sign of bridal modesty over her head, just as it had draped my mother until the day my father died. Her thin brown arms were stacked with gold bracelets, a small red circle was painted on her forehead, and the edges of her feet were tinted with a decorative red dye. I did not embrace her, or kiss her, or take her hand. Instead I asked her, speaking Bengali for the first time in America, if she was hungry.

100 She hesitated, then nodded yes.

101 I told her I had prepared some egg curry at home. "What did they give you to eat on the plane?"

102 "I didn't eat."

103 "All the way from Calcutta?"

104 "The menu said oxtail soup."

105 "But surely there were other items."

106 "The thought of eating an ox's tail made me lose my appetite."

107 When we arrived home, Mala opened up one of her suitcases, and presented me with two pullover sweaters, both made with bright-blue wool, which she had knitted in the course of our separation, one with a V neck, the other covered with cables. I tried them on; both were tight under the arms.

She had also brought me two new pairs of drawstring pajamas, a letter from my brother, and a packet of loose Darjeeling tea. I had no present for her apart from the egg curry. We sat at a bare table, staring at our plates. We ate with our hands, another thing I had not yet done in America.

108 "The house is nice," she said. "Also the egg curry." With her left hand she held the end of her sari to her chest, so it would not slip off her head.

109 "I don't know many recipes."

110 She nodded, peeling the skin off each of her potatoes before eating them. At one point the sari slipped to her shoulders. She readjusted it at once. "There is no need to cover your head," I said. "I don't mind. It doesn't matter here."

111 She kept it covered anyway.

112 I waited to get used to her, to her presence at my side, at my table and in my bed, but a week later we were still strangers. I still was not used to coming home to an apartment that smelled of steamed rice, and finding that the basin in the bathroom was always wiped clean, our two toothbrushes lying side by side, a cake of Pears soap residing in the soap dish. I was not used to the fragrance of the coconut oil she rubbed every other night into her scalp, or the delicate sound her bracelets made as she moved about the apartment. In the mornings she was always awake before I was. The first morning when I came into the kitchen she had heated up the leftovers and set a plate with a spoonful of salt on its edge, assuming I would eat rice for breakfast, as most Bengali husbands did. I told her cereal would do, and the next morning when I came into the kitchen she had already poured the cornflakes into my bowl. One morning she walked with me to MIT, where I gave her a short tour of the campus. On the way we stopped at a hardware store and I made a copy of the key, so that she could let herself into the apartment. The next morning before I left for work she asked me for a few dollars. I parted with them reluctantly, but I knew that this, too, was now normal. When I came home from work there was a potato peeler in the kitchen drawer, and a tablecloth on the table, and chicken curry made with fresh garlic and ginger on the stove. We did not have a television in those days. After dinner I read the newspaper, while Mala sat at the kitchen table, working on a cardigan for herself with more of the blue wool, or writing letters home.

113 At the end of our first week, on Friday, I suggested going out. Mala set down her knitting and disappeared into the bathroom. When she emerged I regretted the suggestion; she had put on a silk sari and extra bracelets, and coiled her hair with a flattering side part on top of her head. She was prepared as if for a party, or at the very least for the cinema, but I had no such destination in mind. The evening was balmy. We walked several blocks down Massachusetts Avenue, looking into the windows of restaurants and shops. Then, without thinking, I led her down the quiet street where for so many nights I had walked alone.

114 "This is where I lived before you came," I said, stopping at Mrs. Croft's chain-link fence.

115 "In such a big house?"

116 "I had a small room upstairs. At the back."

117 "Who else lives there?"

118 "A very old woman."

119 "With her family?"

120 "Alone."

121 "But who takes care of her?"

122 I opened the gate. "For the most part she takes care of herself."

123 I wondered if Mrs. Croft would remember me; I wondered if she had a new boarder to sit with her each evening. When I pressed the bell I expected the same long wait as that day of our first meeting, when I did not have a key. But this time the door was opened almost immediately, by Helen. Mrs. Croft was not sitting on the bench. The bench was gone.

124 "Hello there," Helen said, smiling with her bright pink lips at Mala. "Mother's in the parlor. Will you be visiting awhile?"

125 "As you wish, madame."

126 "Then I think I'll run to the store, if you don't mind. She had a little accident. We can't leave her alone these days, not even for a minute."

127 I locked the door after Helen and walked into the parlor. Mrs. Croft was lying flat on her back, her head on a peach-colored cushion, a thin white quilt spread over her body. Her hands were folded together on her chest. When she saw me she pointed at the sofa, and told me to sit down. I took my place as directed, but Mala wandered over to the piano and sat on the bench, which was now positioned where it belonged.

128 "I broke my hip!" Mrs. Croft announced, as if no time had passed.

129 "Oh dear, madame."

130 "I fell off the bench!"

131 "I am so sorry, madame."

132 "It was the middle of the night! Do you know what I did, boy?"

133 I shook my head.

134 "I called the police!"

135 She stared up at the ceiling and grinned sedately, exposing a crowded row of long gray teeth. "What do you say to that, boy?"

136 As stunned as I was, I knew what I had to say. With no hesitation at all, I cried out, "Splendid!"

137 Mala laughed then. Her voice was full of kindness, her eyes bright with amusement. I had never heard her laugh before, and it was loud enough so that Mrs. Croft heard, too. She turned to Mala and glared.

138 "Who is she, boy?"

139 "She is my wife, madame."

140 Mrs. Croft pressed her head at an angle against the cushion to get a better look. "Can you play the piano?"

141 "No, madame," Mala replied.

142 "Then stand up!"

143 Mala rose to her feet, adjusting the end of her sari over her head and holding it to her chest, and, for the first time since her arrival, I felt sympathy. I remembered my first days in London, learning how to take the Tube to Russell Square, riding an escalator for the first time, unable to understand that when the man cried "piper" it meant "paper," unable to decipher, for a whole year, that the conductor said "Mind the gap" as the train pulled away from each station. Like me, Mala had travelled far from home, not knowing where she was going, or what she would find, for no reason other than to be my wife. As strange as it seemed, I knew in my heart that one day her death would affect me, and stranger still, that mine would affect her. I wanted somehow to explain this to Mrs. Croft, who was still scrutinizing Mala from top to toe with what seemed to be placid disdain. I wondered if Mrs. Croft had ever seen a woman in a sari, with a dot painted on her forehead and bracelets stacked on her wrists. I wondered what she would object to. I wondered if she could see the red dye still vivid on Mala's feet, all but obscured by the bottom edge of her sari. At last Mrs. Croft declared, with the equal measures of disbelief and delight I knew well:

144 "She is a perfect lady!"

145 Now it was I who laughed. I did so quietly, and Mrs. Croft did not hear me. But Mala had heard, and, for the first time, we looked at each other and smiled.

146 I like to think of that moment in Mrs. Croft's parlor as the moment when the distance between Mala and me began to lessen. Although we were not yet fully in love, I like to think of the months that followed as a honeymoon of sorts. Together we explored the city and met other Bengalis, some of whom are still friends today. We discovered that a man named Bill sold fresh fish on Prospect Street, and that a shop in Harvard Square called Cardullo's sold bay leaves and cloves. In the evenings we walked to the Charles River to watch sailboats drift across the water, or had ice-cream cones in Harvard Yard. We bought a camera with which to document our life together, and I took pictures of her posing in front of the Prudential Building, so that she could send them to her parents. At night we kissed, shy at first but quickly bold, and discovered pleasure and solace in each other's arms. I told her about my voyage on the SS *Roma*, and about Finsbury Park and the YMCA, and my evenings on the bench with Mrs. Croft. When I told her stories about my mother, she wept. It was Mala who consoled me when, reading the *Globe* one evening, I came across Mrs. Croft's obituary. I had not thought of her in several months—by then

My Notes

decipher: translate
scrutinizing: inspecting
obscured: covered from view
solace: comfort

My Notes

those six weeks of the summer were already a remote **interlude** in my past—but when I learned of her death I was stricken, so much so that when Mala looked up from her knitting she found me staring at the wall, unable to speak. Mrs. Croft's was the first death I mourned in America, for hers was the first life I had admired; she had left this world at last, ancient and alone, never to return.

147 As for me, I have not strayed much farther. Mala and I live in a town about twenty miles from Boston, on a tree-lined street much like Mrs. Croft's, in a house we own, with a garden that saves us from buying tomatoes in summer, and room for guests. We are American citizens now, so that we can collect social security when it is time. Though we visit Calcutta every few years, and bring back more drawstring pajamas and Darjeeling tea, we have decided to grow old here. I work in a small college library. We have a son who attends Harvard University. Mala no longer drapes the end of her sari over her head, or weeps at night for her parents, but occasionally she weeps for our son. So we drive to Cambridge to visit him, or bring him home for a weekend, so that he can eat rice with us with his hands, and speak in Bengali, things we sometimes worry he will no longer do after we die.

148 Whenever we make that drive, I always take Massachusetts Avenue, in spite of the traffic. I barely recognize the buildings now, but each time I am there I return instantly to those six weeks as if they were only the other day, and I slow down and point to Mrs. Croft's street, saying to my son, Here was my first home in America, where I lived with a woman who was 103. "Remember?" Mala says, and smiles, amazed, as I am, that there was ever a time that we were strangers. My son always expresses his astonishment, not at Mrs. Croft's age but at how little I paid in rent, a fact nearly as **inconceivable** to him as a flag on the moon was to a woman born in 1866. In my son's eyes I see the ambition that had first hurled me across the world. In a few years he will graduate and pave his own way, alone and unprotected. But I remind myself that he has a father who is still living, a mother who is happy and strong. Whenever he is discouraged, I tell him that if I can survive on three continents, then there is no obstacle he cannot conquer. While the astronauts, heroes forever, spent mere hours on the moon, I have remained in this new world for nearly thirty years. I know that my achievement is quite ordinary. I am not the only man to seek his fortune far from home, and certainly I am not the first. Still, there are times I am **bewildered** by each mile I have travelled, each meal I have eaten, each person I have known, each room in which I have slept. As ordinary as it all appears, there are times when it is beyond my imagination.

INDEPENDENT READING LINK
Read and Connect
In this story, the narrator forms a close bond with someone who is different from him in many ways, but also shares some similarities. What kind of relationships does the main character in your independent reading have with the other characters? Are any of the relationships similar to this one? If not, how are they different, and what does that reveal about the character?

Making Observations
- What do you notice about the narrator's perspective?
- If you could speak to the narrator, what question would you like to ask him?

interlude: short period of time
inconceivable: unbelievable
bewildered: amazed

Returning to the Text

• Reread the short story to answer these text-dependent questions.
• Write any additional questions you have about the text in your Reader/Writer Notebook.

1. Why does the narrator feel sympathy for Mala?

_____

_____

_____

_____

2. After meeting Mala, Mrs. Croft states, "She is a perfect lady." What is the significance of the interaction that happens next between the narrator and Mala?

_____

_____

_____

_____

3. Reread the following sentence: "Mrs. Croft's was the first death I mourned in America, for, hers was the first life I had admired; she had left this world at last, ancient and alone, never to return." How does this sentence show the impact of Mrs. Croft on the narrator and the development of the theme?

_____

_____

_____

_____

4. How does the narrator's relationship with Mrs. Croft affect his marriage?

_____

_____

_____

_____

5. What is the overarching significance of the moon landing as a motif? How does the author come back to it at the end of the story?

_____

_____

_____

_____

Working from the Text

6. **Collaborative Conversation:** Reread the narrator's final statement: "Still, there are times I am bewildered by each mile I have travelled, each meal I have eaten, each person I have known, each room in which I have slept. As ordinary as it all appears, there are times when it is beyond my imagination." Turn and talk with a partner about how Lahiri contrasts the bewilderment of the narrator reflecting on his life with his statement that it is all "ordinary."

7. How are the differences between American and Indian culture expressed? How does the narrator's view about them change over time?

8. Turn to a partner and list as many themes as you can that relate to this story. Now look back to the text to see how cultural setting influences these themes. How does Lahiri handle these themes?

9. Now think about the plot. Plot typically follows similar steps across stories.

   • In the exposition, the characters and setting are introduced. On the following chart, label the exposition with details from the story.
   • The rising action is where suspense builds and the story's conflict becomes more complex. What is the rising action of this story? Label it on the chart.
   • The climax is the turning point in the story. Label it on the chart.
   • In the falling action, events after the climax lead to the story's resolution. Write it on the chart.
   • Finally, the denouement is the resolution or outcome of the story. Write a brief summary of the denouement on the chart.

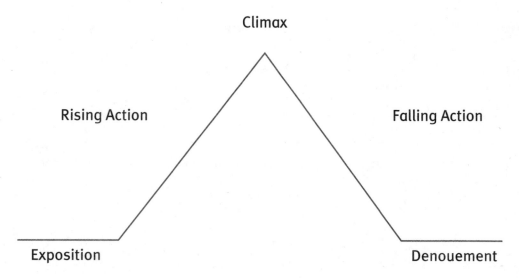

10. Consider the impact the cultural setting has on the plot. Discuss with your partner, making notes in the following chart.

Plot Structure	Impact of Cultural Setting
Exposition	
Rising Action	
Climax	
Falling Action	
Denouement	

☑ Check Your Understanding

The narrator says that surviving three continents is his own personal moon landing. Write a sentence in your Reader/Writer Notebook that describes your personal moon landing or what you hope it will be. Use language that reflects how your culture plays a part in that "moon landing" in the second part of your response.

📝 Writing Prompt: Literary Analysis

Write a paragraph that analyzes the author's use of characterization, plot, and cultural settings in developing themes in this short story. Be sure to:

- Begin with a topic sentence that responds to the prompt and states how the author develops themes through characterization, plot, culture, and settings.
- Provide textual evidence for support.
- Respond using literary terminology and in an appropriately formal register, tone, and voice.

A Journey in the Blink of an Eye

Learning Strategies

Chunking the Text
Discussion Groups
SIFT

My Notes

Learning Targets

- Analyze the use of literary devices, structure, and language to determine the meaning of a text.
- Analyze how historical and cultural settings influence the meaning of text.
- Write a narrative using literary techniques.
- Integrate ideas from multiple texts to build knowledge and vocabulary about how a person's perspectives on a situation may influence his or her emotions.

Preview

In this activity, you will read a short story, use strategies to analyze a text, and then write a narrative using some of the literary techniques studied.

As You Read

- Underline words and phrases that reveal the narrator's perspective. In the margin, write notes about your interpretation of the author's words.
- Circle unknown words and phrases. Try to determine the meaning of the words by using context clues, word parts, or a dictionary.

About the Author

Naguib Mahfouz (1911–2006) was an Egyptian writer of dozens of novels, hundreds of short stories, and more than two hundred articles. Maguib wrote about social issues, politics, and traditional Arab urban life. He combined influences from Eastern and Western cultures. When Mahfouz composed many of his stories, writing about subjects such as God and politics was against the law in Egypt. Some of his writing was so controversial that he received death threats, and in 1994, Mahfouz was stabbed by Islamic militants who were outraged by the treatment of religion in his novels. In 1988, Mahfouz became the first Arabic writer to win the Nobel Peace Prize in Literature and is considered Egypt's greatest modern novelist.

Short Story

Half a Day

by Naguib Mahfouz

1   I proceeded alongside my father, clutching his right hand, running to keep up with long strides he was taking. All my clothes were new: the shoes, the green school uniform, and the red tarboosh[1]. My delight in my new clothes, however, was not altogether **unmarred**, for this was no feast day but the day on which I was to be cast into school for the first time.

2   My mother stood at the window watching our progress, and I would turn toward her from time to time, as though appealing for help. We walked along a street lined with gardens; on both sides were extensive fields planted with crops, prickly pears, henna trees, and a few date palms.

3   "Why school?" I challenged my father openly. "I shall never do anything to annoy you."

4   "I'm not punishing you," he said, laughing. "School's not a punishment. It's the factory that makes useful men out of boys. Don't you want to be like your father and brothers?"

5   I was not convinced. I did not believe there was really any good to be had in tearing me away from the intimacy of my home and throwing me into this building that stood at the end of the road like some huge, high-walled fortress, exceedingly stern and grim.

6   When we arrived at the gate we could see the courtyard, vast and crammed full of boys and girls. "Go in by yourself," said my father, "and join them. Put a smile on your face and be a good example to others."

7   I hesitated and clung to his hand, but he gently pushed me from behind him. "Be a man," he said. "Today you truly begin life. You will find me waiting for you when it's time to leave."

8   I took a few steps, then stopped and looked but saw nothing. Then the faces of boys and girls came into view. I did not know a single one of them, and none of them knew me. I felt I was a stranger who had lost his way. But glances of curiosity were directed towards me, and one boy approached and asked, "Who brought you?"

9   "My father," I whispered.

10   "My father's dead," he said quite simply.

11   I did not know what to say. The gate was closed, letting out a pitiable screech. Some of the children burst into tears. The bell rang. A lady came along,

---

[1] A *tarboosh* is a felt cap, usually red with a tassel, that is worn by Muslim men either by itself or under a turban.

Unit 2 • Persuasion in Literature   219

KNOWLEDGE QUEST

Knowledge Question:

How does a person's perspective on a situation influence his or her emotions?

Across Activities 2.21 and 2.22, you will read two texts about difficult situations at school. While you read and build knowledge about the theme, think about your answer to the Knowledge Question.

My Notes

unmarred: undamaged

My Notes

followed by a group of men. The men began sorting us into ranks. We were formed into an **intricate** pattern in the great courtyard surrounded on three sides by high buildings of several floors; from each floor we were overlooked by a long balcony roofed in wood.

12 "This is your new home," said the woman. "Here too there are mothers and fathers. Here there is everything that is enjoyable and beneficial to knowledge and religion. Dry your tears and face life joyfully."

13 We submitted to the facts, and this **submission** brought a sort of contentment.

14 Living beings were drawn to other living beings, and from the first moments my heart made friends with such boys as were to be my friends and fell in love with such girls as I was to be in love with, so that it seemed my misgivings had had no basis. I had never imagined school would have this rich variety. We played all sorts of different games: swings, the vaulting horse[2], ball games. In the music room we chanted our first songs. We also had our first introduction to language. We saw a globe of the Earth, which revolved and showed the various continents and countries. We started learning the numbers. The story of the Creator of the universe was read to us, we were told of His present world and of His Hereafter, and we heard examples of what He said. We ate delicious food, took a little nap, and woke up to go on with friendship and love, play and learning.

15 As our path revealed itself to us, however, we did not find it as totally sweet and unclouded as we had presumed. Dust-laden winds and unexpected accidents came about suddenly, so we had to be watchful, at the ready, and very patient. It was not all a matter of playing and fooling around. Rivalries could bring about pain and hatred or give rise to fighting. And while the lady would sometimes smile, she would often scowl and scold. Even more frequently she would resort to physical punishment.

16 In addition, the time for changing one's mind was over and gone and there was no question of ever returning to the paradise of home. Nothing lay ahead of us but **exertion**, struggle, and perseverance. Those who were able took advantage of the opportunities for success and happiness that presented themselves amid the worries.

17 The bell rang announcing the passing of the day and the end of work. The **throngs** of children rushed toward the gate, which was opened again. I bade farewell to friends and sweethearts and passed through the gate. I peered around but found no trace of my father, who had promised to be there. I stepped aside to wait. When I had waited for a long time without avail, I decided to return home on my own. After I had taken a few steps, a middle-aged man passed by, and I realized at once that I knew him. He came toward me, smiling, and shook me by the hand, saying, "It's a long time since we last met—how are you?"

intricate: elaborate
submission: obedience or compliance
exertion: physical effort
throngs: large groups

---

[2] A *vaulting horse* is an apparatus for jumping over.

My Notes

18 With a nod of my head, I agreed with him and in turn asked, "And you, how are you?"

19 "As you can see, not all that good, the Almighty be praised!"

20 Again he shook me by the hand and went off. I proceeded a few steps, then came to a startled halt. Good Lord! Where was the street lined with gardens? Where had it disappeared to? When did all these vehicles invade it? And when did all these **hordes** of humanity come to rest upon its surface? How did these hills of refuse come to cover its sides? And where were the fields that bordered it? High buildings had taken over, the street surged with children, and disturbing noises shook the air. At various points stood **conjurers** showing off their tricks and making snakes appear from baskets. Then there was a band announcing the opening of a circus, with clowns and weight lifters walking in front. A line of trucks carrying central security troops crawled majestically by. The siren of a fire engine shrieked, and it was not clear how the vehicle would cleave its way to reach the blazing fire. A battle raged between a taxi driver and his passenger, while the passenger's wife called out for help and no one answered. Good God! I was in a daze. My head spun. I almost went crazy. How could all this have happened in half a day, between early morning and sunset? I would find the answer at home with my father. But where was my home? I could see only tall buildings and hordes of people. I hastened on to the crossroads between the gardens and Abu Khoda³. I had to cross Abu Khoda to reach my house, but the stream of cars would not let up. The fire engine's siren was shrieking at full pitch as it moved at a snail's pace, and I said to myself, "Let the fire take its pleasure in what it consumes." Extremely irritated, I wondered when I would be able to cross. I stood there a long time, until the young lad employed at the ironing shop on the comer came up to me. He stretched out his arm and said **gallantly**, "Grandpa, let me take you across."

🖉 Knowledge Quest

- What do you notice about the narrator's feelings in this story?
- How does the narrator's perspective change?

---

³ *Abu Khoda* is a street in Cairo.

hordes: large, overwhelming groups
conjurers: magicians
gallantly: politely

Returning to the Text

- Reread the short story to answer these text-dependent questions.
- Write any additional questions you have about the short story in your Reader/Writer Notebook.

1. **KQ** Reread paragraph 1. What does the narrator's choice of words tell you about his emotions on his first day of school?

2. **KQ** What is the meaning of the word *pitiable* in paragraph 11? Use context clues and a dictionary to help you decide. Then tell how the "pitiable screech" of the gate closing reflects the narrator's perspective on his situation.

3. **KQ** Reread paragraph 17. What does the narrator realize? How does his perspective change in response to what is happening now?

4. How does the narrator use the end of work in paragraph 17 as a symbol? After reading to the end of the story, what can readers interpret about the story's setting, including time and place?

5. At the end of the story, there is a revelation about the narrator. What is that revelation and how does it connect to the story's theme?

_____

_____

_____

_____

Working from the Text

6. In pairs, chunk the text into three sections, identifying the topic, determining the key details, and then drawing a conclusion from those details. Complete the following chart for each chunk.

Chunk 1 (Paragraphs 1–7)

Topic (Who or what is this section about?)	Key Details	What do we learn from these details?

Chunk 2 (Paragraphs 8–16)

Topic (Who or what is this section about?)	Key Details	What do we learn from these details?

Chunk 3 (Paragraphs 17–20)

Topic (Who or what is this section about?)	Key Details	What do we learn from these details?

7. A theme is a statement about life. To determine theme, consider how all of the elements of a text work together and what ideas about life these elements present. With a partner, brainstorm themes that are developed through the characters, plot, setting, and cultural revelations of this story. Choose one idea and write a thematic statement in your Reader/ Writer Notebook.

SIFT to Find Theme

The acronym SIFT stands for Symbol, Imagery, Figurative Language, and Tone or Theme. You can use this strategy to "sift" through the parts of a story to explore how a writer uses literary elements and stylistic techniques to convey meaning or theme. Identifying these elements is the key to helping you understand the author's perspective and commentary on life—the story's theme.

8. Go back through the story and look for examples of symbols, imagery, figurative language, and tone/theme. Complete the SIFT graphic organizer.

Literary Element	Text Detail	Effect or Meaning of Detail
Symbol		
Imagery		
Figurative Language		
Tone/Theme		

9. In the final paragraph, the author uses rhetorical questions. Turn back to the text, and identify the rhetorical questions. What effect do these questions have? Write your answer in 3–4 sentences.

☑ Focus on the Sentence

Use subordinating conjunctions to write two sentences about "Half a Day."

Though

_____

_____

While

_____

_____

📝 Writing Prompt: Literary

In "The Third and Final Continent" and "Half a Day," both narrators go on a kind of journey. Write a short narrative that centers around a journey, through either time or space. Be sure to:

- Engage and orient the reader by setting out a problem, situation, or observation, establishing one or multiple point(s) of view, and introducing a narrator and/or characters; create a smooth progression of experiences or events.

- Use narrative techniques, such as dialogue, pacing, description, reflection, and multiple plot lines, to develop experiences, events, and/or characters.

- Use a variety of techniques to sequence events so that they build on one another to create a coherent whole.

- Use precise words and phrases, telling details, and sensory language to convey a vivid picture of the experiences, events, setting, and/or characters.

- Provide a conclusion that follows from and reflects on what is experienced, observed, or resolved over the course of the narrative.

Learning Strategies

Graphic Organizer

My Notes

_____

_____

_____

_____

_____

_____

_____

_____

_____

_____

_____

_____

_____

_____

_____

_____

_____

_____

_____

_____

_____

_____

_____

_____

_____

_____

Learning Targets

- Analyze an author's development of characters and setting in an excerpt.
- Analyze how historical and cultural settings affect the meaning of text.
- Write a narrative using literary techniques to develop a complex character.
- Integrate ideas from multiple texts to build knowledge and vocabulary about how a person's perspectives on a situation may influence his or her emotions.

Preview

In this activity, you will read a novel excerpt to determine how the author develops characters through setting and then write a narrative developing a complex character.

About the Author

Mo Yan (b. 1955) is a Chinese writer of short stories, novels, and essays. He had little schooling, working as a cattle farmer beginning at age 11 and then joining the army, where his literary talent was discovered. Mo Yan is a pen name, meaning "don't speak" in Chinese. His work often combines older Chinese literature and oral traditions with contemporary social issues. He sometimes writes in a style of magical realism—a genre of fiction that presents the real world while incorporating elements of magic. However, the excerpt from *Change* in this activity is autobiographical. Mo Yan won the Nobel Prize in Literature in 2012.

As You Read

- Highlight details in the story that tell about characteristics of the narrator. Jot notes in the margin about the characteristics you notice.
- Circle unknown words and phrases. Try to determine the meaning of the words by using context clues, word parts, or a dictionary.

Novel Excerpt

from Change

by **Mo Yan**

1   By rights, I should be narrating events that occurred after 1979, but my thoughts keep carrying me back to that fall afternoon in 1969, when the sun shone brightly, the golden chrysanthemums were in full bloom and the wild geese were on their southern migration. When it reaches that point, I cannot be separated from my thoughts. My memories comprise the "me" of those days

KNOWLEDGE QUEST

Knowledge Question:

How does a person's perspective on a situation influence his or her emotions?

My Notes

a lonely boy who had been expelled from school but who was drawn to the clamour inside the schoolyard.

2   I had slipped in through the untended gate, my heart in my throat, and crossed the long, gloomy corridor to enter the school's central quadrangle, a yard surrounded by buildings. To the left stood an oak pole with a crossbar held on by wire, from which hung a rusty iron bell. Off to the left, two people were playing pingpong across a simple concrete table on a brick stand, watched eagerly by a crowd that was the source of the clamour. It was the school's fall break and, though most of the spectators were teachers, there were also a few of the pretty co-eds who made up the pingpong team and who were the pride of the school. They were in training for a countywide tournament as part of the October First National Day celebration, so instead of leaving school for the break, they'd stayed behind to practice. As children of the state farm Communist Party cadres, they were well developed and fair-skinned, thanks to a nutritious diet. They were also dressed in gaily coloured clothes, and one look told you that they were in a different class from us poor kids.

3   We looked up to them, but they wouldn't give us the time of day. One of the players was the math teacher, Liu Tianguang, a short man with a startlingly large mouth. We'd heard that he could fit his entire fist in that mouth, but none of us had ever seen him do it. An image of him up at the podium yawning grandly often flashed into my mind—that gaping mouth of his really was a sight to behold. One of his nicknames was "Hippo." Now, none of us had ever seen a real hippopotamus, which in Chinese is *hema*, and that sounds like *hama*, for toad, another creature with a large mouth, so it was only natural that we started calling him Toad Liu. That wasn't my invention but, after asking around, he decided it was. Saddling Toad Liu, son of a martyr and deputy chairman of the school's revolutionary committee, with a nickname was such a heinous offence that expelling me from school and kicking me off campus was both reasonable and inevitable.

4   I'd always been a diffident kid with lousy luck who was often too clever for his own good. For example, if I tried to brown-nose one of the teachers, they'd figure I was trying to get them into trouble. I can't count the number of times my mother said to me, "Son, you're the owl that ruins its reputation by announcing good news!" She was right. No one ever associated me with anything good or worthwhile. But let something bad happen, and all fingers pointed to me. People said I was rebellious, that the quality of my thinking was poor, that I hated school and my teachers. They could not have been more wrong! Truth is, I loved school and had special feelings toward my teacher, Big Mouth Liu. That's because I was a kid who was burdened with a large mouth. The boy in one of my stories—"Large Mouth"—was based on yours truly. Teacher Liu and I were, truth be told, fellow sufferers and ought to have enjoyed mutual understanding or, at the very least, mutual sympathy. If there was one person I'd never have given a nickname to, it was him. Anyone could have seen that. Anyone but him. He dragged me by the hair to his office, he kicked me to the floor and yelled: "You…you…you're like a blackbird mocking a black pig!"

clamour: noise
gaily: brightly
saddling: burdening
heinous: terrible

My Notes

5 I tried to explain but he wouldn't let me, and this is how a pretty good boy who was fond of Big Mouth Liu—me, Big Mouth Mo—was expelled from school. Despite the fact that Teacher Liu broadcast my shameful expulsion in front of everyone, I still liked my school so much that I looked for ways to sneak into the schoolyard, beat-up book bag slung over my shoulder, every single day.

6 At first, Teacher Liu personally demanded that I leave. When I refused, he dragged me out by my ear or hair. But I'd sneak right back in before he made it to his office. So then he told some of the bigger boys to do it for him, and, when I still wouldn't leave, they'd pick me up, carry me out beyond the gate and deposit me on the street. But before they were back in their classroom, I was in the schoolyard again, crouching in a corner by the wall, shrunk into myself, both to keep from being spotted and to get a little sympathy as I listened to the cheerful voices and watched the kids jump and play. Pingpong was my favourite. I could watch that till I lost track of where I was, often with tears in my eyes or biting down on my fist. After a while, they gave up trying to drive me away.

⬦ Knowledge Quest
- What are your initial thoughts about the narrator's perspective?
- What surprises you about the narrator's emotions?

Returning to the Text

- Reread the short story to answer these text-dependent questions.
- Write any additional questions you have about the short story in your Reader/Writer Notebook.

1. KQ What does the word *drawn* mean in paragraph 1? Use context clues and a dictionary to help you decide. Then tell how the narrator feels drawn.

   _____

   _____

   _____

   _____

2. What standing does Liu Tianguang hold? How does the reader know?

   _____

   _____

   _____

   _____

3. KQ What is the narrator's perspective on why he was expelled?

   _____

   _____

   _____

   _____

4. KQ Think about the narrators from "Half a Day" and *Change*. What similarities do you see in the way their perspectives on school color their emotional responses to being there?

   _____

   _____

   _____

   _____

KNOWLEDGE QUEST

You can continue to build your knowledge about how a person's perspective on a situation influences his or her emotions by reading related fiction at ZINC Reading Labs. Select the **fiction** filters and type keywords such as *perspective* or *emotions* in the **Search all ZINC articles** field.

 ZINC

 **Knowledge Quest**

Now that you have read "Half a Day" and *Change*, think about what you have learned about how a person's perspective on a situation influences his or her emotions. Then think of a time when you perceived something negatively and found out later your perception was wrong. How did you feel before and after your realization? How might you save yourself from negative feelings in the future? Discuss your ideas with a partner. Then work together to devise a plan of approach for new situations you feel sad, anxious, or angry about.

Working from the Text

5. The author uses both direct and indirect characterization in the story.

  - **Direct characterization** includes details that the narrator states about the characters' personalities.
  - **Indirect characterization** includes details that the narrator reveals about the characters through their speech, thoughts, interactions, behavior, and appearance.
  - Return to the text to determine two instances of direct characterization from the first paragraph and write them in the space provided.

    A.

    B.

6. Complete the following graphic organizer to analyze Mo Yan's direct and indirect characterization of the narrator.

Characterization of the Narrator in *Change*	
Physical Appearance: What does the author tell us about the narrator's appearance?	
Actions: What does the narrator do that reveals things about his personality?	
Self-Identity: How does the narrator describe himself?	
Relationships: What do other people think of the narrator?	

7. How do others' beliefs about the narrator compare or contrast with what he believes about himself? With a partner, fill in the following chart, then discuss how the author uses details to build a complex character.

What Other Characters Believe About the Narrator	What the Narrator States About Himself

8. Both the narrator's mother and teacher use proverbs to describe the narrator. Turn to a partner and discuss what you think each these proverbs might mean. What effect does the use of proverbs have on the reader? Discuss as partners, then share as a whole group.

   • "Son, you're the owl that ruins its reputation by announcing good news!"
   • "[Y]ou're like a blackbird mocking a black pig!"

9. How does the author convey his cultural perspective through his writing?

☑ Check Your Understanding

The excerpt from *Change* and "Half a Day" both describe a young boy going to school. How are these narrators alike and different?

📝 Writing Prompt: Literary

Write a short story (2–4 paragraphs) that builds a complex character. You may choose to use a memorable person you have met in real life as inspiration for your main character. Remember to use characterization, setting, and other literary devices to make your character complex but believable. Be sure to:

• Consider your audience when organizing your narrative.
• Use setting, plot events, and characterization to make your character believable.
• Develop your theme with details, examples, and commentary.

Creating a Narrative

Learning Strategies

Brainstorming
Drafting

Learning Targets

- Plan to write an original short story by brainstorming and conducting research.
- Develop a draft of the beginning of the short story.
- Offer constructive feedback to help group members revise drafts for clarity, development, organization, and effectiveness.

Preview

In this activity, you will conduct research and begin drafting your Embedded Assessment, while working with writing groups.

Brainstorm

1. As you've seen in the stories you've read in this unit, cultural and historical setting can impact characters, plot, and language. To ground your story in its context, you'll need to do some research on the time and location for your story. Record your choice of setting in the space that follows, and write five questions about your setting.

Research

2. Consult print or digital resources to locate the answers to your questions. Record what you learn in the following graphic organizer, and then think about how the answers might impact your story.

Question	Answer	Possible Impact on Story

Outline the Plot

3. Next, outline the plot of your story, deciding who the characters are and what happens. Use the following graphic organizer to outline your plot.

What is the setting of your story?	
Who are the characters in your story? Briefly describe each.	
Summarize the conflict, climax, and resolution.	
What major events occur?	
Based on your list of events, order the scenes in a condensed outline.	

Begin Writing the Narrative

4. Using your graphic and outline, start to draft the beginning of your narrative. Here are a few pointers to keep in mind as you begin writing:

- Use your outline to develop a focused, structured, and coherent draft.
- Use literary elements inspired by those you have read in the previous activities, such as characterization and setting, to develop the theme.

You may find as you begin writing that you need to conduct additional research about the time period or location you have chosen.

☑ Check Your Understanding

Compare and contrast your draft with the outline you created in this activity. Check whether your draft includes well-developed setting, characters, and story elements. Do you need additional research to revise your draft? List two items for improvement in your Reader/Writer Notebook.

Check in with a Peer

Share with a partner the progress you have made so far, and the challenges you have run up against. Then, listen as your partner describes his or her experience. Share any breakthroughs you have had, and give your partner advice on how to solve any problems he or she may be experiencing. You may also use this opportunity to ask your partner questions and request advice.

INDEPENDENT READING LINK

Read and Research

Where is the text you are reading set, and in what time period does it take place? Conduct research that will illuminate this context for you. Develop three questions about the setting, and use print or digital resources to learn more. How does this new knowledge help you deepen your understanding of the text?

My Notes

Learning Targets

- Analyze the use of sensory language to determine the meaning of a text.
- Analyze how historical and cultural settings affect the meaning of a text.
- Write a narrative using sensory language.

Preview

In this activity, you will read a short story and determine how the author uses sensory language to reveal mood, tone, and voice.

About the Author

Jamaica Kincaid (b. 1949) is a Caribbean American author. Born Elaine Potter Richardson on the island of Antigua, she moved to New York City at age 16, working first as a nanny and then pursuing a college education. As a young adult, she became a staff writer for *The New Yorker* and changed her name to Jamaica Kincaid due to family disapproval of her writing career. Many of her stories, including *Annie John*, are somewhat autobiographical, but she cautions her readers that although her writing is influenced by her experiences, her works are fiction.

As You Read

- Underline words that reveal mood and tone, including any sensory language.
- Circle unknown words and phrases. Try to determine the meaning of the words by using context clues, word parts, or a dictionary.

Novel Excerpt

from # Annie John

by **Jamaica Kincaid**

1   My heart now beat fast, and no matter how hard I tried, I couldn't keep my mouth from falling open and my nostrils from spreading to the ends of my face. My old fear of slipping between the boards of the jetty and falling into the dark-green water where the dark-green eels lived came over me. When my father's stomach started to go bad, the doctor had recommended a walk every evening right after he ate his dinner. Sometimes he would take me with him. When he took me with him, we usually went to the jetty, and there he would s and talk to the night watchman about cricket[1] or some other thing that didn't interest me, because it was not personal; they didn't talk about their wives, or

---

[1] *Cricket* is a British bat-and-ball game.

their children, or their parents, or about any of their likes and dislikes. They talked about things in such a strange way, and I didn't see what they found funny, but sometimes they made each other laugh so much that their guffaws would bound out to sea and send back an echo. I was always sorry when we got to the jetty and saw that the night watchman on duty was the one he enjoyed speaking to; it was like being locked up in a book filled with numbers and diagrams and what-ifs. For the thing about not being able to understand and enjoy what they were saying was I had nothing to take my mind off my fear of slipping in between the boards of the jetty.

2   Now, too, I had nothing to take my mind off what was happening to me. My mother and my father—I was leaving them forever. My home on an island—I was leaving it forever. What to make of everything? I felt a familiar hollow space inside. I felt I was being held down against my will. I felt I was burning up from head to toe. I felt that someone was tearing me up into little pieces and soon I would be able to see all the little pieces as they floated out into nothing in the deep blue sea. I didn't know whether to laugh or cry. I could see that it would be better not to think too clearly about any one thing. The launch was being made ready to take me, along with some other passengers, out to the ship that was anchored in the sea. My father paid our fares, and we joined a line of people waiting to board. My mother checked my bag to make sure that I had my passport, the money she had given me, and a sheet of paper placed between some pages in my Bible on which were written the names of the relatives—people I had not known existed—with whom I would live in England. Across from the jetty was a wharf, and some stevedores were loading and unloading barges. I don't know why seeing that struck me so, but suddenly a wave of strong feeling came over me, and my heart swelled with a great gladness as the words "I shall never see this again" spilled out inside me. But then, just as quickly, my heart shriveled up and the words "I shall never see this again" stabbed at me. I don't know what stopped me from falling in a heap at my parents' feet.

3   When we were all on board, the launch headed out to sea. Away from the jetty, the water became the customary blue, and the launch left a wide path in it that looked like a road. I passed by sounds and smells that were so familiar that I had long ago stopped paying any attention to them. But now here they were, and the ever-present "I shall never see this again" bobbed up and down inside me. There was the sound of the seagull diving down into the water and coming up with something silverish in its mouth. There was the smell of the sea and the sight of small pieces of rubbish floating around in it. There were boats filled with fishermen coming in early. There was the sound of their voices as they shouted greetings to each other. There was the hot sun, there was the blue sea, there was the blue sky. Not very far away, there was the white sand of the shore, with the run-down houses all crowded in next to each other, for in some places only poor people lived near the shore. I was seated in the launch between my parents, and when I realized that I was gripping their hands tightly I glanced quickly to see if they were looking at me with scorn, for I felt sure that they must have known of my never-see-this-again feelings. But instead

guffaws: hearty laughter
wharf: area where a ship loads and unloads
stevedores: people who load or unload ships
rubbish: trash

my father kissed me on the forehead and my mother kissed me on the mouth, and they both gave over their hands to me, so that I could grip them as much as I wanted. I was on the verge of feeling that it had all been a mistake, but I remembered that I wasn't a child anymore, and that now when I made up my mind about something I had to see it through. At that moment, we came to the ship, and that was that.

Making Observations

- What do you notice about the event the narrator flashes back to in the first paragraph?
- Why must the narrator leave her home?

Returning to the Text

- Reread the short story to answer these text-dependent questions.
- Write any additional questions you have about the text in your Reader/Writer Notebook.

1. What does the narrator remember about coming to the jetty as a girl? How do her feelings about the jetty then compare or contrast with her feelings in the present?

_____

_____

_____

_____

2. Based on the words you underlined, how does the narrator feel about leaving her home? What details in the text reveal this tone?

_____

_____

_____

_____

3. What theme can be found in the excerpt? How does the author develop this theme?

_____

_____

_____

_____

4. In paragraph 3, the author repeats the phrase "There was/there were." What does this reveal about the narrator? What is conveyed to the reader with this literary device?

_____

_____

_____

_____

5. Why does the narrator determine that despite her anxiety, she must make the journey? What do her words reveal about this decision?

_____

_____

_____

_____

Working from the Text

6. In this story, Annie is a young woman about to embark on a journey. How does the first paragraph establish the narrator's voice? What do you know about the narrator after this paragraph?

7. Sensory language is the use of details that incorporate the five senses—sight, smell, sound, touch, and taste. Authors frequently use sensory language to help the reader visualize the text and form a deeper connection with it. Returning to your highlighted text, complete the following graphic organizer with a partner, using specific examples of how the author uses sensory language to help the reader better understand or experience the text.

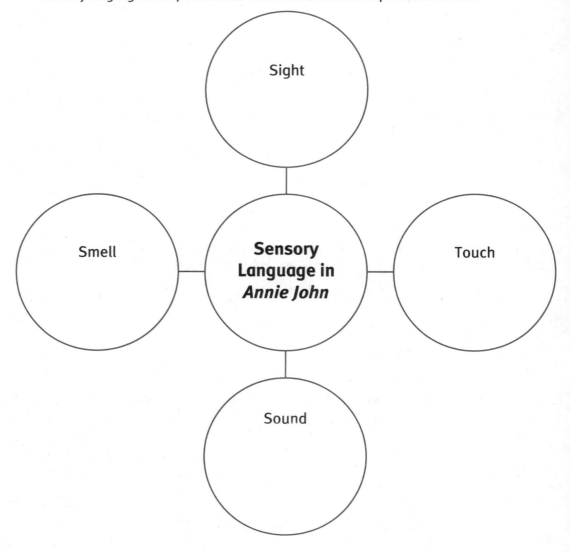

8. Sensory language often helps the reader decipher the voice, tone, and mood of the text. Complete the chart, explaining how each example of sensory language contributes to the voice, tone, and/or mood of the text. You may find that the tone and mood are often intertwined. Note how the sensory language helps the reader both understand the author's attitude and experience a similar mood.

- Voice is the character's speech and thought patterns.
- Tone is how the author feels toward the subject.
- Mood is how the reader feels about the subject or the general feeling created by the text.

Sensory Language	Voice	Tone	Mood

☑ **Check Your Understanding**

What have you learned from Kincaid about the value of using sensory language in writing? Write a short response in your Reader/Writer Notebook.

9. **Collaborative Conversation:** In each of the short stories you've read in this unit, the narrator goes on some kind of journey. How does this narrator feel about her trip? How does she feel about her starting point, and her destination? Compare and contrast this with the characters in the other stories you have read.

10. Continue working on the draft you started in Activity 2.23. Be sure to incorporate sensory details to help the reader visualize your scene, and to establish voice.

Writing a Short Story

 ## ASSIGNMENT

Write an original short story that conveys a specific cultural perspective or historical moment. Conduct research into the time period and setting that you choose in order to convey the setting accurately.

Prewriting and Planning: Take time to review your plan for writing.	■ Is there anything else you wish to include that is not in your outline? ■ Do you need to do any further research?
Drafting: Write your short story using genre characteristics.	■ How will you complete your first draft, using the research you have done? ■ How will you use descriptive sensory details to build your setting and develop your characters? ■ How will you write a satisfying conclusion to your story?
Revising: Look for places to make changes in your writing to improve characterization, setting, plot, and theme.	■ How will you revise to ensure that your story follows a logical order? ■ How will you add sensory or figurative details that improve your characterization? ■ How can you experiment with a variety of syntax and sentence structures?
Editing and Publishing: Confirm that your draft is ready to share with an audience.	■ How will you proofread and edit your essay for proper conventions of standard English capitalization, punctuation, spelling, grammar, and usage? ■ What tools are available for you to further polish and refine your work, such as a dictionary, thesaurus, spell-check, or grammar check? ■ How can the Scoring Guide help you evaluate how well you have met the requirements of the assignment?

Reflection

What have you learned about the writing process? Why is it important to both draft and revise? What did you learn from peer revisions, as both a reader and a writer?

SCORING GUIDE

Scoring Criteria	Exemplary	Proficient	Emerging	Incomplete
Ideas	The narrative • engages the reader through interesting lead-in and details that clearly establish a historical or cultural perspective • uses narrative techniques (dialogue, pacing, description) to develop experiences and characters • provides a conclusion that resolves issues and draws the story to a close.	The narrative • describes an incident and orients the reader to a historical or cultural perspective • uses narrative techniques effectively to develop characters and experiences • provides a clear conclusion to the story.	The narrative • does not describe a cultural perspective or lacks essential details to orient the reader • includes few narrative techniques to develop characters • provides an unsatisfying conclusion that does not resolve the story.	The narrative • does not contain essential details to establish a cultural perspective • does not effectively use narrative techniques to develop the story • does not provide a conclusion.
Structure	The narrative • uses genre characteristics of a short story with well-sequenced events • clearly orients the reader and uses effective transitions to link ideas and events • demonstrates a consistent point of view.	The narrative • uses genre characteristics of a short story and includes a sequence of events • orients the reader and uses transitions to create a coherent whole • uses a mostly consistent point of view.	The narrative • may use some of the genre characteristics of a short story • presents disconnected events and limited coherence • contains a point of view that is not appropriate for the focus of the narrative.	The narrative • does not use genre characteristics of a short story • includes few if any events and no coherence • contains inconsistent and confusing points of view.
Use of Language	The narrative • purposefully uses descriptive language, telling details, and vivid imagery • uses meaningful dialogue when appropriate to advance the narrative • demonstrates error-free spelling and use of standard English conventions.	The narrative • uses descriptive language and telling details • uses direct and/or indirect dialogue when appropriate • demonstrates general command of conventions and spelling; minor errors do not interfere with meaning.	The narrative • uses limited descriptive language or details • contains little or no dialogue • demonstrates limited command of conventions and spelling; errors interfere with meaning.	The narrative • uses no descriptive language or details • contains no effective use of dialogue • contains numerous errors in grammar and conventions that interfere with meaning.

VISUAL PROMPT
In a choir, individual voices come together to create a complex melody. What are some other examples of synthesis you can think of from your own life?

VOICE IN SYNTHESIS

Students in school as well as out of school are "persons" under our Constitution. They are possessed of fundamental rights which the State must respect, just as they themselves must respect their obligations to the State. In our system, students may not be regarded as closed-circuit recipients of only that which the State chooses to communicate . . . Students are entitled to freedom of expression of their views.

—from U.S. Supreme Court Opinion: *Tinker v. Des Moines*

ACTIVITY	CONTENTS	

Texts not included in these materials.

My Independent Reading List

My Notes

Learning Targets

- Make connections between personal experiences and ideas from society and texts.
- Select texts and create a plan for reading independently.

Preview

In this activity, you will explore the essential questions and tasks in Unit 3 and plan your independent reading.

About the Unit

In this unit, you will learn to synthesize—that is, to combine information from multiple sources to write written arguments on current issues. Learning to synthesize allows you to not only restate information from sources but also to evaluate them individually and in comparison and contrast to one another. As you analyze sources and prepare to write your own arguments, you will discover how authors use language, structure, and evidence to convince their audiences.

Essential Questions

Based on your current knowledge, respond to the following questions.

1. What is the relationship between individual freedom and social responsibility

2. What does it mean to have a voice?

3. How does one enter into an ongoing discussion about a subject?

🔲 Planning Independent Reading

The focus of this unit is synthesizing research texts, and you will have the opportunity to practice synthesizing information from multiple texts in class. During your Independent Reading, you have the chance to read other kinds of texts from which to synthesize, including real stories (nonfiction) and imagined ones (fiction). For example, you may choose to read a memoir about a person's struggles with disease or addiction. Then, you may also choose to read an article in a medical or psychological journal about such issues. Develop an Independent Reading Plan, including your reading goals, in your Reader/Writer Notebook.

Stepping into the Parlor

Read this passage from American literary critic Kenneth Burke (1897–1993). As you read, visualize the scene taking place in the imaginary parlor.

Imagine that you enter a parlor. You come late. When you arrive, others have long preceded you, and they are engaged in a heated discussion, a discussion too heated for them to pause and tell you exactly what it is about. In fact, the discussion had already begun long before any of them got there, so that no one present is qualified to retrace for you all the steps that had gone before. You listen for a while, until you decide that you have caught the **tenor** of the argument; then you put in your oar. Someone answers; you answer him; another comes to your defense; another aligns himself against you, to either the embarrassment or gratification of your opponent, depending upon the quality of your ally's assistance. However, the discussion is interminable. The hour grows late, you must depart. And you do depart, with the discussion still vigorously in progress.

In small groups describe what you visualize as you read. Identify words or phrases that are unknown or difficult to understand, and try to define these words in context. Answer the following questions in writing.

4. What does the author mean by the phrase "the tenor of the argument"?

5. What is symbolized by the notion of "[putting] in your oar"?

6. According to Burke, how do you know when it's the right time to enter a conversation?

☑ Check Your Understanding

Think of a time when you entered the middle of a discussion. How did you feel? What strategies did you use to join the conversation? Freewrite for two minutes, applying these experiences to the excerpt from Burke.

ACADEMIC

A speaker's or writer's words carry a **tenor**. The term *tenor* characterizes the intent, tone, or attitude conveyed by the words. When communicating with an audience, it's important to strike the appropriate tenor for the message and the situation.

My Notes

Learning Targets
- Plan and develop an organized draft of a written argument.
- Interact with sources from various viewpoints by taking notes.
- Synthesize information to create a written argument.

Preview

In this activity, you will respond to an opinion prompt in writing, exchange papers, share your responses with at least three other students, and then synthesize responses to create a new piece of writing.

Setting the Stage for a Conversation on Paper

Kenneth Burke used the "Unending Conversation" as a metaphor. Burke sought to give an example of what it's like to contribute to an ongoing academic argument. To enter the parlor as a writer, you must first read what others have said about the topic. Then you must thoughtfully acknowledge others' points of view before contributing your own voice to continue the conversation.

You will now join the "Unending Conversation" by having a conversation on paper. First read and respond to the following prompt.

School officials can place restrictions on how students express themselves through their clothing. Despite most schools having explicit rules regarding dress, every year court cases arise from students claiming that they were unfairly disciplined for what school officials saw as inappropriate or potentially disruptive clothing statements.

1. Write one or two paragraphs stating and supporting your response to the following question:

In your opinion, how much control should a school exercise over students' freedom to express themselves through clothing?

Keep in mind that your response will be shared with classmates. Be mindful of grammar and conventions so that your message is expressed as clearly as possible.

Organizing a Conversation on Paper

2. Proofread your writing, and, if needed, revise your response so it is ready to be shared with classmates.

3. Your teacher will form small groups of three or four students and explain how to perform the next task. As you read other students' writing, you will take notes on their positions, using both summaries and direct quotations. Review the definitions and uses of summaries and quotations that follow.

Summaries are short overviews of source material. You should summarize to:

- establish background.
- describe knowledge from multiple sources.
- determine the main idea of a single source.

Quotations are the exact words an author uses. Quotations must always be punctuated with quotation marks and be cited, crediting the author. You should use direct quotations to:

- strongly support your argument with another author's words.
- disagree with another author.
- compare and contrast points of view.
- discuss research that supports your position.
- highlight powerful text.

4. Exchange papers with another student in your small group. Take notes as you read your classmate's writing. Use the following graphic organizer to organize the opinions of your classmates. Continue to exchange papers with group members until all members have had an opportunity to read and take notes on all other group members' pieces.

Writer's Name	Summary	Direct Quotation	My Reaction

My Notes

Collecting and Organizing Ideas

5. Reconsider your initial opinion. After taking notes, you now have two documents to consider when writing a new response to the original prompt. Think back to the parlor metaphor. How can you, as the writer, synthesize these separate but related pieces of writing and get them to talk to one another for the purpose of refining your own opinion on this topic?

6. Use your notes and consider the following questions to organize your response:

- As you read through your notes, what ideas do you see repeated by several writers?
- Which writers are essentially saying the same thing?
- Which writers take a different direction?
- What is an idea you have not previously considered?
- Who or what point do you agree with?
- Who or what point do you disagree with?
- What do you have to add to the conversation?
- Most important, where are you going to put your oar in and make your point among the current of all of the other voices?

Writing an Argument

Reread the prompt, your original writing, and the notes on your classmates' opinions. After reading other students' responses, develop a new piece of writing that reflects your thinking about the same topic in relation to the opinions of others. Work independently to write a fresh two-paragraph **synthesis** asserting a claim and incorporating at least two of your classmates' voices as presented in their pieces.

- First, write an introduction stating the topic, your opinion, and two sides of the issue.
- Next, complete a two- to three-paragraph synthesis response. You may use this frame as a guide for writing synthesis paragraphs.

When it comes to the topic of _____, most

of us will readily agree that _____. Where

this argument usually ends, however, is on the question of

_____. While some are convinced

that _____, others are convinced that

_____.

- Remember that effective arguments contain claims, evidence, and reasoning. You may assert a complex claim by qualifying your opinion. In addition, you may agree with others' opinions but also make a case for including an exception or a **caveat**.
- Remember to use quotations or paraphrases that reinforce your claim.

VOCABULARY

ACADEMIC

When researching a topic, it is important to use the skill of **synthesis**. By reading a variety of texts and points of view on a topic, the researcher is able to combine this information to write a synthesis stating his or her own educated opinion regarding the subject.

A **caveat** is a cautionary detail or warning. It may be used to give an exception to a broader rule.

Writing Prompt: Argumentative

In your opinion, how much control should a school exercise over the way students dress? Should students have the freedom to express themselves through clothing? Write an argumentative paragraph that expresses your opinion and synthesizes information from multiple sources. Be sure to:

- Assert a claim that explains the extent to which school officials should restrict students' clothing choices.
- Explain how your claim is either supported by others or in conflict with others.
- Include at least one summary statement and one direct quotation.
- Cite the sources you are referencing by using the last names of fellow students.

Writing Checklist

You may use this rubric to evaluate your writing:

_____ Writer's voice is evident, and other sources serve as support or as points to refute.

_____ At least two different sources are cited.

_____ Writing is coherent and shows reasoning that supports a central claim.

_____ Each new point is introduced by a controlling idea statement.

_____ Writing uses a combination of summarization and direct quotations.

_____ Direct quotations are enclosed within quotation marks and are accurate (word-for-word).

_____ Quotations are integrated into the text (introduced by a phrase and followed by analysis).

_____ Citations of sources are either integrated into the sentence or contained in parentheses following the cited words or ideas (by writer's last name).

_____ Draft has been proofread and edited for errors.

☑ Check Your Understanding

When writing your argumentative text, how did you incorporate others' ideas? Why is it important to give credit to the original author?

Reading a Court Case on Freedom of Speech

INDEPENDENT READING LINK

Read and Respond

In this activity, you will make a connection between two texts. Think about the connections you are making with your independent text choices. Write a brief statement in your Reader/Writer Notebook describing a connection you've made between at least two texts from your independent reading and how the connection changes or develops your understanding of each text.

Learning Targets

- Paraphrase and summarize texts, determining the author's position and view.
- Acquire and use content vocabulary and academic vocabulary.

Preview

In this activity, you will read an excerpt of the First Amendment in order to deepen your understanding of freedom of speech. Then you will read a part of a Supreme Court case related to the First Amendment and analyze the meaning of words used in context to understand one justice's position on the case.

Defining Words with Multiple Meanings

Many words have multiple meanings. The precise meaning of the word may be different from one context to another.

1. Write the definitions for the words *opinion*, *right*, and *justice* at the top of a sheet of paper, without consulting any references. If you know more than one definition for each word, write the first definition that comes to mind. Then read the following sentences, which use these words in different contexts.

Word	Sentence	Context-Specific Definition
A: opinion	And the problem for the government in the months ahead is that it is not in complete control of events that may shift public **opinion**. (BBC, March 16, 2015)	
B: opinion	Queen Elizabeth has steadfastly kept her **opinions** to herself during her 63-year reign. (*Newsweek*, March 26, 2015)	
C: opinion	Writing the court's main **opinion**, Justice Anthony Kennedy said the federal judge was wrong when he blocked the transfer. (Reuters, April 28, 2010)	
A: right	But, after five years, I feel like it is now the **right** time for me to leave the band. (BBC, March 26, 2015)	
B: right	Guilt is the discomfort that comes from recognizing that you've done something wrong or failed to do something **right**. (*The New Yorker*, March 26, 2015)	
C: right	Eliminating fraternities or allowing women to join is not an option at public universities where students have the First Amendment **right** to associate. (*Time*, March 26, 2015)	

Word	Sentence	Context-Specific Definition
A: justice	It's a play in which light and dark fight to the death without the insurance of poetic **justice**. (*Los Angeles Times*, August 13, 2014)	
B: justice	Dr. King's funeral message served as a sobering call for **justice**. (*While the World Watched: A Birmingham Bombing Survivor Comes of Age during the Civil Rights Movement*, 2011)	
C: justice	And **Justice** Scalia, who dominates Supreme Court arguments with probing questions laced with sarcasm, gave a fine performance. (*The New York Times*, March 11, 2015)	

2. After your teacher assigns you the letter A, B, or C, reread the sentences that correspond with your assigned letter. Next, write in the graphic organizer new definitions for *opinion*, *right*, and *justice* based on the meaning of each word within your assigned sentences' specific contexts.

3. Complete a think-pair-share with a partner, answering these questions:

* How do the definitions in the graphic organizer compare and contrast with your original out-of-context definitions?
* How does each word's definition change depending on the sentence?
* What context clues lead you to the new definitions?

As You Read

* Identify and underline the central claim of the amendment.
* Circle unknown words and phrases. Try to determine the meaning of the words by using context clues, word parts, or a dictionary.

About the Document

The First Amendment is an amendment, or addition, to the U.S. Constitution that protects basic freedoms in the United States. It was the first part of the Bill of Rights added to the Constitution on December 15, 1791.

Legal Document

Amendment I

Congress shall make no law respecting an establishment of religion, or prohibiting the free exercise thereof; or abridging the freedom of speech, or of the press; or the right of the people peaceably to assemble, and to petition the government for a redress of grievances.

redress: remedy for a wrongdoing

My Notes

Making Observations
- How is the word *right* defined in this piece of text?
- What does this amendment make you think of?

Returning to the Text
- Reread the legal document to answer these questions.
- Write any additional questions you have about the text in your Reader/Writer Notebook.

4. Notice that the First Amendment is one sentence. Who is the subject of the sentence?

_____

_____

_____

5. What do the words "prohibit" and "abridge" mean? According to the First Amendment, what can Congress *not* prohibit or abridge?

_____

_____

_____

_____

6. The First Amendment limits Congress's ability to exercise power over six different rights. What are the six rights?

_____

_____

_____

_____

☑ Check Your Understanding
Before moving on to read about the First Amendment in action, briefly summarize the First Amendment in your own words.

About the Document

The following excerpt is from a 1969 Supreme Court decision, *Tinker v. Des Moines*. Secondary school students in Des Moines, Iowa, wore black armbands to school to protest U.S. involvement in the Vietnam War (1954–1975)—a military conflict between communist North Vietnam and South Vietnam and its ally the United States. People in the United States protested the war due to its length, the high death count, and the lack of a clear and achievable goal. When the students were asked by school administrators to remove the armbands, they refused and were suspended from school. Three of the students and their parents sued the school district for a violation of First Amendment rights, but the court dismissed their complaint. The case was eventually heard by the Supreme Court in 1969.

Mary Beth Tinker and her brother, John Tinker, in 1969

☑ Focus on the Sentence

Reread About the Document and then complete the following chart by answering the reporter's questions: *Who? What? When? Where?* and *Why?* Finally, use your answers to the questions to help you write a one-sentence summary of what you read.

Who? _____

What? _____

When? _____

Where? _____

Why? _____

Summary: _____

_____

As You Read

- Underline the central idea in the text and highlight evidence used to support it.
- Circle unknown words and phrases. Try to determine the meaning of the words by using context clues, word parts, or a dictionary.

My Notes

_____

_____

_____

_____

_____

_____

_____

_____

_____

_____

_____

_____

_____

_____

_____

_____

_____

_____

_____

_____

_____

_____

_____

_____

_____

_____

_____

_____

_____

_____

akin: like

enclaves: communities

totalitarianism: centralized
government where a dictator
requires complete loyalty to the
government with few citizen
rights

Supreme Court Opinion

Tinker v. Des Moines

(Excerpt 1)

1   Mr. Justice Fortas delivered the opinion of the Court.

2   The District Court recognized that the wearing of an armband for the purpose of expressing certain views is the type of symbolic act that is within the Free Speech Clause of the First Amendment. See West Virginia v. Barnette, 319 U.S. 624 (1943); Stromberg v. California, 283 U.S. 359 (1931). Cf. Thornhill v. Alabama, 310 U.S. 88 (1940); Edwards v. South Carolina, 372 U.S. 229 (1963); Brown v. Louisiana, 383 U.S. 131 (1966). As we shall discuss, the wearing of armbands in the circumstances of this case was entirely divorced from actually or potentially disruptive conduct by those participating in it. It was closely **akin** to "pure speech" which, we have repeatedly held, is entitled to comprehensive protection under the First Amendment. Cf. Cox v. Louisiana, 379 U.S. 536, 555 (1965); Adderley v. Florida, 385 U.S. 39 (1966). First Amendment rights, applied in light of the special characteristics of the school environment, are available to teachers and students. It can hardly be argued that either students or teachers shed their constitutional rights to freedom of speech or expression at the schoolhouse gate…

3   In our system, state-operated schools may not be **enclaves** of **totalitarianism**. School officials do not possess absolute authority over their students. Students in school as well as out of school are "persons" under our Constitution. They are possessed of fundamental rights which the State must respect, just as they themselves must respect their obligations to the State. In our system, students may not be regarded as closed-circuit recipients of only that which the State chooses to communicate. They may not be confined to the expression of those sentiments that are officially approved. In the absence of a specific showing of constitutionally valid reasons to regulate their speech, students are entitled to freedom of expression of their views. As Judge Gewin, speaking for the Fifth Circuit, said, school officials cannot suppress "expressions of feelings with which they do not wish to contend." Burnside v. Byars, supra, at 749.

Making Observations
- What do you notice about this court writing as compared and contrasted with other types of writing that are familiar to you?
- What questions do you have after reading this text?

Returning to the Text

- Reread the Supreme Court opinion to answer these text-dependent questions.
- Write any additional questions you have about the text in your Reader/Writer Notebook.

7. Justice Fortas refers to how the District Court views the act of wearing the armbands. How does the District Court interpret that act?

_____

_____

_____

_____

8. What does Fortas list in the second sentence? In what ways are these items related?

_____

_____

_____

_____

9. What pronoun does Fortas use in the third sentence, and what does it represent?

_____

_____

_____

_____

10. Fortas uses the word "divorced" in the third sentence. What two things does he see as divorced from one another?

_____

_____

_____

_____

11. Fortas uses the word "shed" in the last sentence to mean what?

_____

_____

_____

_____

12. Fortas presents an image in the last sentence of students and teachers entering the schoolhouse gate. What point is he making about students and teachers inside and outside of school?

_____

_____

_____

_____

13. A *closed circuit* is a complete electrical circuit around which current flows or a signal circulates as in a loop. What does Fortas mean by saying that students are not "closed-circuit recipients of only that which the State chooses to communicate"?

_____

_____

_____

_____

14. How does Fortas believe students should be perceived?

_____

_____

_____

_____

Working from the Text

15. Return to the text and think of it as a collection of the following three voices:

- Justice Fortas's voice or point of view
- References to the First Amendment
- References to other related court cases

Think of these three voices as elements that are woven together like a braid, supporting the Supreme Court's ruling. Use three highlighter colors to annotate the text, highlighting each of the three voices.

- Color 1: Highlight where Fortas asserts his own voice.
- Color 2: Highlight where Fortas quotes or paraphrases the First Amendment.
- Color 3: Highlight where Fortas cites legal precedents to support his interpretation of the Constitution.

☑ Check Your Understanding

Reread this sentence from the excerpt: *It was closely akin to "pure speech" which, we have repeatedly held, is entitled to comprehensive protection under the First Amendment.*

Write a definition in your Reader/Writer Notebook of the word "pure" as it is used in this context.

Analyzing Rhetoric in a Supreme Court Case

Learning Targets
- Summarize texts for understanding.
- Acquire and use content and academic vocabulary in context.
- Analyze rhetoric in a Supreme Court opinion.

Preview
In the previous activity, you were exposed to some of the language used in a Supreme Court decision. In this activity, you will build on that knowledge to read and work with other excerpts from *Tinker v. Des Moines*.

As You Read
- Define multiple-meaning words in context, using a print or digital dictionary, if necessary.
- Circle unknown words and phrases. Try to determine the meaning of the words by using context clues, word parts, or a dictionary.

Supreme Court Opinion

Tinker v. Des Moines

Excerpt 2)

1   This provision means what it says. We properly read it to permit reasonable regulation of speech-connected activities in carefully restricted circumstances. But we do not confine the **permissible** exercise of First Amendment rights to a telephone booth or the four corners of a pamphlet, or to supervised and ordained discussion in a school classroom.

2   If a regulation were adopted by school officials forbidding discussion of the Vietnam conflict, or the expression by any student of opposition to it anywhere on school property except as part of a prescribed classroom exercise, it would be obvious that the regulation would violate the constitutional rights of students, at least if it could not be justified by a showing that the students' activities would materially and substantially disrupt the work and discipline of the school. Cf. Hammond v. South Carolina State College, 272 F.Supp. 947 (D.C.S.C.1967) (orderly protest meeting on state college campus); Dickey v. Alabama State Board of Education, 273 F.Supp. 613 (D.C.M.D. Ala. 967) (expulsion of student editor of college newspaper). In the circumstances of the present case, the **prohibition** of the silent, passive "witness of the armbands," as one of the children called it, is no less offensive to the Constitution's guarantees. As we have discussed, the record does not demonstrate any facts which might reasonably have led school authorities to forecast substantial disruption of or material interference with school activities, and no disturbances or disorders on the school **premises** in fact occurred. These petitioners merely went about their ordained rounds in school. Their deviation consisted only in wearing on

Learning Strategies
Discussion Groups
Note-taking
SOAPSTone

My Notes

---

permissible: allowable
prohibition: ban
premises: grounds

My Notes

their sleeve a band of black cloth, not more than two inches wide. They wore it to exhibit their disapproval of the Vietnam hostilities and their advocacy of a truce, to make their views known, and, by their example, to influence others to adopt them. They neither interrupted school activities nor sought to intrude in the school affairs or the lives of others. They caused discussion outside of the classrooms, but no interference with work and no disorder. In the circumstances, our Constitution does not permit officials of the State to deny their form of expression.

Making Observations

- What point from this excerpt stands out most to you?
- What is your initial reaction to the stance taken by the Supreme Court in the excerpt?

Returning to the Text

- Reread the Supreme Court opinion to answer these text-dependent questions.
- Write any additional questions you have about the text in your Reader/Writer Notebook.

1. In the second paragraph, what does Fortas mean by "passive'witness of the armbands'"? Why is the word "passive" important?

_____

_____

_____

_____

2. In the second paragraph, Fortas contrasts how a verbal discussion of Vietnam might be perceived differently from the wearing of the armband as a symbolic gesture to protest the war. What point does Fortas make by drawing this comparison?

_____

_____

_____

_____

3. In the second paragraph, Fortas points out that the armbands do not cause disruption or interference with school activities. Why is this important evidence supporting the court's decision?

_____

_____

_____

_____

Working from the Text

4. Working with a partner, return to the text and highlight the same three "voices" you identified in Activity 3.3 with separate color highlighters.

- Color 1: Highlight where Fortas asserts his own voice.
- Color 2: Highlight where Fortas quotes or paraphrases the First Amendment.
- Color 3: Highlight where Fortas cites legal precedents to support his interpretation of the Constitution.

My Notes

5. You have now read two excerpts from Fortas's opinion in the case of *Tinker v. Des Moines*. Skim over both of these excerpts and star the particular sentences you think are the most convincing. In your opinion, what makes these sentences convincing?

6. Share your starred sentences with the class, including your reasons for starring them. Participate in a whole-class discussion about what these sentences have in common.

7. Break into discussion groups to discuss this prompt:

   If Fortas can be more persuasive when writing from a more personal perspective, why do you think he chooses to include references to the Constitution and previous legal cases?

Introducing the Strategy: SOAPSTone

The SOAPSTone strategy is useful for analyzing a nonfiction text. The term SOAPSTone forms an acronym, with each letter reminding you of an element to consider in your analysis:

S: Speaker: What do you know about the speaker?

O: Occasion: What event(s) or situation(s) prompts the creation of the text?

A: Audience: Who is the intended audience?

P: Purpose: What is the author's reason for creating the text? What does he/she want the audience to think or do?

S: Subject: What is the topic of the text?

Tone: What is the speaker's attitude toward the subject?

8. With a partner, use the SOAPSTone strategy to analyze the two excerpts of Justice Fortas's majority opinion (the text from this activity and the text from Activity 3.3). Record your analysis in the Majority Opinion column of the SOAPSTone chart.

	Majority Opinion
Speaker	
Occasion	
Audience	
Purpose	
Subject	
Tone	

My Notes

- Use the SOAPSTone chart to make notes about the reasons Justice Black gives for his dissent.
- Circle unknown words and phrases. Try to determine the meaning of the words by using context clues, word parts, or a dictionary.

Supreme Court Opinion

Tinker v. Des Moines

(Excerpt 3)

by **Mr. Justice Black, dissenting**

Change has been said to be truly the law of life, but sometimes the old and the tried and true are worth holding. The schools of this Nation have undoubtedly contributed to giving us tranquility and to making us a more law-abiding people. Uncontrolled and uncontrollable liberty is an enemy to domestic peace. We cannot close our eyes to the fact that some of the country's greatest problems are crimes committed by the youth, too many of school age. School discipline, like parental discipline, is an **integral** and important part of training our children to be good citizens—to be better citizens. Here a very small number of students have crisply and summarily refused to obey a school order designed to give pupils who want to learn the opportunity to do so. One does not need to be a **prophet** or the son of a prophet to know that, after the Court's holding today, some students in Iowa schools—and, indeed, in all schools—will be ready, able, and willing to defy their teachers on practically all orders. This is the more unfortunate for the schools since groups of students all over the land are already running loose, conducting break-ins, sit-ins, lie-ins, and smash-ins. Many of these student groups, as is all too familiar to all who read the newspapers and watch the television news programs, have already engaged in rioting, property seizures, and destruction. They have picketed schools to force students not to cross their picket lines, and have too often violently attacked earnest but frightened students who wanted an education that the pickets did not want them to get. Students engaged in such activities are apparently confident that they know far more about how to operate public school systems than do their parents, teachers, and elected school officials. It is no answer to say that the particular students here have not yet reached such high points in their demands to attend classes in order to exercise their political pressures. Turned loose with lawsuits for damages and **injunctions** against their teachers as they are here, it is nothing but wishful thinking to imagine that young, immature students will not soon believe it is their right to control the schools, rather than the right of the States that collect the taxes to hire the teachers for the benefit of the pupils. This case, therefore, wholly without constitutional reasons, in my judgment, subjects all the public schools in the country to the whims and caprices of their loudest-mouthed, but maybe not their brightest, students. I, for one, am not fully persuaded that school

integral: necessary and important

prophet: person who knows the future

injunctions: warnings or orders

pupils are wise enough, even with this Court's expert help from Washington, to run the 23,390 public school systems in our 50 States. I wish, therefore, wholly to disclaim any purpose on my part to hold that the Federal Constitution compels the teachers, parents, and elected school officials to surrender control of the American public school system to public school students. I dissent.

Making Observations

- What are your initial thoughts regarding Justice Black's dissenting opinion?
- Which of his points stand out the most to you? Why?

☑ Focus on the Sentence

After reading Justice Black's dissent the first time, write a response in the form of three sentences: a statement, a question, and an exclamation.

Statement: _____

_____

Question: _____

_____

Exclamation: _____

_____

My Notes

Returning to the Text

- Reread the Supreme Court opinion to answer these text-dependent questions.
- Write any additional questions you have about the text in your Reader/Writer Notebook.

9. What is Justice Black's argument about discipline? How is it relevant to the ruling?

_____

_____

_____

_____

10. Justice Black describes those who protest as the "loudest-mouthed, but maybe not their brightest, students" and those who are affected by the protests as "earnest but frightened students." How do these descriptions support his dissenting opinion?

_____

_____

_____

_____

11. As part of Justice Black's dissent, what does he suggest will happen if students are "turned loose with lawsuits for damages and injunctions against their teachers"?

_____

_____

_____

_____

Working from the Text

12. With a partner, use the SOAPSTone strategy to analyze Justice Black's dissenting opinion. Record your answers in the Dissenting Opinion column of the chart.

	Dissenting Opinion
Speaker	
Occasion	
Audience	
Purpose	
Subject	
Tone	

13. The rhetorical triangle may help you frame a discussion on *Tinker v. Des Moines*. The rhetorical triangle is made up of three components, which are present in any persuasive process:

Author: person who generates text

Audience: person who receives text

Text: message conveyed from author to audience

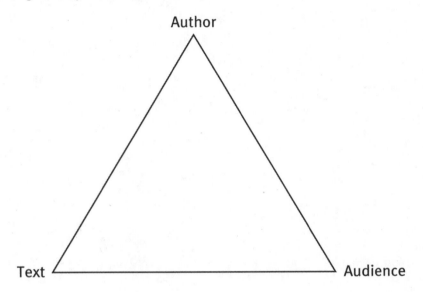

Author

Text — Audience

Use the rhetorical triangle to frame an analytical discussion. Answer the following questions in your discussion group. Take notes during the discussion.

- **Author:** How does Fortas's role as a justice define his responsibility as author?

- **Audience:** Who is the audience for the text? How does consideration of the audience influence the text and how it is written?

Text: What is the message of the text? How does it reflect the author and audience?

 Gaining Perspectives

You have been reading about freedom of speech and how people defend their right to free speech. First, with a partner, discuss why it is important to defend rights to free speech. Then conduct research to answer the following questions.

- How can people defend their First Amendment rights without going all the way to the Supreme Court?
- What role does the media play in free speech?
- How have people in your state and across the United States demonstrated their First Amendment rights? (Find at least one state example and one national example.) What were the outcomes or resolutions to these cases? What similarities and differences do you notice?

Write a summary of your research in your Reader/Writer Notebook. Be prepared to share your findings with the class.

Writing Prompt: Argumentative

Now that you have read the excerpts from *Tinker v. Des Moines*, reread the paragraphs you wrote in response to this writing prompt: *In your opinion, how much control should a school exercise over the way students dress?*

You have already incorporated the opinions of your peers. Expand your response by adding textual evidence from one or more of the *Tinker v. Des Moines* excerpts. You may decide to keep your original claim, or you may change it now that you have read more about this topic. Be sure to:

- Assert a claim that explains the extent to which the government should restrict students' right to protest via clothing.
- Explain how your claim is either supported by others or in conflict with others.
- Include at least one summary statement and one direct quotation.
- Include evidence from the majority and/or dissenting opinion from *Tinker v. Des Moines*.

Check Your Understanding

Supreme Court opinions can be challenging to read and understand. What challenges did you face as you attempted to summarize *Tinker v. Des Moines* for understanding? How did you overcome these challenges? Discuss your ideas with a partner.

Learning Strategies

Graphic Organizer
Marking the Text
Note-taking

My Notes

Learning Targets

- Synthesize information from multimedia texts.
- Write a letter to the editor using a professional writing structure.

Preview

In this activity, you will read a judicial opinion and write a letter to the editor persuading readers of your perspective on the opinion.

1. What do you know about the purpose of vaccinations and how they work? Write what you know about vaccines. Then, in a small group, record each of your group members' responses in the following graphic organizer. Use your group's collaborative knowledge to create a working definition of vaccination recording this definition in the central oval.

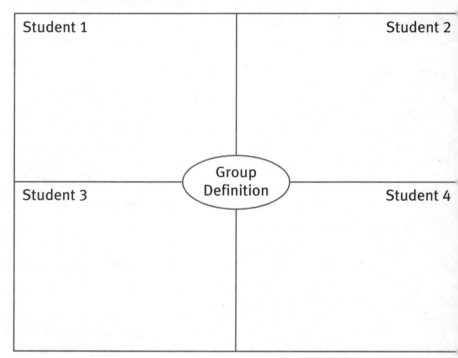

2. Watch the video presented by your teacher that explains how vaccinations work to protect people from viruses. Capture the main ideas about how a vaccine works in your Reader/Writer Notebook.

3. In your small group, review your working definition of a vaccination and expand it by adding information from the video. Then, work as a class to synthesize all of the small groups' definitions to create a succinct explanatio of what a vaccination is and how it works.

INDEPENDENT READING LINK

Read and Respond

In the previous two activities, you have learned to analyze an argument using various strategies. Based on your Independent Reading, identify an argument or claim made by the author, and analyze it using the SOAPSTone strategy. Make notes in your Reader/Writer Notebook.

As You Read

- Underline the primary claim in the document. Put stars where you see supporting evidence for the claim.
- Circle unknown words and phrases. Try to determine the meaning of the words by using context clues, word parts, or a dictionary.

About the Document

In the early 1900s, infectious diseases were the leading cause of death around the world. To combat a smallpox epidemic in Cambridge, Massachusetts, the city's Board of Health in 1902 required all adults be vaccinated or be subject to a fine. When Henning Jacobson was fined after refusing the vaccination, he took his case to the Massachusetts Supreme Court. The court ruled against Jacobson, and he appealed to the Supreme Court of the United States. In 1905, the U.S. Supreme Court established a position on the authority of states to enforce compulsory vaccination laws.

Supreme Court Opinion

from Jacobson v. Massachusetts

1 Mr. Justice Harlan, after making the foregoing statement, delivered the opinion of the court.

2 The defendant insists that his liberty is invaded when the State subjects him to fine or imprisonment for neglecting or refusing to submit to vaccination; that a compulsory vaccination law is unreasonable, **arbitrary** and oppressive, and, therefore, hostile to the inherent right of every freeman to care for his own body and health in such way as to him seems best, and that the execution of such a law against one who objects to vaccination, no matter for what reason, is nothing short of an assault upon his person. But the liberty secured by the Constitution of the United States to every person within its jurisdiction does not import an **absolute** right in each person to be, at all times and in all circumstances, wholly freed from restraint. There are manifold restraints to which every person is necessarily subject for the common good. On any other basis, organized society could not exist with safety to its members. Society based on the rule that each one is a law unto himself would soon be confronted with disorder and anarchy. Real liberty for all could not exist under the operation of a principle which recognizes the right of each individual person to use his own, whether in respect of his person or his property, regardless of the injury that may be done to others. This court

My Notes

arbitrary: random; without reason

absolute: unqualified; permanent

My Notes

has more than once recognized it as a fundamental principle that "persons and property are subjected to all kinds of restraints and burdens, in order to secure the general comfort, health, and prosperity of the State, of the perfect right of the legislature to do which no question ever was, or upon acknowledged general principles ever can be, made so far as natural persons are concerned."

Making Observations

- Is the Supreme Court for or against forcing an individual to get a vaccination in certain cases?
- What are your initial thoughts on the court decision?

Returning to the Text

- Form a small group, and wait for your teacher to assign a letter to your group. Your group will analyze the Supreme Court case using a set of text-dependent questions assigned to you.
- Reread the excerpt to answer the questions. Write any additional questions you have about the text in your Reader/Writer Notebook.

Set A

4. What is "the state"? What does the state do to Jacobson when he refuses to be vaccinated for smallpox?

_____

_____

_____

_____

5. What does *compulsory* mean? How does Jacobson feel about a compulsory vaccination law?

_____

_____

_____

_____

6. What does *inherent* mean? What does Jacobson consider an inherent right?

_____

_____

_____

_____

Set B

7. What does Jacobson consider as an "assault upon his person"?

_____

_____

_____

_____

8. According to this opinion, what are the limits of the "liberty secured by the Constitution"?

_____

_____

_____

_____

9. The word "restraint(s)" appears three times in this excerpt. In this context, what does it mean? What is the author's attitude about restraints?

_____

_____

_____

_____

Set C

10. How is the phrase "common good" used in this excerpt?

_____

_____

_____

_____

11. According to this excerpt, what would happen if we all followed "the rule that each one is a law unto himself"?

_____

_____

_____

_____

12. What has the court recognized more than once?

_____

_____

_____

_____

Working from the Text

13. After your teacher places you in a new group, take turns sharing your answers to the text-dependent questions. You should ask questions, take notes, and annotate your own copy of the text.

14. Work collaboratively with your new group to consider the excerpt as a whole. Identify, mark, and discuss the claim, evidence, reasoning, and acknowledgement of counterclaims.

15. Working as a group, complete the graphic organizer to outline elements of the argument.

Claim	
Counterargument	
Evidence and Reasoning	

☑ Check Your Understanding

According to this excerpt, "disorder and anarchy" would result if we all followed "the rule that each one is a law unto himself." In what ways can you apply this idea to regulations that you face in your everyday life? How does this relate to the essential question: What is the relationship between freedom and responsibility to society? Discuss your response with a partner.

✒ Writing Prompt: Letter to the Editor

Write a letter to the editor from the perspective of someone reading the 1905 court opinion. Your letter should be at least two paragraphs in length. Persuade readers to agree with a particular view on the government's role in requiring vaccination. The letter should focus solely on the 1905 court opinion and how either Jacobson's view or the court's view is correct. Be sure to:

- State your claim clearly, using a formal tone.
- Apply evidence and/or reasoning from the reading to support your claim.
- Include at least one cited, direct quotation from *Jacobson v. Massachusetts*.
- Include a smooth integration of each quotation, with an introductory phrase and follow-up.

Understanding Herd Immunity

Learning Strategies

Marking the Text
Think-Pair-Share

My Notes

Learning Targets

- Synthesize information from multiple texts.
- Analyze characteristics of multimedia texts.

Preview

In this activity, you will view a variety of text types and synthesize them to create a new understanding about vaccinations. From your synthesis, you will write an analysis of a satirical cartoon.

1. Watch the video provided by your teacher. Write one sentence in your Reader/ Writer Notebook narrating what happens in the video. Then turn to a partner and do a think-pair-share about what the phrase *herd immunity* might mean.

2. Remember that a metaphor is a figure of speech that compares two unlike things to make a point. The text you will read sets up an extended metaphor, where the metaphor is developed throughout the entire text. What metaphor does this video illustrate?

About the Author

Eula Biss is an American author of three books and numerous essays. She specializes in science, literature, and creative writing. Biss drew inspiration for *On Immunity: An Inoculation* (2014) from French author Voltaire's satirical novel *Candide* (1759). Like *Candide*, *On Immunity* contains thirty short sections that explore different threads of a central idea. In contrast to *Candide*, which she believes Voltaire wrote "against a certain kind of optimism," Biss attempts to write "for a certain kind of optimism" in *On Immunity*.

As You Read

- Underline rhetorical strategies Biss uses as she discusses herd immunity.
- Circle unknown words and phrases. Try to determine the meaning of the words by using context clues, word parts, or a dictionary.

Opinion Piece

from On Immunity: An Inoculation

by **Eula Biss**

1   If we imagine the action of a vaccine not just in terms of how it affects a single body, but also in terms of how it affects the collective body of a community, it is fair to think of vaccination as a kind of banking of immunity. Contributions to this bank are donations to those who cannot or will not be protected by their own immunity. This is the principle of herd immunity, and it is through herd immunity that mass vaccination becomes far more effective than individual vaccination.

2   Any given vaccine can fail to produce immunity in an individual, and some vaccines, like an influenza vaccine, are less effective than others. But when people are vaccinated with even a relatively ineffective vaccine, viruses have trouble moving from host to host and cease to spread, sparing both the unvaccinated and those in whom vaccination has not produced immunity. This is why the chances of contracting measles can be higher for a vaccinated person living in a largely unvaccinated community than they are for an unvaccinated person living in a largely vaccinated community.

3   The unvaccinated person is protected by the bodies around her, bodies through which disease is not circulating. But a vaccinated person surrounded by bodies that host disease is left **vulnerable** to vaccine failure or fading immunity. We are protected not so much by our own skin, but by what is beyond it. The boundaries between our bodies begin to dissolve here. Donations of blood and organs move between us, exiting one body and entering another, and too with immunity, which is a common trust as much as it is a private account. Those of us who draw on collective immunity owe our health to our neighbors.

Making Observations

- What is one thought you have about herd immunity after reading the first paragraph?
- What questions about vaccinations do you have after reading the excerpt?

vulnerable: defenseless

Returning to the Text

- Reread the opinion piece to answer these text-dependent questions.
- Write any additional questions you have about the text in your Reader/Writer Notebook.

3. What metaphor does Biss use to explain how herd immunity works?

_____

_____

_____

_____

4. How does "draw[ing] on collective immunity" work the same as a person drawing funds from a financial institution?

_____

_____

_____

_____

5. How does the author explain that a vaccinated person living in a largely unvaccinated community is more vulnerable to disease than an unvaccinated person living in a largely vaccinated community?

_____

_____

_____

_____

Working from the Text

6. Reread Biss's explanation of herd immunity while keeping the idea of extended metaphor in mind. Circle each word or phrase related to banking.

7. Think-pair-share with a partner to answer the following question: What role does Biss's banking metaphor play in her opinion piece?

8. With your partner, consider this prompt:

"Banking is like herd immunity because…"

Then write a few sentences completing the thought.

My Notes

9. Join the small group assigned by your teacher. As a group, identify the sentence that best communicates Biss's claim about herd immunity and highlight it in your text.

10. Design a visual representation of Biss's central claim. As a group, quickly sketch the image and then add details.

11. Remaining in groups, view the infographic on how herd immunity works.

About the Document

This is an infographic from the National Institutes of Health promoting mass vaccination. It describes how infectious diseases spread among communities with varying degrees of immunization: no one immunized, some people immunized, and most people immunized.

As You Read

• Underline information that tells you which of the infographic's figures represents people who are immunized.

• Circle unknown words and phrases. Try to determine the meaning of the words by using context clues, word parts, or a dictionary.

Herd Immunity

adapted **from The National Institutes of Health**

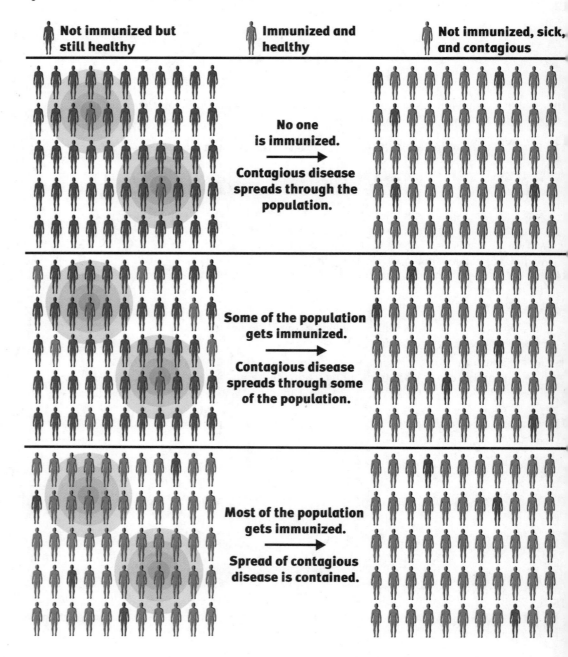

Not immunized but still healthy

Immunized and healthy

Not immunized, sick, and contagious

No one is immunized.

→

Contagious disease spreads through the population.

Some of the population gets immunized.

→

Contagious disease spreads through some of the population.

Most of the population gets immunized.

→

Spread of contagious disease is contained.

Making Observations

- What do you notice about the three sections of the infographic?
- Is there anything omitted from the infographic that you'd like to know?

Returning to the Text

- Look at the infographic again to answer these text-dependent questions.
- Write any additional questions you have about the infographic in your Reader/Writer Notebook.

12. What do the three colors represent?

_____

_____

_____

_____

13. What do the arrows represent?

_____

_____

_____

_____

14. On the left-hand side of the infographic, what do the concentric rings surrounding the red figures represent?

_____

_____

_____

_____

15. How do the words above and below each of the three arrows describe a different situation? What are the three situations?

_____

_____

_____

_____

Working from the Text

16. In your group, discuss and write an answer to the following question in your Reader/Writer Notebooks. Use at least one direct quotation from Biss, integrating it into the explanation and using parenthetical citations.

How does this infographic relate to Biss's explanation of herd immunity?

17. Share explanations about how the infographic relates to Biss's explanation of herd immunity with the whole class. Then return to the essential question: What is the relationship between freedom and responsibility to society? Has your opinion on this topic changed?

VOCABULARY

LITERARY

A **satirist** is someone who writes satire. **Satire** is a genre of literature or art created for the purpose of ridiculing or exposing corruption in society. Some well-known literary examples include *Animal Farm* (1945) by British author George Orwell, which exposes the weaknesses of communism under Russian Premier Joseph Stalin, and *Catch 22* (1961) by American author Joseph Heller—a treatise against the folly of war.

About the Author

James Gillray (1756–1815) was a British satirist and caricaturist. He produced nearly 1,000 prints and caricatures in his lifetime, focusing especially on British politics and social commentary on the rich and foolish. He created *Smallpox—The Speckled Monster*, an illustration, in 1802 when the smallpox vaccination was just beginning to be administered. Due to Gillray's biting wit as a satirist, he was both feared and respected in social circles. His work became iconic and imitated across the world.

Illustration

Smallpox--The Speckled Monster

by **James Gillray**

The COW-POCK — or — the Wonderful Effects of the New Inoculation! — Vide. the Publications of ɣ Anti-Vaccine Society.

Making Observations

- Notice the people around the woman in the center of the illustration. What do their gestures and expressions reveal?
- What does the caption tell or imply?

As You Read

Underline evidence Jenner utilizes to justify his use of the cowpox virus to prevent smallpox.

Circle unknown words and phrases. Try to determine the meaning of the words by using context clues, word parts, or a dictionary.

About the Document

This article is taken from the website for the Jenner Institute, an organization named after Dr. Edward Jenner. Jenner (1749–1823), an English scientist and physician, is credited with introducing the world's first vaccine, to stop the spread of smallpox. The Jenner Institute, founded in 2005, researches and develops new and innovative vaccines.

Informational Text

Vaccination

The Jenner Institute

1   Cowpox is a mild viral infection of cows. It causes a few weeping spots (pocks) on the udders, but little discomfort. Milkmaids occasionally caught cowpox from the cows. Although they felt rather **off-colour** for a few days and developed a small number of pocks (usually on the hand), the disease did not really trouble them.

The First Vaccination

2   A dairymaid, Sarah Nelmes, consulted Jenner in 1796 about a rash on her hand. He diagnosed cowpox rather than smallpox. Sarah confirmed that one of her cows, a Gloucester cow called Blossom, had recently had cowpox. Edward Jenner realised that this was his opportunity to test the protective properties of cowpox by giving it to someone who had not yet suffered smallpox.

3   He chose James Phipps, the eight-year old son of his gardener. On 14th May, he made a few scratches on one of James' arms and rubbed into them some material from one of the pocks on Sarah's hand. A few days later, James became mildly ill with cowpox, but was well again a week later. So Jenner knew that cowpox could pass from person to person as well as from cow to person.

My Notes

---

off-colour: sick

4   The next step was to test whether the cowpox would now protect James from smallpox. On 1st July, Jenner **variolated** the boy. As Jenner anticipated, and undoubtedly to his great relief, James did not develop smallpox on this occasion nor on the many subsequent occasions when his immunity was tested again.

Vaccination Opposition within the Medical Profession

5   Jenner's newly-proven technique for protecting people from smallpox d' not catch on as he anticipated. One reason was a practical one. Cowpox did n occur widely, and doctors who wanted to test the new process had to obtain cowpox matter from Edward Jenner.

6   In an age when infection was not understood, cowpox samples often became contaminated with smallpox itself, because those handling it worked in smallpox hospitals or carried out variolation. This led to claims that cowpo was no safer than smallpox inoculation.

7   There were also many surgeons who did not want Jenner to succeed. The were the variolators whose large incomes were threatened by Jenner's safer an more effective cowpox treatment.

The Anti-Vaccinationists

8   Soon even political cartoonists, such as James Gillray, were publishing engravings that showed people growing cow's heads on their bodies. People became fearful of the possible consequences of receiving material originating from cows, and opposed vaccination on religious grounds saying that they would not be treated with substances originating from God's lowlier creatures

9   Variolation was forbidden by Act of Parliament in 1840, and vaccination with cowpox was made compulsory in 1853. This, in its turn, led to protest marches and vehement opposition from those who demanded freedom of choice.

Making Observations
- What detail in this passage is most surprising to you? Why?
- How does this text build the understanding of vaccines that you have from reading the other texts in this unit?

variolated: pierced the skin of the patient with a needle that was contaminated with smallpox

Returning to the Text

- Revisit the informational text and illustration to answer these text-dependent questions.
- Write any additional questions you have about the text in your Reader/Writer Notebook.

18. How does Gillray's use of irony contrast the illustration's image with its title?

_____

_____

_____

19. How does Gillray use exaggeration to make his point?

_____

_____

_____

20. What do you notice about the physical features of the people?

_____

_____

_____

Working from the Text

21. The purpose of satire is to deride, reveal, or condemn the folly or corruption of a person or society. Satire is generally used within the context of topical issues such as those related to politics. The satirist employs strategies such as:

- **humor**—the use of words to induce laughter through contrast or surprise.
- **irony**—the use of words, situations, or character versus audience knowledge to contrast expectation with reality.
- **exaggeration**—the use of words to suggest something is much better or worse than it is in truth.

Gillray uses satire to make a statement about Jenner's work. Working in pairs, identify which methods of satire Gillray employs. Find evidence of each and discuss with your partner.

22. Reread the Jenner text and consider who is the most likely target of Gillray's satirical illustration. Who is he making fun of in the cartoon? Make a list of ideas.

23. Annotate the text with different colored highlighters to identify references to the different sides of the vaccination issue. What does each of the following think about vaccines: Jenner, the milkmaids, the variolators, and the anti-vaccinationists?

☑ Check Your Understanding

Summarize your analysis of Gillray's claim in a sentence or two. Use evidence from both the illustration and the Jenner text.

Learning Strategies

Debate
Marking the Text
Note-taking

INDEPENDENT READING LINK

Read and Research

In this part of the unit, you have come to understand how exploring many texts related to a topic can help you develop a more complete understanding of that topic. Consider the texts you are reading as part of your Independent Reading. How could you further extend your learning by exploring more perspectives on the same topic? Research media (such as films, documentaries, or graphics) that relate to the topic you are learning about, and choose one to add to your Independent Reading plan. Reflect in writing in your Reader/Writer Notebook about whether this new source changes your thinking on the topic and why or why not.

Learning Targets

- Analyze the author's purpose, audience, and message and how language shapes what the reader perceives.
- Integrate ideas from multiple texts to build knowledge and vocabulary about vaccinations.

Preview

In this activity, you will read two more texts about vaccinations and then synthesize the information to participate in a parlor conversation using the texts from this unit.

As You Read

- Highlight facts Dahl uses to persuade the reader.
- Circle unknown words and phrases. Try to determine the meaning of the words by using context clues, word parts, or a dictionary.

About the Author

British author Roald Dahl (1916–1990) is recognized as one of the greatest storytellers of all time. He wrote successful novellas and short stories for adults, including *Tales of the Unexpected* (1979), but he may be more well-known for his children's stories. The first of these, *James and the Giant Peach* (1961), was followed by *Charlie and the Chocolate Factory* (1964) and a string of other best-selling titles. Despite the enjoyment Dahl still brings to children around the world, he suffered the heartache of losing his daughter to complications resulting from measles. This profound loss sparked him to write about the issue years later.

Letter

Measles: A Dangerous Illness

by **Roald Dahl**

KNOWLEDGE QUEST

Knowledge Question:
How can the views of one person influence others?
In Activity 3.7, you will read a letter and an editorial debating the need for measles vaccinations. While you read and build knowledge about the topic, think about your answer to the Knowledge Question.

1 Olivia, my eldest daughter, caught measles when she was seven years old. As the illness took its usual course I can remember reading to her often in bed and not feeling particularly alarmed about it. Then one morning, when she was well on the road to recovery, I was sitting on her bed showing her how to fashion little animals out of coloured pipe-cleaners, and when it came to her turn to make one herself, I noticed that her fingers and her mind were not working together and she couldn't do anything.

2 "Are you feeling all right?" I asked her.

3 "I feel all sleepy," she said.

4 In an hour, she was unconscious. In twelve hours she was dead.

5 The measles had turned into a terrible thing called measles **encephalitis** and there was nothing the doctors could do to save her. That was twenty-four years ago in 1962, but even now, if a child with measles happens to develop the same deadly reaction from measles as Olivia did, there would still be nothing the doctors could do to help her.

6 On the other hand, there is today something that parents can do to make sure that this sort of tragedy does not happen to a child of theirs. They can insist that their child is immunised against measles. I was unable to do that for Olivia in 1962 because in those days a reliable measles vaccine had not been discovered. Today a good and safe vaccine is available to every family and all you have to do is to ask your doctor to administer it.

7 It is not yet generally accepted that measles can be a dangerous illness. Believe me, it is. In my opinion parents who now refuse to have their children immunised are putting the lives of those children at risk. In America, where measles immunisation is **compulsory**, measles like smallpox, has been virtually wiped out.

8 Here in Britain, because so many parents refuse, either out of obstinacy or ignorance or fear, to allow their children to be immunised, we still have a hundred thousand cases of measles every year. Out of those, more than 10,000 will suffer side effects of one kind or another. At least 10,000 will develop ear or chest infections. About 20 will die.

9 LET THAT SINK IN.

10 Every year around 20 children will die in Britain from measles.

My Notes

encephalitis: inflammation of the brain
compulsory: required

My Notes

11 So what about the risks that your children will run from being immunised? They are almost non-existent. Listen to this. In a district of around 300,000 people, there will be only one child every 250 years who will develop serious side effects from measles immunisation! That is about a million to one chance. I should think there would be more chance of your child choking to death on a chocolate bar than of becoming seriously ill from a measles immunisation.

12 So what on earth are you worrying about? It really is almost a crime to allow your child to go unimmunized.

13 The ideal time to have it done is at 13 months, but it is never too late. All school-children who have not yet had a measles immunisation should beg their parents to arrange for them to have one as soon as possible.

14 Incidentally, I dedicated two of my books to Olivia, the first was "James and the Giant Peach." That was when she was still alive. The second was "The BFG," dedicated to her memory after she had died from measles. You will see her name at the beginning of each of these books. And I know how happy she would be if only she could know that her death had helped to save a good deal of illness and death among other children.

Knowledge Quest
- How does Dahl's letter make you feel?
- What words, phrases, or ideas from the letter stick out to you?

Returning to the Text

- Reread the letter to answer these text-dependent questions.
- Write any additional questions you have about the text in your Reader/Writer Notebook.

1. How does Dahl relate his personal experience to his stance on public vaccination policy?

_____

_____

_____

2. What specific arguments and rhetorical devices does Dahl use to assert his position?

_____

_____

_____

3. **KQ** How does Dahl use ethics, emotion, and logic in his appeal to British parents?

_____

_____

_____

4. **KQ** Why does the author use the word "crime" to refer to a person's decision not to immunize?

_____

_____

_____

As You Read

- Underline factual evidence and circle examples of persuasive techniques.
- Circle unknown words and phrases. Try to determine the meaning of the words by using context clues, word parts, or a dictionary.

About the Author

Dr. Bob Sears is a pediatrician and author based in Dana Point, California. He employs a unique approach to medicine by combining traditional and alternative medical care. He has written many articles and books advocating for delaying or avoiding vaccines, taking a controversial position that contradicts recommendations from the American Academy of Pediatrics.

KNOWLEDGE QUEST

Knowledge Question:
How can the views of one person influence others?

My Notes

Editorial

Mandatory Vaccination Is Not the Answer to Measles

by **Dr. Bob Sears**

February **19, 2015, Orange County Register**

1   Measles. It used to be just a disease. Now it's become a banner under which politicians gather to threaten one of our most sacred rights – the right to give informed consent for medical treatment.

2   Whether you are for vaccines, against them, or neutral, allow me to ask this question: Is vaccination a medical treatment which should fall under the protection of informed consent, or does the government have the right to force them on every American?

3   As a pediatrician, I give patients the MMR vaccine almost every day in my office. And I follow the guidelines of the Centers for Disease Control which mandate that I provide informed consent. The American Medical Association describes informed consent as a patient's right of self-decision and a basic policy in both ethics and law that physicians must honor.

4   If vaccines were harmless to every single person who received them, then I could understand putting this decision in the hands of our elected officials. But here are two **salient** facts:

- About 2,000 severe reactions are reported to the CDC each year which result in prolonged hospitalization, permanent disability, or death. Most reactions aren't even reported, so the true number may be even higher. Yet, because they can't be proven, the medical community denies that they can happen.

- Over $3 billion have been paid out to victims of vaccine reactions. Not $3 million. Not $30 million. Not even $300 million. But $3 billion. Are we paying that much money to victims of pretend reactions? I think not.

5   You might think it's the actual measles outbreak that is responsible for the current political **hysteria**. But it is not. Instead, it is a carefully crafted opportunistic attempt to overstate what measles could potentially do to our nation. It is what politicians, some media outlets, and some in the medical community are trying to portray measles to be. But let's look at the actual facts of the current outbreak:

- As of Feb. 17, there are 141 cases nationwide. Not thousands. According to the Orange County Public Health Department, no new cases have been reported in the OC since Feb. 4.

salient: striking
hysteria: panic

- After the initial **surge**, it is now moving slowly. It is not spreading like wildfire in an exponential explosion of **unprecedented** proportion.

- Last year's 640 cases were an **anomaly** because over 400 occurred in one Amish community in New York and over 100 cases hit an unvaccinated church community in Texas. But for the rest of highly-vaccinated America, last year's measles was business as usual. This year we are off to a tough start, but it's slowing down.

- It has killed no one. It can kill about 1 person in every 1000 cases. Will someone die of measles in the United States in the years to come? Maybe. But it hasn't killed anyone in the past 15 years or more.

- The last time measles hit us hard was 25 years ago. Not last year, not this year, yet.

- It's measles, people. It's not the plague. It's not polio. It's not Ebola. It's measles. If the plague hits, let's force everyone to vaccinate. But measles? Measles? We need something a lot more dangerous than that if we are going to rob each and every patient of the sacred right of informed consent.

6 Let's stop panicking over what measles might do and calmly examine what it is doing. It has a small and **intermittent** presence in our country. It makes people sick, then they get over it. It has complications, but rarely so. Vaccination is important and protective. But it cannot be forced; a parent must give consent.

7 If you would rather make your own medical decisions within the sacred confines of the doctor/patient relationship, then let Sacramento know now. If you would rather give politicians the power to make medical decisions for you, then give them your support. But you better hurry; the outbreak is winding down, and so is the fear. Give them the power before it's too late. I'm sure they'll make plenty of other wise medical decisions for you in the years to come.

⊘ Knowledge Quest

- How would you describe Sears' tone in the editorial?
- Which fact from the editorial influences your position on the topic the most?

surge: rush
unprecedented: never seen before
anomaly: odd occurrence
intermittent: not continuous

Returning to the Text

- Reread the editorial to answer these text-dependent questions.
- Write any additional questions you have about the text in your Reader/Writer Notebook.

5. KQ Why does Sears use the word "sacred" to describe the right to give informed consent?

6. What is the author's purpose for this piece? What does Sears want readers to know?

7. KQ Of what does Sears seek to convince the reader? How does he convince his audience?

8. Look back at the third bullet point under paragraph 5. How does the idea here connect to what you read in the excerpt from *On Immunity*?

9. KQ How are Sears's recommendations different from Dahl's letter? On what do both authors agree?

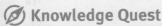

Knowledge Quest

After reading the letter and the editorial about how the views of one person can influence others, think about the reasons someone may lobby against or advocate for the measles vaccine. With a partner, make a T-chart with "Lobby Against" on one side and "Advocate For" on the other. Gather evidence from text you have studied so far that supports both sides. Then discuss sources of text evidence. Why is it important to know where evidence originates? Why is a story or personal anecdote different from a researched fact? When might one type of source sometimes be just as powerful as the other? Share your thoughts, while staying open to your partner's opinions. Then work independently to summarize your discussion.

 INDEPENDENT READING LINK

You can continue to build your knowledge about how the views of one person can influence others by reading other articles at ZINC Reading Labs. Search for keywords such as *peer pressure* or *lobby*.

 ZINC

Working from the Text

10. You will now begin to prepare for a parlor conversation in which you will assume the identities of the authors whose arguments you have read in this unit and discuss vaccination from their points of view. To begin preparing, read Dr. Sears's editorial and consider how Dr. Sears would respond to Roald Dahl. Underline each statement in the Sears piece that seems to be in direct opposition to one of Dahl's points. Compare and contrast your responses with group members. Work with your classmates to collaboratively decide on a single statement with which to begin work.

11. Revisit the Dahl piece to find one quotation that directly opposes the statement your group wrote. Restate Dahl's claim in such a way that it directly responds to the Sears statement, as if Dahl were entering into a debate with Sears.

12. Find another quotation from Sears's writing that can be used to respond to Dahl's point. Continue creating a scripted debate of a few lines (8–10) by finding quotations from Sears and Dahl that argue their claims about vaccinations. Make sure to utilize quotations that respond to points the other speaker is making or that introduce counterpoints. You may quote the texts verbatim or rewrite claims or evidence by paraphrasing or summarizing.

13. Think about the texts and images you have previously analyzed. In what ways might they enter into a conversation or debate like the one your class constructed for Dahl and Sears?

ACADEMIC

When citing a source, one option is to record the words verbatim. To write something verbatim is to transcribe the exact words of the source. When engaging in this practice, it is important to cite the source correctly using a preferred style guide.

VOCABULARY

14. Work with a small group to prepare for a parlor conversation. Review the text from activities 3.5–3.7, and use the following questions as starting points for preparing your discussion:

    - What claim will you argue?
    - What evidence do you have to support this claim?
    - What appeals will you use to argue your point?
    - How will you answer counterpoints?

15. Prepare an index card with notes about the participant your teacher has assigned to your group. Include the following elements:

    - One concise, direct quotation that best captures the participant's claim on the topic of vaccination
    - Relevant background information regarding the participant's stance on vaccination
    - An idea to challenge (record the names of parlor conversation participants with whom the participant will have a difference of opinion, along with explanations of why their positions will be in opposition)
    - Friends to lean on (record the names of parlor conversation participants on whom the participant could call to back up his or her opinions, along with explanations of why those participants would support the claim)

Staging a Parlor Conversation

Participate in a parlor conversation using your index cards and the text and images of this unit. With the other small groups in your classroom, form two concentric circles. Then work within your group to choose one member to represent your group's participant in the inner circle. Remaining group members should sit close to their representative in the outer circle.

To begin the parlor conversation, an inner-circle participant will introduce himself or herself and state a claim. Next, participants who disagree may state a counterclaim, acknowledging the speaker's position and offering evidence from their own argument. Then the first speaker may supply a rebuttal and call on another participant to voice support for his or her position.

The conversation should proceed in this way until every participant in the inner circle has made at least one point (either an original point, an opposing point, or a supporting point). Then the inner-circle students will step out, and a different member of each group will take their places, until all students have had an opportunity to speak.

☑ Check Your Understanding

How did the parlor conversation help you extend your understanding of how the texts on vaccines relate to one another? Discuss your ideas with a partner.

Composing a Synthesis Argument

Learning Targets

- Synthesize information from multiple texts.
- Plan, write, and revise an argument.

Preview

In this activity, you will reexamine the sources from previous activities in this unit to synthesize a response to a prompt about vaccinations. You will then plan, write, and revise an argument stating your opinion.

✍ Writing Prompt: Argumentative

Ever since Jenner experimented with the smallpox vaccine in 1796, mandatory vaccination has been a controversial issue. In an essay that synthesizes at least three of the sources you examined in activities 3.5–3.7, develop a position about how much control you think the government should exercise over an individual's right to make personal decisions regarding vaccination. Be sure to:

- Assert a claim that explains the extent to which the government should have control over people's right to choose to vaccinate or not to vaccinate.
- Explain how your claim is either supported by or in conflict with others.
- Maintain a formal style and objective tone throughout the essay.
- Cite the sources that support your claim, and/or refute sources that do not.
- Revise your draft for clarity, organization, and effectiveness.

Create a Continuum of Positions

1. Within a new assigned group, use index cards to represent each of the texts you have read from activities 3.5–3.7. Use one index card per text and include on it the text's claim and supporting evidence.

Opposed to government interference with vaccination ⟵⟶ In favor of government vaccine mandate

2. Arrange the cards in order so that the card on the far left represents the perspective most strongly opposed to government interference with vaccination. The card on the far right should represent the perspective most strongly in favor of a government mandate regarding vaccinations. Then place the other cards in between, depending on your analysis of where their stances fall in relation to the one on each end. A continuum of opinions will result. Be prepared to explain your reasoning for the positions of the cards.

3. Now, focus on your own views about the government and vaccination. Where do you see yourself in the continuum? Answer the following questions on new index cards:

   - In your opinion, how much control should the government have over whether an individual is vaccinated?
   - What are the main ideas supporting your stance on the government's role in vaccination?
   - Lean on a friend: Which texts will you call on to support your point of view and why?
   - Ideas I will challenge: Which texts will you oppose and why?

Write and Support a Thesis Statement

Now that you have developed a preliminary response to the writing prompt, you will refine your thoughts on the topic and express your ideas in a working thesis statement. A thesis statement is a sentence (sometimes two) that appears in an introduction and acts as a roadmap for the rest of the argument. Your thesis statement will help the reader understand the controversy over compulsory vaccination and the writer's position regarding it. Write your thesis statement by completing the following steps:

- Gather your evidence.
- Narrow your focus while maintaining objectivity.
- Formulate your statement.

4. Begin a working thesis statement by drafting at least three separate thesis statements in your Reader/Writer Notebook. Freewrite under each statement to show how you might support the statement with textual evidence. Then choose the thesis statement you think will be easiest to develop.

5. Select the sources and evidence you will use to develop and support your thesis. Then complete the following chart to narrow your ideas into three supporting ideas with evidence.

Supporting Idea	Evidence

Introduction

The purpose of an introduction is twofold: First, it prepares readers for the thesis and the rest of the essay. Second, it must interest readers enough to cause them to continue reading.

6. You will need to introduce your argument within the context of the vaccine debate. Draft your introduction by summarizing the ongoing debate, giving a brief history, and stating your own view on the topic. Draft your introduction on a separate sheet of paper.

Body Paragraphs

7. Return to the chart that lists your three main supporting ideas with evidence. Consider the best order for presenting the three main ideas. Order them so that the sequence makes logical sense, with one idea building toward the next. Number the rows of your chart to show the order in which you will use the ideas to build the argument. Body paragraphs will expand each of the three main ideas into a full paragraph. Use the quotations and ideas you listed in the Evidence column as material for your writing.

ACADEMIC

When speaking and writing, it is important to elaborate. To elaborate is to expand on a point by providing supporting details. The ability to elaborate lends credibility to one's ideas.

LITERARY

When speaking or writing persuasively, a person generally ends with a call to action. After the speaker or writer makes a claim, supports it with evidence, and addresses counterarguments, the speaker will often ask the audience to change its thinking or perform an action to show its support for the claim.

My Notes

Organize your body paragraphs to include:

- Transitions (connection with the previous paragraph)
- Development of discrete supporting ideas
- Evidence from sources that advance the claim (reference a total of three sources)

You may also use evidence that does not support your claim. Instead, you may elaborate on your claim by refuting a source to advance your argument.

8. Draft the body paragraphs for your argument below your introduction.

Conclusion

9. Reread your introduction and body paragraphs before drafting your conclusion.

Your conclusion should:

- Echo your introduction
- Answer the reader's implied question of "So what?" (Why is this important?)
- Leave the reader with something new to think about
- Serve as a call to action for the reader

10. Draft your conclusion below your body paragraphs.

The Bare Bones Test

11. The Bare Bones Test is a process writers can use for reading their work aloud to a partner. With a partner, follow these steps:

Student 1: Read the introduction to your essay.

Student 2: Write a summary:

Your position on compulsory vaccination is _____

Student 1: Read the first body paragraph.

Student 2: Write a summary statement:

This body paragraph was all about the supporting idea: _____

Student 1: Read the second body paragraph.

Student 2: Write a summary statement:

This body paragraph was all about the supporting idea: _____

Student 1: Read the third body paragraph.

Student 2: Write a summary statement:

This body paragraph was all about the supporting idea: _____

Student 1: Read the conclusion.

Student 2: Write a summary statement:

This conclusion made me think more about _____

After this process, turn to the writer and ask whether you accurately summarized his or her position, recognized the ideas that shaped the body paragraphs, and were left thinking more about a particular idea that the writer intended. If the writer thinks you did not get the "bare bones" of the message, discuss how you think he or she could revise the essay to better communicate these main ideas.

12. Now, conduct the Bare Bones Test again, this time switching roles with your partner.

Revising and Editing

13. Consider the feedback you received from your partner during the Bare Bones Test. Focus on the "big ideas." Use the following checklist as you reflect on and revise your essay:

Criteria	Revision Question	Y/N
Getting the Facts Right	Does the essay do justice to the complexity of the topic, and are the sources represented accurately?	
Connecting the Evidence	Is it clear how the ideas reflected in the sources relate to one another and to your claim?	
Introducing the Essay	Does the introduction provide an overview of the topic?	
Establishing a Claim	Do you clearly assert your own view about the topic?	
Organizing the Body	Are the body paragraphs organized by main ideas that support your claim, and are there smooth transitions between ideas?	
Using Logical Reasoning	Does the essay include a strong, logical line of reasoning?	
Addressing Counterclaims	Does the essay anticipate and address counterclaims?	
Citing Evidence	Do you incorporate evidence from at least three sources to advance your argument, and are the sources cited accurately?	
Summarizing and Quoting	Do you provide a good balance between summarizing and quoting sources?	
Concluding Effectively	Does your conclusion go beyond echoing the ideas presented in the introduction and provide an answer to the reader's "So what?" question?	
Controlling Language	Does the essay demonstrate an effective use of language, with purposeful word choice, syntax, and/or rhetorical appeals?	
Communicating Clearly	Does the essay demonstrate a strong command of grammar and conventions?	

14. After you have revised your essay using the checklist, reconnect with your partner and exchange essays, using the revision checklist to guide the peer review process.

Reflect

15. Consider your work throughout this unit. What skills did you learn or practice that you now feel confident about? What skills would you like to continue to develop?

INDEPENDENT READING LINK

Read and Research

The focus of this part of the unit is research, so it's important to take the time to study the ways in which authors use research. For your Independent Reading, choose a fiction or nonfiction text that required extensive research by the author. For example, you might choose to read a court decision, an investigative report, or a work of historical fiction. As you read, identify the types of sources the author likely used and what his or her research process might have been. Create an Independent Reading Plan with personal reading goals in your Reader/Writer Notebook.

My Notes

_____
_____
_____
_____
_____
_____
_____
_____
_____
_____
_____
_____

Learning Targets
- Understand the details of Embedded Assessment 1.
- Examine how to develop a research plan for a research report.

Preview

In this activity, you will read the assignment for Embedded Assessment 1 and develop a research plan for your research report.

Making Connections

This part of the unit focuses on the research process. Asking questions is part of what makes us human. We ask questions about the world around us and search for information until we eventually arrive at answers. In this part of the unit, you will learn the steps of the research process, including developing a research plan, asking a research question, and choosing the right sources to find information. Through research, you will gain more knowledge and information about a subject.

Unpacking Embedded Assessment 1 and Previewing Embedded Assessment 2

Closely read the assignment for Embedded Assessment 1: Creating an Annotated Bibliography

 Create an annotated bibliography that documents the research you have done for your group project. Each student must submit a bibliography with at least five sources. Include a citation for each source and a brief summary.

Because Embedded Assessment 1 will support Embedded Assessment 2: Presenting a Solution to an Environmental Conflict, you should also preview this assignment:

 Your assignment is to present a solution to the environmental conflict your group has researched. You will create a report and deliver a group presentation designed to contextualize the conflict for your classmates and justify your approach to resolving it.

Find the Scoring Guide and work with your class to paraphrase the expectations for Embedded Assessment 1. Create a graphic organizer to use as a visual reminder of the required skills and concepts. Copy the graphic organizer into your Reader/Writer Notebook, and revisit it after each activity to check your progress.

Research Relay Race

Before you begin your research, it's important to create a plan. Consider the following question:

How do you create the perfect omelet?

1. Imagine that it is your responsibility to find the answer to this question. How would you go about finding its answer? What would your problem-solving process be? Within an assigned small group, work individually to write steps you would take to find the answer this question on sticky notes. You don't have to put the steps in order yet. Just generate as many as you can.

2. When your group members have finished generating ideas, share your ideas with each other. Are there shared ideas more than one group member contributed? Are there some ideas that you want to edit? Are there any ideas that you want to discard?

3. In your group, arrange the steps in order from start to finish by moving sticky notes. Some steps may occur at the same time, and some steps might need to be done more than once, so you may need to be creative about how you place the sticky notes.

4. When your group has finished, call your teacher over and ask whether you have reached the finish line. If you've missed any important steps, your teacher will send you back to the brainstorming stage.

5. As a class, generalize the process you used to answer the omelet question so that it can be used to answer any question. Take notes in the following chart.

RESEARCH PROCESS STEPS	RESOURCES YOU MIGHT USE

6. **Collaborative Conversation:** What are some environmental topics that interest you? What are some ideas you have for a research project? Brainstorm a few topics to share in a class discussion, and listen to your peers as they share their thoughts. Remember to keep an open mind about other people's ideas and take notes, if necessary.

7. Form small groups based on a topic or on areas of shared interest. Remember that each member has a role to play in a group. Assign someone in the group to act as the leader to manage the research and keep everyone on task, as well as to deal with any problems that may arise. Assign another person to act as the note-taker to write down any important questions and ideas. Finally, assign the other group members to ask questions, offer ideas, and organize ideas.

☑ Check Your Understanding

As the roles are assigned for the research process, write down the tasks expected for each group member in your Reader/Writer Notebook. Discuss any roles or responsibilities that might be confusing.

Forming Questions

Learning Targets
- Examine environmental topics to research as a group.
- Generate a question about an environmental issue to research further.

Preview

In this activity, you will brainstorm environmental issues, assign tasks for each member of your research group, and write a research question to answer in your research report.

Learning Strategies

Brainstorming
Discussion Groups
Generating Questions
Graphic Organizer
Sharing and Responding
Writing Groups

Refining Your Topic

1. Brainstorm possible topics for a research report on environmental issues. Use the following diagram to help you understand the difference between local/regional, national, international, and global environmental issues.

Environmental Issues

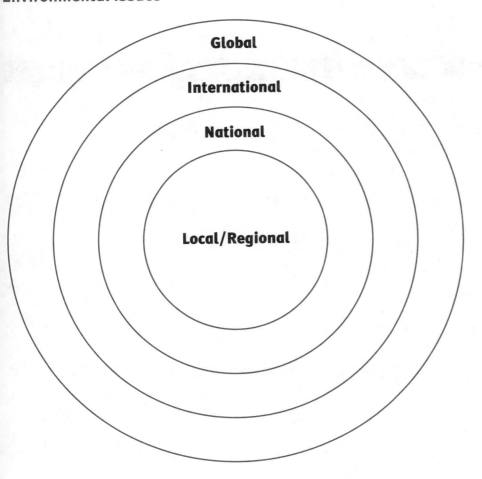

Global

International

National

Local/Regional

My Notes

2. Collaborate with your classmates to chart research ideas your group has brainstormed. As a group, generate some notes on what you already know and would like to learn about each topic.

Regional	Notes	National	Notes

International	Notes	Global	Notes

3. As you look over the list of issues, which ones do you think you might be interested in examining closely? Share your opinions with your group members.

Writing a Research Question

A research question is a clear, focused, concise, and complex question that drives your research. Research questions help you focus your research by providing a path through the research process. Creating research questions will help you work toward supporting a clear thesis.

To write a research question:

Think about your general topic. What do you want to know?

Consider your audience. Keep your audience in mind when developing your question. Would that particular audience be interested in this question?

Start asking questions. Ask open-ended "how" and "why" questions about your general topic to help you think of different areas of your topic.

Evaluate your possible questions. Research questions should not be answerable with a simple "yes" or "no" or by easily found facts. They should, instead, require both research and analysis on the part of the researcher.

Hypothesize possible answers. After you have written your research question, use what you already know to think of possible answers or explanations. This will help guide your research.

4. Write three research questions individually or as a group that you want to answer about the environmental issue you have chosen. Remember that open-ended questions that begin with *how* or *why* are the best questions for a research project.

Making Research Questions Specific

As you generate research questions about your topic, keep in mind that the question should not be too broad in scope. A broad question will provide you with too much information and will make it difficult to choose which information to include. In addition, if your question is too broad and general, an excess of information will create problems later when organizing your notes. Writing a question that is more specific will help narrow your research. However, remember that your question might change once you have researched information about your topic.

Use the following checklist to evaluate your questions:

- ☐ Is the question about a topic that interests me?
- ☐ Does the question begin with *how* or *why*?
- ☐ Is the question researchable?
- ☐ Is my question specific enough to be answered?
- ☐ Can I answer my question using more than one resource?
- ☐ Can I answer my question within the given time frame?

5. Work with your group to evaluate each other's research questions. Use the checklist to determine whether a question is too broad, and suggest ways that it can be rewritten to be more specific.

☑ Check Your Understanding

Which question will your group choose as its focus? Discuss as a group and come to a consensus.

Planning for Research

6. As you plan the research process, discuss the resources your group will use during their research, as well as the expected contribution from each group member. For example, one group member can research information from periodicals at the library while another person looks for information on the Internet. Remember that a good research topic cannot be addressed by reading only one resource, so the research you perform must be thorough. Use the following graphic organizer to help plan your research:

Research Question:		
Group Member	**Task**	**Type of Resources**

Sifting Through Sources

Learning Targets

- Examine different types of sources in both print and digital formats.
- Analyze how to record sources for a bibliography.

Preview

In this activity, you will learn about various types of sources and how to record information depending on the source.

Types of Sources and Ways to Access Them

Once you have decided on a research question, it is time to gather information that helps answer it. Use sources such as encyclopedias, nonfiction books, magazines and newspapers, almanacs, interviews, pamphlets, and brochures. Many sources are available in both print and digital formats.

To find information on the Internet, use a search engine. To use a search engine, choose words and phrases related to your topic and type them into the search field. The keywords should not be so general that they return too much information nor so specific that they return too little. If the results of the search are unsatisfactory, adjust the keywords.

Once you have found a reliable website (URLs ending in *.gov*, *.edu*, or *.org* are generally reliable), use your browser's "bookmark" or "favorites" feature to save the links. You can also organize the links into folders for quick and easy access. Finally, consider printing out the web pages so you can refer to your research when you are away from your computer.

Discuss with your group the strategies you will use to locate good sources.

My Notes

My Notes

☑ Check Your Understanding

Review the different types of sources available for your research. Choose sources you think would be most beneficial, and explain to your group why you think they are important.

Recording Your Sources

As you conduct your research, fill out a table like the one that follows with bibliographic information for every source you use.

Source	
Author	
Book, Magazine, or Newspaper Title	
City of Publication	
Publisher	
Year of Publication	
Website URL	
Notes	

Use index cards to record bibliographic information.

Reflecting on the Process

After recording your sources, return to your small group and share your experiences. Discuss the types of sources you found, as well as any difficulties you faced. In addition, provide feedback and advice about the research process. Finally, share your findings with the class, and discuss any common experiences you had with other groups. Then return to the essential question: Why is responsible use of source materials important? How would you answer this question now?

Evaluating Sources for Credibility

Learning Strategies

Discussion Groups
Graphic Organizer
Questioning the Text
Sharing and Responding
Writing Groups

Learning Targets

- Use multiple print and digital sources.
- Examine how to determine the reliability and credibility of sources.
- Examine sources for fallacies.
- Follow rules for avoiding plagiarism and using citations.

Preview

In this activity, you will learn about the importance of checking the reliability and credibility of your sources by evaluating them for authoritative content, usefulness, and fallacies.

My Notes

The Importance of Evaluating Sources

As you conduct research, it is important to make sure that your sources are reliable. An important distinction between information on the Internet and on the printed page is the reliability of the information. Most printed materials, such as books, newspapers, and magazine articles, are checked for accuracy by editors or fact-checkers. On the other hand, many websites on the Internet are not checked for accuracy by professionals. The information may not be accurate or reliable. As a result, it is important for you to evaluate sources to determine their reliability and credibility before using the information in your research report.

Ensuring That Sources Are Reliable and Credible

Anything can be published on the Internet. Websites often contain information from an unreliable author or include a biased view on a topic or inaccuracies. As a result, you should carefully evaluate sources for credibility.

Reliable websites typically include those with URLs that end in *.gov, .edu,* and *.org,* as well as those maintained by public libraries and the Public Broadcasting Service (PBS). In addition, websites maintained by the government, universities, and professional organizations are generally considered reliable and accurate. Wiki and personal websites are not considered reliable sources and should not be used. However, you can evaluate the sources these websites use to gather their information and use them in your research.

Use the following criteria to evaluate sources for credibility.

URL:
- What is its domain?
   - .com = for-profit business
   - .gov, .mil, .us (or other country code) = government site
   - .edu = educational institution
   - .org = nonprofit organization
- Is this URL someone's personal page?
- Why might using information from a personal page be a problem?
- Do you recognize who is publishing this page? (If not, you may need to investigate further to determine whether the publisher is an expert on the topic and evaluate whether the publisher is biased.)

My Notes

Sponsor:
- Does the website easily give information about the organization or group that sponsors it?
- Does it have a link (often called "About Us") that leads you to that information?
- What do you learn?

Timeliness:
- When was the page last updated? (Usually this is posted at the top or bottom of the page. How current a page is may indicate how accurate or useful the information in it will be.)

Purpose:
- What is the purpose of the page?
- Is the information on the site factual/credible? How do you know?
- Who is its target audience?
- Does it present information or opinion?
- Is it primarily objective or subjective?

Author:
- What credentials does the author have?
- Is this person or group considered an authority on the topic?

Links:
- Does the page provide links?
- Do they work?
- Are they helpful?
- Are they objective or subjective?

1. Use the response sheet as a template to create a similar sheet for each of your sources.

Evaluating Your Sources Response Sheet
List website (title and URL):
What can you tell from the URL?
What can you learn about the page's sponsor?

Evaluating Your Sources Response Sheet
What can you learn about the page's timeliness?
What can you tell about the page's purpose?
What else can you learn about the author?
What can you tell from any links provided?

Understanding Fallacies

Fallacies are ubiquitous in advertising, political discourse, and everyday conversations—and they will continue to be as long as they work as ways to persuade. However, by learning to recognize them when you see them, you can strip away their power. There are many different ways to categorize fallacies and many different names for the various types. The following fallacies (adapted from Brooke Noel Moore and Richard Parker's *Critical Thinking*, 8th ed., 2007) are some of the frequent offenders. Learn these and you'll be ready to see through many of the rhetorical scams that come your way each day.

Post Hoc: Literally meaning "after this," post hoc is a causal fallacy in which a person assumes one thing caused another simply because it happened prior to the other. For example: *The high school soccer team loses an important game the day after they start wearing new uniforms. The coach blames the loss on the new uniforms.*

Slippery Slope: Half an appeal to fear and half a causal fallacy, a slippery slope occurs when someone suggests that one action will lead to an inevitable and undesirable outcome. To say that allowing murals to be painted on the sides of public walls and buildings means that graffiti will soon cover an entire city is a slippery slope argument.

Appeal to Pity: If you have ever asked a teacher to give you a better grade or a second chance because things have been tough recently or because you worked so hard, you're guilty of this one. It refers to an attempt to use compassion or pity to replace a logical argument.

Inappropriate Appeal to Authority: We often rely on experts when we lack our own expertise in a field. But expert testimony can be fallacious in several ways: if the "authority" is not an expert in the field being discussed, if the expert is biased and/or stands to profit from the testimony, if the expert's opinion is not representative of other experts in the field. For example, Linus Pauling, who won Nobel prizes in chemistry and for peace, once said taking vitamin C daily could delay cancer—but his expertise was not in medicine.

Either/Or (or False Dilemma): This fallacy is a conclusion that oversimplifies the argument by suggesting there are only two possible sides or choices, instead of many that involve compromise or creative thinking. For example, a person might say, "Either you're an environmentalist or you hate the planet." Or a person might argue, "Either we ease up on environmental protection or we will see our economy get worse."

Incorrect Premise: All people love dogs. A clean environment is important to owning a dog. Therefore, everyone should live in a clean environment. This example begins with an incorrect premise: All people do not like dogs. So, although the conclusion is valid, the premise it is built on is incorrect.

Hasty Generalization: This fallacy is a conclusion based on insufficient or biased evidence. In other words, it rushes to a conclusion before all relevant facts are available. For example, if your dog likes to eat peanut butter, you might assume that all dogs like to eat peanut butter.

2. Use the table to analyze a source that you have determined to be credible.

	Your Source and Example	Fallacious or Fair?
Post Hoc	"which a person assumes one thing caused another simply because it happend prior to the other. I got a new hockey stick and my team started to win.	Fallacious
Appeal to Pity	"you're guilty of this one it Refers to an attempt to use compassion or Pity to replace a logical argument"	ex: if you ask your mo for more things because things have been tough recently Fallacious/Fair
Inappropriate Appeal to Authority	"if the experts opinion is not representative of other experts in the feild." if a pro hockey told a pro football how to tackle.	Fallacious
Slippery Slope	"when someone suggests that one action will lead to inevetable and undesirable outcome!! If I place a ball on top of a hill it will Roll down	fair
Either/Or	"This fallacy is a conclusion that oversimplifies the argument by suggesting there are only two possible sides or choices".	ex: someone saying i love hockey but anoth saying can you sk or can't skate fair
Incorrect Premise	a false premise is an incorrect proposition that forms the basis of an Argument or assumpion. ex: people that love dogs that thing you need a clean place to take car of them.	Fallacious
Hasty Generalization	based on insuficient or baised evidence, it rushes to collusion." if my cat like cat toys other cats must like them to.	fallacious

Bias and Omission

While some news sources strive hard to present objective coverage of events of the day, other sources present a more subjective point of view, controlling what information is presented even if they avoid being blatantly opinionated. When considering such articles—or any published or online text—as potential sources to support a claim, it's important to first evaluate those sources for their level of bias/credibility and omission. For example, an article about a political issue, such as renewable and nonrenewable sources of energy, might be biased and push only one side of an issue. Or, it could omit necessary information or misdirect the reader away from the missing information. The use of a heavily biased source without acknowledgment (or at least awareness) of bias or omission can greatly undermine your own ethical appeal—especially if someone else challenges your source on the basis of its bias or omission of facts. Can you think of examples of news reporting you thought might be biased? Why did you think that?

3. Check your own sources and research results for bias and omission. Ask yourself the following questions: Is contact information provided? How credible is the source? Is the author or organization providing the information reliable? Does the resource push only one side of an issue or argument, or are several sides presented? When checking multiple resources, do you find that one source omits key information contained in other resources? Record your evaluation in your Reader/Writer Notebook.

✓ Check Your Understanding

Which fallacies have you encountered in your research? With a partner, discuss the different fallacies you have found and how you identified them in your research.

📝 Writing Prompt: Argumentative

Is it important to evaluate all sources for credibility before sharing them on social media? Why or why not? Take a position, and write an argumentative essay that supports your stance. Be sure to:

- State your claim in the beginning sentence.
- Use relevant evidence and valid reasoning to support your claim.
- Provide a concluding statement that supports the claim you have presented.

My Notes

📦 INDEPENDENT READING LINK

Read and Research

Based on your independent reading, generate a simple research question you would like answered, and use reliable sources such as encyclopedias, newspaper and magazines articles, and credible websites to answer your question. Record your findings in your Reader/Writer Notebook.

Learning Strategies

Discussion Groups
Drafting
Graphic Organizer
Sharing and Responding
Summarizing
Think Aloud
Writing Groups

My Notes

Learning Targets

- Write an objective summary.
- Receive peer feedback on a sample citation.

Preview

In this activity, you will begin the research process for your research report and create an entry for your annotated bibliography.

Start with Sources

1. You and your group have developed a question you need to research in preparation for designing a presentation to your classmates. You will each need to find at least three supporting sources, keeping in mind that you are trying to identify a broad range of stakeholder positions relative to your topic.

For each source you collect, you will use the MLA (Modern Language Association) format to create an annotated bibliography entry. Annotated bibliographies are tools for tracking and processing the research work you do.

Entries typically consist of two parts: a complete bibliographic citation for the source and an annotation (brief summary of the source and commentary presenting your response to the source).

For this task, the annotation part of the bibliography will (1) *summarize* the information you found in the source, (2) *analyze* how reliable the source is given the level of subjectivity, its use of evidence, or the narrowness of the perspective it presents, and (3) *assess* the degree to which the source is helpful in your research.

Summarize Effectively

A summary condenses the main ideas and most important details of a longer text into a shorter version. To summarize effectively, read the text carefully and determine the main idea. Then keep track of the details that support the main idea. If possible, use a highlighter to mark the main idea and a different color highlighter to mark the supporting details. Next, restate and condense the main idea and details in your own words. Be sure to write the source and page number on the citation and add a heading explaining what the summary is about. Finally, check the summary for accuracy by comparing it to the source material.

Read the following summary of Excerpt 1 from the *Tinker v. Des Moines* Supreme Court opinion:

Justice Fortas upheld the decision of the District Court, which ruled that wearing an armband to express an opinion is a symbolic act that is protected by the First Amendment. He also ruled that state-operated schools do not possess absolute authority and that teachers and students have freedom of speech inside the school. Schools must also respect the fundamental rights of the students. Schools cannot regulate free speech simply because they disagree with it.

☑ Check Your Understanding

Select another text from the unit and write a summary of it. Exchange your summary with a partner and provide feedback.

Writing an Entry in an Annotated Bibliography

The following are sample entries.

Sample Magazine Entry:

Author(s). "Title of Article." *Magazine Title*. Publication date or issue: page number.

Royte, Elizabeth. "We Know Plastic Is Harming Marine Life. What About Us?" *National Geographic*. June 2018: 97–98.

Royte examines in a fairly objective manner how plastic can be consumed by marine life. The article then questions whether this can cause health issues for humans who consume fish that have eaten plastic. The article contains information about how plastic affects animals, but is inconclusive about the effect it might have on humans. While it asks interesting questions and gives a lot of information about studies, it does not provide a conclusive answer.

Sample Website Entry:

Author(s). "Name of Page." Date of Posting/Revision. Title of website and domain. Name of Institution/Organization Affiliated with Site. Date of access. Web. <electronic address>.

(Note: MLA now considers URLs to be optional.)

Ocean Conservancy, Inc. "The Problem with Plastics." 2018. Oceanconservancy. org. Ocean Conservancy. Web. 27 Nov. 2018. <https://oceanconservancy.org/trash-free-seas/plastics-in-the-ocean/>.

This Web article takes a clear stance, and was written in order to persuade readers to take action to reduce plastics entering the ocean. While it may not be objective, it contains facts that can be checked for accuracy against other sources. This text appeals to readers' emotions, and also uses informal language in some places. It contains links for readers to get involved and to donate money. This source has some authority on the topic, but it also contains bias and is written for the purpose of persuading readers.

Sample Book Entry:

Author(s). *Title of Book*. Place of Publication: Publisher, publication year. Page number(s).

Smith-Llera, Danielle. *Trash Vortex: How Plastic Pollution Is Choking the World's Oceans (Captured Science History Series)*. North Mankato, Minnesota: Capstone Press, 2018.

Smith-Llera's book tells the story of how Captain Charles Morgan discovered evidence of extensive plastic pollution in the Pacific Ocean. It includes a time line of the history of plastics, facts about the variety of products in which plastics are used, explanations of how these products wind up in our oceans, and proof of their harm to both animals and humans. The author is not a scientist herself, but her book includes clearly presented facts that can be checked against other sources. 1–64.

My Notes

LANGUAGE & WRITER'S CRAFT: Citation Styles

The *MLA Handbook for Writers of Research Papers*, published by the Modern Language Association, is one of a number of style guides used in academic and professional writing. Such style guides standardize expectations and rules (called conventions) regarding writing within particular disciplines or fields. As you observe the ways different style guides format bibliographic entries, consider the following:

- When are italics used? When are quotation marks used?
- What punctuation separates the parts of the entries?
- Is the author's first or last name listed first?
- How do you format an entry for a source with no author?

Whether citing references or looking for information on formatting a research paper, consulting a style guide will help you avoid errors.

PRACTICE Correct the errors in the following bibliographic entry to make it conform to MLA style:

> William Ury. The Third Side: Why We Fight and How We Can Stop. New York. Penguin Books, 2000. Print.

Drafting the Embedded Assessment

Use the following template to compile annotated entry drafts for each of your required sources. Once you have completed your annotated entries, compile a complete annotated bibliography as a group. The bibliography should be in alphabetical order. You will also need to complete a source evaluation sheet for each online resource you use. Use a standard format for citation.

Source 1:

Annotation:

Source 2:

Annotation:

Source 3:

Annotation:

My Notes

2. Once you have completed a sample entry for your annotated bibliography, exchange the citation with a partner to get feedback. Mark your partner's citation with feedback on the following criteria:

- Does the entry include the title, author, and/or website of the source?
- Does the entry include a main idea and supporting details?
- Does the entry include an assessment of how the source was helpful in the research?
- Does the entry include a reflection of how the source is objective or too subjective?
- Does the summary follow MLA guidelines?

Based on these areas, how should your partner revise the summary to make it more comprehensive and accurate? Make notes and offer specific suggestions on how to revise the entry to be included in the annotated bibliography.

☑ Check Your Understanding

Revise your own entry to reflect the feedback you receive. Annotate it to show how you have made it better.

Creating an Annotated Bibliography

 ASSIGNMENT

Create an annotated bibliography that documents the research you have done for your group project. Each student must submit a bibliography with at least five sources. Include a citation for each source and a brief summary and evaluation.

Planning and Prewriting: Take time to make a plan for your annotated bibliography.	▪ Which sources will you choose to annotate? ▪ What information will you include for each annotation? ▪ How will you take notes to summarize, analyze, and assess the information you will include in the annotation?
Drafting and Revising: Write your annotated bibliography.	▪ How will you summarize the information found in the source? ▪ How was the source helpful in your research? ▪ How will you determine if the source was subjective or too narrow for your report? ▪ How can you format your citation to fit MLA style?
Editing and Publishing: Prepare a final draft for publication.	▪ How will you proofread and edit your annotated bibliography for proper conventions of standard English capitalization, punctuation, spelling, grammar, and usage? ▪ What tools are available for you to further polish and refine your work, such as a dictionary, thesaurus, spellcheck, or grammar check? ▪ How can the Scoring Guide help you evaluate how well you have met the requirements of the assignment?

Reflection

After completing this Embedded Assessment, think about how you went about accomplishing this task, and respond to the following:

• How did you decide which sources would be most helpful in answering your research question?

• Did you find it easy or difficult to summarize information and then evaluate it for your annotated bibliography? Why?

• Why is the responsible use of source materials important?

SCORING GUIDE

Scoring Criteria	Exemplary	Proficient	Emerging	Incomplete
Ideas	The bibliography • contains a well-written summary of relevant source information • contains a clear description of how each source is relevant to the research project • contains a thorough analysis of the reliability and credibility of each source.	The bibliography • contains a summary of source information • contains a description of how each source is relevant to the research project • contains an analysis of the reliability and credibility of each source.	The bibliography • contains a minimal summary of the information contained in the source • contains an inadequate description of how each source is relevant to the research project • contains an incomplete analysis of the reliability and credibility of each source.	The bibliography • contains minimal or no summary of the information contained in sources • does not contain a description of how each source is relevant to the research project • does not contain an analysis of the reliability and credibility of each source.
Structure	The bibliography • contains five or more sources • precisely conforms to MLA style.	The bibliography • contains five sources • follows MLA conventions.	The bibliography • may be missing sources or have incorrect citations • strays from MLA conventions in some places.	The bibliography • is missing sources • does not follow MLA conventions.
Use of Language	The bibliography • is written in a academic tone with precise diction that demonstrates a clear understanding of the research topic • demonstrates command of the conventions of standard English grammar, usage, and language.	The bibliography • is written in an academic tone with some use of precise diction • shows an appropriate use of conventions; some minor errors are evident.	The bibliography • is written in an informal or inconsistent tone • contains errors in conventions, many of which interfere with meaning.	The bibliography • is written in an informal tone • contains extensive errors in grammar, punctuation, and conventions.

My Notes

Learning Targets
- Preview the second Embedded Assessment.
- Explore how research can be presented visually in film and infographics.
- Develop a preliminary presentation plan.

Preview

In this activity, you will begin studying strategies to create a multimedia presentation.

Making Connections

In the middle part of the unit, you used the research process to create an annotated bibliography. In this part, you will use the sources from your annotated bibliography to plan a research report and multimedia presentation about your solution to an environmental conflict.

Unpacking Embedded Assessment 2

Closely read the assignment for Embedded Assessment 2 to identify and analyze the components of the assignment.

 Your assignment is to present a solution to the environmental conflict your group has researched. You will deliver a group presentation designed to contextualize the conflict for your classmates and justify your approach to resolving it.

Using the assignment and Scoring Guide, work with your class to analyze the prompt and create a graphic organizer to use as a visual reminder of the required concepts (what you need to know) and skills (what you need to do). Copy the graphic organizer into your Reader/Writer Notebook.

After each activity, use the graphic organizer to reflect on what you have learned and what you still need to learn to be successful in the Embedded Assessment.

Elements of an Argument in Film

1. In the first column of the graphic organizer that follows, paraphrase each of the elements listed.

2. As you view the film, take notes on how each of the elements is represented a short documentary film.

Elements of Argument	Film Title:
Hook:	
Claim:	
Support:	
Concessions/Refutations:	
Call to Action:	

As You Read

- Place a star next to data or other facts that give the reader documented research.
- Circle unknown words and phrases. Try to determine the meaning of the words by using context clues, word parts, or a dictionary.

My Notes

Infographic

Reducing Your Bottled Water Footprint

REDUCING YOUR BOTTLED WATER FOOTPRINT

Eating local saves water, but might not be possible 100% of the time for everyone in the U.S., with seasonal vegetables and the need to import things like bananas and coffee. However, almost everyone can **REDUCE THEIR WATER FOOTPRINT BY DRINKING LOCAL.**

How much water do we use each day?

Water consumption goes beyond how long you run the tap. Everything you eat and use – including granola bars, books, cars, and everything in between – has a "water footprint."

10-25
gallons per 5 minute shower[1]

2
gals/min from the avg. faucet[1]

the avg. U.S. consumer uses as much as **1,320** gals/day[2]

My Notes

What is bottled Water anyway?

44%

MUNICIPAL TAP WATER
that has undergone
further purification.

56%

SPRING WATER
derived from
underground springs.

The U.S. is the world's largest consumer of
bottled water. In 2011 we bought a record
9.1 billion gallons of bottled water nationwide,
equaling **29.2 gallons** per person.[3]

**9.1 billion
gallons**

Environmental impact of bottled Water

NATURAL RESOURCES

Polyethylene Terephthalate (PET)

Nearly all water bottles are made from PET
a plastic produced from crude oil.[6]

OIL

 **3x THE WATER**

The amount of water used to produce
the bottle can be up to 3 times higher
than the actual amount of water in
the bottle.[6]

RECYCLING VS TRASH

 **100%**
RECYCLABLE

27%
ACTUALLY
RECYCLED

 **35
BILLION**
IN TRASH

My Notes

RECYCLING RATES FOR WATER BOTTLES AREN'T HIGH.
Only 27% of water bottles are recycled in the U.S., despite PET being 100% recyclable.[9] Unfortunately, 35 billion plastic water bottles are thrown in the trash each year in the U.S.[7]

LANDFILLS & OCEANS

Bottles that aren't recycled end up in landfills, where they never truly degrade, and in oceans where they break down and can be ingested by birds and other marine life.[3] Bottles also end up in incinerators, and litter streets and parks across the country.

RECYCLED GOODS

Recycled bottles are shredded and melted into pellets, which can be used to make hundreds of items, such as fleece, t-shirts, car bumpers, dog beds and even other plastic bottles.[10]

DID YOU KNOW?

Trash covers up to 40% of the ocean's surface
90% is plastic[7]

In the ocean, water bottles can break down into such small pieces that just one 1-liter water bottle could end up on every mile of beach in the world.[7]

CARBON FOOTPRINT

82.8g OF CO2

The total carbon footprint of one 500 ml (16.9 oz) bottle of water is 82.8g of CO_2. This figure includes producing the PET bottle, distribution and transportation, the cardboard tray used in its packaging, and the energy used by the retailor.[5]

WATER FROM OVERSEAS >>> CAN HAVE A HIGHER FOOTPRINT

Fiji water travels up to **5,000 miles** to reach San Francisco. French brands travel up to **6,200 miles** to get there.[5]

My Notes

Do we even need bottled water?

AROUND THE WORLD

In many areas of the world, the drinking water is unsafe, making sources like bottled water a necessity.

IN THE U.S.

Most drinking water in the U.S. is completely safe. Utility companies are required to test municipal water hundreds of times a month for more than 100 chemicals. If you're still not sure, check the consumer confidence report that the EPA requires utility companies to provide.[11]

BOTTOM LINE

Nearly half of bottled water is just tap water.

500x $

Bottled water can be up to 500 times as expensive as your tap water.[12]

Imagine how much you could save with a reusable water bottle!

SOURCES
1 http://www.treehugger.com/green-home/11-clever-ways-conserve-at-home.html
2 http://waterfootprint.org/en/water-footprint/personal-water-footprint/
3 http://www.gracelinks.org/2379/bottled-water-and-water-conservation
4 http://phys.org/news156506896.html
5 http://elua.com/wp-content/uploads/2013/08/Elua-Bottled-Water-and-Our-Environment.pdf
6 http://www.dw.de/life-cycle-of-a-plastic-water-bottle/g-17266360
7 http://ecowatch.com/2014/04/07/22-facts-plastic-pollution-10-things-can-do-about-it/
8 http://www.container-recycling.org/index.php/issues/bottled-water/91-media/outsidenews/275-down-the-drain
9 http://www.mrcpolymers.com/PlasticRecyclingFacts.php
10 http://www.napcor.com/PET/whatispet.html
11 http://www.consumerreports.org/cro/water-filters/buying-guide.htm
12 http://thewaterproject.org/bottled-water-on-campus

WHEELS FOR WISHES

wheelsforwishes.org/bottled-water-footprint

Making Observations

- What detail of the infographic stood out to you?
- What is something you learned from the infographic that surprised you?

☑ Focus on the Sentence

After closely reading the infographic the first time, write an initial response to the information you have learned. Respond by writing one of each sentence type below, drawing on information from the graphic.

Statement: _____

_____

Question: _____

_____

Exclamation: _____

_____

Command: _____

_____

Working from the Text

3. Use the SMELL strategy to independently analyze the infographic.

Sender-Receiver Relationship: To what audience is the infographic directed? What is the attitude toward the target audience?

Message: What is the infographic's central claim? What content does it use to support that claim?

Effect: Emotional Strategy: What emotional appeals are included? What seems to be their desired effect? Are they fallacious? Consider both images and actual words.

Logical Strategies: What logical arguments/appeals are included? What is their effect? Are they fallacious? Consider both images and actual words.

Language: How can you compare the language in the film to the language in the infographic? What similarities and differences do you notice?

4. How credible is this infographic? What details help you to determine this?

☑ Check Your Understanding

Compare and contrast the strategies that support claims in the film and the infographic and consider how you can use these strategies in a multimedia presentation. Record your ideas in your Reader/Writer Notebook.

5. In small groups, list the strategies the filmmakers and the infographic designers use to support their claims. Discuss which strategies are most effective and why. Consider which strategies are the most memorable, and analyze what makes them memorable. In what ways do each of these strategies support specific presentation tools?

📦 INDEPENDENT READING LINK

Read and Respond

The focus of this second part of the unit is presenting research visually, so it's important to take the time to study the ways in which authors display research. For your Independent Reading, choose a fiction or nonfiction text that required extensive research by the author. For example, you might choose to read a science report, a journal article, or historical fiction. As you read, identify ways in which the author presents research visually. Create an Independent Reading Plan with personal reading goals in your Reader/Writer Notebook.

My Notes

6. Use the following questions to help your group choose a presentation tool: *Which presentation tool do you want to use? How could you incorporate multimedia elements into your presentation? How do the filmmakers and infographic designers use language and images in compelling ways? What parts of the rubric look challenging? What skills does each group member bring to the project? How will you divide the challenge in a way that correlates to each group member's strengths?*

☑ Check Your Understanding

Join with another small group to provide feedback on each group's plan. Use the rubric for guidance as you give feedback.

After both teams have shared and received feedback, reflect on the experience, recording your ideas in your Reader/Writer Notebook. What ideas did the other group spark?

Learning Targets

- Examine the genre characteristics of a report.
- Plan and draft a report.
- Revisit research to modify a research question.

Preview

In this activity, you will analyze a mentor text to help you draft your report.

As You Read

- Put checkmarks next to genre characteristics, such as subheads, numbered lists, and sources.
- Circle unknown words and phrases. Try to determine the meaning of the words by using context clues, word parts, or a dictionary.

About the Author

The United Nations Environment Programme is an agency of the United Nations that develops and promotes environmental policies around the world. It was founded in 1972 after the United Nations Conference on the Human Environment. The United Nations Environment Programme works on issues including climate change, chemicals and waste, resource consumption, and disasters and conflicts.

Research Report

from Single-Use Plastics: A Roadmap for Sustainability

by the United Nations Environment Programme

Executive summary

1   The benefits of plastic are undeniable. The material is cheap, lightweight and easy to make. These qualities have led to a boom in the production of plastic over the past century. This trend will continue as global plastic production skyrockets over the next 10 to 15 years. We are already unable to cope with the amount of plastic waste we generate, unless we rethink the way we manufacture, use and manage plastics. Ultimately, tackling one of the biggest environmental scourges of our time will require governments to regulate, businesses to innovate and individuals to act.

2   This paper sets out the latest thinking on how we can achieve this. It looks at what governments, businesses and individuals have achieved at national and sub-national levels to curb the consumption of single-use plastics.

My Notes

My Notes

It offers lessons that may be useful for policymakers who are considering regulating the production and use of single-use plastics.

The Age of Plastic: Why we need to change

3   Since the 1950s, the production of plastic has outpaced that of almost every other material. Much of the plastic we produce is designed to be thrown away after being used only once. As a result, plastic packaging accounts for about half of the plastic waste in the world. Most of this waste is generated in Asia, while America, Japan and the European Union are the world's largest producers of plastic packaging waste per capita.

4   Our ability to cope with plastic waste is already overwhelmed. Only nine per cent of the nine billion tonnes of plastic the world has ever produced has been recycled. Most ends up in landfills, dumps or in the environment. If current consumption patterns and waste management practices continue, then by 2050 there will be around 12 billion tonnes of plastic litter in landfills and the environment. By this time, if the growth in plastic production continues at its current rate, then the plastics industry may account for 20 per cent of the world's total oil consumption.

5   Most plastics do not biodegrade. Instead, they slowly break down into smaller fragments known as microplastics. Studies suggest that plastic bags and containers made of expanded polystyrene foam (commonly referred to as "Styrofoam") can take up to thousands of years to decompose, contaminating soil and water.

6   The most common single-use plastics found in the environment are, in order of magnitude, cigarette butts, plastic drinking bottles, plastic bottle caps, food wrappers, plastic grocery bags, plastic lids, straws and stirrers, other types of plastic bags, and foam take-away containers. These are the waste products of a throwaway culture that treats plastic as a disposable material rather than a valuable resource to be harnessed.

7   Plastic waste causes a plethora of problems when it leaks into the environment. Plastic bags can block waterways and exacerbate natural disasters. By clogging sewers and providing breeding grounds for mosquitoes and pests, plastic bags can increase the transmission of vector-borne diseases like malaria. High concentrations of plastic materials, particularly plastic bags, have been found blocking the airways and stomachs of hundreds of species. Plastic bags are often ingested by turtles and dolphins who mistake them for food. There is evidence that the toxic chemicals added during the manufacture of plastic transfer to animal tissue, eventually entering the human food chain. Styrofoam products, which contain carcinogenic chemicals like styrene and benzene, are highly toxic if ingested, damaging the nervous systems, lungs and reproductive organs. The toxins in Styrofoam containers can leach into food and drinks. In poor countries, plastic waste is often burned for heat or cooking, exposing people to toxic emissions. Disposing of plastic waste by burning it in open-air pits releases harmful gases like furan and dioxin.

exacerbate: worsen
carcinogenic: cancer-causing

8   The economic damage caused by plastic waste is vast. Plastic litter in the Asia-Pacific region alone costs its tourism, fishing and shipping industries $1.3 billion per year. In Europe, cleaning plastic waste from coasts and beaches costs about €630 million per year. Studies suggest that the total economic damage to the world's marine ecosystem caused by plastic amounts to at least $13 billion every year. The economic, health and environmental reasons to act are clear.

Key findings and recommendations

9   Plastic bag bans, if properly planned and enforced, can effectively counter one of the causes of plastic overuse. Nevertheless, to tackle the roots of the problem, governments need to improve waste management practices and introduce financial incentives to change the habits of consumers, retailers and manufacturers, enacting strong policies that push for a more circular model of design and production of plastics. They must finance more research and development of alternative materials, raise awareness among consumers, fund innovation, ensure plastic products are properly labelled and carefully weigh possible solutions to the current crisis. Governments must engage a broad range of stakeholders in the decision-making process as they seek to tackle the crisis. To meet the rising tide of plastics, we urgently need strong government leadership and **intervention**.

Photographer Justin Hofman calls this "a photo I wish didn't exist." Seahorses often grip natural objects such as seaweed to help them move through water, but this seahorse off the coast of Sumbawa, Indonesia, has found a plastic cotton swab to embrace.

intervention: involvement that changes or stops an action

10   Governments around the world are increasingly awake to the scale of plastic pollution. More than 60 countries have introduced bans and **levies** to curb single-use plastic waste. Plastic bags and, to a certain extent, foamed plastic products like Styrofoam have been the main focus of government action so far. This is understandable. These plastic products are often the most visible forms of plastic pollution. It is estimated that one[1] to 5 trillion[2] plastic bags are consumed worldwide each year. Five trillion is almost 10 million plastic bags per minute. If tied together, all these plastic bags could be wrapped around the world seven times every hour.

11   It is too early to draw robust conclusions on the environmental impact that bans and levies have had. In 50 per cent of cases, information about their impact is lacking, partly because some countries have adopted them only recently and partly because monitoring is inadequate. In countries that do have data, about 30 per cent have registered drastic drops in the consumption of plastic bags within the first year. The remaining 20 per cent of countries have reported little to no change.

12   Of the countries that have reported little to no impact, the main problems appear to be (i) a lack of enforcement and (ii) a lack of affordable alternatives. The latter has led to cases of smuggling and the rise of black markets for plastic bags or to the use of thicker plastic bags that are not covered by the bans. This has increased environmental problems in some cases.

13   Public-private partnerships and voluntary agreements can be good alternatives to bans. Voluntary reduction strategies allow citizens time to change their consumption patterns and provide an opportunity for affordable and eco-friendly alternatives to hit the market. The promotion and adoption of reusable bags is an example of a reduction strategy where the choice lies with the consumer. This strategy has changed consumer behaviour and reduced the use of **conventional** plastic bags in many regions.

14   Given the broad range of possible actions to curb single-use plastics and their mixed impact, UN Environment has drawn up a **10-step roadmap for governments** that are looking adopt similar measures or improve on current ones. The steps are based on the experiences of 60 countries around the globe:

1. **Target the most problematic single-use plastics** by conducting a baseline assessment to identify the most problematic single-use plastics, as well as the current causes, extent and impacts of their mismanagement.

2. **Consider the best actions to tackle the problem** (e.g. through regulatory, economic, awareness, voluntary actions), given the country's socio-economic standing and considering their appropriateness in addressing the specific problems identified.

levies: monies collected by a government

conventional: ordinary; usual

---

[1] Earth Policy Institute (2014). http://www.earth-policy.org/press_room/C68/plastic_bags_fact_sheet

[2] The Worldwatch Institute estimates that 4–5 trillion plastic bags were produced in 2002, ranging from large trash bags to thick shopping totes to flimsy grocery sacks. Assuming that the number has remained stable since then, the value used is the upper estimate of 5 trillion. http://www.theworldcounts.com/counters/waste_pollution_facts/plastic_bags_used_per_year

3. **Assess the** potential social, economic and environmental **impacts** (positive and negative) of the preferred short-listed instruments/actions. How will the poor be affected? What impact will the preferred course of action have on different **sectors** and industries?

4. **Identify and engage key stakeholder groups**—retailers, consumers, industry representatives, local government, manufacturers, civil society, environmental groups, tourism associations—to ensure broad buy-in. Evidence-based studies are also necessary to defeat opposition from the plastics industry.

5. **Raise public awareness** about the harm caused by single-used plastics. Clearly explain the decision and any **punitive** measures that will follow.

6. **Promote alternatives.** Before the ban or levy comes into force, assess the availability of alternatives. Ensure that the pre-conditions for their uptake in the market are in place. Provide economic incentives to encourage the uptake of eco-friendly and fit-for-purpose alternatives that do not cause more harm. Support can include tax rebates, research and development funds, technology **incubation**, public-private partnerships, and support to projects that recycle single-use items and turn waste into a resource that can be used again. Reduce or abolish taxes on the import of materials used to make alternatives.

7. **Provide incentives to industry** by introducing tax rebates or other conditions to support its transition. Governments will face resistance from the plastics industry, including importers and distributors of plastic packaging. Give them time to adapt.

8. **Use revenues** collected from taxes or levies on single-use plastics to maximize the public good. Support environmental projects or boost local recycling with the funds. Create jobs in the plastic recycling sector with seed funding.

9. **Enforce** the measure chosen effectively, by making sure that there is clear allocation of roles and responsibilities.

10. **Monitor** and **adjust** the chosen measure if necessary and update the public on progress.

Making Observations
- What are your initial thoughts about the research report?
- What questions do you have after reading the text?

My Notes

---

sectors: segments or parts
punitive: punishing
incubation: development

Returning to the Text

- Reread the research report to answer these text-dependent questions.
- Write any additional questions you have about the text in your Reader/Writer Notebook.

1. What is the meaning of the word "plethora" as it is used in paragraph 7?

2. What effects does the author attribute to the leaking of plastics into the environment?

3. Identify two of the author's proposed solutions to curb the negative impact of plastics in the environment.

4. In what ways have some environmental bans and levies backfired?

5. Who is the author's intended audience? What evidence directs you to this conclusion?

Working from the Text

6. Your teacher will provide the full report for "Single-Use Plastics: A Roadmap for Sustainability." Begin by studying its Table of Contents to understand what information the report contains and how it is organized. Skim and scan the report to further analyze the contents and information about the organization. Note the visual elements and how they assist in the document's organization.

7. Complete the graphic organizer to show how the report synthesizes evidence to present a claim.

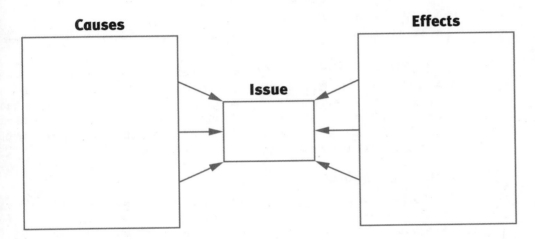

Causes → **Issue** ← **Effects**

8. Use the graphic organizer to plan your own report.

Elements of Argument	Key Points/Information to Include
Hook: • Grab attention and establish your subject.	
Claim: • State your basic position.	
Reasons and Evidence: • Present reasons that support your position on the issue. • Provide sufficient supporting evidence from your sources, including background information that explains your concerns.	
Counterclaims: • Build credibility by objectively discussing the other side. • Concede common ground on which you can agree. • Refute central claims held by the other side.	
Call to Action: • Propose the solutions you support and suggest what the benefits of adopting them might be—or the consequences of failing to do so.	

📝 Writing Prompt: Argumentative

Using evidence from the sources in your annotated bibliography, draft an introduction and two supporting paragraphs of an original report. Be sure to:

- Synthesize information from the sources in your annotated bibliography.
- Implement appropriate structure for the audience, purpose, and topic of your piece.
- Incorporate appropriate genre characteristics, including a hook, a claim, and reasons and evidence.

☑ Check Your Understanding

After drafting your first three paragraphs, go back and mark any argumentative writing characteristics you included. You should have a hook, a claim, reasons and evidence, and possibly a counterclaim. If you do not have a counterclaim yet, make a note to include at least one when you continue writing your report. Make note of any other details that are missing, and be sure to include them in future drafts.

Reflect and Revise

Now that you have written your report's first three paragraphs, revisit your research question and consider whether revising it to make it more specific would help you find more or better support for the claim in your draft. For example, if your original research question was "Does single-use plastic harm the environment?" you might change it to "How can we reduce the harm that single-use plastic has on the environment?" to find more support for the claim.

With this revision in place, review the sources in your annotated bibliography to find information gaps. Ask yourself what additional resources you might need to support your claim, and create a plan to obtain them.

Then reflect on the essential question: *What does it mean to have a voice?* Think about your own voice in this report, and how your voice might have an impact on others.

Visual Evidence

Learning Strategies

Graphic Organizer
Jigsaw
OPTIC

Learning Targets

- Evaluate and create graphs, charts, and other visuals.
- Conduct additional research.

Preview

In this activity, you will examine five different visuals and use your research to create your own visuals.

As You Read

- Jot down questions you have about data and research as you read.
- Circle unknown words and phrases. Try to determine the meaning of the words by using context clues, word parts, or a dictionary.

Infographics

from Single-Use Plastics: A Roadmap for Sustainability

by the United Nations Environment Programme

Figure 1

Plastics replacing the traditionally used materials

Product	Previous typical packaging material		Current typical packaging material	
Milk, edible oil	▶ Glass, metal		▶ 3 or 5 layer film pouches	
Toiletries (soap/shampoos)	▶ Paper, glass		▶ Plastic pouches or films	
Cement, fertiliser	▶ Jute		▶ PP/HDPE woven sack	
Toothpaste	▶ Metal		▶ Plastic lamitube	

Figure 2

Global plastic production by industrial sector, 2015

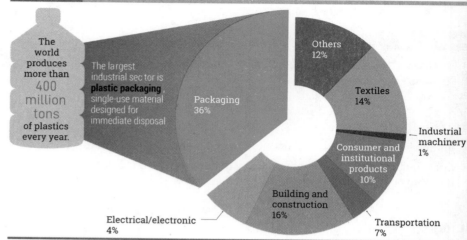

Source: *Adapted from Geyer, Jambeck, and Law, 2017*

Figure 3

Distribution of single-use plastic production by region (2014)

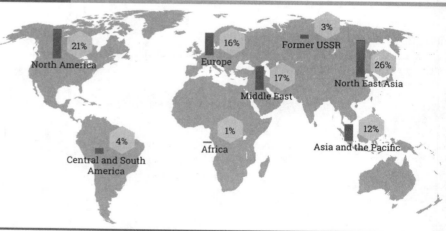

Source: *Adapted from ICIS Supply and demand database (2014)*

Figure 4

Global primary plastics waste generation, 1950–2015

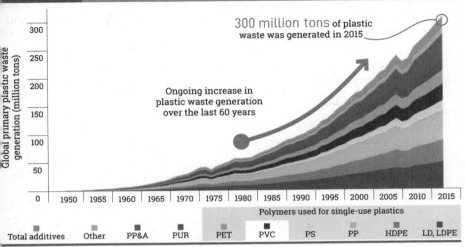

Source: Adapted from Geyer, Jambeck, and Law, 2017

Figure 5

Plastic packaging waste generation, 2014

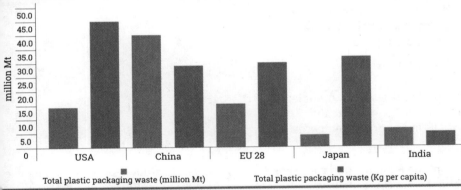

Source: Adapted from Geyer, Jambeck, and Law, 2017

Making Observations
- What do you notice about the use of color in these infographics?
- Which of the infographics do you find to be the clearest to read?

Taking an OPTIC Look at Graphics

1. Follow your teacher's instructions to form a Home Base group.

2. Move as directed by your teacher into an Expert group, in which you will work to analyze one of the figures from "Single-Use Plastics: A Roadmap for Sustainability." Use the following OPTIC chart to guide your analysis.

Overview Write notes on what the visual appears to be about.	
Parts Zoom in on the parts of the visual, and describe any elements or details that seem important.	
Title Highlight the words of the title of the visual (if one is available).	
Interrelationships Use the title as the theory and the parts of the visual as clues to detect and specify how the elements of the graphic are related.	
Conclusion Draw a conclusion about the visual as a whole. What does the visual mean? Summarize the message of the visuals in one or two sentences.	

3. Prepare to present the findings from your Expert group analysis to students in your Home Base group. Think about what could make your presentation effective or ineffective and list your ideas in the following chart.

Effective Presentation	Ineffective Presentation

4. Return to your Home Base group to present your analysis of the figure your Expert group was assigned. As each person takes a turn presenting, the rest of the group will evaluate the presentation and then give feedback to the presenter.

5. Meet with your research group. Share your revised research question from the previous activity. Then create a plan for conducting additional research to answer your revised research question and for presenting research findings in a graph, a chart, or another visual for Embedded Assessment 2. Each member of your research group will create at least one visual.

☑ Check Your Understanding

Reflect on the use of visuals in a presentation by responding to the questions in the following diagram.

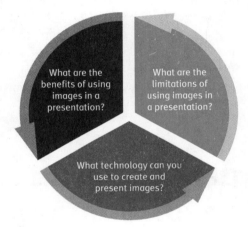

Reflect and Revise

6. Study your preliminary presentation plan from Activity 3.14. Add the creation of visuals to your plan. Then brainstorm any other multimedia tools you might want to include (e.g., interactive responses, videos, photographs, animated simulations) and update your plan to include them.

 Gaining Perspectives

In the last few activities, you have read about issues people face every day as they make eco-friendly choices that will help future generations. With a partner, monitor your state's actions concerning sustainability initiatives. Examples of actions to monitor include online communications, social media campaigns, emails, text messages, and direct mail or signage.

Keep these questions in mind:

- Where can you go to find information about your state's actions?
- Are you surprised by your state's actions? Why or why not?
- What trends do you notice?
- What more can people in your state do to foster sustainability?

When you are finished researching sustainable efforts in your state, create a brief presentation of the data and show it to your class.

INDEPENDENT READING LINK

Read and Research

Do some research on the topic of your independent reading. Create a mini-research plan in advance to identify your primary research questions about the topic. This plan may also lead you to additional research questions. Synthesize that information into a visual representation and put it in your Reader/Writer Notebook. Be sure to include a title that addresses the central idea of the visual.

My Notes

My Notes

Learning Targets

- Evaluate how an author addresses counterclaims and proposes solutions in a report.
- Conduct additional research to identify and respond to opposition and propose solutions.
- Integrate ideas from multiple texts to build knowledge and vocabulary about how people and businesses are persuaded to participate in an activitist movement.

Preview

In this activity, you will use a mentor text to help you formulate counterclaims and solutions.

As You Read

- Put a star next to the author's solutions to the problem.
- Circle unknown words and phrases. Try to determine the meaning of the words by using context clues, word parts, or a dictionary.

Research Report

from Single-Use Plastics: A Roadmap for Sustainability

by the United Nations Environment Programme

Waste management system improvements

1   Bans on plastic bags and Styrofoam items can effectively counter some of the symptoms of plastic overuse. However, better waste management systems, along with circular thinking, can help achieve long-term plastics in the environment.

Promotion of eco-friendly alternatives

2   By working together with industry, governments can support the development and promotion of sustainable alternatives in order to phase out single-use plastics progressively.

3   By introducing economic incentives, supporting projects which upscale or recycle single-use items and stimulating the creation of micro-enterprises[1], governments can contribute to the uptake of eco-friendly alternatives to single-use plastics. More details are provided as part of the Roadmap for Policymaker in section 5.3.6.

KNOWLEDGE QUEST

Knowledge Question:

How are people and businesses persuaded to participate in an activist movement?

Across Activities 3.17 and 3.18, you will read two research reports about public awareness of sustainable materials. While you read and build knowledge about the topic, think about your answer to the Knowledge Question.

sustainable: continuous or recurring

---

[1] A *micro-enterprise* is a very small business.

Social awareness and public pressure

4   Social awareness and education are essential to shape and encourage changes in consumer behaviour, but a gradual, transformational process is necessary. A longstanding change in cultural attitudes towards environmental matters is often not attainable through brief or stand-alone awareness campaigns. It is instead best achieved through embedding messaging in regular **didactic** practices and school curriculums from a very young age. Public awareness strategies can include a wide range of activities designed to persuade and educate. These strategies may focus not only on the reuse and recycling of resources, but also on encouraging responsible use and **minimization** of waste generation and litter. The relevance of education and awareness is highlighted in several case studies in section 4 as well as in the concluding chapter.

5   Public pressure can act as a trigger for policy decision-making. In Bali for instance, the "Bye Bye Plastic Bags" initiative is a social campaign lead by youth to mobilize people in Bali to say no to plastic bags. Two teenagers campaigned for over four years to get plastic bags banned from the island, starting with a petition that collected over 100,000 signatures. Despite initial resistance from the local government, the governor eventually signed a memorandum of understanding to phase out plastic bags by 2018.

6   Similarly, in New Zealand, a petition launched by a group of high school students calling on the central government to impose a NZD 0.10 levy on all plastic bags in supermarkets gained more than 17,000 signatures. The public support for action led mayors from across New Zealand to sign an open letter, asking the central government to impose a nation-wide plastic bag levy. Since the change in the ruling party following the general elections in September 2017, the government has been considering levies and bans for single-use plastic bags, although no official announcement has yet been made.

7   Public pressure is also widely recognized as **precipitating** private sector choices, given that demand drives supply.

Voluntary reduction strategies and agreements

8   Reduction strategies are another option to lessen the number of plastic bags and the amount of single-use plastic packaging. As opposed to bans and taxes, the value of reduction strategies is that they do not attempt to force sudden changes in the market. They build on the understanding that for the change to be long-lasting, it needs to be voluntary and based on choice. These strategies recognize the complexity of needs linked to bag usage, often leaving the choice up to the consumers. For the reduction strategies to be successful, adequate social awareness is necessary, as discussed in section 3.1.

9   The promotion and adoption of reusable bags as alternatives to plastic bags is an example of a reduction strategy where the choice rests with the consumer. This strategy has been effective in many local and national **contexts** to change consumer behaviour and reduce the use of conventional plastic carrier bags. Linked with social pressure and image, in Canada for instance,

didactic: teaching
minimization: reduction
precipitating: bringing about quickly
contexts: environments or settings

My Notes

reusable bags have been widely embraced, as they were promoted as the "green" choice and often offered free of charge as a promotional item by various organizations.

10   Voluntary agreements are another example of reduction strategies driven by the supply side. Voluntary agreements between the government and producers/retailers can act as an alternative to bans and be an effective instrument demonstrating public-private collaboration (see the Austria case study in section 4.1.2). Retailers and producers are indeed critical partners in effecting behavioural change by building awareness and providing alternatives.

11   For instance, in New Zealand in 2017, given the considerable public pressure from various groups to act on single-use plastic bags, and considering the lengthy process needed for a law to be enacted, the Ministry of Environment decided to pursue a voluntary agreement. Officials engaged with the two largest supermarket chains to encourage them to either charge for, or voluntarily ban, single-use carrier bags. Soon after the meetings, both chains announced the complete phase-out of such bags by the end of 2018.

Policy instruments

12   Policy interventions to reduce single-use plastic bags and Styrofoam products have been implemented at national and subnational levels. Governments have introduced different policy tools, from bans, to economic instruments such as taxes (see Table 1).

13   Governments around the world have defined and regulated the thickness of the plastic bags allowed or banned. For instance, the European Union has defined "lightweight" bags as those with a thickness not exceeding 50 microns (0.05 millimetres).

⊘ Knowledge Quest
- Who is the target audience of this report?
- Where did you find yourself agreeing with the author?

☑ Focus on the Sentence
Write sentences using the vocabulary from the text and the following subordinating conjunctions.

unless/sustainable: _____

_____

although/minimization: _____

_____

Returning to the Text

- Reread the research report to answer these text-dependent questions.
- Write any additional questions you have about the text in your Reader/Writer Notebook.

1. How do the headings in the report support its organization?

_____

_____

_____

_____

2. What is the effect of the parallelism in paragraphs 2 and 3?

_____

_____

_____

_____

3. How does the author use case studies to support a claim?

_____

_____

_____

_____

4. KQ Why does the author support reduction strategies and voluntary agreements over bans?

_____

_____

_____

_____

5. KQ What does the word "pressure" mean in paragraph 7? Use context clues and a dictionary to help you decide. Then tell how public pressure on a private sector often brings about change in the private sector.

_____

_____

_____

_____

6. **KQ** Although bans on plastic have had some success, why doesn't the author argue in favor of them?

_____

_____

_____

_____

Working from the Text

7. Consider how the author addresses a counterclaim in the mentor text. Note how the author increases the ethical appeal, or credibility, by including an argument that someone might make against the claim. By addressing and refuting it, the author gains credibility and strengthens the claim. Find examples of counterclaim, concessions, refutation, and solution in the mentor text and add them to the graphic organizer. Refer to the text you underlined and starred to help guide you.

Elements of Argument	Textual Evidence
Counterclaim	
Concession	
Refutation	
Solution	

8. Review the three paragraphs of your report. Mark any counterclaims, concessions, refutations, or solutions that you have included so far. If any of these are missing, make a note to include them in the rest of your report.

9. In the graphic organizer, fill in examples of your own. Compare and contrast these examples to the ones from the mentor text. Ask yourself whether your examples are as strong. Where do you need to strengthen your argument? What strategies will you use to do that?

Elements of Argument	Textual Evidence
Counterclaim	
Concession	
Refutation	
Solution	

10. Conduct additional research to complete a personal graphic organizer in your Reader/Writer Notebook and strengthen your report.

☑ Check Your Understanding

What are the benefits of addressing counterclaims? Be sure to support your response in your Reader/Writer Notebook with examples from the mentor text. Then, discuss as a class some of the best examples from your graphic organizers.

📝 Writing Prompt: Argumentative

Use details from the research collected in your graphic organizer to draft the final two paragraphs of your report. In these paragraphs, you will need to respond to counterclaims and propose solutions. Be sure to:

- Include specific details, examples, and commentary that reflect depth of thought.
- Critique each step of the research process, and implement changes as needed to strengthen your claim and supporting evidence.
- Produce a draft with strong organization.

My Notes

My Notes

Learning Targets

- Use a variety of source integration strategies to maintain the flow of ideas in your writing.
- Avoid plagiarism and maintain accuracy by properly citing research in writing and speech.
- Integrate ideas from multiple texts about how people and businesses are persuaded to participate in an activist movement.

Preview

In this activity, you will learn how to avoid plagiarism and use a variety of source integration strategies in your writing.

As You Read

- Underline the main idea of this excerpt. Put stars where you would like to learn about something mentioned.
- Circle unknown words and phrases. Try to determine the meaning of the words by using context clues, word parts, or a dictionary.

About the Author

Natalie Hansford is a graduate of New York University's College of Arts and Science with a Bachelor of Arts degree in psychology and journalism. She grew up in Orange Beach, Alabama, and became interested in how humans' everyday habits can harm the environment when she took an Environmental Social Movements course while studying abroad in Berlin, Germany. The class watched the documentary *Before the Flood*, which discusses the dangers of palm oil production, and the experience compelled Hansford to research the topic for a midterm paper. She continues to explore ways in which humans can limit our impact on the natural world.

Research Report

The Danger of Palm Oil Production

by **Natalie Hansford**

1   As shown in the Leonardo DiCaprio produced documentary *Before the Flood*, Walgreens, Burger King, Kraft, and Tyson are just some of the large American-based companies that harvest palm oil for the creation of their products. However, many environmental organizations insist this oil—and the resulting

KNOWLEDGE QUEST

Knowledge Question:

How are people and businesses persuaded to participate in an activist movement?

products—are typically gathered by unsustainable means. If this is true, then up to half of the typical American household is made up of these environmentally unfriendly products ("What's the Issue"). The popularity of palm oil has had far-reaching negative effects on our environment, inspiring environmental organizations to work toward more sustainable production practices.

The effects of palm oil production

2   Palm oil comes from the fruit of African palm trees. Today, these trees are grown in Africa, Asia, and the Americas. However, 85% of palm oil is produced solely from forests in Indonesia and Malaysia ("What's the Issue"). Therefore, these two countries face the highest risk of palm oil-related deforestation. Due to this deforestation, environmental group Say No to Palm Oil reports that "a third of all mammal species in Indonesia are considered to be critically endangered," with orangutans being the most at risk. According to Say No to Palm Oil, between 1000 to 5000 of these primates are killed each year as a result of the search for palm oil.

3   The production of palm oil also affects another mammal species: humans. In the rural regions of Southeast Asia, the industry creates job opportunities for the poor. However, in some cases, it also leads to harsh child labor conditions and negatively affects the indigenous people ("What's the Issue"). Indonesia is home to around 40 million indigenous people, whose land is often taken from them without permission. As a result, they are left homeless.

4   This issue impacts regions beyond Southeast Asia. Due to the far-reaching effects of deforestation, palm oil production has become a global concern. Say No to Palm Oil reports that the burning of forests and forest undergrowth for palm oil has made Indonesia "the third highest greenhouse gas emitter in the world." The contribution of this gas has, in turn, added to the acceleration of climate change.

Organizations working towards change

5   From 2004 to 2016, the number of organizations concerned with the negative effects of palm oil production has grown significantly. The Roundtable on Sustainable Palm Oil (RSPO) was created in 2004. On its official website, the organization states its goal as transforming "markets to make sustainable palm oil the norm." It takes responsibility for the production of 11.45 million tonnes of certified sustainable palm oil. The RSPO has been shown to, at least in the long-run, benefit companies which adhere to their certification standards ("What's The Issue"). It also allows all members of civil society—not simply company owners, but producers and consumers—to benefit from safer methods of palm oil production ("What's the Issue").

6   The Palm Oil Innovation Group (POIG) was created in order to build upon the existing RSPO standards ("About POIG"). POIG focuses on developing new models for palm oil production. The hope is that, if the standards for palm oil production are altered, then companies will be forced into sustainable practices ("About POIG").

My Notes

7   The World Wildlife Fund (WWF) works closely with the RSPO and POIG. According to the organization's website, they encourage companies to use sustainable palm oil in their products by posting palm oil buyer scorecards. The WWF also works to eliminate incentives for environmentally harmful palm oil production ("Palm Oil").

8   Some proponents of this sustainable reformation are not working as part of a single large organization. Thomas King, the founder of Say No to Palm Oil, has been involved in the Orangutan Project and the Jane Goodall Institute Australia ("About"). But his initiative, started in 2010, is separate from these organizations. While King urges followers to support all pro-sustainable palm oil groups, his personal focus is on inspiring citizens to take their own action. Say No to Palm Oil offers a 28-Day Palm Oil Challenge, as well as volunteer opportunities in Southeast Asia ("What Can I Do?").

9   However, some environmentalists view the work of these groups as a "greenwashing scheme." That is to say, they believe the sustainable production of palm oil can be used to deceive society into thinking companies are being environmentally friendly when they are, in fact, maintaining the same harmful status quo. According to journalist Ben Block, following RSPO regulations, forest that is not considered "high-value" can be removed. Between the countries involved in palm oil production, there is not a single consensus on what "high-value" means. Therefore, the various companies involved in production can interpret the term for their own benefit ("Can 'Sustainable' Palm Oil Slow Deforestation?").

10   Greenpeace International believes the RSPO certification has too many loopholes to truly be effective ("Can 'Sustainable' Palm Oil Slow Deforestation?"). In September 2016, Greenpeace reported that IOI, a Malaysian palm oil supplier that had recently been certified by RSPO, was going against sustainable policies ("What Does Greenpeace's Palm Oil Report Mean?"). Therefore, there may be a reason to have concerns about "greenwashing."

11   Despite any perceived flaws regarding the RSPO, the group has consistently been at the leading edge of palm oil production reform. One may wonder why a group like the RSPO is more influential than one like Say No to Palm Oil. It could be because the RSPO was created six years before the latter group. However, there is another possible answer: the RSPO provides a link between businesses and the everyday citizens affected by these companies. By insisting on safer palm oil practices, the RSPO holds businessmen accountable for their actions. Say No to Palm Oil, on the other hand, encourages individual to take responsibility for their planet's health, a goal which is not always easy for a single person.

The future of palm oil sustainability

12 Palm oil production poses challenges to the mammals and indigenous people who call the forests of Southeast Asia home. Furthermore, this practice increases the rate of universal climate change. In response to this concern, organizations like the RSPO, POIG, WWF, and Say No to Palm Oil have been working toward more sustainable palm oil creation methods—and, through this, a more sustainable planet. Out of all the organizations, the RSPO appears to have had the most success with its work. However, is placing all responsibilities on large companies really the long-term answer?

13 Changing policies and practices within ruling bodies is a natural solution for ceasing environmentally unfriendly behavior. However, it is when individuals do not take responsibility and care for their environment that such companies are able to harm the planet. Unlike the RSPO, Say No to Palm Oil provides pertinent educational sources, allowing people to do research and come to their own conclusions about this environmental hazard. By giving agency to the everyday citizen, this organization is letting those who believe they lack a voice or the time know that they do indeed possess both.

14 So maybe one should not ask how effective current sustainable palm oil efforts have been. Instead they should ask what they themselves are doing to save the forests, the indigenous people, and this earth.

Works cited

"About." *Say No to Palm Oil*, saynotopalmoil.com/About.

"About POIG." *POIG*, poig.org.

"About Us." *RSPO*, rspo.org/about.

Before the Flood. Directed by Fisher Stevens, National Geographic Documentary Films, 2016.

Block, Ben. "Can 'Sustainable' Palm Oil Slow Deforestation?" *Worldwatch Institute*, worldwatch.org/node/6082.

Michail, Niamh. "What Does Greenpeace's Palm Oil Report Mean for IOI & RSPO?" *Food Navigator*, foodnavigator.com/Article/2016/09/28/What-does-Greenpeace-s-palm-oil-report-mean-for-IOI-RSPO.

"Palm Oil." *WWF*, worldwildlife.org/industries/palm-oil.

"What Can I Do?" *Say No To Palm Oil*, saynotopalmoil.com/What_can_i_do.

"What's The Issue." *Say No to Palm Oil*, saynotopalmoil.com/Whats_the_issue.

Ø Knowledge Quest

- What is your initial reaction to the author's report?
- How would you describe the approach the author uses to persuade people to participate in an activist movement?

Returning to the Text

- Reread the research report to answer these text-dependent questions.
- Write any additional questions you have about the text in your Reader/Writer Notebook.

1. What do the details of this research report suggest is its key idea?

_____

_____

_____

_____

2. How does the author use structural elements to organize the text and inform readers?

_____

_____

_____

_____

3. What effects have unsustainable oil extraction practices had on the environment and people of Southeast Asia?

_____

_____

_____

_____

4. **KQ** What is a greenwashing scheme? Think about how this phrase relates to the idea of being "green" (or environmentally conscious) and the figurative meaning of *whitewashing*. Then tell how a greenwashing scheme influences people and whether its influence is a good or bad thing.

_____

_____

_____

_____

My Notes

. KQ What view do the authors of "Single-Use Plastics: A Roadmap for Sustainability" and "The Dangers of Palm Oil Production" share about how public perception affects an activist movement?

_____

_____

_____

_____

Ø Knowledge Quest

After reading two reports about how people and businesses are persuaded to participate in an activist movement, think about the reasons a person might decide to adopt or reject a new habit that promotes sustainability. With a partner, select a sustainable habit, such as trying reusable grocery bags. Then work out a list of actions that you could take to persuade others to adopt the habit. Evaluate each action by discussing the following questions: *Why is this action persuasive? Who might have a negative reaction to it, and why?* Then write a summary of your discussion in your Reader/Writer Notebook.

INDEPENDENT READING LINK

You can continue to build your knowledge about how people and businesses are persuaded to participate in an activist movement by reading other articles at ZINC Reading Labs. Search for keywords such as *activism* or *persuasion*.

ZINC

Working with Sources in an Academic Essay

build credibility for their claims, writers need to document their supporting vidence, whether they're using statistics, expert testimony, or even ideas taken om multiple sources. While different publications and professions use their own tyle guides for how to do this, the Modern Language Association (MLA) guidelines re typically used in language arts classes. MLA style also provides writers with a ystem for referencing their sources through parenthetical citation in their essays nd in works cited pages.

lost importantly, the use of MLA style can protect writers from accusations of *lagiarism*, which is the purposeful or accidental use of source material by other vriters without giving credit. Consider the following excerpt from page 13 of a nited Nations Environment Programme report.

> Plastic bags can choke waterways and exacerbate natural disasters. In 1988, poor drainage resulting from plastic bag litter clogging drains contributed to devastating floods in Bangladesh, causing several deaths as two-thirds of the country was submerged (see case study 4.3.2).

> Styrofoam products, due to their low density and light weight—like plastic bags—can be blown away by the wind. They can float in water and break down into smaller pieces that are highly toxic if ingested.

According to 2015 estimates, 16 of the top 20 countries contributing to marine plastic litter are middle-income countries, whose economic growth is outpacing waste management infrastructure development (Giacovelli 13).

Giacovelli, Claudia. "Single-Use Plastics: A Roadmap for Sustainability." United Nations Environment Programme. 2018. wedocs.unep.org/ bitstream/handle/20.500.11822/25496/singleUsePlastic_sustainability. pdf?sequence=1&isAllowed=y.

6. Which of the following would be considered plagiarism if it did not include a source citation? Discuss your ideas with a partner.

- Plastic bags can block waterways and worsen the impact of natural disasters.
- Styrofoam products can float in water as well as break into smaller pieces that are toxic if ingested.
- Wind and other forces of nature easily disperse Styrofoam products because they are so lightweight.

Options for Citing Sources

If you determine that a source citation is needed, you have options for how to document the source. Be sure to vary your source integration to maintain good flow in your writing.

Option A: Use a parenthetical citation to cover the source information.

Example: Styrofoam products can float in water as well as break into smaller pieces that are toxic if ingested (Giacovelli 13).

Option B: Use either footnotes or endnotes to provide source information.

Example: Styrofoam products can float in water as well as break into smaller pieces that are toxic if ingested.[1]

Option C: Start with some of the source information.

Example: Studies show that Styrofoam products can float in water as well as break into smaller pieces that are toxic if ingested (Giacovelli 13).

Option D: End with some of the source information.

Example: Styrofoam products can float in water as well as break into smaller pieces that are toxic if ingested, according to the United Nations Environment Programme (Giacovelli 13).

Option E: Insert some of the source information somewhere midsentence.

Example: Styrofoam products can float in water, studies show, as well as break into smaller pieces that are toxic if ingested (Giacovelli 13).

Option F: Insert an appositive or adjectival phrase to add credentials or clarify information.

Example: Styrofoam products—ubiquitous materials worldwide—can float in water as well as break into smaller pieces that are toxic if ingested (Giacovelli 13).

7. Revise the following sentence after paraphrasing it in your Reader/Writer Notebook to incorporate appropriate source information using at least two different options.

> **Original text:** In developing countries with inadequate solid waste management regulations, plastic bag litter can aggravate pandemics. By blocking sewage systems and providing breeding grounds for mosquitoes and other pests, plastic bags can raise the risk of transmission of vector-borne diseases such as malaria.[39]

> **Paraphrased text:**

> **Option 1:**

> **Option 2:**

iting Sources Accurately

nother key ethical issue when using sources is the accuracy of the information eing presented. Consider the information in the following infographic.

Global flow of plastic packaging waste, 2015

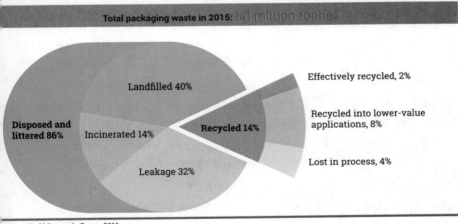

Total packaging waste in 2015: 141 million tonnes

Disposed and littered 86%
Landfilled 40%
Incinerated 14%
Leakage 32%
Recycled 14%
Effectively recycled, 2%
Recycled into lower-value applications, 8%
Lost in process, 4%

urce: *World Economic Forum, 2016*

8. Using texts you have read in this unit and the information in the table, how ethical is each of the following references?

Example: Of the total packaging waste in 2015, 14 percent was incinerated.

Example: Only 14 percent of total packaging waste was able to be recycled in 2015.

Example: Eighty-six percent of packaging waste in 2015 was disposed and littered.

Revise each of these examples and add a source citation in your Reader/Writer Notebook. Paraphrase or use direct quotations to ensure you are ethically crediting your source.

My Notes

Working with Sources in an Oral Presentation

While using evidence in an argument is crucial to its effectiveness, the information has to be cited so that the source is evident. In speaking, this tends to take a different form than in writing. Since you do not include parenthetical citations when speaking, what information should you include to indicate that your information is reliable?

As a speaker, it is particularly important that you give a thorough citation of your source. Audience members may want to find the source for further investigation, and they have no way to do so except by using information offered in your speech.

General tips on citing sources within your speech or oral presentation:

- Do not say "quote, unquote" when you offer a direct quotation. Use brief pauses to frame the quote, instead. You may say "quote" if you are trying to emphasize the quote.
- Provide enough information about each source so that your audience could, with a little effort, find it.
- If your source is unknown to your audience, provide enough information about the source for the audience to perceive it as credible. Typically, you would provide this credentialing of the source by stating the source's expertise and qualifications to discuss the topic.

Citation Examples

From a book with one author:

Typically include: Author, brief credentials, date, and title

"Dr. Derek Bok, President Emeritus of Harvard University, in his 2005 book *Our Underachieving Colleges*, wrote. ..."

From a website:

Typically include: Site title, credentials, and date last updated (some websites may not be updated on a regular basis)

"One of the most active developers of neurotechnology, Cyberkinetics, claims on their website last updated on March 24, 2006, that. ..."

From a TV or radio show:

Typically include: Name of show, date it aired, title of story, and name of reporter

"On March 24, 2006, National Public Radio's Morning Edition aired a story by reporter Christopher Joyce titled, 'Greenland Glaciers Moving More Quickly to the Ocean.' In the story, experts claimed. ..."

From an interview you performed:

Typically include: Name, date, credentials

"In a personal interview conducted on February 12, 2006, with Charlotte Maddux, director of the local chapter of the American Cancer Society, she told me. ..."

My Notes

from a print magazine:

Typically include: Name of publication, name of reporter, and date

"According to a feature article written by reporter Kelli Brown about the rising costs of medicine in the March 27, 2006, issue of *Time* magazine. ..."

from a newspaper:

Typically include: Name of reporter, name of publication, date, and version (i.e., print or electronic version). Providing additional information may give credibility to the source.

"In a front-page article in the January 17, 2006, edition of the *Washington Post* that looked ahead to President Bush's second term, reporter Dana Milbank quoted White House Chief of Staff, Andrew H. Card, Jr., who said, 'President Bush. ...'"

from a reference work:

Typically include: Title, credentials, and date of publication

"The 2005 edition of *Simmons Market Research*, considered by most to be the nation's leading authority on the behavior of the American consumer, notes. ..."

9. With your group members, identify specific pieces of evidence you are taking from sources in your research. For each, decide which type of source citation is most appropriate to establishing credibility and reliability. Revise to cite each source, using the Citation Examples.

☑ Check Your Understanding

Exchange reports with a partner and highlight all references to specific evidence, quotations, or ideas from sources. Add editing suggestions for accurate citation of sources, where needed. Be sure to vary the use of direct and indirect quotations and vary your syntax to enhance the flow of the writing.

Select key evidence that you will use to present your stakeholder's concerns to your group. Make a plan for how you will integrate oral source citations for this evidence.

Peer Presenting

Learning Strategies

Brainstorming
Graphic Organizer
Outlining

Learning Targets

- Publish and present a report to peers.
- Revise and formalize a group presentation plan.

Preview

In this activity, you will develop a rubric to evaluate reports.

My Notes

Creating a Rubric

Rubrics provide specific criteria that teachers will use to grade a project or measure understanding and growth. These tools are highly beneficial to students because they provide clear guidelines to help create a successful piece of work.

Your final reports will be evaluated in three areas: ideas, structure, and effectiveness of language. Ideas include a clear, thoroughly explained claim with strong supporting evidence. Structure evaluates your overall organization. Use of language covers making effective choices for meaning, as well as examining sentence structure. In your small groups, brainstorm what you would expect to see in exemplary reports that contain strong ideas, structure, and language. Then study several examples of rubrics and refine your ideas. Thoughtfully, complete the rest of the rubric.

Evaluating Your Report

1. Share a copy of your report with each member of your group and your teacher.

2. Practice scoring your report using the rubric your team created. Then practice scoring your group members' papers. Take some time to reflect on patterns you notice in one another's work. What are your collective strengths and weaknesses? What elements need the most revision? Which of your group members' strategies might improve your report?

Collaborative Conversation

3. Use an app or program to create a "mini presentation" of three or more slides. Use your original visual from Activity 3.16 along with at least two other forms of media to support your delivery of the report.

4. Present the slides to your research group. Rather than reading them aloud, highlight your main points using the mini presentation as support, taking care to make effective choices for communicating the slides' meaning. Consider the feedback of your group members to help guide your revisions.

5. After all of the reports are presented, use the following graphic organizer to outline and plan for a presentation that synthesizes the reports with one clear thesis with a logical progression of evidence. Consider creating a digital version of the graphic organizer so that information can be easily shifted or edited. Or, you may want to hand-draw the graphic organizer and affix removable sticky notes to each section.

Thesis Statement:

Evidence 1	Evidence 2	Evidence 3	Evidence 4

☑ Check Your Understanding

Now that you have your details in a specific, logical order, use the rubric you created to reassess your report. Are there still areas that need improvement? How can you move to *exemplary* in each category?

🎁 Independent Reading Checkpoint

Use the rubric you created to score an excerpt from your independent reading text. In your Reader/Writer Notebook, evaluate this excerpt. Reflect on its strengths and weaknesses. Ask yourself: *Has anything been omitted? Do I detect any bias? How does the author support his or her claims? How does the author address counterclaims? How can I transfer the strategies the author uses into my own future work?*

Presenting a Solution to an Environmental Conflict

 ASSIGNMENT

Your assignment is to present a solution to the environmental conflict your group has researched. You will deliver a group presentation designed to contextualize the conflict for your classmates and justify your approach to resolving it.

Planning: Collaborate with your group to evaluate evidence and potential solutions.	▪ How will you use logic, evidence, and rhetorical appeals to advocate your stakeholders' concerns? ▪ How will you integrate oral source citations to cite your research, including paraphrased and quoted text? ▪ How will your group identify common ground, significant obstacles, and potential solutions—and evaluate which solutions might actually work?
Drafting and Organizing: Draft a policy proposal and organize a collaborative presentation.	▪ How will you work cooperatively to develop and revise a plan that bridges gaps and melds arguments together into a policy proposal? ▪ How will your group collaborate to create a joint presentation that explains the process and the resulting conclusions to the rest of the class? ▪ What background information will you provide to give a context for the conflict? ▪ How will you engage your audience with a hook and provide an effective conclusion with a clear call to action? ▪ How will you select an organizing structure appropriate to purpose, audience, topic, and context? ▪ Which stakeholder positions will you present to the class (use at least three)? ▪ What evidence and citations will you include to develop claims, counterclaims, and reasons? ▪ How will you argue for a proposed solution to the problem, one that respects the wishes of all stakeholders as completely as possible and that has a positive impact?
Rehearsing and Presenting: Use effective speaking and listening to prepare, present, and observe.	▪ How can you apply effective speaking skills to rehearse an appropriate mode of delivery? ▪ How will you involve all group members in the presentation? ▪ How can you use a multimedia delivery to engage your audience? ▪ How will you take notes to demonstrate your understanding, questioning, and evaluating of your peers' presentations in a meaningful way?

Reflection

After completing this Embedded Assessment, think about how you went about accomplishing this task, and respond to the following:

- How does the issue of individual rights versus social responsibility contribute to the debate surrounding your topic? How much consideration did you have to give this issue when formulating your report?

- How persuasive is your own proposal compared and contrasted to others? What content, organization, delivery, or media enhanced persuasiveness or credibility?

SCORING GUIDE

Scoring Criteria	Exemplary	Proficient	Emerging	Incomplete
Ideas	The presentation • supports a strong policy proposal with a clear explanation of a variety of stakeholder positions • argues persuasively for an insightful potential solution • develops claims, counterclaims, and reasons with evidence and citations from a variety of credible sources.	The presentation • supports a policy proposal with an adequate explanation of several stakeholder positions • argues persuasively, for the most part, for a logical potential solution • develops claims, counterclaims, and reasons with sufficient evidence and citations from reliable sources.	The presentation • has an inadequate policy proposal; includes partial explanation of stakeholder positions • uses an inconsistently persuasive argument; solution is illogical • develops claims, counterclaims, and reasons insufficiently; may use limited or unreliable sources.	The presentation • has no policy proposal and/or lacks stakeholder positions • does not propose a potential solution • does not develop an argument and/or provides little or no evidence of research.
Structure	The presentation • demonstrates extensive evidence of collaboration and preparation • has an engaging introduction that thoroughly explains the conflict • follows a smooth and effective organizational structure • concludes with a clear call to action.	The presentation • demonstrates adequate evidence of collaboration and preparation • has an introduction that explains the conflict • follows a logical organizational structure • includes an adequate conclusion.	The presentation • demonstrates insufficient or uneven collaboration and/or preparation • has a weak introduction • uses a flawed or illogical organizational structure • includes a weak or partial conclusion.	The presentation • demonstrates a lack of collaboration or preparation • lacks an introduction • has little or no organizational structure • lacks a conclusion.
Use of Language	The presentation • uses persuasive language and precise diction • demonstrates command of the conventions of standard English grammar, usage, and language • cites and evaluates sources thoroughly in an annotated bibliography • integrates oral citations smoothly.	The presentation • uses appropriate language and some precise diction • demonstrates adequate command of the conventions of standard English • cites and evaluates sources in an annotated bibliography • includes adequate oral citations.	The presentation • uses inappropriate language; may use basic diction • demonstrates partial command of the conventions of standard English • begins to cite and/or evaluate sources in an annotated bibliography; may use improper format • includes inadequate oral citations.	The presentation • does not communicate; vague or confusing • has frequent errors in standard English grammar, usage, and language • lacks an annotated bibliography • lacks oral citations.

PRAISE, MOCK, MOURN

O ray of sunlight,
most beautiful that ever shone
on Thebes, city of the seven gates,
you've appeared at last . . . .

–from *Antigone*, by Sophocles

GOALS

- To use context to distinguish among denotative, connotative, and figurative meanings of words
- To analyze the effects of meter and rhyme schemes in poetry
- To analyze how the author's use of language informs and shapes the perception of readers
- To write literary texts such as fiction and poetry using genre characteristics and craft
- To perform a scene using vocal and visual delivery

VOCABULARY

LITERARY
dynamic character
elegy
imagery
mood
sarcasm
stage directions
static character
stichomythia
tone
voice

My Independent Reading List

Learning Strategy

Note-taking

My Notes

Learning Targets
- Preview the Essential Questions for the unit.
- Create a plan for reading independently.

Preview

In this activity, you will explore the essential questions and tasks for this unit and create a plan for your own independent reading.

About the Unit

Across time periods and regions, authors have used a variety of techniques to communicate universal purposes including praise, mockery, and mourning. In this unit, you will study the tools authors use to achieve these purposes and the effects their choices make. You'll also hone your own ability to express these purposes in creative writing and performance. You will begin the unit by studying a variety of poetic forms and analyzing them closely.

Essential Questions

Based on your current knowledge, respond to the following Essential Questions.

1. Why are humans inclined to respond to people, objects, or events with praise, mockery, or mourning?

2. How can authors use language to create an effect on their readers?

3. How can a performer communicate a character's perspective through oral and visual interpretation?

🎲 Planning Independent Reading

The focus of this unit is the exploration of praise, mockery, and mourning in world literature as these human responses to people, objects, and events are presented in drama, poetry, and fiction, and you will have the chance to expand your study of these purposes using a wide range of texts. In your Independent Reading, you have the opportunity to read longer works of fiction or nonfiction from a variety of time periods and cultures. Reading longer works will expose you to the numerous ways in which authors establish these purposes in their writing. Record your plan in your Reader/ Writer Notebook.

Three Celebrations of Food

Learning Targets
- Analyze how an author's use of language creates an effect on the reader.
- Analyze the meter and rhyme of a poem.

Preview
In this activity, you will read and analyze three odes about food, noting characteristics of the texts.

Praise
1. You'll begin this unit by examining how authors praise or celebrate something or someone. Before you begin reading, make a list of words that you associate with the word *praise*, including synonyms and figures of speech. Then, create a symbol or emoji that represents the word *praise*.

As You Read
- Highlight **imagery** based on sensory details in the text.
- Circle unknown words and phrases. Try to determine the meaning of the words by using context clues, word parts, or a dictionary.

Learning Strategies
Choral Reading
Discussion Groups
Graphic Organizer

VOCABULARY

LITERARY
Imagery is a type of figurative language in literary works that makes use of sensory language (words that appeal to the five senses) to represent ideas, actions, or objects in a text.

About the Author

Carol Coffee Reposa (b. 1943) is an author who was the poet laureate of Texas in 2018. After teaching literature and creative writing to college students for more than three decades, she became the poetry editor of *Voices de La Luna*, a Texas literary journal. For Reposa, great poetry is a gateway to invention. "You have to say new things or to say old things in a new way. One thing you can't do is say old things in old ways," she explains.

Poetry

Vegetable Love in Texas
by Carol Coffee Reposa

> Farmers say
>
> There are two things
>
> Money can't buy:
>
> Love and homegrown tomatoes.

My Notes

My Notes

5 I pick them carefully.

They glow in my hands, shimmer

Beneath their **patina** of warm dust

Like **talismen.**

Perhaps they are.

10 Summer here is a **crucible**

That melts us down

Each day,

The sky a sheet of metal

Baking cars, houses, streets.

15 Out in the country

Water-starved **maize**

Shrivels into artifacts.

A **desiccated** cache

Of shredded life.

20 Farmers study archeology

In limp straw hats.

But still I have

This feeble harvest,

Serendipity in red:

25 Red like a favorite dress,

Warm like a dance,

Lush like a kiss long desired,

Firm like a vow, the hope of rain.

Making Observations
- Which words in this poem stand out to you?
- What do you notice about the structure of the poem?

patina: coating
talismen: magical objects
crucible: container for melting
maize: corn
desiccated: dried up
serendipity: good fortune

Returning to the Text

- Reread the poem to answer these text-dependent questions.
- Write any additional questions you have about the text in your Reader/Writer Notebook.

2. How does the speaker compare and contrast summer with the tomato she picks?

it the best time of year and nothing can be the same

3. What words does Reposa use to describe tomatoes? What connotations do these words have?

glow shimmer patina talismen

4. Reread line 24. Why does the speaker call the tomato harvest "serendipity"?

to say that tomatos have a good fortune.

My Notes

Rhyme and Meter

Many poems contain specific rhyme and meter. Rhyme is the repetition of similar sounds, often the ending sounds of words. Frequently poetry employs rhyme schemes, specific arrangements of rhyme that form a pattern. Meter is the rhythm of a poem, the way the syllables are counted.

The poem you will read next includes imperfect rhymes. In slant rhymes, the end consonants of two words match but the vowel sounds before the ending consonant aren't necessarily the same. In eye rhymes, two words that have similar spellings but not pronunciations are paired (think: mood and flood). Sometimes slant and eye rhymes are also called half rhymes.

As You Read

- Underline each rhyme in the poem.
- Circle unknown words and phrases. Try to determine the meaning of the words by using context clues, word parts, or a dictionary.

About the Author

Jonathan Swift (1667–1745) was an Irish poet, essayist, and writer. He wrote satire—a type of literature that ridicules the shortcomings of individuals or institutions in an attempt to make a point. After living in England for most of his life, Swift returned to Dublin, Ireland, to serve as the dean of St. Patrick's Cathedral. Over the course of his 30 years as dean, he wrote most of his well-recognized works. Swift's poems are straightforward, using literary devices such as allusion sparingly and employing logical arguments to support his points.

Poetry

Mutton

by **Jonathan Swift**

Gently stir and blow the fire,

Lay the mutton down to roast,

Dress it quickly, I desire,

In the dripping put a toast,

5   That I hunger may remove —

Mutton is the meat I love.

On the dresser see it lie;

Oh, the charming white and red;

Finer meat ne'er met the eye,

10 On the sweetest grass it fed:

Let the jack go swiftly round,

Let me have it nice and brown'd.

On the table spread the cloth,

Let the knives be sharp and clean,

15 Pickles get and salad both,

Let them each be fresh and green.

With small beer, good ale and wine,

Oh ye gods! how I shall dine.

Making Observations

- What descriptive words in the poem catch your attention?
- How does the speaker feel about mutton?

Returning to the Text

- Reread the poem to answer these text-dependent questions.
- Write any additional questions you have about the text in your Reader/Writer Notebook.

5. Identify any half rhymes in the poem. What effect do these have on the poem?

it makes the poem smooth and so readers can keep Reading it unstead of Pausin most of the time

6. Reread the line "Let the knives be sharp and clean." What image does this evoke?

nice and clean and set up for a good dinner and so everything is perfect

7. What do you think Swift was trying to convey in this poem? Cite evidence in the text to support your answer.

he was citing that everything should be clean and perfect for anything

As You Read

- Underline details about sights, smells, and sounds.
- Circle unknown words and phrases. Try to determine the meaning of the words by using context clues, word parts, or a dictionary.

About the Author

Marcus Jackson is an American writer and poet. He studied creative writing, earning an undergraduate degree from the University of Toledo and studying at New York University. His poems have been published in many places, notably *The New Yorker* and *Harvard Review*. Jackson's poetry has focused on giving voices to those who are not largely represented in American poetry.

Poetry

Ode to Kool-Aid

by **Marcus Jackson**

You turn the kitchen
tap's metallic stream
into tropical drink,
extra sugar whirlpooling
5 to the pitcher-bottom
like gypsum sand.
Purplesaurus Rex, Roarin'
Rock-A-Dile Red, Ice Blue
Island Twist, Sharkleberry Fin;
10 on our tongues, each version
keeps a section, like tiles
on the elemental table.
In ninth grade, Sandra
employed a jug of Black Cherry

---

gypsum: white or colorless mineral

15 to dye her straightened

bangs burgundy.

When toddlers swallow you,

their top lips mustache in color

as if they've kissed paint.

20 The trendy folks can savor

all that imported mango nectar

and health-market juice.

We need factory-crafted packets,

unpronounceable ingredients,

25 a logo cute enough to hug,

a drink unnaturally sweet

so that, on the porch,

as summer sun recedes,

Granddad takes out his teeth

30 to make more mouth to admit you.

Making Observations

• What emotions do you feel while reading the poem?

• What images catch your attention?

Returning to the Text

- Reread the poem to answer these text-dependent questions.
- Write any additional questions you have about the text in your Reader/Writer Notebook.

8. What imagery does the speaker use in lines 17–19? How does this contribute to the mood of the poem?

that cool aid stays on top of your lip every time you drink it.

9. What does the narrator compare Kool-Aid to in lines 20–24? What is the effect of this contrast?

that we need more of it because it's a hit to the world

10. What is the impact of the image in the final two lines of the poem?

~~takes~~ saying he wants more room so, he could drink more of it.

Working from the Text

11. As you reread each of the poems aloud, make notes of the images you see in your mind. In what ways do the poet's choice of words and phrases, figurative language, and rhyme and meter help you create these mental images?

they help me because it gives a very good discription of what there saying

12. What is the rhyme scheme of the poem "Mutton"? What effect does the rhyme scheme have on its meaning?

the Rythem is words that make the dring sound amazing lik nectur, sweet, savor,

Examining Author's Craft

Authors make choices in their writing that reveal their feelings and influence their readers in certain ways. Looking at the choices an author makes can help you appreciate his or her writing, especially in poetry. Three elements that can be revealed through an author's language choices are tone, mood, and voice. Analyzing a poem's tone, mood, and voice will help you make meaning from the poem.

13. Highlight words in each of the poems that contribute to the tone, mood, and voice of the poem. Make notes in the My Notes section about words that stand out to you and how they affect the poem's meaning.

14. In the poem "Vegetable Love in Texas," what tone (attitude toward the subject) does the speaker use to describe the color of the tomatoes? What words help reveal the tone to the reader?

    she was using a light tone and strong words to describe why home tomatos are better

15. Form small groups. Look at the words you highlighted in each of the poems. What words did your group highlight? Look at each poem together one at a time starting with "Vegetable Love in Texas." Complete the following graphic organizer to organize your analysis of these words.

"Vegetable Love in Texas"	Mood Created	Voice	Tone Revealed Toward Subject

"Mutton"	Mood Created	Voice	Tone Revealed Toward Subject

"Ode to Kool-Aid"	Mood Created	Voice	Tone Revealed Toward Subject

6. Collaborative Conversation: What do these poems have in common? What is unique about each one?

7. Based on what you've read today, what do the genre characteristics of odes seem to be? Do you have any observations about the structure or the language? What are some ways that poets communicate praise in an ode?

INDEPENDENT READING LINK

Read and Connect

Think about the imagery of the texts you are reading in class and those from your independent reading. Choose one example from your independent reading, and write a brief statement about the imagery (sensory language) and the tone, theme, or voice it creates.

Check Your Understanding

Choose one of the poems and complete the following sentence starter using information from the poem you chose.

In the poem _____, the poet uses words such as _____ and _____ to create a mood (or tone) of _____.

My Notes

Learning Strategies

Graphic Organizer
Marking the Text

My Notes

Learning Targets

- Analyze conventions, features, and structure of poetry.
- Write an ode using characteristics, structure, and conventions of poetic odes.

Preview

In this activity, you will read and analyze "Ode to the Cat" by Pablo Neruda, then write your own ode based on what you have learned about the characteristics, structure, and conventions of poetic odes.

As You Read

- Underline characteristics of the ode that tell readers the cat is celebrated.
- Circle unknown words and phrases. Try to determine the meaning of the word by using context clues, word parts, or a dictionary.

About the Author

Pablo Neruda (1904–1973), born Neftalí Ricardo Eliécer Reyes Basoalto, was a Chilean poet who was considered one of the greatest Spanish-language poets of his time. Neruda began writing as a young man, and he won several literary competitions in high school. He began writing under a pseudonym because his family did not approve of his writing, but he eventually became a world-famous poet, diplomat, and politician in the Communist Party. He won the Nobel Prize in Literature in 1971.

Poetry

Ode to the Cat

by **Pablo Neruda**
translated by **Ken Krabbenhoft**

> There was something wrong
>
> with the animals:
>
> their tails were too long, and they had
>
> unfortunate heads.
>
> 5 Then they started coming together,
>
> little by little
>
> fitting together to make a landscape,

developing birthmarks, grace, pep.

But the cat,

10 only the cat

turned out finished,

and proud:

born in a state of total completion,

it sticks to itself and knows exactly what it wants.

15 Man would like to be fish or fowl,

snakes would rather have wings

and dogs are would-be lions.

Engineers want to be poets,

flies **emulate** swallows,

20 and poets try hard to act like flies.

But the cat

wants nothing more than to be a cat,

and every cat is pure cat

from its whiskers to its tail,

25 from sixth sense to squirming rat,

from nighttime to its golden eyes.

Nothing hangs together

quite like a cat:

neither flowers nor the moon

30 have

such consistency.

It's a thing by itself,

like the sun or a topaz,

and the elastic curve of its back,

35 which is both subtle and confident,

is like the curve of a sailing ship's prow.

The cat's yellow eyes

are the only

slot

emulate: copy

My Notes

40 for depositing the coins of night.
O little
emperor without a realm,
conqueror without a homeland,
diminutive parlor tiger, nuptial

45 sultan of heavens,
roofed in erotic tiles:
when you pass
in rough weather
and poise

50 four nimble paws
on the ground,
sniffing,
suspicious
of all earthly things,

55 (because everything
feels filthy
to the cat's **immaculate** paw),
you claim
the touch of love in the air.

60 O freelance household
beast, arrogant
vestige of night,
lazy, agile
and strange,

65 O fathomless cat,
secret police
of human chambers,
and badge
of

70 vanished velvet!
Surely there is nothing

diminutive: small
immaculate: clean
vestige: sign

enigmatic

in your manner,

maybe you aren't a mystery after all.

75 You're known to everyone, you belong

to the least mysterious **tenant**.

Everyone may believe it,

believes they're master,

owner, uncle

80 or companion,

to a cat,

some cat's colleague,

disciple or friend.

But not me.

85 I'm not a believer.

I don't know a thing about cats.

I know everything else, including life and its archipelago,

seas and unpredictable cities,

plant life,

90 the pistil and its scandals,

the pluses and minuses of math.

I know the earth's volcanic protrusions

and the crocodile's unreal hide,

the fireman's unseen kindness

95 And the priest's blue **atavism**.

But cats I can't figure out.

My mind slides on their indifference.

Their eyes hold **ciphers** of gold.

Making Observations
- What images do you picture in your mind as you read?
- What is the speaker's opinion of cats?

tenant: occupant
atavism: ancestor
ciphers: codes

Returning to the Text

- Reread the poem to answer these text-dependent questions.
- Write any additional questions you have about the text in your Reader/Writer Notebook.

1. Why does Neruda mention other animals in the poem?

2. Reread lines 75–85. What does the speaker say about those who believe they understand cats? What does the speaker believe?

3. How does Neruda describe the cat's eyes throughout the poem? What effect does his choice of words have?

4. How would you describe the structure of the poem? What effect does this create?

5. What do you notice about the length of the lines in this poem? What effect does this create?

4.3

Working from the Text

6. In lines 41–76, Neruda shifts to address the cat directly. In your Reader/Writer Notebook, list the ways in which the poet addresses the cat (beginning with "O little emperor...") and the imagery associated with each address.

7. Neruda describes the cat both by stating what the cat is like and by stating what it is not like. Return to the text and highlight words and phrases that personify or provide characteristics of the cat in one color. Highlight non-qualities in a different color.

8. Complete a graphic organizer that describes what the cat in the poem is and is not.

The cat is ...	The cat is not ...

9. Choose an object or person and generate a list of descriptive words for that subject. Be sure to also include things that are like your subject, and things that your subject is not like. Write down these words and phrases in your Reader/Writer Notebook in preparation for the writing prompt.

☑ Check Your Understanding

In a few sentences, describe what purpose Neruda's use of irregular structure achieves.

📝 Writing Prompt: Literary

Write an ode on the subject you selected in Working from the Text. Use the descriptive words you generated in the final step. Be sure to:

- Plan and revise to include appropriate structure.
- Write using characteristics of the genre, such as rhyme and sensory language.
- Include the characteristics of an ode, such as by giving the poem a traditional structure or by using word choices that glorify or celebrate your subject.

My Notes

#9 my mom
amazing
funny
out going
loving
sweet
kind
positive

Scorn in Antigone

Learning Strategies

Graphic Organizer
Small Group Discussion

My Notes

Learning Targets

- Analyze the author's purpose, intended audience, and message.
- Determine how language shapes the reader's perception.

Preview

In this activity, you will read an excerpt from *Antigone*, then analyze it for how the language mocks.

Mock

1. What do you think of when you hear the word *mock*? List synonyms for the word *mock*, and then compare your list with a partner. What connotations does *mock* have? Design a symbol or emoji that represents the word.

Synopsis

Later in this unit, you will read the full text of *Antigone*, a play written by the Gre playwright Sophocles around 440 BCE. Despite its origins in Athens nearly 2,500 years ago, the play continues to resonate with contemporary audiences around the world. Set against a backdrop of civic unrest and uprising in the city-state of Athens, the play examines questions about the power of the state, the role of lav and the duty of citizens to rebel against unjust laws.

In the play, Antigone sneaks out of the city to bury her brother Polyneices's body against the orders of the ruler Creon, who sees Polyneices as a traitor undeservi of a proper burial. Antigone tells Creon that it is more important to follow the law of the gods than to obey the law of the king. In response, Creon orders his guard to place Antigone in a cave with no food or water, essentially condemning her to death. In the excerpt that follows, Creon meets with Teiresias, a blind prophet skilled in the ancient art of augury, or predicting the future based on the flight patterns of birds. In this scene, he relays a bold warning to the king.

As You Read

- Underline words and phrases that contribute to mood, voice, and tone.
- Circle unknown words and phrases. Try to determine the meaning of the word by using context clues, word parts, or a dictionary.

About the Author

Few records exist that tell the story of the life of Sophocles (c. 496 BCE– 406 BCE), one of the great playwrights of the golden age of ancient Greece. He spent his life in the historically and politically important city-state of Athens, where he benefited from family wealth, good social connections, an excellent education, a winning personality, and a talent for writing plays that perfectly captured the spirit of his time and place. He wrote over 100 plays, but only seven remain. Sophocles, along with

Aeschylus and Euripides, is considered a master of Greek tragedy. During his time, ancient Greece was known to be in its golden age of art and forward thinking. Sophocles is credited with several innovations to the dramatic form. Increasing the number of characters in a play, for example, allowed him to make the plots more complex and interesting to audiences. By focusing on characters' fatal flaws, poor decisions, and moral dilemmas, he created suspenseful plays that also evoked audiences' sympathies.

Play

Antigone

by **Sophocles**

TEIRESIAS

You'll know—once you hear the tokens of my art.

In Greek myths, Teiresias could predict the future based on flights of birds.

INDEPENDENT READING LINK

Read and Recommend
Consider the language used in both the text you read in this activity and your independent reading selection. Write a five-line text advertisement for your peers explaining how your independent reading text uses language to shape perception.

TEIRESIAS.

defiled: made unclean
intransigence: unwillingness to compromise

1135   As I was sitting in my ancient place
        receiving omens from the flights of birds
        who all come there where I can hear them,
        I note among those birds an unknown cry—
        evil, unintelligible, angry screaming.

1140   I knew that they were tearing at each other
        with murderous claws. The noisy wings
        revealed that all too well. I was afraid.
        So right away up on the blazing altar
        I set up burnt offerings. But Hephaestus[1]

1145   failed to shine out from the sacrifice—
        dark slime poured out onto the embers,
        oozing from the thighs, which smoked and spat,
        bile was sprayed high up into the air,
        and the melting thighs lost all the fat

1150   which they'd been wrapped in. The rites had failed—
        there was no prophecy revealed in them.
        I learned that from this boy, who is my guide,
        as I guide other men. Our state is sick—
        your policies have done this. In the city

1155   our altars and our hearths have been **defiled**,
        all of them, with rotting flesh brought there
        by birds and dogs from Oedipus' son,[2]
        who lies there miserably dead. The gods
        no longer will accept our sacrifice,

1160   our prayers, our thigh bones burned in fire.
        No bird will shriek out a clear sign to us,
        for they have gorged themselves on fat and blood
        from a man who's dead. Consider this, my son.
        All men make mistakes—that's not uncommon.

1165   But when they do, they're no longer foolish
        or subject to bad luck if they try to fix
        the evil into which they've fallen,
        once they give up their **intransigence**.

---

[1] *Hephaestus* is the Greek god of fire and metalworking.
[2] *Oedipus' son* is Polyneices.

Men who put their stubbornness on show
1170 invite accusations of stupidity.
Make concessions to the dead—don't ever stab
a man who's just been killed. What's the glory
in killing a dead person one more time?
I've been concerned for you. It's good advice.
1175 Learning can be pleasant when a man speaks well,
especially when he seeks your benefit.

Making Observations

- What do you notice about how Teiresias speaks to Creon?
- What questions do you have after reading the excerpt?

Returning to the Text

- Reread the poem to answer these text-dependent questions.
- Write any additional questions you have about the text in your Reader/Writer Notebook.

2. What words does Teiresias use to convey his fright?

3. What omen does Teiresias interpret, and what is the meaning of the sign?

4. Beginning in line 1135, how does Teiresias connect his vision directly to Creon? How can Creon change the course?

5. What is the purpose of Teiresias's speech as it relates to Creon?

_____

_____

_____

_____

Working from the Text

6. Look back at the words and phrases you underlined as you read. Use the graphic organizer to analyze some of the words and phrases you selected from the reading.

Word/Phrase	Mood, Voice, or Tone	Possible Message
"murderous claws"		

7. Consider how the language in this excerpt differs from the language you studied in the texts in Activities 4.2 and 4.3. What do you notice about diction that is used to communicate mockery, and how does it differ from diction used to praise?

8. How does Teiresias highlight Creon's flaws? Identify the turning point in the text, highlighting the point when Teiresias stops sharing his own prophecy and indicates to Creon that the vision is about him. What is the impact of Teiresias's language here? Discuss in a small group.

☑ Check Your Understanding

Think about an authority figure you could write a scornful note to. What kinds of words might you use in your note to communicate your scorn?

Playing with Convention in a Sonnet

Learning Targets

- Analyze poetry for structure and meter.
- Analyze the use of satire.
- Analyze how an author draws on and transforms source material in a specific work.

Preview

In this activity, you will read and analyze two sonnets: one written by Petrarch and one written by William Shakespeare.

Petrarchan Sonnets

A Petrarchan sonnet is a structured way of writing poetry that is attributed to the Italian poet Petrarch. A Petrarchan sonnet always has fourteen lines divided into two sections. The first section is an octave, which is an eight-line stanza that follows an ABBAABBA rhyming pattern. The second section is a sestet, which is a six-line stanza whose rhyming pattern may vary. Often Petrarch's sestets follow a CDCDCD or CDECDE rhyming pattern.

In Petrarchan sonnets, the octave usually presents a conflict the speaker is dealing with and the sestet presents the resolution. The main message of the sonnet is summed up in the final two or three lines of the sestet.

As You Read

- Highlight rhyming words at the ends of lines. Use a different color for each rhyme.
- Circle unknown words and phrases. Try to determine the meaning of the words by using context clues, word parts, or a dictionary.

About the Author

Petrarch (1304–1374) is one of the best-loved poets of world literature. Originally from Arezzo, Tuscany, Petrarch is also considered one of the fathers of the modern Italian language. As a young adult, he studied law, but he began to pursue a career in literature when he realized it was his passion. His love poems, most of which are sonnets, are addressed to a woman named Laura de Noves, whom he met in 1327 and remembered for the rest of his life. Petrarch's poems can also be found under the name Francesco Petrarca.

My Notes

My Notes

Poem/Sonnet

Sonnet 90

by **Petrarch**

translated by **Morris Bishop**

She used to let her golden hair fly free
For the wind to toy and tangle and molest;
Her eyes were brighter than the radiant west.
(**Seldom** they shine so now.) I used to see

5   Pity look out of those deep eyes on me.
("It was false pity," you would now protest.)
I had love's tinder heaped within my breast;
What wonder that the flame burnt furiously?
She did not walk in any **mortal** way,

10 But with angelic progress; when she spoke,
Unearthly voices sang in **unison**.
She seemed **divine** among the dreary folk
Of earth. You say she is not so today?
Well, though the **bow**'s unbent, the wound bleeds on.

Making Observations
- What emotion does this sonnet express?
- What does this sonnet make you think of?

seldom: not very often
mortal: human
unison: sounds that have the same pitch
divine: of God
bow: curved piece of wood with ends held in line by a tight string

Shakespearean Sonnets

Beginning in the early 1590s, Shakespeare experimented with, and eventually perfected, sonnets. Sonnets originated in Italy, but they took on a distinguishing English form. They became the most popular form of poetry of Shakespeare's time in England. English sonnets feature three rhymed quatrains (four lines) followed by a rhymed couplet (two lines). In fourteen lines, the poet could create a complex theme, resolved in the final two lines. Shakespeare's sonnets, like most of his works, focus on love, beauty, the effects of time, and mortality.

Shakespeare uses different patterns of language in his poetry. Verse is a poetic form of expression that involves separate lines of specific length, usually determined by syllables. Iambic pentameter is a rhyme scheme in which each line of the poem consists of ten syllables. Shakespeare wrote all but one of his sonnets in iambic pentameter. The syllables are divided into five pairs (called *iambs* or *iambic feet*). An iamb is made up of an unstressed syllable and then a stressed syllable—for example: good BYE. Here's an example from "Sonnet 18":

> Shall I/ com PARE/ thee TO/ a SUM/ mer's DAY?
> Thou ART/ more LOVE/ ly AND/ more TEM/ per ATE

As You Read

- Underline words and phrases that show Shakespeare's tone.
- Circle unknown words and phrases. Try to determine the meaning of the words by using context clues, word parts, or a dictionary.

About the Author

William Shakespeare (1564–1616) is perhaps the most famous poet and playwright of all time. While the facts of his life are uncertain, historians have pieced together a history from his writing, church records, legal documents, and references to him in other writings of the time. Shakespeare lived during the Elizabethan period in England, a time of literary and artistic richness. Shakespeare began to focus on poetry after the 1592 plague outbreak. The London theater and other public places closed for health and safety, so Shakespeare had two options: stay and find work or tour with a theatrical company abroad. Shakespeare chose to write poetry.

Poetry

Sonnet 130

by **William Shakespeare**

My mistress' eyes are nothing like the sun;

Coral is far more red than her lips' red;

If snow be white, why then her breasts are **dun;**

If hairs be wires, black wires grow on her head.

5　I have seen roses **damasked,** red and white,

But no such roses see I in her cheeks;

And in some perfumes is there more delight

Than in the breath that from my mistress **reeks.**

I love to hear her speak, yet well I know

10　That music hath a far more pleasing sound;

I grant I never saw a goddess go;

My mistress, when she walks, treads on the ground.

And yet, by heaven, I think my love as rare

As any she **belied** with false compare.

Making Observations

- What is your first impression of the speaker?
- What images do you see in your mind as you read?

Returning to the Text

- Reread the poem to answer these text-dependent questions.
- Write any additional questions you have about the text in your Reader/Writer Notebook.

1. How are the structures of Petrarch's and Shakespeare's sonnets similar?

---

dun: dull gray-brown
damasked: patterned
reeks: smells
belied: misrepresented

2. How does the speaker of Petrarch's sonnet describe his love interest's eyes, and what problem does his description point out?

_____

_____

_____

_____

3. How does the speaker in Shakespeare's sonnet describe his mistress's eyes? What effect does this opening have?

_____

_____

_____

_____

4. Both Petrarch and Shakespeare compare a love interest's walk to something else. How is Shakespeare's comparison different from Petrarch's?

_____

_____

_____

_____

5. How are the resolutions in the sonnets alike and different? How does Shakespeare's final message to the reader differ from Petrarch's?

_____

_____

_____

_____

6. Whom or what is the speaker mocking in Shakespeare's poem?

_____

_____

_____

_____

My Notes

Working from the Text

7. In small groups, complete a choral read of Shakespeare's sonnet. What elements of iambic pentameter can you detect? Where does the poem seem deviate in meter and for what purpose?

8. Analyze the development of Shakespeare's sonnet. How do the ideas progress throughout the poem?

Structure	Analysis
Lines 1–4 (quatrain 1)	
Lines 5–8 (quatrain 2)	
Lines 9–12 (quatrain 3)	
Lines 13–14 (couplet)	

Identifying Literary Devices: Satire

9. Satire is a type of literature that ridicules the shortcomings of individuals or institutions in an attempt to make a point. Traditional sonnets in Elizabethan England were modeled on Petrarchan sonnets, which use flowery language. Highlight the flowery language that Shakespeare uses in this sonnet.

10. Discuss with a partner: How does Shakespeare employ irony and sarcasm to mock typical Petrarchan odes? What lines reveal that Shakespeare is mocking over-the-top flattery in praising his mistress, though the sonnet might seem to be mocking her at first? Return to the essential question, "How can authors use language to create an effect on their readers?"

VOCABULARY

LITERARY

Sarcasm is a form of irony used in literature to mock or ridicule in order to make a point.

☑ Focus on the Sentence

In preparation for your analysis of Shakespeare's use of satire, you will need to craft a thesis statement. Answer the following questions and then put them together into a sentence to create your thesis.

Who? (author): _____

Does what? (employs what literary device): _____

In order to do what?: _____

Now combine what you wrote into a thesis statement.

_____

11. To support your thesis statement, you need to back up your main idea with facts and evidence from the text. In the chart, list evidence from each sonnet that supports your thesis. In the left column, cite a phrase or line from the poem; in the right column, provide a brief analysis for why it supports your thesis.

Text Evidence	Analysis

☑ Check Your Understanding

In a few sentences, explain what purpose Shakespeare might have had for using satire.

✍ Writing Prompt: Literary Analysis

Write a paragraph that analyzes Shakespeare's use of satire in achieving the sonnet's purpose. Be sure to:

- Begin with a thesis that responds to the prompt and states how Shakespeare uses satire to achieve his purpose.
- Provide textual evidence for support.
- Respond using literary terminology and in an appropriately formal tone, register, and voice.

Sorrow in an Elegy

Learning Targets

- Examine how word choice contributes to a poem's mood, voice, and tone.
- Analyze how a poet uses meter, rhyme, and diction to convey a message and to shape the perception of readers.

Preview

In this activity, you will read an elegy, or a poem of mourning, and closely analyze the poet's masterful use of language to express sorrow.

VOCABULARY

LITERARY

An **elegy** is a poem of mourning, often written after someone has died. The word *elegy* comes from the Greek word *elegos*, or a "song of lament." Classical Greek elegies consisted of couplets with a very specific meter. While elegies in English often consist of couplets, the genre is not strictly bound to any particular use of rhyme or meter.

Mourn

1. What do you associate with the word *mourn*? What other words do you think of when you hear *mourn*? Make a list, and compare with a partner. Then create a symbol or emoji that evokes the ideas you discussed.

As You Read

- Annotate the text by underlining words and phrases that convey a particular mood, voice, or tone.
- Circle unknown words and phrases. Try to determine the meaning of the words by using context clues, word parts, or a dictionary.

About the Author

Wystan Hugh Auden (1907–1973) was born in York, England, and grew up in the industrial city of Birmingham. The son of a physician, Auden showed an early interest in the sciences but changed course to study English at Oxford. After a period of time working as a teacher in Britain and traveling to Germany, Iceland, Spain, and China, Auden emigrated to the United States just before the start of the Second World War, in 1939. His first book of poetry, called simply *Poems*, was published in 1928. Since then, Auden has been widely appreciated for his intellectual vigor, mastery of technique, and versatility as a poet, librettist, critic, essayist, and playwright. Several of his works have come into wide public view through media representations, including the poem "Funeral Blues," which was featured in the 1994 film *Four Weddings and a Funeral*.

My Notes

Poetry

Funeral Blues

by **W. H. Auden**

Stop all the clocks, cut off the telephone.

Prevent the dog from barking with a juicy bone,

Silence the pianos and with muffled drum

Bring out the coffin, let the mourners come.

5 Let aeroplanes circle moaning overhead

Scribbling in the sky the message He is Dead,

Put crêpe bows round the white necks of the public doves,

Let the traffic policemen wear black cotton gloves.

He was my North, my South, my East and West,

10 My working week and my Sunday rest

My noon, my midnight, my talk, my song;

I thought that love would last forever, I was wrong.

The stars are not wanted now; put out every one,

Pack up the moon and dismantle the sun.

15 Pour away the ocean and sweep up the wood;

For nothing now can ever come to any good.

Making Observations

• What are your first thoughts about the elegy?

• What images from the poem can you picture in your mind?

Returning to the Text

- Reread the poem to answer these text-dependent questions.
- Write any additional questions you have about the text in your Reader/Writer Notebook.

2. How does each line in the first stanza begin? What does the poet achieve by beginning the poem this way?

_____

_____

_____

_____

3. Revisit your annotations for the first two stanzas. Which images can you picture in your mind? What do these images have in common and what message do they convey?

_____

_____

_____

_____

4. Reread the third stanza. What does the text say explicitly, and what does that imply about the speaker's relationship with the person who has died?

_____

_____

_____

_____

5. What is the poem's rhyme scheme and meter? How do these choices of rhyme and meter connect to the poet's purpose, audience, and message?

_____

_____

_____

_____

6. How does the structure and imagery established in the first stanza repeat later in the poem, especially in the final stanza? What mood and tone do these lines help the readers experience?

_____

_____

_____

_____

Working from the Text

7. Think about the mental images you made while reading "Funeral Blues." How does the depiction of the poem in this illustration differ from your visualization?

ILLUSTRATED BY NATHAN GELGUD

8. Poets choose their words carefully, but not every word serves the same purpose. Look carefully at Auden's diction in "Funeral Blues." In the graphic organizer, record examples of words or phrases that most clearly convey the mood or tone of the poem.

Words or Phrases (include line numbers)	Analysis of Tone: What is the speaker's attitude?	Analysis of Mood: What feelings do the words evoke?

9. With a partner, choose the phrase, line, or couplet from the poem that you think most powerfully conveys the poem's tone and mood. Create an illustration to visually represent it.

10. Present your illustration to your classmates, using academic vocabulary to explain it. How do the words you selected contribute to the poem's overall message? How does your illustration get that message across to viewers?

11. You've now read poems that praise, mock, and mourn. What differences do you notice between these poems? Consider how authors use language to create these different effects? Return to the essential question: "Why are humans inclined to respond to people, objects, or events with praise, mockery, or mourning?"

☑ Check Your Understanding

Quickwrite: Revisit the unit essential question with the poem "Funeral Blues" in mind: "How can authors use language to create an effect on their readers?"

 Gaining Perspectives

In "Funeral Blues," the narrator grieves as he shares personal feelings about the loss of a loved one. While grieving is natural after a loss, for some people grief can lead to depression. Depression is a common disorder with various symptoms, such as chronic sadness, hopelessness, anxiety, irritability, and/or apathy (lack of interest in things that used to bring pleasure). People experiencing depression should speak to a trusted friend or family member, a counselor, or a nurse or doctor about such symptoms. Think about how you might learn more about the difference between grief and depression. With a partner, research and discuss where you could find expert advice on how to help a friend who recently lost someone and who may be suffering from depression. Then write a summary of your discussion in your Reader/Writer Notebook.

Two Responses to War

Learning Strategy

Close Reading
Marking the Text
TP-CASTT

Learning Targets

- Analyze the author's use of language and literary devices in a poem.
- Write a literary analysis exploring how language choices are used to advance the author's purpose.
- Integrate ideas from multiple texts to build knowledge and vocabulary about wars and war heroes.

Preview

In this activity, you will read two poems about war and analyze the authors' uses of language, literary devices, and other structural features to convey messages to the audience. Then you will write a literary analysis.

As You Read

- Underline examples of irony *I* (where reality contrasts with expectation), sarcasm *S* (comment intended to bring pain or abuse to the listener), or satire *Sa* (ridicule of person, place, or event).
- Circle unknown words and phrases. Try to determine the meaning of the words by using context clues, word parts, or a dictionary.

About the Author

Dunya Mikhail (b. 1965) is an Iraqi American poet. Born in Baghdad, Mikhail worked as a journalist in Iraq, where she was declared an enemy of the state by its brutal president, Saddam Hussein (1937–2006). She immigrated to the United States, forced to flee from the Iraqi government. Mikhail's writing is centered on themes of war, exile, and loss. She believes that coming of age as a writer in heavily censored Iraq influenced her use of metaphors and layered meaning in her poetry.

My Notes

KNOWLEDGE QUEST

Knowledge Question:

How might a war "live on" long after it is over?

In Activity 4.7, you will read two poems about the effects of war. While you read and build knowledge about the topic, think about your answer to the Knowledge Question.

My Notes

Poetry

The War Works Hard

by **Dunya Mikhail**

translated by **Elizabeth Winslow**

How magnificent the war is! S

How eager

and efficient!

Early in the morning,

5   it wakes up the sirens

and dispatches ambulances

to various places,

swings corpses through the air,

rolls stretchers to the wounded,

10   summons rain   I

from the eyes of mothers,   I

digs into the earth   I

dislodging many things   I

from under the ruins…   I

15   Some are lifeless and glistening,

others are pale and still throbbing…

It produces the most questions

in the minds of children,

entertains the gods   Sa

20   by shooting and missiles

into the sky,

sows mines in the fields   I

and reaps punctures and blisters,   I

urges families to **emigrate,**   I

25   stands beside the clergymen

as they curse the devil   Sa

(poor devil, he remains   Sa

with one hand in the searing fire)…

The war continues working, day and night.

emigrate: leave a country

30 It inspires **tyrants**
    to deliver long speeches,
    awards medals to generals
    and themes to poets.
    It contributes to the industry
35 of artificial limbs,
    provides food for flies,
    adds pages to the history books,
    achieves equality
    between killer and killed,
40 teaches lovers to write letters,
    accustoms young women to waiting,
    fills the newspapers
    with articles and pictures,
    builds new houses
45 for the orphans,
    invigorates the coffin makers,
    gives grave diggers
    a pat on the back
    and paints a smile on the leader's face.
50 The war works with unparalleled **diligence**!
    Yet no one gives it
    a word of praise.

Knowledge Quest

- What do you notice about the author's descriptions of war?
- What detail about the effects of war stands out for you?

INDEPENDENT READING LINK

Read and Discuss

Think about the language used by the authors of both the poems you have read in class and your independent reading. How has the author of your independent reading selection used literary devices such as irony, sarcasm, or satire to achieve his or her purpose? Discuss with a partner.

tyrants: absolute rulers
invigorates: energizes
diligence: energetic effort

Returning to the Text

- Reread the poem to answer these text-dependent questions.
- Write any additional questions you have about the text in your Reader/Writer Notebook.

1. KQ Describe how lines 1–14 portray war. What impact does this description have?

   it Describes how war is so good when in reality war is terrible all though w can declair dominites bat PeoPel die in war

2. KQ What does "magnificent" mean in line 1? Use context clues and a dictionary to help you decide. Then tell what you think the author's purpose is in using the word to describe the scope and effects of war.

   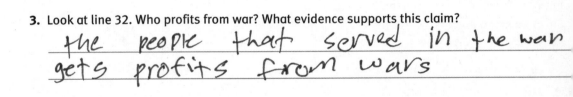

   the way they used "magnificent" was how brave and how eager war can be

3. Look at line 32. Who profits from war? What evidence supports this claim?

   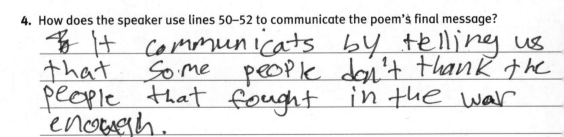

   the people that served in the war gets profits from wars

4. How does the speaker use lines 50–52 to communicate the poem's final message?

   It communicats by telling us that some people don't thank the people that fought in the war enough.

Working from the Text

5. Where in this poem can you find elements of praise? What about mockery and mourning?

6. Look at the punctuation used in the poem. In a group, discuss the author's use of exclamation points. How does the punctuation contribute to the overall mood and tone of the poem?

7. What is the primary literary device used in lines 50–52? What effect does it create?

8. Personification is a literary device that gives human characteristics to something nonhuman. In this poem, the speaker personifies war. What images of the war "working hard" does the speaker provide in the poem? In your Reader/Writer Notebook, list examples of language the speaker uses to personify war. Share and discuss your findings with your classmates.

As You Read

- Underline examples of irony.
- Put a star next to sections with sensory language.
- Circle unknown words and phrases. Try to determine the meaning of the words by using context clues, word parts, or a dictionary.

About the Author

Rita Dove (1952–) was born in Akron, Ohio. In 1976, she won the Pulitzer Price for Poetry for her collection of poems *Thomas and Beulah*. She has served as the nation's Poet Laureate, read her poetry at the White House under several different presidents, taught creative writing for many years, and appeared on several television programs.

KNOWLEDGE QUEST

Knowledge Question:
How might a war "live on" long after it is over?

My Notes

Arlington National Cemetery in Virginia

milk tooth: baby tooth

Poetry

Grape Sherbet

by **Rita Dove**

The day? Memorial.
After the grill
Dad appears with his masterpiece—
swirled snow, gelled light.
5   We cheer. The recipe's
a secret and he fights
a smile, his cap turned up
so the bib resembles a duck.
That morning we galloped
10 through the grassed-over mounds
and named each stone
for a lost **milk tooth**. Each dollop
of sherbet, later,
is a miracle,
15 like salt on a melon that makes it sweeter.
Everyone agrees—it's wonderful!
It's just how we imagined lavender
would taste. The diabetic grandmother
stares from the porch,
20 a torch
of pure refusal.
We thought no one was lying
there under our feet,
we thought it

25   was a joke. I've been trying

to remember the taste,

but it doesn't exist.

Now I see why

you bothered,

30   father.

⊘ Knowledge Quest

- What interests you about the author's attitude toward war?
- How do you feel after reading about the effects of war from a child's perspective?

Returning to the Text

- Reread the poem to answer these text-dependent questions.
- Write any additional questions you have about the text in your Reader/Writer Notebook.

9. KQ   What does *memorial* mean, and what is Memorial Day?

_____

_____

_____

_____

10. What do lines 1–4 depict? What mood do they create?

_____

_____

_____

_____

11. What does the author's use of diction and syntax reveal about the speaker in the poem?

_____

_____

_____

_____

My Notes

12. What is the significance of the line "I've been trying to remember the taste, but it doesn't exist"? How does this affect the overall meaning and mood of the poem?

_____

_____

_____

_____

_____

13. **KQ** In "The War Works Hard," war lives on by producing "questions / in the minds of children." What kinds of questions did war produce in the mind of the speaker of "Grape Sherbet" when she was a child? Why might her questions have been different from those of the children in "The War Works Hard"?

_____

_____

_____

_____

_____

_____

INDEPENDENT READING LINK

You can continue to build your knowledge about this theme by reading related poetry at ZINC Reading Labs.

Select the **poetry** filters and type keywords such as *war* in the **Search all ZINC articles** field.

Knowledge Quest

After reading "The War Works Hard" and "Grape Sherbet," discuss with a partner the similarities and differences between how the two poems show that a war "lives on" long after it is over. How are the poems' speakers alike? How are they different? How are their revelations about war or its aftermath alike and different? Take notes during your discussion. Then write a few paragraphs comparing and contrasting the poems' messages about the lasting effects of war. Be sure to:

- Refer to the poems you read for this Knowledge Quest and cite text evidence.
- Use transitions that clearly indicate comparison and contrast, such as *similarly*, *likewise*, in *contrast*, and *unlike*.

Working from the Text

14. In poetry, a word or phrase often has a meaning that is bigger than its literal meaning. Look at the beginning of the poem. What larger purpose does the word "memorial" serve in the context of the poem?

15. TP-CASTT is a method of poetry analysis through Title, Paraphrase, Connotation, Attitude, Shifts, Title (based on the context of the poem), and Theme. With a partner, complete the TP-CASTT chart for "Grape Sherbet."

Title (With no knowledge of the poem, make a prediction based on its title.)	
Paraphrase (Translate the poem line by line literally.)	
Connotation (Translate the poem's figurative language and literary devices for hidden meanings.)	
Attitude (Note the speaker's attitude, the author's attitude, and how the poem makes the reader feel.)	
Shifts (Note where the attitudes change.)	
Title (Examine the title based on the context of the poem.)	
Theme (Describe what the poem is about and the lesson.)	

16. What does the sweetness of the grape sherbet allude to about the father?

17. Compare the poems "The War Works Hard" and "Grape Sherbet" in your pairs, answering the following questions:

   - What do the war and grape sherbet represent?
   - What elements of praise, mourning, or mockery are present in each poem?
   - How can you compare and contrast the poets' use of language?

☑ Check Your Understanding

Why do you think poets layer meanings rather than explicitly stating their thoughts? Record your thoughts in your Reader/Writer Notebook, then discuss with a partner.

📝 Writing Prompt: Literary Analysis

Choose one of the poems in this activity to analyze. Write two paragraphs that analyze the poet's use of language to achieve her purpose. Be sure to:

- Begin with a thesis that responds to the prompt.
- Provide textual evidence for support.
- Respond using literary terminology and in an appropriately formal tone, register, and voice.

---

18. When drafting your response, first write your thesis. Then, you can use the following outline to plan your paragraphs:

   - Topic sentence (connect to the thesis)
   - Context for a quotation from the text supporting the topic sentence
   - Quotation from the text (cite appropriately)
   - Analysis of how the quotation supports the topic sentence/thesis
   - Closing sentence with transition

Writing a Literary Analysis of a Poem

Learning Targets

- Analyze the author's purpose through language and literary elements.
- Write a literary analysis.

Preview

In this activity, you will write a literary analysis of the poem "One Art," analyzing the author's use of literary elements to evoke praise, mockery, and mourning.

1. You will be applying your understanding of praising, mocking, and mourning in poetry in Elizabeth Bishop's poem "One Art." Read the following writing prompt before you begin.

Writing Prompt: Literary Analysis

Read the poem "One Art" by Elizabeth Bishop. Analyze how the author evokes praise, mockery, and mourning in the poem through language, rhyme, meter, and structure. Be sure to:

- Begin with a thesis that responds to the prompt.
- Provide textual evidence for support.
- Analyze how the author's use of language and structure informs and shapes the mood, voice, tone, and perception of its reader.
- Respond using literary terminology and in an appropriately formal tone, register, and voice.

As You Read

- Underline words and phrases that repeat throughout the poem.
- Circle unknown words and phrases. Try to determine the meaning of the words by using context clues, word parts, or a dictionary.

About the Author

Elizabeth Bishop (1911–1979) was a respected poet during her lifetime, yet she was not well known until after her death. Since then, her reputation has risen, and she is now considered one of the greatest 20th-century American poets. After the death of her father when she was one year old and the institutionalization of her mother when she was five years old, Bishop was raised by both sets of her grandparents, in Nova Scotia and in Massachusetts. A perfectionist when it came to revisions, Bishop published only 101 poems during her writing career. She received the Pulitzer Prize in 1956 and the National Book Award in 1970.

My Notes

Poetry

One Art

by **Elizabeth Bishop**

The art of losing isn't hard to master;
so many things seem filled with the intent
to be lost that their loss is no disaster.

Lose something every day. Accept the fluster
5   of lost door keys, the hour badly spent.
The art of losing isn't hard to master.

Then practice losing farther, losing faster:
places, and names, and where it was you meant
to travel. None of these will bring disaster.

10   I lost my mother's watch. And look! my last, or
next-to-last, of three loved houses went.
The art of losing isn't hard to master.

I lost two cities, lovely ones. And, vaster,
some realms I owned, two rivers, a continent.
15   I miss them, but it wasn't a disaster.

—Even losing you (the joking voice, a gesture
I love) I shan't have lied. It's evident
the art of losing's not too hard to master
though it may look like (*Write* it!) like disaster.

Making Observations
- What words stood out to you as you read the poem, and what made them stand out?
- What images made the biggest impression on you?

Writing an Analysis

2. Read the poem. Annotate it for elements of TP-CASTT, then complete the TP-CASTT chart.

Title (With no knowledge of the poem, make a prediction based on its title.)	something about a piece of art
Paraphrase (Translate the poem line by line literally.)	1. losing isnt hard to master
Connotation (Translate the poem's figurative language and literary devices for hidden meanings.)	
Attitude (Note the speaker's attitude, the author's attitude, and how the poem makes the reader feel.)	
Shifts (Note where the attitudes change.)	
Title (Examine the title based on the context of the poem.)	the title means ~~something~~ a piece of life like losing in life is a art
Theme (Describe what the poem is about and the lesson.)	losing isnt hard it comes by a lot in life. every day

3. With a partner, compare and contrast your poem annotations and TP-CASTT charts. Fill in missing information, and discuss points about which you have different ideas.

4. Write your thesis. You can revise your thesis as needed.

5. Draft an outline for your essay. You can use the following outline to plan your paragraphs:

   - Topic sentence (connect to the thesis)
   - Context for a quotation from the text supporting the topic sentence
   - Quotation from the text (cite appropriately)
   - Analysis of how the quotation supports the topic sentence/thesis
   - Closing sentence with transition

6. Write a draft of your analysis using your outline.

7. In small groups, trade drafts to review. Use the following checklist to provide peer feedback.

✓ Comprehension of the poem

Comments _____

_____

_____

✓ Analysis of details from the text (Is it complete and accurate?)

Comments _____

_____

_____

✓ Analysis of literary techniques used in the text (Is it complete and accurate?)

Comments _____

_____

_____

✓ Analysis of textual evidence

- Quotations
- Paraphrasing
- Appropriate citations

Comments _____

_____

_____

8. Revise and finalize your analysis based on the peer feedback and your own ideas regarding the development of the draft.

My Notes

Learning Targets

- Analyze the development of characterization, plot, and theme.
- Write a short illustrated story.

Preview

In this activity, you will read an excerpt from a graphic novel and use your understanding of its elements to create your own panel drawings.

Making Connections

In this next part of the unit, you will continue to look at how authors praise, mock, and mourn, but in two new genres: short story and graphic novel. Then you will do some creative writing of your own that conveys at least one of these purposes.

Unpacking Embedded Assessment 1

Read the assignment for Embedded Assessment 1: Writing an Analysis of a Piece of Creative Writing closely to identify and analyze the components of the assignment.

 Your assignment is to complete the creative writing piece that you started in Activity 4.12 and to write an analysis of your piece. Your analysis should document the choices you make in your creative writing that serve the purpose of praise, mockery, or mourning.

Using the assignment and Scoring Guide, work with your class to analyze the prompt and create a graphic organizer to use as a visual reminder of the required concepts (what you need to know) and skills (what you need to do). Copy the graphic organizer in your Reader/Writer Notebook.

After each activity, use this graphic to guide reflection about what you have learned and what you still need to learn in order to be successful on the Embedded Assessment.

Features of a Graphic Novel

Graphic novels are cartoon drawings that tell a story and are published as a book. As you explore *Persepolis*, you should note the distinct features that characterize the genre. Following is a list of terms to use when referring to the novel in both your writing and speaking.

Panel: squares or rectangles that contain a single image

Gutters: space between panels

Dialogue Balloons: contain communication between/among characters

Thought Bubbles: contain a character's thoughts shared only with the reader

Captions: provide information about the scene or character

Sound Effects: visual clues about sounds in the scene

eview the excerpt of the graphic novel to identify its features. Then label the
llowing image using the terms provided.

s You Read

Record details regarding key narrative elements of the story in the My
Notes space.

Circle unknown words and phrases. Try to determine the meaning of the words
by using context clues, word parts, or a dictionary.

About the Author

Marjane Satrapi (b. 1969) grew up in Tehran, Iran. As a
child, she observed the increasing loss of civil liberties
in her country. At the age of 14, her parents sent her to
Austria to escape the turmoil in Iran caused, in part, by
a clash between Eastern and Western lifestyles. After
returning to Iran for a brief period as an adult, Satrapi
moved to France, where she works as an illustrator,
graphic novelist, and author of children's books.

My Notes

Graphic Novel

PERSEPOLIS *by* **Marjane Satr**

My Notes

My Notes

My Notes

HE TOOK PHOTOS EVERY DAY. IT WAS STRICTLY FORBIDDEN. HE HAD EVEN BEEN ARRESTED ONCE BUT ESCAPED AT THE LAST MINUTE.
WE WAITED FOR HIM FOR HOURS. THERE WAS THE SAME SILENCE AS BEFORE A STORM.
I THOUGHT THAT MY FATHER WAS DEAD, THAT THEY HAD SHOT HIM.
HELLO, I'M HOME!
EBY!
THANK GOD!

My Notes

Making Observations

- What details stand out to you after reading the excerpt?
- What questions does the story raise for you?

Returning to the Text

- Return to the graphic novel excerpt to answer these text-dependent questions.
- Write any additional questions you have about the text in your Reader/Writer Notebook.

1. What is the purpose of the graphic novel? How do the words and format of the graphic novel relate to that purpose?

2. Look at the panel in which the narrator is pressed between her mother and grandmother. What can you infer from the art that is not stated directly in the text? What clues can you use to make this inference?

3. Why does the narrator compare the wait for her father to come home to "the same silence as before a storm"?

4. What do you notice about the dominance of black or white in each illustration? How do the illustrations support the text of the story?

5. Why does the grandmother say, "If I die now at least I'll be a martyr! Grandma martyr!"

6. At one point in the excerpt, the author switches from showing what is happening in the narrator's house to showing the historical events that the grandmother is describing. Why do you think she chooses to show this flashback?

_____

_____

_____

_____

7. At the end of the excerpt, we see the narrator reading a book called *The Reasons for the Revolution* and saying that she decided to read all the books she could. How does this help bring this part of the story to a satisfying close?

_____

_____

_____

_____

Working from the Text

8. Use the following graphic organizer to sort your annotations.

Narrative Elements	Details from the Narrative	Characteristics of the Graphic Novel
Setting		
Character		
Point of View		

Narrative Elements	Details from the Narrative	Characteristics of the Graphic Novel
Sequence of Events		
Theme		

9. **Collaborative Conversation:** In your group, discuss any elements of praise, mockery, or mourning you notice in the graphic novel. Why do you think the author writes for these purposes? What might she have been trying to communicate?

10. How does Satrapi use visuals to enhance the elements of praise, mockery, and mourning in this excerpt? List some examples.

📝 Writing Prompt: Literary

Create a short illustrated story, using a series of panel drawings. You may choose to write your own narrative or create panels for a scene from your independent reading. Use at least one of the visual techniques you listed in step 10 to convey praise, mockery, or mourning. Be sure to:

- Include narrative elements of setting, character, point of view, sequence of events, and theme throughout the panels.
- Use dialogue balloons and captions to inform the perception of readers.
- Edit your captions and dialogue to correctly use coordinating and subordinating conjunctions.

Mourning in the Afternoon

Learning Targets

- Analyze how an author uses diction to achieve a specific mood and tone.
- Draft a short scene using strong diction and vivid descriptions.

Preview

In this activity, you will read a short story about a family in mourning and begin developing a story of your own.

As You Read

- Jot down questions you have about the story in the My Notes section.
- Underline specific sensory details in the story that help you create a strong mental image.
- Circle unknown words and phrases. Try to determine the meaning of the words by using context clues, word parts, or a dictionary.

About the Author

Gabriel García Márquez (1927–2014), a Colombian journalist and novelist, is perhaps most famous for introducing readers to magical realism—a type of fiction that combines fantasy and conventional storytelling. García Márquez's family greatly influenced his work. He grew up with his grandparents and was inspired by his grandmother's storytelling. He is perhaps best known for his novels *Love in the Time of Cholera*—which is based partly on his parents' early relationship—and *One Hundred Years of Solitude*. In 1982, he was awarded the Nobel Prize in Literature.

Short Story

Tuesday Siesta

by **Gabriel García Márquez**
translated by **J. S. Bernstein**

1   The train emerged from the quivering tunnel of sandy rocks, began to cross the symmetrical, interminable banana plantations, and the air became humid and they couldn't feel the sea breeze any more. A stifling blast of smoke came in the car window. On the narrow road parallel to the railway there were oxcarts loaded with green bunches of bananas. Beyond the road, in uncultivated spaces set at odd intervals there were offices with electric fans,

My Notes

interminable: never-ending

My Notes

red-brick buildings, and residences with chairs and little white tables on the terraces among dusty palm trees and rosebushes. It was eleven in the morning, and the heat had not yet begun.

2 "You'd better close the window," the woman said. "Your hair will get full of soot."

3 The girl tried to, but the shade wouldn't move because of the rust.

4 They were the only passengers in the lone third-class car. Since the smoke of the locomotive kept coming through the window, the girl left her seat and put down the only things they had with them: a plastic sack with some things to eat and a bouquet of flowers wrapped in newspaper. She sat on the opposite seat, away from the window, facing her mother. They were both in severe and poor mourning clothes.

5 The girl was twelve years old, and it was the first time she'd ever been on a train. The woman seemed too old to be her mother, because of the blue veins on her eyelids and her small, soft, and shapeless body, in a dress cut like a cassock.[1] She was riding with her spinal column braced firmly against the back of the seat, and held a peeling patent-leather handbag in her lap with both hands. She bore the conscientious serenity of someone accustomed to poverty.

6 By twelve the heat had begun. The train stopped for ten minutes to take on water at a station where there was no town. Outside, in the mysterious silence of the plantations, the shadows seemed clean. But the still air inside the car smelled like untanned leather. The train did not pick up speed. It stopped at two identical towns with wooden houses painted bright colors. The woman's head nodded and she sank into sleep. The girl took off her shoes. Then she went to the washroom to put the bouquet of flowers in some water.

7 When she came back to her seat, her mother was waiting to eat. She gave her a piece of cheese, half a corn-meal pancake, and a cookie, and took an equal portion out of the plastic sack for herself. While they ate, the train crossed an iron bridge very slowly and passed a town just like the ones before, except that in this one there was a crowd in the plaza. A band was playing a lively tune under the oppressive sun. At the other side of town the plantations ended in a plain which was cracked from the drought.

8 The woman stopped eating.

9 "Put on your shoes," she said.

10 The girl looked outside. She saw nothing but the deserted plain, where the train began to pick up speed again, but she put the last piece of cookie into the sack and quickly put on her shoes. The woman gave her a comb.

11 "Comb your hair," she said.

12 The train whistle began to blow while the girl was combing her hair. The woman dried the sweat from her neck and wiped the oil from her face with

oppressive: severe

[1] A *cassock* is a long garment worn by clergy.

her fingers. When the girl stopped combing, the train was passing the outlying houses of a town larger but sadder than the earlier ones.

13 "If you feel like doing anything, do it now," said the woman. "Later, don't take a drink anywhere even if you're dying of thirst. Above all, no crying."

14 The girl nodded her head. A dry, burning wind came in the window, together with the locomotive's whistle and the clatter of the old cars. The woman folded the plastic bag with the rest of the food and put it in the handbag. For a moment a complete picture of the town, on that bright August Tuesday, shone in the window. The girl wrapped the flowers in the soaking-wet newspapers, moved a little farther away from the window, and stared at her mother. She received a pleasant expression in return. The train began to whistle and slowed down. A moment later it stopped.

15 There was no one at the station. On the other side of the street, on the sidewalk shaded by the almond trees, only the pool hall was open. The town was floating in the heat. The woman and the girl got off the train and crossed the abandoned station—the tile split apart by the grass growing up between—and over to the shady side of the street.

16 It was almost two. At that hour, weighted down by drowsiness, the town was taking a siesta. The stores, the town offices, the public school were closed at eleven, and didn't reopen until a little before four, when the train went back. Only the hotel across from the station, with its bar and pool hall, and the telegraph office at one side of the plaza stayed open. The houses, most of them built on the banana company's model, had their doors locked from inside and their blinds drawn. In some of them it was so hot that the residents ate lunch in the patio. Others leaned a chair against the wall, in the shade of the almond trees, and took their siesta right out in the street.

17 Keeping to the protective shade of the almond trees, the woman and the girl entered the town without disturbing the siesta. They went directly to the parish house. The woman scratched the metal grating on the door with her fingernail, waited a moment, and scratched again. An electric fan was humming inside. They did not hear the steps. They hardly heard the slight creaking of a door, and immediately a cautious voice, right next to the metal grating: "Who is it?" The woman tried to see through the grating.

18 "I need the priest," she said.

19 "He's sleeping now."

20 "It's an emergency, "the woman insisted.

21 Her voice showed a calm determination.

22 The door was opened a little way, noiselessly, and a plump, older woman appeared, with very pale skin and hair the color of iron. Her eyes seemed too small behind her thick eyeglasses.

23 "Come in," she said, and opened the door all the way.

24 They entered a room permeated with an old smell of flowers. The woman of the house led them to a wooden bench and signaled them to sit down. The girl did so, but her mother remained standing, absent-mindedly, with both hands clutching the handbag. No noise could be heard above the electric fan.

25 The woman of the house reappeared at the door at the far end of the room. "He says you should come back after three," she said in a very low voice. "He just lay down five minutes ago."

26 "The train leaves at three-thirty," said the woman.

27 It was a brief and self-assured reply, but her voice remained pleasant, full of undertones. The woman of the house smiled for the first time.

28 "All right," she said.

29 When the far door closed again, the woman sat down next to her daughter. The narrow waiting room was poor, neat, and clean. On the other side of the wooden railing which divided the room, there was a worktable, a plain one with an oilcloth cover, and on top of the table a primitive typewriter next to a vase of flowers. The parish records were beyond. You could see that it was an office kept in order by a spinster.

30 The far door opened and this time the priest appeared, cleaning his glasses with a handkerchief. Only when he put them on was it evident that he was the brother of the woman who had opened the door.

31 "How can I help you?" he asked.

32 "The keys to the cemetery," said the woman.

33 The girl was seated with the flowers in her lap and her feet crossed under the bench. The priest looked at her, then looked at the woman, and then through the wire mesh of the window at the bright, cloudless sky.

34 "In this heat," he said. "You could have waited until the sun went down."

35 The woman moved her head silently. The priest crossed to the other side of the railing, took out of the cabinet a notebook covered in oilcloth, a wooden penholder, and an inkwell, and sat down at the table. There was more than enough hair on his hands to account for what was missing on his head.

36 "Which grave are you going to visit?" he asked.

37 "Carlos Centeno's," said the woman.

38 "Who?"

39 "Carlos Centeno," the woman repeated.

40 The priest still did not understand.

41 "He's the thief who was killed here last week," said the woman in the same tone of voice. "I am his mother."

42 The priest scrutinized her. She stared at him with quiet self-control, and the Father blushed. He lowered his head and began to write. As he filled the page, he asked the woman to identify herself, and she replied unhesitatingly, with precise details, as if she were reading them. The Father began to sweat. The girl unhooked the buckle of her left shoe, slipped her heel out of it, and rested it on the bench rail. She did the same with the right one.

43 It had all started the Monday of the previous week, at three in the morning, a few blocks from there. Rebecca, a lonely widow who lived in a house full of odds and ends, heard above the sound of the drizzling rain someone trying to force the front door from the outside. She got up, rummaged around in her closet for an ancient revolver that no one had fired since the days of Colonel Aureliano Buendía, and went into the living room without turning on the lights. Orienting herself not so much by the noise at the lock as by a terror developed in her by twenty-eight years of loneliness, she fixed in her imagination not only the spot where the door was but also the exact height of the lock. She clutched the weapon with both hands, closed her eyes, and squeezed the trigger. It was the first time in her life that she had fired a gun. Immediately after the explosion, she could hear nothing except the murmur of the drizzle on the galvanized roof. Then she heard a little metallic bump on the cement porch, and a very low voice, pleasant but terribly exhausted: "Ah, Mother." The man they found dead in front of the house in the morning, his nose blown to bits, wore a flannel shirt with colored stripes, everyday pants with a rope for a belt, and was barefoot. No one in town knew him.

44 "So his name was Carlos Centeno," murmured the Father when he finished writing.

45 "Centeno Ayala," said the woman. "He was my only boy."

scrutinized: closely examined

46   The priest went back to the cabinet. Two big rusty keys hung on the inside of the door; the girl imagined, as her mother had when she was a girl and as the priest himself must have imagined at some time, that they were Saint Peter's keys. He took them down, put them on the open notebook on the railing, and pointed with his forefinger to a place on the page he had just written, looking at the woman.

47   "Sign here."

48   The woman scribbled her name, holding the handbag under her arm. The girl picked up the flowers, came to the railing shuffling her feet, and watched her mother attentively.

49   The priest sighed. "Didn't you ever try to get him on the right track?"

50   The woman answered when she finished signing.

51   "He was a very good man."

52   The priest looked first at the woman and then at the girl, and realized with a kind of pious amazement that they were not about to cry. The woman continued in the same tone:

53   "I told him never to steal anything that anyone needed to eat, and he minded me. On the other hand, before, when he used to box, he used to spend three days in bed, exhausted from being punched."

54   "All his teeth had to be pulled out," interrupted the girl.

55   "That's right," the woman agreed. "Every mouthful I ate those days tasted of the beatings my son got on Saturday nights."

56   "God's will is inscrutable," said the Father.

57   But he said it without much conviction partly because experience had made him a little skeptical and partly because of the heat. He suggested that they cover their heads to guard against sunstroke. Yawning, and now almost completely asleep, he gave them instructions about how to find Carlos Centeno's grave. When they came back, they didn't have to knock. They should put the key under the door; and in the same place, if they could, they should put an offering for the church. The woman listened to his directions with great attention, but thanked him without smiling.

58   The Father had noticed that there was someone looking inside, his nose pressed against the metal grating, even before he opened the door to the street. Outside was a group of children. When the door was opened wide, the children scattered. Ordinarily, at that hour there was no one in the street. Now there were not only children. There were groups of people under the almond trees. The Father scanned the street swimming in the heat and then he understood. Softly, he closed the door again.

59   "Wait a moment," he said without looking at the woman.

inscrutable: mysterious

60 His sister appeared at the far door with a black jacket over her nightshirt and her hair down over her shoulders. She looked silently at the Father.

61 "What was it?" he asked.

62 "The people have noticed," murmured his sister.

63 "You'd better go out by the door to the patio," said the Father.

64 "It's the same there," said his sister. "Everybody is at the windows."

65 The woman seemed not to have understood until then. She tried to look into the street through the metal grating. Then she took the bouquet of flowers from the girl and began to move toward the door. The girl followed her.

66 "Wait until the sun goes down," said the Father.

67 "You'll melt," said his sister, motionless at the back of the room. "Wait and I'll lend you a parasol."

68 "Thank you," replied the woman. "We're all right this way."

69 She took the girl by the hand and went into the street.

Making Observations
- Which details related to the setting stand out to you?
- What are your first impressions of the mother?

Returning to the Text

- Reread the short story to answer these text-dependent questions.
- Write any additional questions you have about the text in your Reader/Writer Notebook.

1. Use context clues to explain what a *siesta* is.

_____

_____

_____

_____

2. What conclusions can you draw about the mother based on her behavior toward the priest during the siesta?

_____

_____

_____

_____

3. What is the mother's tone as she speaks to her daughter in the beginning? What effect does this have?

_____

_____

_____

_____

4. How does the author juxtapose the townspeople to the mother to deepen her characterization?

_____

_____

_____

5. How does the author build theme through characterization?

_____

_____

_____

_____

☑ Focus on the Sentence

Use your notes and discussions about "Tuesday Siesta" to write three different types of sentences.

Write one statement about the conflict the mother faces.

_____

_____

Write a question you would like to ask the mother.

_____

_____

Write a piece of advice for the mother in the form of a command.

_____

_____

Working from the Text

6. Study the imagery based on sensory language related to the setting of the story. Include an example in the graphic organizer and identify the mood (atmosphere or emotional setting) it creates.

Examples of Imagery	Mood

7. How does the physical description of the mother develop her character? Include a quotation from the story to support your response.

Physical Description	Characterization

8. Study the excerpt in the graphic organizer. Analyze the effects of the author's syntax.

Author's Syntax	Effects
"If you feel like doing anything, do it now," said the woman. "Later, don't take a drink anywhere even if you're dying of thirst. Above all, no crying."	

9. What tone does the author use in the mother's retelling of the facts of her son's death?

10. Where in this story can you find elements of praise? What about mockery and mourning?

☑ Check Your Understanding

Make a connection between the mother in "Tuesday Siesta" and another character you have read about this year.

> ### ✍ Writing Prompt: Literary
>
> In "Tuesday Siesta," the author explores the mourning process of a family. Write a short scene in which a character mourns something or someone. Be sure to:
>
> - Use narrative techniques including dialogue and description to develop a conflict and characters.
> - Use imagery, diction, and syntax to create mood.
> - Use a variety of sentences to develop your narrative.

Language Checkpoint: Using Subordination and Coordination

Understanding Subordination and Coordination

To understand subordination and coordination, you must first understand independent and dependent clauses.

Independent clause: a phrase that contains a subject and a verb and expresses a complete thought; can stand alone as a complete sentence

Example: They were the only passengers in the lone third-class car.

Dependent (or subordinate) clause: a phrase that contains a subject and verb but does not express a complete thought; cannot stand alone as a complete sentence

Example: Since the smoke of the locomotive kept coming through the window

1. Read the following clauses and identify whether they are independent or dependent.

	Clause	I/D
a.	A mother and daughter travel to town to visit the cemetery.	
b.	Although they interrupted the town's siesta	
c.	The short story explores the idea of mourning.	

Using Coordinating Conjunctions

Coordinating conjunctions are words that join two or more words (or phrases) of equal importance.

The Seven Coordinating Conjunctions			
and	for	or	yet
but	nor	so	

2. Use each coordinating conjunction one time to complete the sentences. Choose the best option based on context.

- The mother requested a meeting with the priest, _____ the caretaker told her to come back later.
- The caretaker was surprised when the mother said it was an emergency, _____ most people appeared to respect the wishes of the priest immediately.
- The mother was already looked down on by society, _____ she did not fear additional scorn.
- The caretaker went to fetch the priest, _____ he promptly returned to see what the problem was.
- When the mother requested the keys to the cemetery, the priest had to choose to give her the keys _____ question why she wanted them so badly.
- The mother did not appear ashamed, _____ did she hesitate to claim the thief as her son.
- The mother explained how she had raised her son, _____ the priest still felt the need to ask if she had tried to get him on a better path.

Using Subordinating Conjunctions

Subordinating conjunctions are words that join two clauses, making one of them subordinate to, o
less important than, the other.

Quick Guide to Subordinating Conjunctions			
after	before	in order to	when
although (though)	even if	since	whenever
as (as if)	even though	unless	whether
because	if	until	while

3. Read the following independent clauses. Choose a subordinating conjunction to join them, and write your sentence.

- Soot and humid air filled the train.
- The daughter obeyed her mother's requests.

4. Show your sentence to a partner. Did you use the same subordinating conjunction? If not, how does the meaning of the sentence change?

5. For each of the following sentences, select the subordinating conjunction that would clearly tie the dependent clause to the independent one. Make sure that the word fits the meaning within the sentence.

- _____ she came back to her seat, her mother was waiting to eat. (Although, Before, When)
- _____ he filled the page, he asked the woman to identify herself, and she replied unhesitatingly, with precise details, as if she were reading them. (As, Before, Whenever)

6. Share your answers with a partner, and be prepared to explain why your answer is correct. Discuss how each subordinating conjunction changes the meaning of the sentence.

7. With your partner, look back at the sample sentences you have seen in this activity. What punctuation mark do you notice in most of the sentences? Where is it placed? Write down the pattern you notice.

Revising

Revise the passage to correct errors of subordination and coordination.

[1] Carlos Centeno Ayala resorted to being a thief because he was extremely poor.
[2] Although his mother warned him not to steal from anyone who really needed the food, Carlos made a fatal error. [3] He tried to rob a widow, so her years of living alone had encouraged her to keep a gun. [4] Since the morning came, Carlos was found dead and barefoot.

1. a. NO CHANGE
   b. thief, and
   c. thief, because
   d. thief, or
2. a. NO CHANGE
   b. Because
   c. After
   d. When
3. a. NO CHANGE
   b. widow, but
   c. widow, for
   d. widow, yet
4. a. NO CHANGE
   b. When
   c. Since
   d. While

☑ Check Your Understanding

In Activity 4.11, you will peer edit a classmate's writing. Look for ways to combine sentences or fix incomplete sentences using coordinating and subordinating conjunctions. Suggest which conjunctions you would choose, and explain to the student why the conjunctions make the writing clearer. Then add an item to your **Editor's Checklist** to help you remember to check your writing for coordinating and subordinating conjunctions.

Practice

Return to the scene that you wrote at the end of Activity 4.10. If you did not use any coordinating conjunctions, find two sentences you can combine. If you did not use any subordinating conjunctions, find an opportunity to use one. If you already used conjunctions, be sure you used ones that make sense and that you punctuated them properly.

Writing to Praise, Mock, or Mourn

Learning Strategies

Drafting
Graphic Organizer
Webbing
Writer's Checklist

Learning Targets

- Create a text that praises, mocks, or mourns.
- Apply peer suggestions to help you create a final draft of your composition.

Preview

In this activity, you will write and revise a literary text that praises, mocks, or mourns a person, object, or event.

1. Reading helps us become better writers, and writing helps us become better readers. In this activity, you'll draft a piece of creative writing where you'll draw on understanding of how authors communicate praise, mockery, and mourning. By doing so, you'll place yourself in the shoes of the authors you've read in this unit. Read the following prompt before you begin.

Writing Prompt: Literary

Think back on how the texts in this unit have conveyed praise, mockery, or mourning. Choose one of these three purposes and create a literary text that illustrates this purpose. You can choose from any of the genres studied in this unit, including poetry, drama, short story, and graphic novel. Be sure to:

- Choose diction and syntax that effectively create mood, voice, and tone appropriate to your purpose.
- Use literary devices appropriate to the genre you select.
- Use language that informs and shapes the perception of your reader.

Brainstorming

2. Before you begin writing, take time to brainstorm some ideas. Use the following web organizer to list people, objects, or events you might praise, mock, or mourn.

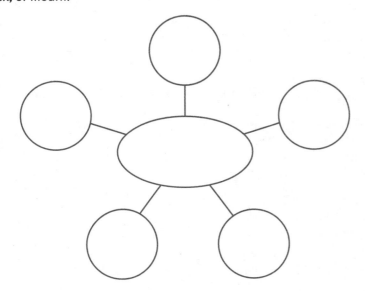

INDEPENDENT READING LINK

Read and Discuss

Choose a passage from your independent reading book and rewrite it for the purpose of praise, mockery, or mourning. Then share your writing with a classmate. Have your classmate rewrite it using one of the remaining purposes—praise, mockery, or mourning—while you rewrite his/hers. Discuss how these purposes transform the text and what effect they have on the reader.

My Notes

3. Highlight the ideas in your web organizer that resonate with you. Then, discuss these highlighted topics with a partner to narrow your focus to one idea you want to pursue. As you review genre characteristics, consider whether your topic will be successful for the format you've chosen.

Genre Characteristics

4. After you have selected your topic, use the graphic organizer below to help you organize ideas for your draft. Note that not every genre characteristic will apply to the genre you select. Identify the rows that are relevant to your genre, and use those rows to plan your writing.

Genre Characteristics	Questions to Ask Yourself	My Details
Setting	• What is the most logical time and place for my story? • What sensory details will make my setting unique? • What type of imagery will I use to set the mood (atmosphere or emotional setting)?	
Plot	• What are the conflicts in my story? • How are these conflicts resolved? • What do these conflicts reveal about character and theme?	
Character	• Who are my characters and what makes them interesting? • What are my characters' motivations? • How do my characters speak and work with others?	
Point of View	• Who is the story's narrator? • Does the point of view make sense given the purpose of the story?	
Imagery	• Are my sensory details specific and clear? • Do my details serve the purpose to praise, mock, or mourn? • Do my details establish the right mood (atmosphere or emotional setting) for the story?	
Dialogue	• Do I show rather than tell? • Is each character's dialogue distinct? • How does dialogue move the story forward?	
Theme	• What lesson does the main character learn in the story? • How does the character learn this lesson? • Does the theme have universal applications?	
Visual Techniques	• In what ways do the relative size of the panels emphasize important story elements? • Would sound or motion effects help convey movement? • Which sensory details can be conveyed visually?	

Draft

5. Once you have completed your graphic organizer, use a computer to start writing your first draft. Use your graphic organizer to help you fill in the details of your story. Be sure to include clear details that serve the purpose to praise, mock, or mourn.

Peer Revision

6. Work with an assigned group of four or five to begin a round of peer revision. Group members will take on different roles (reader, writer, or listener) as they review each other's writing. Use the chart to help you get the most out of each role. As groups members review your draft, use a computer to make notes directly on your draft. After the review, show your notes to group members so that you can be sure you understood their suggestions. Then save the draft with your notes from the peer review so that you can reference it later as you make revisions.

The purpose of peer revision is to:

- Provide a safe environment in which to share your stories.
- Receive meaningful feedback to help you improve your story in specific areas.
- Learn specific strategies for revision.

Group Member Role	Guidelines	Discussion/Response Starters
The Reader: Reads the text aloud, then starts the discussion.	The reader shares his/her understanding of the story with the writer. The reader provides feedback for revision.	Compliments: • You have strong word choice, such as . . . • Your descriptions make me feel . . . • Your writing reminds me of . . .
The Listeners: Take notes on the reader's comments. Prepare questions for the writer. Offer additional constructive statements.	The listeners focus on positive and constructive statements to describe the writing. The listeners rely on the graphic organizer from step 4 to give productive feedback.	Comments and Suggestions: • I enjoyed the part when . . . • I was confused when . . . • How will you resolve (a specific issue)? • Where do you see your text going from here?
The Writer: Listens to the read aloud, takes notes, and answers questions and concerns.	The writer listens carefully to comments to ensure that the readers are getting the essence of the story. The writer asks questions to ensure comprehension of suggestions. The writer considers advice to improve writing, and incorporates at least some of the feedback into the revision.	Questions: • What areas need more development? • Which parts are confusing or ineffective? • What strategies can I use to improve this part?

Final Draft

7. Revise your composition using both the suggestions from your peer revision group and your new ideas. Be sure to read your draft aloud, highlighting any areas that seem clunky or unnecessary. Continue until you are happy with the final product. Be sure to take the time to polish your text, as you will be analyzing it in the next activity. Consult the Areas for Revision checklist as you make changes:

Areas for Revision	Questions to Ask Yourself
Praise, Mock, or Mourn	• Do I convey the clear purpose to praise, mock, or mourn in the story? • Do I incorporate suggestions from my peer group? • Is my word choice optimal? How does my diction create specific connotations?
Setting and Plot	• Do I have a clear setting? • Does my setting help establish mood? • Is my narrative believable?
Characters and Point of View	• Do I introduce characters effectively? • Do I have a strong, complex protagonist? • Does the story clearly establish a point of view?
Imagery	• Is the imagery purposeful? • What mood does my imagery evoke? • Is my language fresh or cliché?
Dialogue	• Is my dialogue varied and interesting? • Do my characters have unique ways of speaking? • Does my dialogue move the story forward?
Theme	• Have I established a thought-provoking theme?
Visual Technique (for graphic novel-style stories only)	• Have I used visual techniques such as color, scale, and motion to create an effect on the reader?

8. After you finish your final draft, compare and contrast it with your first draft. Reflect on some the changes and how they advance the narrative more effectively.

ⓘ Independent Reading Checkpoint

Review your independent reading text and analyze how the author uses literary devices such as imagery, irony, sarcasm, and satire to shape the reader's perception of a person, character, event, or idea. Consider whether the author's intent was to praise, mock, or mourn or to do something else. Then write a literary analysis of the text that includes a thesis statement about the author's purpose for writing and support it with examples from the text that show how the author used literary devices to steer the reader's thinking and communicate the theme of his or her work. Use your notes from this unit's Independent Reading Links to help you.

ASSIGNMENT

Your assignment is to write an analysis of your creative writing piece, or of another text from this unit. Your analysis should examine the choices made that serve the purpose of praise, mockery, or mourning.

Planning and Prewriting: Take time to make a plan for your essay.	■ How can you draft a thesis that explains the ways in which the purpose of praise, mockery, or mourning drives the text?
	■ What textual support can you find for your thesis?
	■ How can you use an outline to plan the structure of your essay?
Drafting and Revising: Write your analytical essay.	■ How will you introduce your topic, organize your ideas, and provide a thoughtful concluding statement?
	■ How will you integrate textual evidence from your literary text with commentary about how the evidence supports your thesis and topic sentences?
	■ How will you demonstrate your understanding of genre characteristics of literary texts?
Editing and Publishing: Prepare a final draft for publication.	■ What strategies or tools, such as Peer Editing or an Editor's Checklist, will you use to help you edit and proofread your essay for proper conventions of standard English capitalization, punctuation, spelling, grammar, and usage?
	■ What tools are available for you to further polish and refine your work, such as a style guide, dictionary, thesaurus, spell-check, or grammar check?
	■ How can the Scoring Guide help you evaluate how well you have met the requirements of the assignment?

Reflection

After completing this Embedded Assessment, think about how you went about accomplishing this task, and respond to the following questions:

- Why do works written for the purpose of praise, mockery, or mourning cross time and cultures?
- How does your experience of writing your own work in Activity 4.11 help you understand how these themes are conveyed in a new way?

SCORING GUIDE

Scoring Criteria	Exemplary	Proficient	Emerging	Incomplete
Ideas	The essay • thoroughly examines the effect of praise, mockery, or mourning on character development, plot, and theme • accurately analyzes characterization • smoothly integrates relevant textual evidence, including details, quotations, and examples.	The essay • examines the effect of praise, mockery, or mourning • adequately analyzes characterization • includes sufficient textual evidence, including details, quotations, and examples.	The essay • confuses the effect of praise, mockery, or mourning on character development, plot, and theme • provides some analysis of characterization • provides insufficient textual evidence (e.g., details, quotations, examples).	The essay • does not examine the effect of praise, mockery, or mourning on character development, plot, and theme • lacks analysis of characterization • provides inaccurate or no textual evidence (e.g., details, quotations, examples).
Structure	The essay • uses an effective organizational structure with a logical progression of ideas • introduces the topic engagingly, links supporting ideas, and provides a thoughtful conclusion • uses appropriate and varied transitions.	The essay • uses an adequate organizational structure with a logical progression of ideas • introduces the topic, links supporting ideas, and provides a conclusion • uses effective transitions.	The essay • uses an inconsistent organizational structure • does not introduce the topic, link supporting ideas, and/or provide a conclusion • uses weak, repetitive, or insufficient transitions.	The essay • does not follow an obvious organizational structure • does not introduce the topic, link supporting ideas, and/or provide a conclusion • uses few, if any, transitions.
Use of Language	The essay • uses precise language and a variety of sentence structures • maintains an academic voice and objective tone • demonstrates command of conventions with few errors in grammar, usage, capitalization, punctuation, and spelling.	The essay • uses some precise language and different sentence structures • generally maintains an academic voice and objective tone • demonstrates adequate command of conventions; few errors in grammar, capitalization, punctuation, or spelling.	The essay • uses vague language and simple sentences • does not establish or maintain an academic voice • demonstrates partial command of conventions; errors in grammar, usage, capitalization, punctuation, and/or spelling interfere with meaning.	The essay • uses inappropriate language and simpl or incomplete sentences • does not use academic voice • demonstrates little command of conventions; serious errors in grammar, usage, capitalization, punctuation, and/or spelling confuse meaning.

ntroducing Greek Drama

Learning Targets

- Identify the knowledge and skills necessary to complete Embedded Assessment 2 successfully.
- Reflect on understanding of vocabulary, essential questions, and character relationships.
- Preview a play by learning background information about tragedy and Sophocles's Theban plays.

Preview

In this activity, you will read the assignment for Embedded Assessment 2 and gather background information about Greek drama and Greek playwright Sophocles.

Making Connections

n this part of the unit, you will learn about Greek drama by reading *Antigone*. s you read the play, you will examine the major characters and analyze their nteractions with one another. You will also explore the concept of the tragic hero nd how the play develops this characterization. You will also practice performing ialogues, and then perform a scene from *Antigone* with a group.

Unpacking Embedded Assessment 2

Read the assignment for Embedded Assessment 2: Performing a Scene from *Antigone*:

Your assignment is to choose a scene from *Antigone* with your group, mark the text for visual and vocal delivery, and then perform it in front of the class. Your performance should demonstrate an analysis of each character's feelings and motivations. You will also be responsible for carefully viewing your classmates' performances and providing feedback.

In your own words, summarize what you will need to know to complete this assessment successfully. With your class, create a graphic organizer to represent the skills and knowledge you will need to complete the tasks identified in the Embedded Assessment.

ntroduction to Greek Drama

1. Following are five texts about ancient Greece and Greek tragedies. With your group, mark the text of one of the following topics as assigned by your teacher by highlighting key information.

Learning Strategies

Discussion Groups
Graphic Organizer
Jigsaw
Marking the Text
Paraphrasing

My Notes

My Notes

Greek Theater

- Tragedies were produced as part of a religious festival every year in Athens.
- Awards were given to the playwright who presented the best series of three dramas.
- Plays were performed in vast outdoor amphitheaters that could seat 40,000 people.
- All actors were men. The Greek word for actor is *hypokrites*. They wore masks with built-in megaphones so they could be heard; they also wore platform shoes for added height.
- The stage was a slightly raised platform. Actors' movements were bold and definite.
- The Chorus—a group of actors who moved and sang together—acted as one character and spoke in unison during the Choral Odes, which separated the scenes of the drama.
- The Chorus set the mood, summarized the action, represented a point of view, sided with various characters, or warned of disaster.
- Greek theater incorporated unities of time, place, and action, which meant that there were no scene changes and no complicated subplots; the plays took place in one day and in one place and focused on one event.
- Violent action took place offstage; messengers told the audience what happened.
- The audience knew the story ahead of time. The emotion of the characters was what they came to see.

Sophocles

- He was one of three great Greek tragic playwrights (along with Aeschylus and Euripides). He wrote during the "golden age" of Greece.
- He was born in 496 BCE, and he lived for 90 years.
- Although only seven of his plays remain, he wrote more than 100.
- He served his city of Colonus, near Athens, in various capacities.
- He entered his plays in contests, winning his first at the age of 28 (and defeating Aeschylus in that contest).
- He was awarded first prize about 20 times and second prize all the other times.
- He added a third actor to the cast of his plays—before this, all dramas played with only two characters other than the chorus.

Tragedy and the Tragic Hero

- Tragedy is a difficult and rewarding form of drama, which was made into an art by the Greeks.
- Tragedy involves the downfall of a hero, usually ending with his or her destruction or death.

Aristotle's *Poetics* on Tragedy

- Tragedy arouses the emotions of pity and fear, wonder and awe.
- The main character is a tragic hero who must be a man or woman capable of great suffering.
- The downfall of the hero usually ends with his or her destruction or death.

- The plot involves intense emotion, with a horrible truth that leads to release or *catharsis* (purification).
- The drama does not leave the audience in depression, but with a deeper understanding of life.

Aristotle's *Poetics* on the Tragic Hero

- The tragic hero is a man or woman of noble stature.
- The tragic hero is a good person who is brought down by an "act of injustice" (*hamartia*) because they know no better or believe that a greater good will be served by their actions.
- The hero has a tragic flaw (weakness), such as pride, quickness to anger, or misjudgment.
- The hero has free choice, which makes the downfall his or her own fault, but experiences misfortune that is not entirely deserved.
- The hero gains self-knowledge or understanding before the downfall, and therefore experiences redemption.

Antigone and Her Family Background

- *Antigone* is a complete play, but it is part of a cycle of three plays, including *Oedipus Rex* and *Oedipus at Colonus*, written by Sophocles about the generations of the Cadmus family.
- The plays deal with the curse placed upon the family for a crime committed against the gods. The curse begins with a prophecy to King Laius and Queen Jocasta of Thebes that their son, Oedipus, will kill his father and marry his own mother.
- To avoid fulfillment of the prophecy, the baby Oedipus is left in the mountains to die of exposure, but he is found and raised by the king and queen of Corinth.
- Later Oedipus unknowingly kills his father and wins the hand of Jocasta, the widowed queen, thus fulfilling the prophecy. They have four children, Antigone, Ismene, Eteocles, and Polyneices.
- When Jocasta discovers the truth, she hangs herself. When Oedipus discovers the truth, he blinds and exiles himself. He leaves his brother-in-law, Creon, to look after his children.
- Before he dies, Oedipus leaves orders that his two sons are to share the kingship; however, Eteocles, the first to reign, refuses to step down. Polyneices, his brother, attacks the city and his brother. They kill each other in battle.
- Creon becomes king and orders Eteocles buried with religious rites and honors. He orders that Polyneices be left unburied and uncovered for birds and animals to feed on his body. According to Greek beliefs, his soul could thus never rest. Antigone buries her brother against the order of her uncle. Thus begins the play's action.

Pronunciation Guide

Refer to online resources for explanations and examples of correct pronunciation of Greek names, such as the following helpful instructions:

- The final *e* is always pronounced: Athene = a-THEE-neh.
- *Ch* is pronounced like *k*, never as in *church*.
- *C* is pronounced soft (like *s*) before *e* and *i* sounds; otherwise it is pronounced hard (like *k*): Polyneices = poly-NI-ses.
- The same applies to *g*; soft (as in *giant*) before *e* and *i* sounds, hard (as in *gate*) otherwise.
- *Th* is always smooth, as in *thigh*, never rough, as in *they*: Athene = a-THEE-neh.
- Pronounce the vowels as in English, but you will be a little closer to the ancient pronunciation if you pronounce them as in Romance languages (Italian or Spanish, for example).
- *Ae* and *oe* can be pronounced like *e*.
- General rules of accent:
  - If a name has two syllables, accent the first.
  - If a name has three or more syllables, then typically either the second-to-last syllable or the third-to-last syllable is accented.

    Aphrodite = ah-froh-DI-tee

    Herodotus = huh-ROD-uh-tus

    Thermopylae = ther-MO-pih-lee

    Aeschylus = ES-kih-lus or EE-skih-lus

    Thucydides = thoo-SIH-di-des

2. After completing your research, work with your group to prepare a presentation. Your presentation should summarize what you have learned and highlight key details about your topic. When viewing the presentations of others, be sure to take notes that you can refer to during the trivia game.

Antigone Plot Summary

3. Read the following plot summary of *Antigone*, then paraphrase the main points of the story with a partner.

After the death of King Oedipus in Colonus, his two sons—Eteocles and Polyneices—die in battle fighting for the throne of Thebes. Creon, Antigone's uncle, becomes king of Thebes and announces that Eteocles will be given a proper burial. However, he orders that Polyneices, who he considers a traitor, is to be left to rot on the field of battle. Antigone, the sister of Eteocles and Polyneices, discusses the ruling with her sister, Ismene, and decides to defy the order and give Polyneices a proper burial. When she is caught, Creon throws Antigone in prison and condemns her to death. Haemon (Creon's son and Antigone's fiancé), the blind prophet Teiresias, and the Chorus beg Creon to release Antigone from prison. Creon relents, but it is too late. Antigone has killed herself in her jail cell. Haemon kills himself in despair, as does Creon's wife when she learns what has happened to her son. At the end, Creon is left to rule Thebes alone.

INDEPENDENT READING LINK

Read and Research

In this activity, you've learned information about the play *Antigone*, which you will begin reading in the next activity. Think about your independent reading. What things could you research that would help you more deeply understand the text you're reading? Conduct inquiry into two topics, and record what you learn in your Reader/Writer notebook. Then, reflect on whether the information helps you understand your independent reading more fully.

Antigone (1882) by British painter Frederic Leighton (1830–1896)

Trivia Game

About the Author	It's a Tragedy	Greek Theater	Antigone and Her Family
200 Points The author of *Oedipus Rex*, *Oedipus at Colonus*, and *Antigone*	**200 Points** Civilization that made tragedy into an art	**200 Points** City where tragedies were produced as part of a religious festival	**200 Points** The other two plays in the series with *Antigone*
400 Points The number of Sophocles's plays that exist today out of a total of more than 100	**400 Points** Downfall, usually by destruction or death	**400 Points** The part of a Greek play usually chanted (or sung) in unison	**400 Points** The King and Queen of Thebes
600 Points The nickname of the time period in ancient Greece when Sophocles wrote his plays	**600 Points** Pity and fear, wonder and awe	**600 Points** Masks with built-in megaphones and platform shoes	**600 Points** "Your son will kill his father and marry his own mother."
900 Points Sophocles's age when he won his first drama competition	**900 Points** A single flaw in character, or *hamartia*	**900 Points** A group of actors that move and sing together, acting as one character	**900 Points** Both mother and wife of Oedipus
1,000 Points The number of actors Sophocles cast in his plays	**1,000 Points** Horrible truth that leads to release	**1,000 Points** The Greek word for *actor*	**1,000 Points** "Bury Eteocles but not Polyneices."

Graphic Organizer
Marking the Text
Skimming/Scanning
Think-Pair-Share

VOCABULARY

LITERARY

Stage directions are instructions written into the script of a play that indicate stage actions, movements of performers, or production requirements.

My Notes

Learning Targets

- Examine the use of stage directions and the Greek Chorus.
- Analyze the characters of Antigone and Ismene, as well as their motivations and conflicts.

Preview

In this activity, you will begin reading the Greek tragedy *Antigone* and analyzing the characters of Antigone and Ismene in the opening scene.

Stage Directions

Stage directions are often placed within parentheses and printed in italics. When reading a play script, use this text feature to help you visualize the story's setting and characters' movements. Note: "left" and "right" directions are from the actor's point of view as he or she faces the audience. Skim/scan the text of the opening scene of *Antigone*. What key information is provided by the stage directions?

As You Read

- Highlight passages that reveal each character's motivation throughout the scene.
- Circle unknown words and phrases. Try to determine the meaning of the words by using context clues, word parts, or a dictionary.

Play

Antigone

by **Sophocles**

Antigone, daughter of Oedipus

Ismene, daughter of Oedipus, sister of Antigone

Creon, king of Thebes

Eurydice, wife of Creon

Haemon, son of Creon and Eurydice, engaged to Antigone

Teiresias, an old blind prophet

Boy, a young lad guiding Teiresias

Guard, a soldier serving Creon

Messenger

Chorus, Theban Elders

Attendants

[Thebes,[1] in front of the palace, which stands in the background, its main doors facing the audience. Enter Antigone leading Ismene away from the palace]

---

[1] *Thebes* is an influential city in ancient Greece.

ANTIGONE: Now, dear Ismene, my own blood sister,
do you have any sense of all the troubles
Zeus keeps bringing on the two of us,
as long as we're alive? All that misery
5 which stems from Oedipus? There's no suffering,
no shame, no ruin—not one dishonour—
which I have not seen in all the troubles
you and I go through. What's this they're saying now,
something our general has had proclaimed
10 throughout the city? Do you know of it?
Have you heard? Or have you just missed the news?
Dishonours which better fit our enemies
are now being piled up on the ones we love.

ISMENE: I've had no word at all, Antigone,
15 nothing good or bad about our family,
not since we two lost both our brothers,
killed on the same day by a double blow.
And since the Argive² army, just last night,
has gone away, I don't know any more
20 if I've been lucky or face total ruin.

ANTIGONE: I know that. That's why I brought you here,
outside the gates, so only you can hear.

ISMENE: What is it? The way you look makes it seem
you're thinking of some dark and gloomy news.

25 **ANTIGONE:** Look—what's Creon doing with our two brothers?
He's honouring one with a full funeral
and treating the other one disgracefully!
Eteocles, they say, has had his burial
according to our customary rites,
30 to win him honour with the dead below.
But as for Polyneices, who perished
so miserably, an order has gone out

---

² The *Argive army* refers to the city of Argos, where Polyneices raises an army to fight his brother Eteocles for the throne.

GRAMMAR & USAGE

Parallel Structure
Parallel structure is the use of similar word patterns to express ideas of equal importance. It creates rhythm that can serve to create emphasis. Notice this example from lines 5 and 6: "There's no suffering, no shame, no ruin…" Here, Sophocles uses the repeated word pattern of "no" followed by a noun in each listed item. What does this structure emphasize about Antigone's experience?

My Notes

My Notes

throughout the city—that's what people say.
He's to have no funeral or **lament**,
35 but to be left unburied and unwept,
a sweet treasure[3] for the birds to look at,
for them to feed on to their heart's content.
That's what people say the noble Creon
has announced to you and me—I mean to me—
40 and now he's coming to proclaim the fact,
to state it clearly to those who have not heard.
For Creon this matter's really serious.
Anyone who acts against the order
will be stoned to death before the city.
45 Now you know, and you'll quickly demonstrate
whether you are nobly born, or else
a girl unworthy of her splendid ancestors.

ISMENE: Oh my poor sister, if that's what's happening,
what can I say that would be any help
50 to ease the situation or resolve it?

ANTIGONE: Think whether you will work with me in this
and act together.

ISMENE: In what kind of work?
What do you mean?

55 **ANTIGONE:** Will you help these hands
take up Polyneices' corpse and bury it?

ISMENE: What? You're going to bury Polyneices,
when that's been made a crime for all in Thebes?

ANTIGONE: Yes. I'll do my duty to my brother—
60 and yours as well, if you're not prepared to.
I won't be caught betraying him.

---

lament: expression of grief

[3] *Sweet treasure* refers to Polyneices's body left unburied, which birds and other creatures will gorge on.

ISMENE: You're too **rash**.
Has Creon not expressly banned that act?

ANTIGONE: Yes. But he's no right to keep me from what's mine.

65 **ISMENE:** O dear. Think, Antigone. Consider
how our father died, hated and disgraced,
when those mistakes which his own search revealed
forced him to turn his hand against himself
and stab out both his eyes. Then that woman,
70 his mother and his wife—her double role—
destroyed her own life in a twisted noose.
Then there's our own two brothers, both butchered
in a single day—that ill-fated pair
with their own hands slaughtered one another
75 and brought about their common doom.
Now, the two of us are left here quite alone.
Think how we'll die far worse than all the rest,
if we defy the law and move against
the king's decree,[4] against his royal power.
80 We must remember that by birth we're women,
and, as such, we shouldn't fight with men.

My Notes

Actors Alexandria King and Ava McCoy in a 2018 production of the play *Antigone* by the Classical Theatre of Harlem in Harlem, New York

rash: impulsive

[4] A *king's decree* is a rule or edict issued by the king.

Since those who rule are much more powerful,
we must obey in this and in events
which bring us even harsher agonies.

85   So I'll ask those underground for pardon—
since I'm being compelled, I will obey
those in control. That's what I'm forced to do.
It makes no sense to try to do too much.

ANTIGONE: I wouldn't urge you to. No. Not even

90   if you were keen to act. Doing this with you
would bring me no joy. So be what you want.
I'll still bury him. It would be fine to die
while doing that. I'll lie there with him,
with a man I love, pure and innocent,

95   for all my crime. My honours for the dead
must last much longer than for those up here.
I'll lie down there forever. As for you,
well, if you wish, you can show contempt
for those laws the gods all hold in honour.

100 **ISMENE:** I'm not disrespecting them. But I can't act
against the state. That's not in my nature.

ANTIGONE: Let that be your excuse. I'm going now
to make a burial mound for my dear brother.

ISMENE: Oh poor Antigone, I'm so afraid for you.

105 **ANTIGONE:** Don't fear for me. Set your own fate in order.

ISMENE: Make sure you don't reveal to anyone
what you intend. Keep it closely hidden.
I'll do the same.

ANTIGONE: No, no. Announce the fact—if you don't let
everybody know,

110 I'll despise your silence even more.

keen: eager

ISMENE: Your heart is hot to do cold deeds.

ANTIGONE: But I know, I'll please the ones I'm duty bound to please.

ISMENE: Yes, if you can. But you're after something
which you're incapable of carrying out.

115 **ANTIGONE:** Well, when my strength is gone, then I'll give up.

ISMENE: A vain attempt should not be made at all.

ANTIGONE: I'll hate you if you're going to talk that way.
And you'll rightly earn the loathing of the dead.
So leave me and my foolishness alone—
120 we'll get through this fearful thing. I won't suffer
anything as bad as a disgraceful death.

ISMENE: All right then, go, if that's what you think right.
But remember this—even though your mission
makes no sense, your friends do truly love you.
[Exit Antigone and Ismene. Enter the Chorus of Theban elders]

Making Observations
• What have we learned so far about Antigone and Ismene?
• What events have taken place before the play even begins?

Returning to the Text

- Reread the scene to answer these text-dependent questions.
- Write any additional questions you have about the text in your Reader/Writer Notebook.

1. Read lines 25–47 carefully. How does Antigone summarize Creon's proclamation? How will th ruling affect her family?

2. In lines 65–75, why does Ismene recount their family's history to her sister? What might her purpose be?

3. The conflict between Antigone and Ismene is clearly stated in lines 89–99. Explain this conflic and how it advances the plot. Consider what you learned about ancient Greek beliefs in the last activity.

4. What effect is created by the juxtaposition of the terms *hate* and *love* in lines 117 and 124? What does the use of these terms reveal about each sister?

5. How does the play build tension and conflict between the two sisters?

Working from the Text

6. Reread the opening scene between Antigone and Ismene. Take notes regarding the two sisters in the graphic organizer. Be sure to cite line numbers when noting textual evidence.

Character Analysis in the Opening Scene

Character	Indirect Characterization That Defines Each Character	Quotations That Show Character Intent or Emotion	Adjectives to Describe the Character (include textual evidence)
Antigone			
Ismene			

7. Summarize the characterization (character details), intent, and emotion of both characters. Discuss your ideas with a partner.

8. A requirement for effective oral performance is strong vocal delivery. Review the elements of vocal delivery and explain why each one is critical to an oral performance.

Elements of Vocal Delivery	Explanation of Importance to an Oral Performance
Tone	
Pitch	
Volume	
Pace	
Pause	
Articulation	
Pronunciation	

My Notes

_____

_____

_____

_____

_____

_____

_____

_____

_____

_____

_____

_____

_____

VOCABULARY

LITERARY

In drama, **stichomythia** is the delivery of dialogue in a rapid, fast-paced manner, with actors speaking emotionally and leaving very little time between speakers.

INDEPENDENT READING LINK

Read and Connect

Ask a partner to work with you. Choose a dialogue from your Independent Reading text. If possible, use a dialogue that includes stichomythia, or rapid speech. Practice reading the conversation with your partner, and then read it to a small group. Repeat the activity with your partner's Independent Reading text.

9. With a partner or small group as assigned by your teacher, choose a section of the text and plan how you will deliver your character's lines.

Tone	
Pitch	
Volume	
Pace	
Pause	
Articulation	
Pronunciation	

10. Rehearse your scene with appropriate vocal delivery. In this opening scene, Antigone and Ismene quickly build tension and conflict between their characters with their rapid speech, or **stichomythia.** Practice this convention as you read and incorporate appropriate gestures.

☑ Check Your Understanding

As your partner or group member practices stichomythia, make sure they focus on the vocal elements of articulation and pronunciation. Why might articulation and pronunciation be the most difficult vocal elements to follow when practicing stichomythia? Discuss your ideas.

Chorus Lines

Learning Targets

- Analyze the structure of a traditional ode.
- Determine how language contributes to tone, voice, and mood.
- Integrate ideas from multiple texts to build knowledge and vocabulary about the role of the Greek Chorus in a traditional Greek play.

Preview

In this activity, you will be introduced to a traditional Greek ode from *Antigone* and learn how classic odes have inspired modern ones.

Learning Strategies

Marking the Text
Summarizing

My Notes

The Greek Chorus

In Greek drama, the choral odes have many purposes. Even though the Chorus is composed of a number of individuals, it functions as one character. Onstage this is shown in the way Chorus members dress. For example, they frequently wear similar costumes and may also have similar masks to show that they represent a single character.

One member of the Chorus serves as the Chorus Leader. That person participates in a dialogue between himself/herself and the rest of the Chorus, or represents the Chorus when speaking to another character.

Greek Odes

As you may have inferred during Activity 4.2, an ode is a poem that addresses a particular subject. Odes have a standardized structure and typically describe an event, an individual, or another subject with praise. Greek odes were originally poems that were performed set to music, often accompanied by the *aulos*, or lyre, an ancient Greek instrument. This is part of the reason why odes are classified as lyric poetry (expressive of the speaker's emotions).

Classic Greek odes have three main parts to their structure:

- Strophe—a formal opening
- Antistrophe—a "mirroring" stanza that has the same meter and length as the opening
- Epode—the closing section with a new meter and length

Classic odes have inspired modern poetry, including the three poems you read in Activity 4.2. Although modern poets tend to use more irregular forms, they are connected to their Greek predecessors. In this activity, you'll look at an ode from the Greek drama *Antigone*. Though it is written in classical Greek form, it may be difficult to decipher the form because it is translated from its original Greek language.

As You Read

- Label and use brackets to mark the parts of a classic Greek ode.
- Circle unknown words and phrases. Try to determine the meaning of the words by using context clues, word parts, or a dictionary.

KNOWLEDGE QUEST

Knowledge Question:

How do the members of a Greek Chorus work together to perform in front of an audience?

In Activity 4.14, you will read a play that includes a traditional Greek Chorus and view an image about the makeup of a Greek Chorus. While you read and build knowledge about the topic, think about your answer to the Knowledge Question.

My Notes

Play

Antigone

by **Sophocles**

FIRST ODE[1]

125 **CHORUS—Strophe 1**[2]**:** O ray of sunlight,

most beautiful that ever shone

on Thebes, city of the seven gates,

you've appeared at last,

you glowing eye of golden day,

130 moving above the streams of Dirce,[3]

driving into headlong flight

the white-shield warrior from Argos,

who marched here fully armed,

now forced back by your sharper power.

135 **CHORUS LEADER:** Against our land he marched,

sent here by the warring claims

of Polyneices, with piercing screams,

an eagle flying above our land,

covered wings as white as snow,

140 and **hordes** of warriors in arms,

helmets topped with horsehair crests.

CHORUS—Antistrophe 1[4]**:** Standing above our homes,

he ranged around our seven gates,

with threats to swallow us

145 and spears thirsting to kill.

Before his jaws had had their fill

and gorged themselves on Theban blood,

before Hephaistos'[5] pine-torch flames

had seized our towers, our fortress crown,

---

[1] The *First Ode* is typical of a traditional ode, which is a choral song chanted by the Chorus in a Greek tragedy.

[2] *Strophe 1* is part of the ode the Chorus chants while moving from right to left across the stage.

[3] *Streams of Dirce* refers to a stream near Thebes.

[4] *Antistrophe 1* is part of the ode the Chorus chants while moving back across the stage from left to right.

[5] *Hephaistos* is the blacksmith of the gods; he hammers out lightning bolts for Zeus.

hordes: masses

150 he went back, driven in retreat.

Behind him rings the din of war—

his enemy, the Theban dragon-snake,

too difficult for him to overcome.

CHORUS LEADER: Zeus hates an arrogant boasting tongue.

155 Seeing them march here in a mighty stream,

in all their clanging golden pride,

he hurled his fire and struck the man,

up there, on our battlements, as he began

to scream aloud his victory.

160 **CHORUS—Strophe 2:** The man swung down, torch still in hand,

and smashed into **unyielding** earth—

the one who not so long ago attacked,

who launched his furious, enraged assault,

to blast us, breathing raging storms.

165 But things turned out not as he'd hoped.

Great war god Ares[6] assisted us—

he smashed them down and doomed them all

to a very different fate.

In ancient times, the theater was a popular place to go. Traditional Greek theaters were built with rows of auditorium seating and a flat floor in the center of the structure. This flat part of the floor, called the orchestra, is where the Chorus stood. Most Greek plays had a Chorus of up to about 15 people. The main actors performed on an elevated stage above the floor, called a logeion.

unyielding: rigid

---

[6] *Ares* is the god of war.

My Notes

CHORUS LEADER: Seven captains at seven gates
170 matched against seven equal warriors
paid Zeus[7] their full bronze tribute,
the god who turns the battle tide,
all but that pair of wretched men,
born of one father and one mother, too—
175 who set their conquering spears against each other
and then both shared a common death.

CHORUS—Antistrophe 2: Now victory with her glorious name
has come, bringing joy to well-armed Thebes.
The battle's done—let's strive now to forget
180 with songs and dancing all night long,
with Bacchus[8] leading us to make Thebes shake.

Knowledge Quest
- What did you notice from the scene and the illustration about the way a Greek Chorus performs?
- What details from the Chorus members' dialogue stand out for you?

Focus on the Sentence
Write four different sentence types from the point of view of the Chorus or the Chorus Leader. Use information from the play to write the sentences.

Statement: _____

_____

Question: _____

_____

Exclamation: _____

_____

Command: _____

---

[7] *Zeus* is the supreme ruler of all the gods on Mount Olympus; he is also known as the weather god who controls thunder, lightning, and rain.
[8] *Bacchus* is the Roman god of wine; he equates to Dionysius, the Greek god of wine.

Returning to the Text

- Reread the scene to answer these text-dependent questions.
- Write any additional questions you have about the text in your Reader/Writer Notebook.

1. In Strophe 1, what helps the reader understand the Chorus's position on the battle?

_____

_____

_____

_____

2. KQ Contrast the imagery used by the Chorus and the Chorus Leader in Strophe 1. How do these images show the different tones, or attitudes, that the speakers have?

_____

_____

_____

_____

3. KQ The word *Antistrophe* contains the word part *anti-*, meaning "opposite." In what way is the Chorus's behavior during an Antistrophe the opposite of its behavior during a Strophe? Also, what does the opposite movement show?

_____

_____

_____

_____

4. How does the tone (attitude toward the subject) change in Strophe 2?

_____

_____

_____

5. In lines 166–168, what does the Chorus mean by saying "he . . . doomed them all to a very different fate"? Include pertinent details from preceding lines in your answer.

_____

_____

_____

_____

INDEPENDENT READING LINK

You an continue to build your knowledge about the role of a Greek chorus by reading other articles at ZINC Reading Labs. Search for keywords such as *Greek hero*.

 ZINC

6. **KQ** What do the illustration and caption tell you about the position of a Greek Chorus relative to the main actors of the play, and what is the effect of this positioning?

_____

_____

_____

_____

⊘ Knowledge Quest

After reading the scene from *Antigone* and viewing the image of a Greek Chorus, think about what you learned about how the members of a Greek Chorus work together to perform in front of an audience. With a partner, discuss your thoughts on the role of a Greek Chorus and how it is represented in both what they say and how they move. Begin your discussion by answering the following questions: *What does the Chorus tell the audience? What purposes do the different Chorus members serve? How might a traditional Greek play be different if the Chorus were missing?* Be sure to:

- Respond to the questions appropriately, citing evidence to support your answers.
- Generate questions of your own to include in the discussion.
- Express connections to the comments and evidence your partner brings to the discussion.

☑ Focus on the Sentence

Read the following short sentence. Then expand it by providing more details as prompted by the questions.

The ode from *Antigone* celebrates something.

What? _____

How? _____

_____

_____

Working from the Text

7. Analyze an assigned section of the ode (Strophe 1, Antistrophe 1, Strophe 2, Antistrophe 2) for organization, imagery, and meaning. Write a short summary of the section in your Reader/Writer Notebook.

8. Share your summary with group, and exchange ideas about the organization, imagery, and meaning of each section. Then look at the overall structure of the ode. How do the individual parts come together to create the whole?

9. In your small group, look for ways the ode contrasts sorrow for those killed in battle with celebration that the city is victorious. Discuss how this contrast contributes to the tone and voice of the ode.

☑ Check Your Understanding

What elements of praise, mockery, or mourning can you find in this text? How does Sophocles create this effect?

Learning Strategies

Graphic Organizer
Marking the Text
Summarizing
Think-Pair-Share

Learning Targets

- Analyze the difference between dynamic and static characters.
- Examine the character of Creon, including his attitude, actions, and emotions.

Preview

In this activity, you will continue reading *Antigone* and analyze the attitude and emotions of Creon, the king of Thebes.

LITERARY

A **dynamic character** in literature is one who changes in response to the events of a narrative. A **static character** remains the same throughout the narrative.

Dynamic and Static Characters

Remember that one of the elements of Greek drama is the use of masks to portray a character's attitude or emotions. A **dynamic character** may need multiple masks over the course of a performance, while a **static character** may not.

As You Read

- Highlight evidence of Creon's character traits and how they evolve throughout the events of the scene.
- Circle unknown words and phrases. Try to determine the meaning of the words by using context clues, word parts, or a dictionary.

My Notes

Play

Antigone

by **Sophocles**

[The palace doors are thrown open and guards appear at the doors]

    CHORUS LEADER: But here comes Creon, new king of our land,
    son of Menoikeos. Thanks to the gods,
    who've brought about our new good fortune.
185 What plan of action does he have in mind?
    What's made him hold this special meeting,
    with elders summoned by a general call?
    [Enter Creon from the palace]

    CREON: Men, after much tossing of our ship of state,
    the gods have safely set things right again.
190 Of all the citizens I've summoned you,
    because I know how well you showed respect
    for the eternal power of the throne,

first with Laius and again with Oedipus,
once he restored our city. When he died,
195 you stood by his children, firm in loyalty.
Now his sons have perished in a single day,
killing each other with their own two hands,
a double slaughter, stained with brother's blood.
And so I have the throne, all royal power,
200 for I'm the one most closely linked by blood
to those who have been killed. It's impossible
to really know a man, to know his soul,
his mind and will, before one witnesses
his skill in governing and making laws.
205 For me, a man who rules the entire state
and does not take the best advice there is,
but through fear keeps his mouth forever shut,
such a man is the very worst of men—
and always will be. And a man who thinks
210 more highly of a friend than of his country,
well, he means nothing to me. Let Zeus know,
the god who always watches everything,
I would not stay silent if I saw disaster
moving here against the citizens,
215 a threat to their security. For anyone
who acts against the state, its enemy,
I'd never make my friend. For I know well
our country is a ship which keeps us safe,
and only when it sails its proper course
220 do we make friends. These are the principles
I'll use in order to protect our state.
That's why I've announced to all citizens
my orders for the sons of Oedipus—
Eteocles, who perished in the fight
225 to save our city, the best and bravest
of our spearmen, will have his burial,
with all those purifying rituals
which accompany the noblest corpses,
as they move below. As for his brother—
230 that Polyneices, who returned from exile,
eager to wipe out in all-consuming fire

his ancestral city and its native gods,
keen to seize upon his family's blood
and lead men into slavery—for him,
235 the proclamation in the state declares
he'll have no burial mound, no funeral rites,
and no lament. He'll be left unburied,
his body there for birds and dogs to eat,
a clear reminder of his shameful fate.
240 That's my decision. For I'll never act
to respect an evil man with honours
in preference to a man who's acted well.
Anyone who's well **disposed** towards our state,
alive or dead, that man I will respect.

245 **CHORUS LEADER:** Son of Menoikeos, if that's your will
for this city's friends and enemies,
it seems to me you now control all laws
concerning those who've died and us as well—
the ones who are still living.

250 **CREON:** See to it then, and act as guardians of what's been proclaimed.

CHORUS: Give that task to younger men to deal with.

CREON: There are men assigned to oversee the corpse.

CHORUS LEADER: Then what remains that you would have us do?

CREON: Don't yield to those who **contravene** my orders.

255 **CHORUS LEADER:** No one is such a fool that he loves death.

CREON: Yes, that will be his full reward, indeed.
And yet men have often been destroyed
because they hoped to profit in some way.
[Enter a guard, coming toward the palace]

GUARD: My lord, I can't say I've come out of breath
260 by running here, making my feet move fast.

disposed: inclined
contravene: oppose, or act
contrary to

Many times I stopped to think things over—
and then I'd turn around, retrace my steps.
My mind was saying many things to me,
"You fool, why go to where you know for sure
265 your punishment awaits?"—"And now, poor man,
why are you hesitating yet again?
If Creon finds this out from someone else,
how will you escape being hurt?" Such matters
kept my mind preoccupied. And so I went,
270 slowly and reluctantly, and thus made
a short road turn into a lengthy one.
But then the view that I should come to you
won out. If what I have to say is nothing,
I'll say it nonetheless. For I've come here
275 clinging to the hope that I'll not suffer
anything that's not part of my destiny.

Actors Jean Vilar (1912–1971) and Georges Wilson (1921–2010) in a 1960 production of *Antigone* by Théâtre National Populaire in Paris

CREON: What's happening that's made you so upset?

GUARD: I want to tell you first about myself.
I did not do it. And I didn't see
280   the one who did. So it would be unjust
if I should come to grief.

CREON: You **hedge** so much. Clearly you have news of something
ominous.

GUARD: Yes. Strange things that make me pause a lot.

CREON: Why not say it and then go—just leave.

285   **GUARD:** All right, I'll tell you. It's about the corpse.
Someone has buried it and disappeared,
after spreading thirsty dust onto the flesh
and undertaking all appropriate rites.

CREON: What are you saying? What man would dare this?

290   **GUARD:** I don't know. There was no sign of digging,
no marks of any pick axe or a mattock.
The ground was dry and hard and very smooth,
without a wheel track. Whoever did it
left no trace. When the first man on day watch
295   revealed it to us, we were all amazed.
The corpse was hidden, but not in a tomb.
It was lightly covered up with dirt,
as if someone wanted to **avert** a curse.
There was no trace of a wild animal
300   or dogs who'd come to rip the corpse apart.
Then the words flew round among us all,
with every guard accusing someone else.
We were about to fight, to come to blows—
no one was there to put a stop to it.
305   Every one of us was responsible,
but none of us was clearly in the wrong.
In our defence we pleaded ignorance.

hedge: avoid giving a clear response
avert: prevent

Then we each stated we were quite prepared
to pick up red-hot iron, walk through flames,
310 or swear by all the gods that we'd not done it,
we'd no idea how the act was planned,
or how it had been carried out. At last,
when all our searching had proved useless,
one man spoke up, and his words forced us all
315 to drop our faces to the ground in fear.
We couldn't see things working out for us,
whether we agreed or disagreed with him.
He said we must report this act to you—
we must not hide it. And his view **prevailed**.
320 I was the unlucky man who won the prize,
the luck of the draw. That's why I'm now here,
not of my own free will or by your choice.
I know that—for no one likes a messenger
who comes bearing unwelcome news with him.

325 **CHORUS LEADER:** My lord, I've been wondering for some time now—
could this act not be something from the gods?

CREON: Stop now—before what you're about to say
enrages me completely and reveals
that you're not only old but stupid, too.
330 No one can tolerate what you've just said,
when you claim gods might care about this corpse.
Would they pay extraordinary honours
and bury as a man who'd served them well,
someone who came to burn their offerings,
335 their pillared temples, to torch their lands
and scatter all its laws? Or do you see
gods paying respect to evil men? No, no.
For quite a while some people in the town
have secretly been muttering against me.
340 They don't agree with what I have decreed.
They shake their heads and have not kept their necks
under my yoke, as they are duty bound to do
if they were men who are content with me.
I well know that these guards were led astray—

> **prevailed:** won out

My Notes

345 such men urged them to carry out this act
for money. To foster evil actions,
to make them commonplace among all men,
nothing is as powerful as money.
It destroys cities, driving men from home.

350 Money trains and twists the minds in worthy men,
so they then undertake disgraceful acts.
Money teaches men to live as scoundrels,
familiar with every **profane** enterprise.
But those who carry out such acts for cash

355 sooner or later see how for their crimes
they pay the penalty. For if great Zeus
still has my respect, then understand this—
I swear to you on oath—unless you find
the one whose hands really buried him,

360 unless you bring him here before my eyes,
then death for you will never be enough.
No, not before you're hung up still alive
and you confess to this gross, violent act.
That way you'll understand in future days,

365 when there's a profit to be gained from theft,
you'll learn that it's not good to be in love
with every kind of monetary gain.
You'll know more men are ruined than are saved
when they earn profits from dishonest schemes.

370 **GUARD:** Do I have your permission to speak now,
or do I just turn around and go away?

CREON: But I find your voice so irritating—
don't you realize that?

GUARD: Where does it hurt? Is it in your ears or in your mind?

375 **CREON:** Why try to question where I feel my pain?

GUARD: The man who did it—he upsets your mind.
I offend your ears.

---

profane: vulgar or improper

CREON: My, my, it's clear to see
it's natural for you to chatter on.

380 GUARD: Perhaps. But I never did this.

CREON: This and more—you sold your life for silver.

GUARD: How strange and sad when the one who sorts this out gets it all wrong.

CREON: Well, enjoy your sophisticated views.
But if you don't reveal to me who did this,
385 you'll just confirm how much your treasonous gains
have made you suffer.
[Exit Creon back into the palace. The doors close behind him]

GUARD: Well, I hope he's found. That would be best. But whether caught or not—
and that's something sheer chance will bring about—
you won't see me coming here again.
390 This time, against all hope and expectation,
I'm still unhurt. I owe the gods great thanks.
[Exit the Guard away from the palace]

SECOND ODE

CHORUS—Strophe 1: There are many strange and wonderful things,
He moves across the white-capped ocean seas
blasted by winter storms, carving his way
395 under the surging waves engulfing him.
With his teams of horses he wears down
the unwearied and immortal earth,
the oldest of the gods, harassing her,
as year by year his ploughs move back and forth.

400 CHORUS—Antistrophe 1: He snares the light-winged flocks of birds,
herds of wild beasts, creatures from deep seas,
trapped in the fine mesh of his hunting nets.
O resourceful man, whose skill can overcome
ferocious beasts roaming mountain heights.

405 He curbs the rough-haired horses with his bit
and tames the inexhaustible mountain bulls,
setting their savage necks beneath his yoke.

CHORUS—Strophe 2: He's taught himself speech and wind-swift thought,
trained his feelings for communal civic life,
410 learning to escape the icy shafts of frost,
volleys of pelting rain in winter storms,
the harsh life lived under the open sky.
That's man—so resourceful in all he does.
There's no event his skill cannot confront—
415 other than death—that alone he cannot shun,
although for many baffling sicknesses
he has discovered his own remedies.

CHORUS—Antistrophe 2: The qualities of his inventive skills
bring arts beyond his dreams and lead him on,
420 sometimes to evil and sometimes to good.
If he treats his country's laws with due respect
and honours justice by swearing on the gods,
he wins high honours in his city.
But when he grows bold and turns to evil,
425 then he has no city. A man like that—
let him not share my home or know my mind.

Making Observations

- What characters do we meet in this scene?
- What actions take place?

eturning to the Text

Reread the scene to answer these text-dependent questions.

Write any additional questions you have about the text in your Reader/Writer Notebook.

1. In line 188, what does Creon mean by the metaphorical phrase "after much tossing of our ship of state"?

2. What is Creon's definition of an effective ruler? Cite evidence from the text to support your analysis.

3. Reread lines 245–249. Using evidence from the text, discuss how the Chorus's view of Creon's control seems to have changed from the beginning of the scene.

4. Explain the hyperbole in lines 308–312. What emotion does this exaggerated imagery imply?

5. Compare and contrast Creon's attitude toward the Chorus in lines 327–343 to his speech at the start of this scene (lines 190–194). How has his tone shifted?

6. Why does the Chorus use the metaphor of moving "across the white-capped ocean seas" (line 393) to describe how humans move through life?

_____

_____

_____

_____

Working from the Text

7. Summarize the main idea for each part of the Second Ode.

8. Complete the following graphic organizer using the evidence of Creon's attitude or emotions that you highlighted in the text.

Lines 182–324

Emotions, Characteristics	What Creon Says
What Creon Does	What Others Say About Creon

Lines 325–386 (and following stage directions)

Emotions, Actions	What Creon Says
What Creon Does	What Others Say About Creon

9. What gestures or visual elements would help you to portray Creon? Brainstorm in groups, as assigned by your teacher, and practice reading lines 327–369 using gestures.

☑ Check Your Understanding

With a partner, summarize Creon's point of view in two or three sentences, and describe how it conflicts with Antigone's point of view. Do you think one character is more "right" than the other? Explain.

LANGUAGE & WRITER'S CRAFT: Consulting a Style Manual

Careful writers not only learn the art of writing; they also learn the mechanics. One way to do that is to consult style manuals about questions of style. Many different manuals exist. Following are a few you may find helpful. Check with your teacher to see whether she or he has a preference for the style manual you use.

- *Chicago Manual of Style*
- *Elements of Style*
- *MLA Handbook*
- *MLA Style Manual*
- *New York Times Manual of Style and Usage*
- *New Oxford Style Manual/New Hart' s Rules*
- *Turabian*

In addition to this list, there are many online resources that are useful, including Purdue University's Online Writing Lab. Research other possible online sources and bookmark them for future reference.

PRACTICE The underlined words and phrases in the following paragraph contain style errors. Use a style manual—either online or print—to identify and correct the errors.

2,000 years ago, Sophocles wrote the three well known dramas we call the theban plays. He did not write them in chronological order; instead, he began with "Antigone," which takes place last.

Writing Prompt: Informational

From your notes, write a paragraph to explain Creon's attitudes and emotions and how they change throughout the scene. Be sure to:

- Include a well-stated topic sentence.
- Include details and textual evidence that highlight Creon's attitude or emotions.
- Use a logical organizational structure, and employ transitions effectively to move from one key point to the next.

10. After you write your paragraph, share it with a discussion group.

ACTIVITY
4.16 Conflicting Motivations

Learning Strategies

Graphic Organizer
Marking the Text
Predicting

My Notes

Learning Targets

- Examine character motivations and beliefs.
- Make predictions about how character interaction will advance the plot.

Preview

In this activity, you will continue reading *Antigone* and analyze the motivations of Antigone and Creon.

Character Motivations

1. Before you read the next section, use the following graphic organizer to review Antigone's and Creon's underlying motivations.

Antigone	Creon
Concern about the burial of Polyneices:	
Attitude about the power of the gods:	

2. Up to this point in the play, the drama's two main characters have not been on stage at the same time. What is the effect of Sophocles's choice to not have the two main characters interact on the stage at this point in the plot? I your Reader/Writer Notebook, predict how you think the plot will unfold whe Antigone and Creon are together on the stage.

3. Use your notes to draft a statement about how the conflict between Antigon and Creon conveys a theme related to justice.

4. Predict how the interaction of these two characters will advance the plot of the play.

As You Read

- Mark the text for evidence of each character's motivations and beliefs.
- Circle unknown words and phrases. Try to determine the meaning of the word by using context clues, word parts, or a dictionary.

ay

Antigone

· **Sophocles**

nter the Guard, with Antigone]

CHORUS LEADER: What's this? I fear some omen from the gods.
I can't deny what I see here so clearly—
that young girl there—it's Antigone.

430 Oh you poor girl, daughter of Oedipus,
child of a such a father, so unfortunate,
what's going on? Surely they've not brought you here
because you've disobeyed the royal laws,
because they've caught you acting foolishly?

435 **GUARD**: This here's the one who carried out the act.
We caught her as she was burying the corpse.
Where's Creon?
[The palace doors open. Enter Creon with attendants.]

CHORUS LEADER: He's coming from the house—and just in time.

CREON: Why have I come "just in time"? What's happening? What is it?

440 **GUARD**: My lord, human beings should never take an oath
there's something they'll not do—for later thoughts
contradict what they first meant. I'd have sworn
I'd not soon venture here again. Back then,
the threats you made brought me a lot of grief.

445 But there's no joy as great as what we pray for
against all hope. And so I have come back,
breaking that oath I swore. I bring this girl,
captured while she was honouring the grave.
This time we did not draw lots. No. This time

450 I was the lucky man, not someone else.
And now, my lord, take her for questioning.
Convict her. Do as you wish. As for me,
by rights I'm free and clear of all this trouble.

My Notes

CREON: This girl here—how did you catch her? And where?

455 GUARD: She was burying that man. Now you know all there is to know

CREON: Do you understand just what you're saying? Are your words the truth?

GUARD: We saw this girl giving that dead man's corpse
full burial rites—an act you'd made illegal.
460 Is what I say simple and clear enough?

CREON: How did you see her, catch her in the act?

GUARD: It happened this way. When we got there,
after hearing those awful threats from you,
we swept off all the dust covering the corpse,
465 so the damp body was completely bare.
Then we sat down on rising ground up wind,
to escape the body's putrid rotting stench.
We traded insults just to stay awake,
in case someone was careless on the job.
470 That's how we spent the time right up 'til noon,
when the sun's bright circle in the sky
had moved half way and it was burning hot.
Then suddenly a swirling windstorm came,
whipping clouds of dust up from the ground,
475 filling the plain—some heaven-sent trouble.
In that level place the dirt storm damaged
all the forest growth, and the air around
was filled with dust for miles. We shut our mouths
and just endured this **scourge** sent from the gods.
480 A long time passed. The storm came to an end.
That's when we saw the girl. She was shrieking—
a distressing painful cry, just like a bird
who's seen an empty nest, its fledglings gone.
That's how she was when she saw the naked corpse.
485 She screamed out a lament, and then she swore,
calling evil curses down upon the ones
who'd done this. Then right away her hands

scourge: instrument of suffering

threw on the thirsty dust. She lifted up
a finely made bronze jug and then three times
490 poured out her tributes to the dead.
When we saw that, we rushed up right away
and grabbed her. She was not afraid at all.
We charged her with her previous offence
as well as this one. She just kept standing there,
495 denying nothing. That made me happy—
though it was painful, too. For it's a joy
escaping troubles which affect oneself,
but painful to bring evil on one's friends.
But all that is of less concern to me
500 than my own safety.

CREON: You there—you with your face
bent down towards the ground, what do you say?
Do you deny you did this or admit it?

ANTIGONE: I admit I did it. I won't deny that.

505 CREON: [to the Guard] You're dismissed—go where you want. You're
free—
no serious charges made against you.
[Exit the Guard. Creon turns to interrogate Antigone]
Tell me briefly—not in some lengthy speech—
were you aware there was a proclamation
forbidding what you did?

510 **ANTIGONE:** I'd heard of it. How could I not? It was public knowledge.

CREON: And yet you dared to break those very laws?

ANTIGONE: Yes. Zeus did not announce those laws to me.
And Justice living with the gods below
sent no such laws for men. I did not think
515 anything which you proclaimed strong enough
to let a mortal override the gods
and their unwritten and unchanging laws.
They're not just for today or yesterday,

My Notes

but exist forever, and no one knows

520 where they first appeared. So I did not mean

to let a fear of any human will

lead to my punishment among the gods.

I know all too well I'm going to die—

how could I not?—it makes no difference

525 what you decree. And if I have to die

before my time, well, I count that a gain.

When someone has to live the way I do,

surrounded by so many evil things,

how can she fail to find a benefit

530 in death? And so for me meeting this fate

won't bring any pain. But if I'd allowed

my own mother's dead son to just lie there,

an unburied corpse, then I'd feel distress.

What's going on here does not hurt me at all.

535 If you think what I'm doing now is stupid,

perhaps I'm being charged with foolishness

by someone who's a fool.

CHORUS LEADER: It's clear enough the spirit in this girl is passionate—

her father was the same. She has no sense

540 of compromise in times of trouble.

CREON: *[to the Chorus Leader]* But you should know the most
    obdurate wills

are those most prone to break. The strongest iron

tempered in the fire to make it really hard—

that's the kind you see most often shatter.

545 I'm well aware the most tempestuous horses

are tamed by one small bit. Pride has no place

in anyone who is his neighbour's slave.

This girl here was already very insolent

in contravening laws we had proclaimed.

550 Here she again displays her proud contempt—

having done the act, she now boasts of it.

She laughs at what she's done. Well, in this case,

if she gets her way and goes unpunished,

then she's the man here, not me. No. She may be

WORD CONNECTIONS

Multiple-Meaning Word
The word **passionate** has several meanings related to one idea: having or showing strong emotions. Can you figure out the variations in tone or meaning of this word? Which meaning is most accurate for the context used in line 538?

obdurate: hardhearted or inflexible
tempered: hardened
insolent: disrespectful

555 my sister's child, closer to me by blood

than anyone belonging to my house

who worships Zeus Herkeios[1] in my home,

but she'll not escape my harshest punishment—

her sister, too, whom I accuse as well.

560 She had an equal part in all their plans

to do this burial. Go summon her here.

I saw her just now inside the palace,

her mind out of control, some kind of fit.

[Exit attendants into the palace to fetch Ismene]

When people hatch their mischief in the dark

565 their minds often convict them in advance,

betraying their treachery. How I despise

a person caught committing evil acts

who then desires to glorify the crime.

ANTIGONE: Take me and kill me—what more do you want?

570 **CREON**: Me? Nothing. With that I have everything.

ANTIGONE: Then why delay? There's nothing in your words

that I enjoy—may that always be the case!

And what I say displeases you as much.

But where could I gain greater glory

575 than setting my own brother in his grave?

All those here would confirm this pleases them

if their lips weren't sealed by fear—being king,

which offers all sorts of various benefits,

means you can talk and act just as you wish.

580 **CREON**: In all of Thebes, you're the only one

who looks at things that way.

ANTIGONE: They share my views, but they keep their mouths shut

just for you.

CREON: These views of yours—so different from the rest—

---

[1] *Zeus Herkeios* refers to an altar where sacrifices and liquid gifts were offered to Zeus; Zeus was the Divine protector of the house and the fence surrounding it; *herkos* means "fence" in Greek.

My Notes

don't they bring you any sense of shame?

585 ANTIGONE: No—there's nothing shameful in honouring my mother's children.

CREON: You had a brother killed fighting for the other side.

ANTIGONE: Yes—from the same mother and father, too.

CREON: Why then give tributes which insult his name?

590 ANTIGONE: But the one who died was not some slave—it was his own brother.

CREON: Yes, he will, if you give equal honours to a wicked man.

ANTIGONE: But the one who died was not some slave—it was his own brother.

CREON: Who was destroying this country—the other one went to his death defending it.

Athol Fugard's play *The Island* (1974) is set in a South African prison during the apartheid era. Here, two prisoners stage a performance of *Antigone*. In this 2003 production, South African actors John Kani (left) plays Creon, and Winston Ntshona (right) plays Antigone at the Brooklyn Academy of Music in New York.

595 **ANTIGONE**: That may be, but Hades[2] still desires equal rites for both.

CREON: A good man does not wish what we give him
to be the same an evil man receives.

ANTIGONE: Who knows? In the world below perhaps
such actions are no crime.

600 **CREON**: An enemy can never be a friend, not even in death.

ANTIGONE: But my nature is to love. I cannot hate.

CREON: Then go down to the dead. If you must love,
love them. No woman's going to govern me—
no, no—not while I'm still alive.
[Enter two attendants from the house bringing Ismene to Creon]

605 **CHORUS LEADER**: Ismene's coming. There—right by the door.
She's crying. How she must love her sister!
From her forehead a cloud casts its shadow
down across her darkly flushing face—
and drops its rain onto her lovely cheeks.

610 **CREON**: You there—you snake lurking in my house,
sucking out my life's blood so secretly.
I'd no idea I was nurturing two pests,
who aimed to rise against my throne. Come here.
Tell me this—do you admit you played your part
615 in this burial, or will you swear an oath
you had no knowledge of it?

ISMENE: I did it—I admit it, and she'll back me up.
So I bear the guilt as well.

ANTIGONE: No, no—justice will not allow you to say that.
620 You didn't want to. I didn't work with you.

My Notes

---

[2] _Hades_ is the King of the Underworld and god of the dead.

ISMENE: But now you're in trouble, I'm not ashamed
of suffering, too, as your companion.
ANTIGONE: Hades and the dead can say who did it—
I don't love a friend whose love is only words.

625 ISMENE: You're my sister. Don't dishonour me.
Let me respect the dead and die with you.

ANTIGONE: Don't try to share my death or make a claim
to actions which you did not do. I'll die—
and that will be enough.

630 ISMENE: But if you're gone, what is there in life for me to love?

ANTIGONE: Ask Creon. He's the one you care about.

ISMENE: Why hurt me like this? It doesn't help you.

ANTIGONE: If I am mocking you, it pains me, too.

ISMENE: Even now is there some way I can help?

635 ANTIGONE: Save yourself. I won't envy your escape.

ISMENE: I feel so wretched leaving you to die.

ANTIGONE: But you chose life—it was my choice to die.

ISMENE: But not before I'd said those words just now.

ANTIGONE: Some people may approve of how you think—
640 others will believe my judgment's good.

ISMENE: But the mistake's the same for both of us.

ANTIGONE: Be brave. You're alive. But my spirit died
some time ago so I might help the dead.

CREON: I'd say one of these girls has just revealed

645 how mad she is—the other's been that way
  since she was born.
  ISMENE: My lord, whatever good sense people have by birth no longer
    stays with them
  once their lives go wrong—it abandons them.

  CREON: In your case, that's true, once you made your choice
650 to act in evil ways with wicked people.

  ISMENE: How could I live alone, without her here?

  CREON: Don't speak of her being here. Her life is over.

  ISMENE: You're going to kill your own son's bride?

  CREON: Why not? There are other fields for him to plough.

655 **ISMENE:** No one will make him a more loving wife
  than she will.

  CREON: I have no desire my son should have an evil wife.

  ANTIGONE: Dearest Haemon, how your father wrongs you.

  CREON: I've had enough of this—you and your marriage.

660 **ISMENE:** You really want that? You're going to take her from him?

  CREON: No, not me. Hades is the one who'll stop the marriage.

  CHORUS LEADER: So she must die—that seems decided on.

  CREON: Yes—for you and me the matter's closed.
  [Creon turns to address his attendants]
  No more delay. You slaves, take them inside.
665 From this point on they must act like women
  and have no liberty to wander off.
  Even bold men run when they see Hades
  coming close to them to snatch their lives.

[The attendants take Antigone and Ismene into the palace, leaving Creon and the Chorus on stage]

THIRD ODE

CHORUS—Strophe 1: Those who live without tasting evil

670 have happy lives—for when the gods
shake a house to its foundations,
then **inevitable** disasters strike,
falling upon whole families,
just as a surging ocean swell

675 running before cruel Thracian winds
across the dark trench of the sea
churns up the deep black sand
and crashes headlong on the cliffs,
which scream in pain against the wind.

680 **CHORUS—Antistrophe 1:** I see this house's age-old sorrows,
the house of Labdakos'[3] children,
sorrows falling on the sorrows of the dead,
one generation bringing no relief
to generations after it—some god

685 strikes at them—on and on without an end.
For now the light which has been shining
over the last roots of Oedipus' house
is being cut down with a bloody knife
belonging to the gods below—

690 for foolish talk and frenzy in the soul.

CHORUS—Strophe 2: Oh Zeus, what human trespasses
can check your power? Even Sleep,
who casts his nets on everything,
cannot master that—nor can the months,

695 the tireless months the gods control.
A **sovereign** who cannot grow old,
you hold Olympus as your own,
in all its glittering magnificence.
From now on into all future time,

700 as in the past, your law holds firm.

inevitable: sure to happen
sovereign: king

---

3 *Labdakos* is father to Laius, grandfather to Oedipus.

It never enters lives of human beings
in its full force without disaster.
CHORUS—Antistrophe 2: Hope ranging far and wide brings comfort
to many men—but then hope can deceive,
705 delusions born of volatile desire.
It comes upon the man who's ignorant
until his foot is seared in burning fire.
Someone's wisdom has revealed to us
this famous saying—sometimes the gods
710 lure a man's mind forward to disaster, and he
thinks evil's something good. But then he
lives only the briefest time free of catastrophe.

Making Observations
- What major events happen in this scene?
- What emotions do you think Antigone and Creon feel at this point in the play?

Returning to the Text
- Reread the scene to answer these text-dependent questions.
- Write any additional questions you have about the text in your Reader/Writer Notebook.

5. In lines 440–453, what are the Guard's feelings about returning to speak to Creon? Why does he refer to himself as "the lucky man" in line 450?

_____
_____
_____
_____

6. Why is the windstorm significant in the development of the plot? What explanation does the Guard give for its cause?

_____
_____
_____
_____

7. Why does Antigone admit what she has done even though she knows Creon will punish her? Provide evidence from the text to support your inference.

_____

_____

_____

_____

8. What is the meaning of the metaphors Creon uses in lines 542–546? What do they imply about how he will treat Antigone?

_____

_____

_____

_____

9. How and why has Ismene's attitude changed since the beginning of the play?

_____

_____

_____

_____

As You Read

- The following painting illustrates a scene from *Antigone*. Identify characters and determine their actions by using what you know from the play along with what is depicted in the painting.
- Write notes in the margin about how the image depicts the characters' internal and external traits.

Antigone from *Antigone* by Sophocles (oil on canvas)
By Marie Spartali Stillman, (1844–1927)

Making Observations

- What are the characters in the painting doing?
- What does the image show you about the characters' emotions?

Returning to the Image

- View the image again to answer these questions.
- Write any additional questions you have about the image in your Reader/Writer Notebook.

10. What scene in Antigone does the painting depict? Why might Ismene be looking over her shoulder?

_____

_____

_____

_____

11. How does the painting give more information about the play *Antigone* to someone who might read it?

_____

_____

_____

_____

12. What emotions depicted in the painting are different from those described in the play? How does reading the play help you interpret Antigone's thoughts and emotions in the painting?

_____

_____

_____

_____

Working from the Text

13. Revisit the prediction in your Reader/Writer Notebook about how you thought the plot would unfold as Creon and Antigone confronted each other on stage. Describe their interaction and their differing motivations.

14. Mark text evidence that supports your inferences about the motivations of Creon and Antigone by highlighting, underlining, or annotating the text.

15. Work with your group to paraphrase and analyze the motivation behind what each character says in the scene between the Guard, Creon, Antigone, and Ismene.

Textual Evidence: What the Character Says	Analysis: What Motivates the Character
Guard:	
Creon:	
Antigone:	
Ismene:	

16. Work collaboratively in a small group to prepare for a performance of the scene (lines 427–668). First, decide who will play each role. Then consider your character's motivations and how you will portray them through your delivery. Mark the text for pauses, tone, pace, and volume to convey important ideas and key details.

17. Rehearse the scene and present it to other groups.

18. Provide feedback to other groups. What did the group do well? What could they do differently next time? Look at the scoring rubric for Embedded Assessment 2 as you prepare your feedback.

Language Checkpoint: Recognizing Frequently Confused Words

Recognizing Frequently Confused Words

When writers want to be taken seriously, they must be sure they have used the words they intended to use. Many English words are frequently confused with each other.

1. **Quickwrite:** Think about the words *to*, *two*, and *too*. Writers often confuse these words. Why do you think that is?

To/Two/Too

Word	Definition/Use	Example from *Antigone*
to	begins a prepositional phrase or infinitive (a verb phrase)	"And if I have **to** die before my time, well, I count that a gain." (lines 525–526)
two	a number	"we **two** lost both our brothers, killed on the same day by a double blow." (lines 16–17)
too	also or exceedingly	"But now you're in trouble, I'm not ashamed of suffering, **too**, as your companion." (lines 621–622)

2. Fill in the word *to/two/too* that should complete each sentence.

- Haemon, the king's son, proposed _____ Antigone on the night of the ball.
- The _____ sisters had _____ brothers who were both killed in battle.
- Antigone was going _____ do what she thought would please the gods over what would please the king, so she buried her brother against the king's wishes.
- Antigone is brought before the king, and eventually Ismene comes before him, _____. Ismene tries _____ defend her sister's actions.
- However, Antigone rejects her sister's attempts to help because Ismene failed _____ help her bury their brother.

Then/Than

Word	Definition/Use	Example from *Antigone*
then	1) an adverb relating to time 2) the result of something	"Well, in this case, if she gets her way and goes unpunished, **then** she's the man here, not me." (lines 552–554)
than	used when making comparisons	"She may be my sister's child, closer to me by blood **than** anyone belonging to my house." (lines 554–556)

3. Write a sentence or two about the play *Antigone* using the words *then* and *than*.:

- then:

- than:

That/Which

Word	Definition/Use	Example from *Antigone*
that	used when introducing a clause of information that is necessary for understanding the sentence. No extra punctuation is needed.	"You must remember **that** by birth we're women, and, as such, we shouldn't fight with men." (lines 80–81)
which	used to introduce a clause of extra information not necessary for understanding. Set off the clause with commas.	"All those here would confirm this pleases them if their lips weren't sealed by fear—being king, **which** offers all sorts of various benefits, means you can talk and act just as you wish." (lines 576–579)

Review the examples above. In the first example, we need the information "that by birth we're women" as part of the sentence or it would not make sense. The second example does not need the clause "which offers all sorts of various benefits," so it is set off by commas and begins with the word *which*.

4. Complete the following sentences with the words *that* or *which*.

- Antigone wants to see _____ her brother is given a proper burial at any cost.
- At first Ismene does not support Antigone's decision, _____ is punishable by death, to disobey the king's commands.
- The Guard feels sorry for Antigone, but not enough to wish _____ she hadn't been caught.
- Creon's declaration of Antigone's death, _____ he was too stubborn to change, set in motion events leading to the death of his own son.

Except/Accept

Word	Definition/Use	Example for *Antigone*
except	to exclude or to leave out; can be used as a verb, adverb, or preposition	Everyone **except** Antigone obeyed the king's orders.
accept	to take in or receive or to acknowledge as true	King Creon could not **accept** the idea of giving Polyneices a proper burial.

5. Write a sentence of dialogue that Antigone and Creon could have said to each other. Use the words *except* and *accept* in your sentences.

- Antigone:

- Creon :

6. Share your sentences with a partner, and check to make sure your partner's sentences are correct. Revise sentences, as needed, in the space provided.

Revising

Read the paragraph about *Antigone*, and select which revision would correct the sentence. Circle your answer. If the sentence does not require a revision, select "No Change."

The play *Antigone* is a tragedy like *Romeo and Juliet*, meaning the main character is brought down by a tragic flaw or circumstance. In this case, it's a matter of disobedience. In the opening scene, the reader is told that Antigone will stand alone against the king and (1) <u>then</u> die young. Evidently, spilling the beans in the beginning of a play is a trend in storytelling because famous playwrights Sophocles and Shakespeare both use this technique on more (2) <u>then</u> one occasion. However, their style of writing does not stop the audience from wanting (3) <u>too</u> keep watching (4) <u>to</u> see what will happen next. Today, not (5) <u>to</u> many writers use this strategy; however, watching movie previews can leave observers feeling like they have already seen (6) <u>to</u> much.	**1. a)** than **b)** NO CHANGE **2. a)** than **b)** NO CHANGE **3. a)** to **b)** two **c)** NO CHANGE **4. a)** two **b)** too **c)** NO CHANGE **5. a)** to **b)** two **c)** NO CHANGE **6. a)** to **b)** two **c)** NO CHANGE

7. Go over your answers with a partner. Did you make the same choices? Work together to resolve any differences and summarize your discussion the space provided.

☑ Check Your Understanding

For each set of words, write either a question you can ask yourself to remember which word you want to use or a phrase that will help you remember which word is which.

to/two/too:

then/than:

that/which:

except/accept:

Practice

Read the following sample of a student response to the play. Make corrections as necessary to the frequently confused words by rewriting the paragraph in the space that follows.

Antigone is a very stubborn character. However, her motives are good. She wants <u>too</u> make sure her brother is treated respectfully in death, but <u>than</u> she disobeys the king's orders <u>two</u>. She is not willing to <u>except</u> treating Polyneices badly because of choices he made while living, which is why he is killed in the first place. Rather than follow the king's wishes, she follows her <u>heart. Which</u> gets her into trouble. She doesn't care, though. She <u>excepts</u> her sentence of death and does not waver.

An Epic Foil

Learning Targets

- Discuss the use of foil characters and their interactions with other characters.
- Examine the staging in a play and practice incorporating staging in a performance.

Preview

In this activity, you will continue reading *Antigone* and analyze the interaction between Creon and Haemon, as well as the words, thoughts, and actions of the characters.

Foil Characters

1. Consider the three characters who have interacted with Creon so far. How is each one different from Creon? Discuss your ideas with a partner and take notes about each in the space provided.

   Guard:

   Antigone:

   Ismene:

2. Which of these characters do you think serves as the strongest foil for Creon? How does this foil help develop and highlight Creon's character? Continue discussing your ideas with your partner.

As You Read

- Highlight evidence of Haemon's character traits in one color and Creon's character traits in another color.
- Circle unknown words and phrases. Try to determine the meaning of the words by using context clues, word parts, or a dictionary.

My Notes

Play

Antigone

by **Sophocles**

[The palace doors open]

CHORUS LEADER: Here comes Haemon,
your only living son. Is he grieving
715 the fate of Antigone, his bride,
bitter that his marriage hopes are gone?

CREON: We'll soon find out—more accurately
than any prophet here could indicate.
[Enter Haemon from the palace]
My son, have you heard the sentence that's been passed
720 upon your bride? And have you now come here
angry at your father? Or are you loyal to me,
on my side no matter what I do?

HAEMON: Father, I'm yours. For me your judgments
and the ways you act on them are good—
725 I shall follow them. I'll not consider
any marriage a greater benefit
than your fine leadership.

CREON: Indeed, my son,
that's how your heart should always be resolved,
730 to stand behind your father's judgment on every
issue. That's what men pray for—
obedient children growing up at home
who will pay back their father's enemies,
evil to them for evil done to him,
735 while honouring his friends as much as he does.
A man who fathers useless children—
what can one say of him except he's bred
troubles for himself, and much to laugh at
for those who fight against him? So, my son,
740 don't ever throw good sense aside for pleasure,

My Notes

for some woman's sake. You understand
how such embraces can turn freezing cold
when an evil woman shares your life at home.
What greater wound is there than a false friend?
745 So spit this girl out—she's your enemy.
Let her marry someone else in Hades.
Since I caught her clearly disobeying,
the only **culprit** in the entire city,
I won't **perjure** myself before the state.
750 No—I'll kill her. And so let her appeal
to Zeus, the god of blood relationships.
If I foster any lack of full respect
in my own family, I surely do the same
with those who are not linked to me by blood.
755 The man who acts well with his household
will be found a just man in the city.
I'd trust such a man to govern wisely
or to be content with someone ruling him.
And in the thick of battle at his post
760 he'll stand firm beside his fellow soldier,
a loyal, brave man. But anyone who's proud
and violates our laws or thinks he'll tell
our leaders what to do, a man like that
wins no praise from me. No. We must obey
765 whatever man the city puts in charge,
no matter what the issue—great or small,
just or unjust. For there's no greater evil
than a lack of leadership. That destroys
whole cities, turns households into ruins,
770 and in war makes soldiers break and run away.
When men succeed, what keeps their lives secure
in almost every case is their obedience.
That's why they must support those in control,
and never let some woman beat us down.
775 If we must fall from power, let that come
at some man's hand—at least, we won't be called
inferior to any woman.

---

culprit: person who has
committed a crime
perjure: make a liar of

My Notes

CHORUS LEADER: Unless we're being deceived by our old age,
what you've just said seems reasonable to us.

780 HAEMON: Father, the gods instill good sense in men—
the greatest of all the things which we possess.
I could not find your words somehow not right—
I hope that's something I never learn to do.
But other words might be good, as well.
785 Because of who you are, you can't perceive
all the things men say or do—or their complaints.
Your gaze makes citizens afraid—they can't
say anything you would not like to hear
But in the darkness I can hear them talk—.
790 the city is upset about the girl.
They say of all women here she least deserves
the worst of deaths for her most glorious act.
When in the slaughter her own brother died,
she did not just leave him there unburied,
795 to be ripped apart by carrion dogs or birds.
Surely she deserves some golden honour?
That's the dark secret rumour people speak.
For me, father, nothing is more valuable
than your well being. For any children,
800 what could be a greater honour to them
than their father's thriving reputation?
A father feels the same about his sons.
So don't let your mind dwell on just one thought,
that what you say is right and nothing else.
805 A man who thinks that only he is wise,
that he can speak and think like no one else,
when such men are exposed, then all can see
their emptiness inside. For any man,
even if he's wise, there's nothing shameful
810 in learning many things, staying flexible.
You notice how in winter floods the trees
which bend before the storm preserve their twigs.
The ones who stand against it are destroyed,
root and branch. In the same way, those sailors
815 who keep their sails stretched tight, never easing off,

make their ship capsize—and from that point on
sail with their rowing benches all submerged.
So end your anger. Permit yourself to change.
For if I, as a younger man, may state
820 my views, I'd say it would be for the best
if men by nature understood all things—
if not, and that is usually the case,
when men speak well, it good to learn from them.

CHORUS LEADER: My lord, if what he's said is relevant,
825 it seems appropriate to learn from him,
and you too, Haemon, listen to the king.
The things which you both said were excellent.

CREON: And men my age—are we then going to school
to learn what's wise from men as young as him?

830 **HAEMON:** There's nothing wrong in that. And if I'm young,
don't think about my age—look at what I do.

CREON: And what you do—does that include this,
honouring those who act against our laws?

HAEMON: I would not encourage anyone
835 to show respect to evil men.

CREON: And her—
is she not suffering from the same disease?

HAEMON: The people here in Thebes all say the same—
they deny she is.

840 **CREON:** So the city now
will instruct me how I am to govern?

HAEMON: Now you're talking like someone far too young.
Don't you see that?

CREON: Am I to rule this land

845 at someone else's whim or by myself?

HAEMON: A city which belongs to just one man
is no true city.

CREON: According to our laws,
does not the ruler own the city?

850 **HAEMON:** By yourself you'd make an excellent king
but in a desert.

CREON: It seems as if this boy
is fighting on the woman's side.

HAEMON: That's true—
855 if you're the woman. I'm concerned for you.

CREON: You're the worst there is—you set your judgment up
against your father.

HAEMON: No, not when I see
you making a mistake and being unjust.

860 **CREON:** Is it a mistake to honour my own rule?

Actors Nikitas Tsakiroglou, Ioanna Papa, and Stavros Zalmas in a 2016 production of
Antigone at Dimotiko Theatro Kipou in Thessaloniki, Greece

HAEMON: You're not honouring that by trampling on
the gods' prerogatives.

CREON: You foul creature—
you're worse than any woman.

365 **HAEMON:** You'll not catch me
giving way to some disgrace.

CREON: But your words
all speak on her behalf.

HAEMON: And yours and mine—
370 and for the gods below.

CREON: You woman's slave—
don't try to win me over.

HAEMON: What do you want—
to speak and never hear someone reply?

75 **CREON:** You'll never marry her while she's alive.

HAEMON: Then she'll die—and in her death kill someone else.

CREON: Are you so insolent you threaten me?

HAEMON: Where's the threat in challenging a bad decree?

CREON: You'll regret parading what you think like this—
80 you—a person with an empty brain!

HAEMON: If you were not my father, I might say
you were not thinking straight.

CREON: Would you, indeed?
Well, then, by Olympus, I'll have you know
35 you'll be sorry for demeaning me
with all these insults.
[Creon turns to his attendants]

prerogatives: exclusive rights or
privileges

Go bring her out—
that hateful creature, so she can die right here,
with him present, before her bridegroom's eyes.

890 HAEMON: No. Don't ever hope for that. She'll not die
with me just standing there. And as for you—
your eyes will never see my face again.
So let your rage charge on among your friends
who want to stand by you in this.
[Exit Haemon, running back into the palace]

895 CHORUS LEADER: My lord, Haemon left in such a hurry.
He's angry—in a young man at his age
the mind turns bitter when he's feeling hurt.

CREON: Let him dream up or carry out great deeds
beyond the power of man, he'll not save these girls—
900 their fate is sealed.

CHORUS LEADER: Are you going to kill them both?

CREON: No—not the one whose hands are clean. You're right.

CHORUS LEADER: How do you plan to kill Antigone?

CREON: I'll take her on a path no people use,
905 and hide her in a cavern in the rocks,
while still alive. I'll set out provisions,
as much as piety requires, to make sure
the city is not totally corrupted.
Then she can speak her prayers to Hades,
910 the only god she worships, for success
avoiding death—or else, at least, she'll learn,
although too late, how it's a waste of time
to work to honour those whom Hades holds.

INDEPENDENT READING LINK

Read and Research

Review the notes you have been taking in your Reader/Writer Notebook about your independent reading. Is there a topic connected to Greek drama that you would like to learn more about? Do you want to learn more about Sophocles or other Greek playwrights? Choose a topic and generate questions for an informal inquiry about the subject. Locate relevant sources and conduct research about your topic. Then share your findings with the class in the form of an oral or written report.

piety: devotion to religion; fulfillment of religious obligations

Making Observations
- What are your thoughts about Creon and Haemon?
- What about this scene stands out most to you?

Returning to the Text

Reread the scene to answer these text-dependent questions.

Write any additional questions you have about the text in your Reader/Writer Notebook.

1. Reread lines 731–735. How does this statement help you understand what Creon expects from his son in this situation?

    _____

    _____

    _____

    _____

2. Haemon delivers a well-organized and moving argument to Creon in defense of Antigone in lines 780–823. Identify the different rhetorical appeals you can find in it.

    _____

    _____

    _____

    _____

3. In lines 840–851, what are Creon and Haemon arguing about? What prejudices does Creon reveal, and what do they tell you about Creon's character?

    _____

    _____

    _____

    _____

4. One of the characteristics of a tragic hero is "a good person who is brought down by an 'act of injustice.'" Explain why Creon's choice of death for Antigone is an "act of injustice."

    _____

    _____

    _____

    _____

Working from the Text

5. Look back at the text. Where you can you find elements of praise, mockery, and mourning? How might you convey these in a performance?

6. Work collaboratively in a small group to plan and perform the scene you just read among Creon, Haemon, and the Chorus Leader by marking the text for pauses, emphasis, volume, and tone to convey the words, thoughts, and actions of the characters. Be sure to think about how each character could adapt his or her speech to reflect or enhance the meaning of the action taking place in the scene.

7. Work together to stage the scene, including deciding on the positions of the actors and the use of props, costumes, lighting, sound effects, and makeup.

8. Rehearse the scene with your group. Provide feedback to your peers on ways to improve the performance. Consider these questions as you provide feedback:

   - Did the performance clearly convey the character's motivations?
   - Was the vocal presentation effective? What would improve it?
   - How did each character adapt his or her speech for the scene?
   - Were effective visual techniques used? If not, what technique can you suggest?

☑ Check Your Understanding

Reflect on your group's performance of the scene in your Reader/Writer Notebook. What did your group do well? Does the staging improve or detract from the performance? How would you interpret the scene differently next time? Then return to the essential question: How can a performer communicate perspective through oral and visual interpretation?

Odes to Love and Death

Learning Targets

- Analyze choral odes for author's purpose, literary elements, and theme.
- Present well-reasoned ideas supported with textual evidence in discussion groups.

Preview

In this activity, you will review the purpose of choral odes in Greek drama and analyze their function in *Antigone*.

Analyzing Choral Odes

1. Review the Introduction to Greek Drama information in Activity 4.12. List the various purposes of choral odes:

   -
   -
   -
   -
   -
   -

2. Reflect on the three odes you have read so far. Then complete the first three rows of the Purposes of the Choral Odes graphic organizer in the Working from the Text section of this activity.

As You Read

Annotate in the margins with inferences regarding the ancient Greeks' beliefs about love and death. Underline text evidence to support your inferences.

Circle unknown words and phrases. Try to determine the meaning of the words by using context clues, word parts, or a dictionary.

Learning Strategies

Graphic Organizer
Marking the Text
Summarizing
Think Aloud
Think-Pair-Share

My Notes

_____
_____
_____
_____
_____
_____
_____
_____
_____
_____
_____
_____
_____
_____
_____
_____
_____
_____

WORD CONNECTIONS

Word Relationships

The Choral Leader says that Antigone is "going to her bridal room" (line 932). He uses this as a *euphemism*, a word or phrase used in place of another word or phrase that is considered too harsh. In this context, the phrase *bridal room* refers to the place where Antigone is going to die. What is the effect of the Choral Leader using this euphemism?

squanders: wastes
perverting: corrupting

Play

Antigone

by **Sophocles**

FOURTH ODE

CHORUS—Strophe: O Eros,[1] the conqueror in every fight,
915　Eros, who **squanders** all men's wealth,
　　who sleeps at night on girls' soft cheeks,
　　and roams across the ocean seas
　　and through the shepherd's hut—
　　no immortal god escapes from you,
920　nor any man, who lives but for a day.
　　And the one whom you possess goes mad.

CHORUS—Antistrophe: Even in good men you twist their minds,
　　perverting them to their own ruin.
　　You provoke these men to family strife.
925　The bride's desire seen glittering in her eyes—
　　that conquers everything, its power
　　enthroned beside eternal laws, for there
　　the goddess Aphrodite works her will,
　　whose ways are irresistible.

[Antigone enters from the palace with attendants who are taking her away to her execution]

930　**CHORUS LEADER:** When I look at her I forget my place.
　　I lose restraint and can't hold back my tears—
　　Antigone going to her bridal room
　　where all are laid to rest in death.

COMMOS

ANTIGONE—Strophe 1: Look at me, my native citizens,
935　as I go on my final journey,
　　as I gaze upon the sunlight one last time,
　　which I'll never see again—for Hades,
　　who brings all people to their final sleep,

---

[1] *Eros* is the god of love and son of Aphrodite.

leads me on, while I'm still living,

940 down to the shores of Acheron.[2]

I've not yet had my bridal chant,

nor has any wedding song been sung—

for my marriage is to Acheron.

CHORUS: Surely you carry fame with you and praise,

945 as you move to the deep home of the dead.

You were not stricken by lethal disease

or paid your wages with a sword.

No. You were in charge of your own fate.

So of all living human beings, you alone

950 make your way down to Hades still alive.

ANTIGONE: I've heard about a guest of ours,

daughter of Tantalus,[3] from Phrygia—

she went to an excruciating death

in Sipylus,[4] right on the mountain peak.

955 The stone there, just like clinging ivy,

wore her down, and now, so people say,

the snow and rain never leave her there,

as she laments. Below her weeping eyes

her neck is wet with tears. God brings me

960 to a final rest which most resembles hers.

CHORUS—Antistrophe 1: But Niobe[5] was a goddess, born divine—

and we are human beings, a race which dies.

But still, it's a fine thing for a woman,

once she's dead, to have it said she shared,

965 in life and death, the fate of demi-gods.

ANTIGONE: Oh, you are mocking me! Why me—

by our fathers' gods—why do you all,

my own city and the richest men of Thebes,

---

[2] *Acheron* is a river in Hades across which the dead are ferried.

[3] *Tantalus,* the son of Zeus, is punished by being "tantalized" by food and drink that are always just out of his reach.

[4] *Sipylus* is the mountain ruled by Tantalus; it is the location of the weeping stone formation of Niobe.

[5] *Niobe* is the daughter of Tantalus; all her children are killed, and she is turned to stone; her rock formation appears to weep tears for her children as it rains.

My Notes

insult me now right to my face,

970 without waiting for my death?

Well at least I have Dirce's springs,

the holy grounds of Thebes,

a city full of splendid chariots,

to witness how no friends lament for me

975 as I move on—you see the laws

which lead me to my rock-bound prison,

a tomb made just for me. Alas!

In my wretchedness I have no home,

not with human beings or corpses,

980 not with the living or the dead.

CHORUS—Strophe 2: You pushed your daring to the limit, my child,

and tripped against Justice's high altar—

perhaps your agonies are paying back.

some compensation for your father.

985 **ANTIGONE—Antistrophe 2:** Now there you touch on my most
painful thought—

my father's destiny—always on my mind,

along with that whole fate which sticks to us,

the splendid house of Labdakos—the curse

arising from a mother's marriage bed,

990 when she had sex with her own son, my father.

From what kind of parents was I born,

their wretched daughter? I go to them,

unmarried and accursed, an outcast.

Alas, too, for my brother Polyneices,

995 who made a fatal marriage and then died—

and with that death killed me while still alive.

CHORUS: To be piously **devout** shows reverence,

but powerful men, who in their persons

incorporate authority, cannot bear

1000 anyone to break their rules. Hence, you die

because of your own selfish will.

ANTIGONE—Epode: Without lament, without a friend,

and with no marriage song, I'm being led

devout: religious

in this miserable state, along my final road.

1005 So wretched that I no longer have the right

to look upon the sun, that sacred eye.

But my fate prompts no tears, and no

friend mourns.

CREON: Don't you know that no one faced with death

1010 would ever stop the singing and the groans,

if that would help? Take her and shut her up,

as I have ordered, in her tomb's embrace.

And get it done as quickly as you can.

Then leave her there alone, all by herself—

1015 she can sort out whether she wants suicide

or remains alive, buried in a place like that.

As far as she's concerned, we bear no guilt.

But she's lost her place living here with us.

ANTIGONE: Oh my tomb and bridal chamber—

1020 my eternal hollow dwelling place,

where I go to join my people. Most of them

have perished—Persephone[6] has welcomed them

among the dead. I'm the last one, dying here

the most evil death by far, as I move down

1025 before the time allotted for my life is done.

But I go nourishing the vital hope

my father will be pleased to see me come,

and you, too, my mother, will welcome me,

as well as you, my own dear brother.

1030 When you died, with my own hands I washed you.

I arranged your corpse and at the grave mound

poured out **libations**. But now, Polyneices,

this is my reward for covering your corpse.

However, for wise people I was right

1035 to honour you. I'd never have done it

for children of my own, not as their mother,

nor for a dead husband lying in decay—

no, not in defiance of the citizens.

libations: liquid gifts to a god

6 *Persephone* is the goddess of the underworld; she is abducted by Hades and forced to spend one third of each year there, which is the winter when nothing blooms or grows.

What law do I appeal to, claiming this?
1040 If my husband died, there'd be another one,
and if I were to lose a child of mine
I'd have another with some other man.
But since my father and my mother, too,
are hidden away in Hades' house,
1045 I'll never have another living brother.
That was the law I used to honour you.
But Creon thought that I was in the wrong
and acting recklessly for you, my brother.
Now he seizes me by force and leads me here—
1050 no wedding and no bridal song, no share
in married life or raising children.
Instead I go in sorrow to my grave,
without my friends, to die while still alive.
What holy justice have I violated?
1055 In my wretchedness, why should I still look
up to the gods? Which one can I invoke
to bring me help, when for my reverence
they charge me with impiety? Well, then,
if this is something fine among the gods,
1060 I'll come to recognize that I've done wrong.
But if these people here are being unjust

Actor Micari in Japanese director Satoshi Miyagi's production of *Antigone* at the Festival d'Avignon in 2017 in France

may they endure no greater punishment
than the injustices they're doing to me.

CHORUS LEADER: The same storm blasts continue to attack
065 the mind in this young girl.

CREON: Then those escorting her
will be sorry they're so slow.

ANTIGONE: Alas, then,
those words mean death is very near at hand.

1070 **CREON:** I won't encourage you or cheer you up,
by saying the sentence won't be carried out.

ANTIGONE: O city of my fathers
in this land of Thebes—
and my ancestral gods,
1075 I am being led away.
No more delaying for me.
Look on me, you lords of Thebes,
the last survivor of your royal house,
see what I have to undergo,
1080 the kind of men who do this to me,
for paying **reverence** to true piety.
[*Antigone is led away under escort*]

FIFTH ODE

CHORUS—Strophe 1: In her brass-bound room fair Danae[7] as well
endured her separation from the heaven's light,
a prisoner hidden in a chamber like a tomb,
1085 although she, too, came from a noble line.
And she, my child, had in her care
the liquid streaming golden seed of Zeus.
But the power of fate is full of mystery.
There's no evading it, no, not with wealth,

reverence: respect or honor

---

7 *Danae* is the daughter of a king; Zeus falls in love with her and they have a son, Perseus.

1090 or war, or walls, or black sea-beaten ships.

CHORUS—Antistrophe 1: And the hot-tempered child of Dryas,[8]

king of the Edonians, was put in prison,

closed up in the rocks by Dionysus,[9]

for his angry mocking of the god.

1095 There the dreadful flower of his rage

slowly withered, and he came to know

the god who in his frenzy he had mocked

with his own tongue. For he had tried

to hold in check women in that frenzy

1100 inspired by the god, the Bacchanalian fire.

More than that—he'd made the Muses angry,

challenging the gods who love the flute.

CHORUS—Strophe 2: Beside the black rocks where the twin seas meet,

by Thracian Salmydessos at the Bosphorus,

1105 close to the place where Ares dwells,

the war god witnessed the unholy wounds

which blinded the two sons of Phineus,[10]

inflicted by his savage wife—the sightless holes

cried out for someone to avenge those blows

1110 made with her sharpened comb in blood-stained hands.

CHORUS—Antistrophe 2: In their misery they wept, lamenting

their wretched suffering, sons of a mother

whose marriage had gone wrong. And yet,

she was an offspring of an ancient family,

1115 the race of Erechtheus, raised far away,

in caves surrounded by her father's winds,

Boreas' child, a girl who raced with horses

across steep hills—child of the gods.

But she, too, my child, suffered much

1120 from the immortal Fates.

---

[8] The *child of Dryas* is Dryas's son, who objects to the worship of Dionysus and is imprisoned and driven mad; later, he is blinded by Zeus as additional punishment.

[9] *Dionysus* is the Greek god of wine and son of Zeus.

[10] *Phineus* is the King of Thrace, who imprisons his first wife Cleopatra; his new wife blinds Cleopatra's two sons out of jealousy.

Making Observations

- What happens between Creon and Antigone in this scene?
- What details do you notice about Creon or Antigone that someone else may have missed?

Returning to the Text

- Reread the scene to answer these text-dependent questions.
- Write any additional questions you have about the text in your Reader/Writer Notebook.

3. How does Antigone think the public views her fate in lines 966–980? Why does she have this impression? Is it accurate? Support your answers with textual evidence.

_____

_____

_____

_____

4. What justification does Antigone give for burying Polyneices even though she says she would not have done it for other members of her family?

_____

_____

_____

_____

5. How do Creon and Antigone ultimately see themselves and their roles in this scene? Provide evidence from the text to support your answer.

_____

_____

_____

_____

6. Several times in the scene, Antigone's tomb is referred to as her bridal chamber. How might this affect the mood of the audience or reader?

_____

_____

_____

_____

7. In lines 1095–1096, what does the Chorus mean by "the dreadful flower of his rage slowly withered"?

_____

_____

_____

_____

Working from the Text

8. Use the following graphic organizer to analyze the purpose of the odes in *Antigone*.

Purposes of the Choral Odes			
Ode	**Summary of Content**	**Connection to the Previous Scene**	**Functional Purpose of the Ode**
1	Polyneices and his army try to defeat Thebes at its seven gates; Eteocles and Thebans defend it along with Zeus's power, with brother killing brother.	The ode provides a description of troubles that precede the play's beginning and adds explanation of Antigone's and Ismene's descriptions of war.	The scene serves as a bridge between Scene I, where Antigone and Ismene are introduced, and the entrance of Creon.
2			
3			
4			

Ode	Summary of Content	Connection to the Previous Scene	Functional Purpose of the Ode

Purposes of the Choral Odes

9. After working on the graphic organizer, use the following questions to guide a group discussion of the ideas in this passage. Provide textual support for your opinions.

- What attitudes and ideas about love and death are conveyed in this scene?
- How are these ideas similar to or different from your culture's attitude toward love or death?
- How do the different characters and their interactions help develop themes related to love and death?

Learning Strategies

Graphic Organizer
Marking the Text
Think-Pair-Share

My Notes

Learning Targets
- Analyze the development of a tragic hero over the course of a play.
- Plan for the performance of a scene from *Antigone*.

Preview

In this activity, you will analyze the development of Creon as a tragic hero over the course of the play.

As You Read
- Underline text evidence that shows Creon's development as a tragic hero.
- Circle unknown words and phrases. Try to determine the meaning of the word by using context clues, word parts, or a dictionary.

Play

Antigone

by **Sophocles**

[Enter Teiresias, led by a young boy]

TEIRESIAS: Lords of Thebes, we two have walked a common path,
one person's vision serving both of us.
The blind require a guide to find their way.

CREON: What news do you have, old Teiresias?

1125 **TEIRESIAS:** I'll tell you—and you obey the prophet.

CREON: I've not rejected your advice before.

TEIRESIAS: That's the reason why you've steered the city
on its proper course.

CREON: From my experience
1130 I can confirm the help you give.

TEIRESIAS: Then know this—
your luck is once more on fate's razor edge.

CREON: What? What you've just said makes me nervous.

INDEPENDENT READING LINK

Read and Discuss

After you identify the tragic hero in the play *Antigone*, think about your independent reading selection. Use the characteristics of a tragic hero to identify the character in your independent reading who might be considered a tragic hero. Share your thoughts with a small group of peers.

TEIRESIAS: You'll know—once you hear the tokens of my art.

1135 As I was sitting in my ancient place
receiving omens from the flights of birds
who all come there where I can hear them,
I note among those birds an unknown cry—
evil, unintelligible, angry screaming.

1140 I knew that they were tearing at each other
with murderous claws. The noisy wings
revealed that all too well. I was afraid.
So right away up on the blazing altar
I set up burnt offerings. But Hephaestus

1145 failed to shine out from the sacrifice—
dark slime poured out onto the embers,
oozing from the thighs, which smoked and spat,
bile was sprayed high up into the air,
and the melting thighs lost all the fat

1150 which they'd been wrapped in. The rites had failed—
there was no prophecy revealed in them.
I learned that from this boy, who is my guide,
as I guide other men. Our state is sick—
your policies have done this. In the city

1155 our altars and our hearths have been **defiled**,
all of them, with rotting flesh brought there
by birds and dogs from Oedipus' son,
who lies there miserably dead. The gods
no longer will accept our sacrifice,

1160 our prayers, our thigh bones burned in fire.
No bird will shriek out a clear sign to us,
for they have gorged themselves on fat and blood
from a man who's dead. Consider this, my son.
All men make mistakes—that's not uncommon.

1165 But when they do, they're no longer foolish
or subject to bad luck if they try to fix
the evil into which they've fallen,
once they give up their **intransigence**.
Men who put their stubbornness on show

1170 invite accusations of stupidity.
Make concessions to the dead—don't ever stab
a man who's just been killed. What's the glory

My Notes

_____

_____

_____

_____

_____

_____

_____

_____

_____

_____

_____

_____

GRAMMAR & USAGE

Syntax
The way clauses and phrases are arranged into sentences—a writer's **syntax**—greatly affects the pacing and mood of a text. Study the sentence structure of lines 1135–1139. Notice this sentence is a five-line complex sentence. What are the structures of the three sentences beginning with line 1140 and ending with line 1142? How would you describe the general pattern of sentence structures here? How does this overall pattern affect the pace and mood of Teiresias's argument and help him make his point?

defiled: made unclean

intransigence: unwillingness to compromise

My Notes

in killing a dead person one more time?
I've been concerned for you. It's good advice.
1175 Learning can be pleasant when a man speaks well,
especially when he seeks your benefit.

CREON: Old man, you're all like archers shooting at me—
For you all I've now become your target—
even prophets have been aiming at me.
1180 I've long been bought and sold as merchandise
among that tribe. Well, go make your profits.
If it's what you want, then trade with Sardis
for their golden-silver alloy—or for gold
from India, but you'll never hide that corpse
1185 in any grave. Even if Zeus' eagles
should choose to seize his festering body
and take it up, right to the throne of Zeus,
not even then would I, in trembling fear
of some defilement, permit that corpse
1190 a burial. For I know well that no man
has the power to pollute the gods.
But, old Teiresias, among human beings
the wisest suffer a disgraceful fall
when, to promote themselves, they use fine words
1195 to spread around abusive insults.

TEIRESIAS: Alas, does any man know or think about …

CREON: *[interrupting]* Think what? What sort of **pithy** common thought
are you about to utter?

TEIRESIAS: [ignoring the interruption] … how good advice
is valuable—worth more than all possessions.

1200 **CREON:** I think that's true, as much as foolishness
is what harms us most.

TEIRESIAS: Yet that's the sickness
now infecting you.

pithy: short and clever

CREON: I have no desire
1205 to **denigrate** a prophet when I speak.

TEIRESIAS: But that's what you are doing, when you claim
my oracles are false.

CREON: The tribe of prophets—
all of them—are fond of money.

1210 **TEIRESIAS:** And kings?
Their tribe loves to benefit dishonestly.

CREON: You know you're speaking of the man who rules you.

TEIRESIAS: I know—thanks to me you saved the city
and now are in control.

1215 **CREON:** You're a wise prophet,
but you love doing wrong.

TEIRESIAS: You'll force me
to speak of secrets locked inside my heart.

CREON: Do it—just don't speak to benefit yourself.

1220 **TEIRESIAS:** I don't think that I'll be doing that—
not as far as you're concerned.

CREON: You can be sure
you won't change my mind to make yourself more rich.

TEIRESIAS: Then understand this well—you will not see
1225 the sun race through its cycle many times
before you lose a child of your own loins,
a corpse in payment for these corpses.
You've thrown down to those below someone
from up above—in your arrogance
1230 you've moved a living soul into a grave,
leaving here a body owned by gods below—

denigrate: slander

unburied, dispossessed, unsanctified.
That's no concern of yours or gods above.
In this you violate the ones below.

1235 And so destroying avengers wait for you,
Furies of Hades and the gods, who'll see
you caught up in this very wickedness.
Now see if I speak as someone who's been bribed.
It won't be long before in your own house

1240 the men and women all cry out in sorrow,
and cities rise in hate against you—all those
whose mangled soldiers have had burial rites
from dogs, wild animals, or flying birds
who carry the unholy stench back home,

1245 to every city hearth. Like an archer,
I shoot these arrows now into your heart
because you have provoked me. I'm angry—
so my aim is good. You'll not escape their pain.
Boy, lead us home so he can vent his rage

1250 on younger men and keep a quieter tongue
and a more temperate mind than he has now.
[Exit Teiresias, led by the young boy]

CHORUS LEADER: My lord, my lord, such dreadful prophecies—
and now he's gone. Since my hair changed colour
from black to white, I know here in the city

1255 he's never uttered a false prophecy.

CREON: I know that, too—and it disturbs my mind.
It's dreadful to give way, but to resist
and let destruction hammer down my spirit—
that's a fearful option, too.

1260 **CHORUS LEADER:** Son of Menoikeos,
you need to listen to some good advice.

CREON: Tell me what to do. Speak up. I'll do it.

CHORUS LEADER: Go and release the girl from her rock tomb.
Then prepare a grave for that unburied corpse.

1265 **CREON:** This is your advice? You think I should concede?

CHORUS LEADER: Yes, my lord, as fast as possible.
Swift footed injuries sent from the gods
hack down those who act imprudently.

CREON: Alas—it's difficult. But I'll give up.
1270 I'll not do what I'd set my heart upon.
It's not right to fight against necessity.

CHORUS LEADER: Go now and get this done. Don't give the work
to other men to do.

CREON: I'll go just as I am.
1275 Come, you servants, each and every one of you.
Come on. Bring axes with you. Go there quickly—
up to the higher ground. I've changed my mind.
Since I'm the one who tied her up, I'll go
and set her free myself. Now I'm afraid.
1280 Until one dies the best thing well may be
to follow our established laws.
[Creon and his attendants hurry off stage]

SIXTH ODE

CHORUS—Strophe 1: Oh you with many names,
you glory of that Theban bride,
and child of thundering Zeus,
1285 you who cherish famous Italy,
and rule the welcoming valley lands
of Eleusian Deo—
O Bacchus—you who dwell
in the bacchants' mother city Thebes,
1290 beside Ismenus'[1] flowing streams,
on land sown with the teeth
of that fierce dragon.

My Notes

_____

_____

_____

_____

_____

_____

_____

_____

_____

_____

_____

_____

_____

_____

_____

_____

_____

_____

_____

_____

_____

[1] *Ismenus* is a river near Thebes, which is sacred to Apollo.

CHORUS—Antistrophe 1: Above the double mountain peaks,
the torches flashing through the murky smoke
1295 have seen you where Corcyian nymphs
move on as they worship you
by the Kastalian stream.
And from the ivy-covered slopes
of Nysa's hills, from the green shore
1300 so rich in vines, you come to us,
visiting our Theban ways,
while deathless voices all cry out
in honour of your name, "Evoe."[2]

CHORUS—Strophe 2: You honour Thebes, our city,
1305 above all others, you and your mother
blasted by that lightning strike.
And now when all our people here
are captive to a foul disease,
on your healing feet you come
1310 across the moaning strait
or over the Parnassian hill.

CHORUS—Antistrophe 2: You who lead the dance,
among the fire-breathing stars,
who guard the voices in the night,
1315 child born of Zeus, oh my lord,
appear with your attendant Thyiads,
who dance in frenzy all night long,
for you their patron, Iacchus.[3]
[Enter a Messenger]

MESSENGER: All you here who live beside the home
1320 of Amphion and Cadmus—in human life
there's no set place which I would praise or blame.
The lucky and unlucky rise or fall
by chance day after day—and how these things
are fixed for men no one can prophesy.

---

[2] *Evoe* is similar to hallelujah, a cry of joy shouted by worshippers at festivals.
[3] *Iacchus* is another name for Dionysus.

325 For Creon, in my view, was once a man
   we all looked up to. For he saved the state,
   this land of Cadmus, from its enemies.
   He took control and reigned as its sole king—
   and prospered with the birth of noble children.
330 Now all is gone. For when a man has lost
   what gives him pleasure, I don't include him
   among the living—he's a breathing corpse.
   Pile up a massive fortune in your home,
   if that's what you want—live like a king.
335 If there's no pleasure in it, I'd not give
   to any man a vapour's shadow for it,
   not compared to human joy.

CHORUS LEADER: Have you come with news of some fresh trouble
in our house of kings?

1340 **MESSENGER:** They're dead—
   and those alive bear the responsibility
   for those who've died.

CHORUS LEADER: Who did the killing?
Who's lying dead? Tell us.

1345 **MESSENGER:** Haemon has been killed.
   No stranger shed his blood.

CHORUS LEADER: At his father's hand?
Or did he kill himself?

MESSENGER: By his own hand—
1350 angry at his father for the murder.

CHORUS LEADER: Teiresias, how your words have proven true!

MESSENGER: That's how things stand. Consider what comes next.

CHORUS LEADER: I see Creon's wife, poor Eurydice—
she's coming from the house—either by chance,

1355 or else she's heard there's news about her son.
[Enter Eurydice from the palace with some attendants]

EURYDICE: Citizens of Thebes, I heard you talking,
as I was walking out, going off to pray,
to ask for help from goddess Pallas.
While I was unfastening the gate,
1360 I heard someone speaking of bad news
about my family. I was terrified.
I collapsed, fainting back into the arms
of my attendants. So tell the news again—
I'll listen. I'm no stranger to misfortune.

1365 **MESSENGER:** Dear lady, I'll speak of what I saw,
omitting not one detail of the truth.
Why should I ease your mind with a report
which turns out later to be incorrect?
The truth is always best. I went to the plain,
1370 accompanying your husband as his guide.
Polyneices' corpse, still unlamented,
was lying there, the greatest distance off,
torn apart by dogs. We prayed to Pluto
and to Hecate, goddess of the road,
1375 for their good will and to restrain their rage.
We gave the corpse a ritual wash, and burned
what was left of it on fresh-cut branches.
We piled up a high tomb of his native earth.
Then we moved to the young girl's rocky cave,
1380 the hollow cavern of that bride of death.
From far away one man heard a voice
coming from the chamber where we'd put her
without a funeral—a piercing cry.
He went to tell our master Creon,
1385 who, as he approached the place, heard the sound,
an unintelligible scream of sorrow.
He groaned and then spoke out these bitter words,
"Has misery made me a prophet now?
And am I travelling along a road
1390 that takes me to the worst of all disasters?

I've just heard the voice of my own son.
You servants, go ahead—get up there fast.
Remove the stones piled in the entrance way,
then stand beside the tomb and look in there
1395 to see if that was Haemon's voice I heard,
or if the gods have been deceiving me."
Following what our desperate master asked,
we looked. In the furthest corner of the tomb
we saw Antigone hanging by the neck,
1400 held up in a noose—fine woven linen.
Haemon had his arms around her waist—
he was embracing her and crying out
in sorrow for the loss of his own bride,
now among the dead, his father's work,
1405 and for his horrifying marriage bed.
Creon saw him, let out a fearful groan,
then went inside and called out anxiously,
"You unhappy boy, what have you done?
What are you thinking? Have you lost your mind?
1410 Come out, my child—I'm begging you—please come."
But the boy just stared at him with savage eyes,
spat in his face and, without saying a word,
drew his two-edged sword. Creon moved away,
so the boy's blow failed to strike his father.
1415 Angry at himself, the ill-fated lad
right then and there leaned into his own sword,
driving half the blade between his ribs.
While still conscious he embraced the girl
in his weak arms, and, as he breathed his last,
1420 he coughed up streams of blood on her fair cheek.
Now he lies there, corpse on corpse, his marriage
has been fulfilled in chambers of the dead.
The unfortunate boy has shown all men
how, of all the evils which afflict mankind,
1425 the most disastrous one is thoughtlessness.

[*Eurydice turns and slowly returns into the palace*]

CHORUS LEADER: What do you make of that? The queen's gone back.
She left without a word, good or bad.

My Notes

MESSENGER: I'm surprised myself. It's about her son—
she heard that terrible report. I hope
1430 she's gone because she doesn't think it right
to mourn for him in public. In the home,
surrounded by her servants, she'll arrange
a period of mourning for the house.
She's discreet and has experience—
1435 she won't make mistakes.

CHORUS LEADER: I'm not sure of that.
To me her staying silent was extreme—
it seems to point to something ominous,
just like a vain excess of grief.

1440 **MESSENGER:** I'll go in.
We'll find out if she's hiding something secret,
deep within her passionate heart. You're right—
excessive silence can be dangerous.
[The Messenger goes up the stairs into the palace. Enter Creon from the side,
with attendants. Creon is holding the body of Haemon.]

CHORUS LEADER: Here comes the king in person—carrying
1445 in his arms, if it's right to speak of this,
a clear reminder that this evil comes
not from some stranger, but his own mistakes.

CREON: Aaiii—mistakes made by a foolish mind,
cruel mistakes that bring on death.
1450 You see us here, all in one family—
the killer and the killed.
Oh the profanity of what I planned.
Alas, my son, you died so young—
a death before your time.
1455 Aaiii ... aaiii ... you're dead ... gone—
not your own foolishness but mine.

CHORUS LEADER: Alas, it seems you've learned to see what's right—
but far too late.

WORD CONNECTIONS

Multiple-Meaning Word
The word **vain** has several meanings. Look up the different meanings in a dictionary and then decide which meaning best fits the context in line 1439, "Just like a vain excess of grief." *Vain* is also a homonym, or a word that sounds the same as another word or words. What are the differences among *vain*, *vein*, and *vane*? Consider their meanings and their parts of speech.

ominous: threatening
profanity: offense

CREON: Aaiiii … I've learned it in my pain.

1460 Some god clutching a great weight struck my head,

then hurled me onto paths in wilderness,

throwing down and casting underfoot

what brought me joy.

So sad … so sad …

1465 the wretched agony of human life.

[*The Messenger reappears from the palace*]

MESSENGER: My lord, you come like one who stores up evil,

what you hold in your arms and what you'll see

before too long inside the house.

CREON: What's that?

1470 Is there something still more evil than all this?

MESSENGER: Your wife is dead—blood mother of that corpse—

slaughtered with a sword—her wounds are very new,

poor lady.

CREON: Aaiiii … a gathering place for death …

My Notes

Syrian refugees performing in an Arabic production of Antigone in 2014 in Beirut, Lebanon

My Notes

1475 no sacrifice can bring this to an end.
Why are you destroying me? You there—
you bringer of this dreadful news, this agony,
what are you saying now? Aaiii ...
You kill a man then kill him once again.
1480 What are you saying, boy? What news?
A slaughter heaped on slaughter—
my wife, alas ... she's dead?

MESSENGER: [Opening the palace doors, revealing the body of Eurydice]
Look here. No longer is she concealed inside.

CREON: Alas, how miserable I feel—to look upon
1485 this second horror. What remains for me,
what's fate still got in store? I've just held
my own son in my arms, and now I see
right here in front of me another corpse.
Alas for this suffering mother.
1490 Alas, my son.

MESSENGER: Stabbed with a sharp sword at the altar,
she let her darkening eyesight fail,
once she had cried out in sorrow
for the glorious fate of Megareos,[4]
1495 who died some time ago, and then again
for Haemon, and then, with her last breath,
she called out evil things against you,
the killer of your sons.

CREON: Aaaii ... My fear now makes me tremble.
1500 Why won't someone now strike out at me,
pierce my heart with a double bladed sword?
How miserable I am ... aaiii ...
how full of misery and pain ...

---

[4] *Megareos* is the youngest son of Creon and Eurydice; he is an inexperienced solder who dies in battle.

My Notes

MESSENGER: By this woman who lies dead you stand charged
505 with the deaths of both your sons.

CREON: What about her?
How did she die so violently?

MESSENGER: She killed herself,
with her own hands she stabbed her belly,
510 once she heard her son's unhappy fate.

CREON: Alas for me … the guilt for all of this is mine—
it can never be removed from me or passed
to any other mortal man. I, and I alone …
I murdered you … I speak the truth.
515 Servants—hurry and lead me off,
get me away from here, for now
what I am in life is nothing.

CHORUS LEADER: What you advise is good—if good can come
with all these evils. When we face such things
520 the less we say the better.

CREON: Let that day come, oh let it come,
the fairest of all destinies for me,
the one which brings on my last day.
Oh, let it come, so that I never see
1525 another dawn.

CHORUS LEADER: That's something for the times ahead.
Now we need to deal with what confronts us here.
What's yet to come is the concern of those
whose task it is to deal with it.

1530 **CREON:** In that prayer
I included everything I most desire.

CHORUS: Pray for nothing.
There's no release for mortal human beings,
not from events which destiny has set.

My Notes

1535 **CREON:** Then take this foolish man away from here.

I killed you, my son, without intending to,

and you, as well, my wife. How useless I am now.

I don't know where to look or find support.

Everything I touch goes wrong, and on my head

1540 fate climbs up with its overwhelming load.

[The Attendants help Creon move up the stairs into the palace, taking Haemon's body with them]

CHORUS: The most important part of true success

is wisdom—not to act impiously

towards the gods, for boasts of arrogant men

bring on great blows of punishment—

1545 so in old age men can discover wisdom.

Making Observations
- What major events take place in this scene?
- What emotions do you feel as you read this final passage?

Returning to the Text
- Reread the scene to answer these text-dependent questions.
- Write any additional questions you have about the text in your Reader/Writer Notebook.

1. In line 1132, Teiresias tells Creon that his "luck is once more on fate's razor edge." What does this metaphor mean? How should Creon react?

2. What indications do you have that Teiresias is truly a prophet? What do you think the signs he has interpreted mean? Annotate any clues that point to h being a true prophet.

3. Reread lines 1177–1195 and annotate any patterns you see in Creon's language. What excuse does Creon give for refusing to listen to Teiresias's advice? When has he made this accusation before, and what does this pattern of behavior say about his character?

_____

_____

_____

_____

4. Creon introduces the metaphor of the archer and the target in line 1177. How does Teiresias turn this metaphor against Creon, starting in line 1245?

_____

_____

_____

_____

5. The turning point for Creon begins in lines 1256–1262. Trace the development of this change in his conversation with the Chorus Leader. What characteristics of the tragic hero do these lines illustrate?

_____

_____

_____

_____

6. How does the Messenger describe Creon in lines 1325–1337? Does this description sound like that of a tragic hero? Explain.

_____

_____

_____

_____

7. Beginning with line 1365, what are the key events that the Messenger shares with Eurydice, Creon's wife?

_____

_____

_____

_____

8. What does Creon mean when he asks in lines 1485–1486, "What remains for me, what's fate still got in store?"

_____

_____

_____

9. How does the Chorus's line "There's no release for mortal human beings, not from events which destiny has set" (lines 1533–1534) relate to Creon's question about fate in line 1485?

_____

_____

_____

10. In lines 1457–1458, the Chorus Leader tells Creon, "Alas, it seems you've learned to see what's right—but far too late." What chances is Creon given throughout the play to "see what's right," and how does he respond? How does this relate to the unfolding of the tragedy?

_____

_____

_____

_____

11. What final message does the Chorus deliver, and how could you interpret this as the theme of the play?

_____

_____

_____

_____

Working from the Text

12. Review the characteristics of a tragic hero listed in Activity 4.13. Explain in your Reader/Writer Notebook which character in the play so far could be considered a tragic hero. List at least three reasons why the character meets the definition.

3. Work with a partner or small group to complete the graphic organizer. Find textual evidence to support your analysis of Creon as a tragic hero.

Creon as a Tragic Hero	
Characteristics of the Tragic Hero	**Where/When Has Creon Demonstrated These Qualities?**
Person of noble stature	
Good person who is brought down by an "act of injustice" (*hamartia*) because he knows no better or believes that a greater good will be served by his actions	
Has a weakness, or tragic flaw, such as pride, quickness to anger, or misjudgment	
Has free choice that makes his downfall his own fault	
Experiences misfortune that is not entirely deserved	
Gains self-knowledge or understanding before his downfall, and therefore experiences redemption	

4. How can you compare the character of Creon from *Antigone* to Okonkwo in *Things Fall Apart*?

5. Return to the Purposes of the Choral Odes graphic organizer in Activity 4.18 and complete the section for the Sixth Ode.

6. **Collaborative Conversation:** Working in a small group, go back to the photographs of the different performances of *Antigone*. Why do you think the unit includes photographs from many different productions? What can you hypothesize about the play? How does this connect to the essential question, "Why are humans inclined to respond to people, objects, or events with praise, mockery, or mourning?"

Preparing for the Embedded Assessment

17. With your group, choose a scene from *Antigone* for Embedded Assessment 2 and mark the text for vocal delivery. In addition, annotate areas of the text that reveal the characters' feelings and motivations. Be sure to look at the scoring guide as you develop your plan for the performance.

🎲 Independent Reading Checkpoint

Review the plays you selected for your independent reading. Prepare an informal presentation that briefly describes the plays you chose, including their characters, plots, settings, and so on. Then explain to the class how plays are similar to and different from other forms of entertainment, such as books and movies. For example, how is the story conveyed in a play versus other forms of entertainment? What are the limitations of theater? How does the audience learn about the characters, plot, and setting in a play? How is it different from a novel or movie?

Performing a Scene from *Antigone*

ASSIGNMENT

Your assignment is to choose a scene from *Antigone* with your group, mark the text for visual and vocal delivery, and then perform it in front of the class. Your performance should demonstrate an analysis of each character's feelings and motivations. You will also be responsible for carefully viewing your classmates' performances and providing feedback.

Planning: With your group, prepare to perform your scene.	■ How will you select a scene from *Antigone*? ■ What is the meaning of each of your character's lines? ■ How will you mark the text to indicate vocal and visual delivery? ■ How will you use vocal delivery to express your character's feelings and motivations? ■ How will you use visual delivery and staging to interpret the scene? ■ How will you and your group make notes and plan your performance?
Rehearsing: Memorize your lines and rehearse the performance with your group.	■ How will you demonstrate an understanding of each character's feelings and motivations? ■ While your partner is speaking, how should your character react? ■ How can you speak to your partner's character while both of you face the audience? ■ How can you make the scene more understandable and interesting for your audience with visual and vocal delivery? ■ How can you enhance your scene with set design, costumes, props, or music? ■ How can the Scoring Guide help you evaluate how well your performance will meet the requirements of the assignment?
Performing and Listening: Perform your scene for an audience of your peers and take notes on your classmates' performances.	■ How can you convey the feelings and motivations of the characters? ■ Who are the characters involved? ■ What is the scene about? ■ How can you use peer responding to help you improve your performance? ■ What were the best performances you saw, and what made them effective?

Reflection

Write a reflection in your Reader/Writer Notebook evaluating your overall performance.

- What steps did you take to help yourself understand the scene and plan your performance?
- What were the strengths and challenges of your overall performance?
- How did you feel about performing and speaking in front of others before this unit?
- How did different performers emphasize the feelings and motivations of the characters?

SCORING GUIDE

Scoring Criteria	Exemplary	Proficient	Emerging	Incomplete
Ideas	The performance • conveys a strong analysis of the feelings and motivations of the characters • conveys an insightful interpretation, and meaning is cleverly communicated through visual and vocal delivery • uses a variety of effective staging elements (set design, lighting, sound, props, etc.).	The performance • conveys an adequate analysis of the feelings and motivations of the characters • conveys an effective interpretation, and meaning is communicated through visual and vocal delivery • uses some staging elements (set design, lighting, sound, props, etc.).	The performance • conveys a partial or uneven analysis of the feelings and motivations of the characters • conveys an adequate interpretation, and meaning is passably communicated through visual and vocal delivery • uses a staging element (set design, lighting, sound, props, etc.), but it does not enhance the performance.	The performance • does not convey an analysis of the feeling and motivations of the characters • lacks an adequate interpretation, and meaning is not communicated throug visual and vocal delivery • does not use any staging elements (set design, lighting, soun props, etc.).
Structure	The performance • includes detailed scene annotations with performance notes and a creative plan for the performance • notes show excellent evidence of listening to and evaluating peer performances • reflection demonstrates insightful commentary on strengths, challenges, growth, and evaluation of performances. • demonstrates extensive evidence of collaboration.	The performance • includes an annotated scene with performance notes and a plan for the performance • notes show adequate evidence of listening to and evaluating peer performances • reflection demonstrates adequate commentary on strengths, challenges, growth, and evaluation of performances. • demonstrates adequate evidence of collaboration.	The performance • includes some scene annotations with performance notes and elements of a plan for the performance • notes show some evidence of listening to and evaluating peer performances • reflection demonstrates little commentary on strengths, challenges, growth, and evaluation of performances. • demonstrates uneven or ineffective evidence of collaboration.	The performance • includes no scene annotations with performance notes an elements of a plan for the performance • notes show no evidence of listening to and evaluating pee performances • reflection does not demonstrate commentary on strengths, challenges, growth, and evaluatio of performances. • demonstrates no evidence of collaboration.
Use of Language	The performance • uses language that delivers a faithful and dramatic representation through visual and vocal delivery • demonstrates an accurate memorization of lines.	The performance • uses language that delivers a faithful representation through visual and vocal delivery • demonstrates an adequate memorization of lines.	The performance • includes mispronunciations, mumbled words, and/or language that does not correctly represent the scene • demonstrates inefficient ability to memorize lines.	The performance • uses language that does not include significant parts of the scene and/or shows unclear visual and vocal delivery • demonstrates no abili to memorize lines.

Resources

Independent Reading

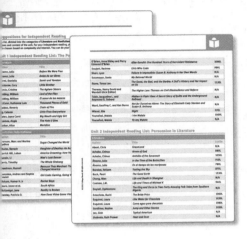

Learning Strategies

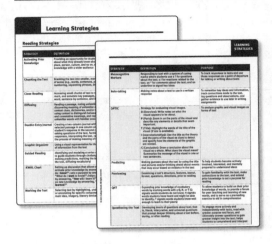

Graphic Organizers

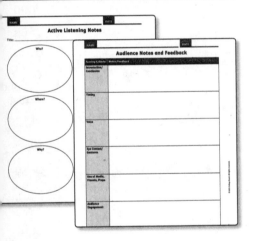

English-Spanish Glossary

Index of Skills

Index of Authors and Titles

Suggestions for Independent Reading

This list, divided into the categories of **Literature** and **Nonfiction/Informational Text**, comprises titles related to the themes and content of the unit. For your independent reading, you can select from this wide array of titles, which have been chosen based on complexity and interest. You can do your own research and select titles that intrigue you.

Unit 1 Independent Reading List: The Power of Argument

Literature		
Author	Title	Lexile
Álvarez, Julia	*Before We Were Free*	890L
Álvarez, Julia	*Antes de ser libres*	N/A
Carmi, Daniella	*Samir and Yonatan*	810L
Doctorow, Cory	*Little Brother*	900L
Garcia, Cristina	*The Agüero Sisters*	1000L
Golding, William	*Lord of the Flies*	770L
Golding, William	*El senor de las moscas*	760L
McCunn, Ruthanne Lum	*Thousand Pieces of Gold*	940L
Naidoo, Beverly	*Chain of Fire*	910L
Ng, Celeste	*Little Fires Everywhere*	N/A
Oates, Joyce Carol	*Big Mouth and Ugly Girl*	720L
Thomas, Angie	*The Hate U Give*	HL590
Walker, Alice	*Meridian*	1010L

Nonfiction/Informational		
Author	Title	Lexile
Aronson, Marc and Marina Budhos	*Sugar Changed the World*	1130L
Bhutto, Benazir	*Daughter of Destiny: An Autobiography*	N/A
Carrick Hill, Laban	*America Dreaming: How Youth Changed America in the Sixties*	1190L
Cunxin, Li	*Mao's Last Dancer*	810L
Ferris, Timothy	*The Whole Shebang*	N/A
Freedman, Russell	*Because They Marched: The People's Campaign for Voting Rights That Changed America*	1160L
Gonzales, Andrea and Sophie Houser	*Girl Code: Gaming, Going Viral, and Getting It Done*	1030L
Hickam, Homer H. Jr	*Rocket Boys*	N/A
Laure, Jason et al.	*South Africa*	1020L
McGonigal, Jane	*Reality Is Broken*	N/A
Netzley, Patricia D.	*How Does Video Game Violence Affect Society?*	1390L

O'Brien, Anne Sibley and Perry Edmond O'Brien	After Gandhi: One Hundred Years of Nonviolent Resistance	1080L
Saujani, Reshma	Girls Who Code	990L
Sherr, Lynn	Failure Is Impossible: Susan B. Anthony in Her Own Words	N/A
Sotomayor, Sonia	My Beloved World	N/A
Stone, Tanya Lee	The Good, the Bad, and the Barbie: A Doll's History and Her Impact on Us	1120L
Thoreau, Henry David and Wendell Glick (Editor)	The Higher Law: Thoreau on Civil Disobedience and Reform	N/A
Tobin, Jacqueline L. and Raymond G. Dobard	Hidden in Plain View: A Secret Story of Quilts and the Underground Railroad	N/A
Ward, Geoffrey C. and Ken Burns	Not for Ourselves Alone: The Story of Elizabeth Cady Stanton and Susan B. Anthony	N/A
Wiesel, Elie	Night	570L
Yousafzai, Malala	I Am Malala	1000L
Yousafzai, Malala	Yo soy Malala	N/A

Unit 2 Independent Reading List: Persuasion in Literature

Literature		
Author	Title	Lexile
Abani, Chris	GraceLand	N/A
Achebe, Chinua	Arrow of God	880L
Achebe, Chinua	Anthills of the Savannah	1030L
Álvarez, Julia	In the Time of the Butterflies	910L
Álvarez, Julia	En el tiempo de las mariposas	780L
Barakat, Ibtisam	Tasting the Sky	870L
Buck, Pearl	The Good Earth	1530L
Cheng, Nien	Life and Death in Shanghai	N/A
Coetzee, J.M.	Life and Times of Michael K	940L
Dayrell, Elphinstone	The King and the Ju Ju Tree: Forty Amazing Folk Tales from Southern Nigeria	N/A
Emecheta, Buchi	The Bride Price	1060L
Esquivel, Laura	Like Water for Chocolate	1030L
Esquivel, Laura	Como agua para chocolate	1080L
Gordimer, Nadine	Jump and Other Stories	1030L
Jen, Gish	Typical American	N/A
Jhabvala, Ruth Prawer	Heat and Dust	N/A

Jin, Ha	*Ocean of Words*	790L
Jin, Ha	*Waiting*	N/A
Kincaid, Jamaica	*A Small Place*	N/A
Kingsolver, Barbara	*The Poisonwood Bible*	960L
Kingsolver, Barbara	*La biblia envenenada*	N/A
Knowles, John	*A Separate Peace*	1110L
Lahiri, Jhumpa	*The Namesake*	1210L
Le Guin, Ursula K.	*Always Coming Home*	N/A
Park, Linda Sue	*A Single Shard*	920L
Tan, Amy	*The Bonesetter's Daughter*	800L

Nonfiction/Informational

Author	Title	Lexile
Álvarez, Julia	*Something to Declare*	1100L
Brown, Dee	*Bury My Heart at Wounded Knee*	1160L
Bryson, Bill	*Notes from a Small Island*	N/A
Kurlansky, Mark	*The Story of Salt*	1100L
Lee, Sungju and Susan McClelland	*Every Falling Star: The True Story of How I Survived and Escaped North Korea*	880L
Nabhan, Gary Paul	*Why Some Like It Hot: Food, Genes, and Cultural Diversity*	N/A
Pham, Andrew	*Catfish and Mandala: A Two-Wheeled Voyage Through the Landscape and Memory of Vietnam*	N/A
Reef, Catherine	*Frida and Diego—Art, Love, Life*	1080L
Seierstad, Asne	*The Bookseller of Kabul*	N/A
Uwiringiyimana, Sandra and Abigail Pesta	*How Dare the Sun Rise: Memoirs of a War Child*	HL790l

nit 3 Independent Reading List: Voice in Synthesis

Literature

Author	Title	Lexile
Alexie, Sherman	*The Absolutely True Diary of a Part-Time Indian*	600L
Danticat, Edwidge	*Behind the Mountains*	940L
Eggers, Dave	*What Is the What*	N/A
Hudson, Jan	*Sweetgrass*	640L
Kidd, Sue Monk	*The Secret Life of Bees*	840L
Kidd, Sue Monk	*La vida secreta de las abejas*	N/A
Klass, David	*California Blue*	820L
Lake, Nick	*In Darkness*	800L
Reynolds, Jason	*Long Way Down*	HL720L
Silko, Leslie Marmon	*Ceremony*	890L
Stockett, Kathryn	*The Help*	930L
Temple, Frances	*Taste of Salt: A Story of Modern Haiti*	650L
Zoboi, Ibi	*Pride*	HL760L

Nonfiction/Informational

Author	Title	Lexile
Ali, Nujood	*I Am Nujood: Age 10 and Divorced*	N/A
Al-Windawi, Thura	*Thura's Diary: My Life in Wartime Iraq*	990L
Beal, Merrill D.	*I Will Fight No More Forever: Chief Joseph and the Nez Perce War*	1130L
Coates, Ta-Nehisi	*Between the World and Me*	1090L
Freedman, Russell	*We Will Not Be Silent: The White Rose Student Resistance Movement That Defied Adolf Hitler*	630L
Gonick, Larry	*Cartoon Guide to the Environment*	N/A
Haelle, Tara	*Vaccination Investigation: The History and Science of Vaccines*	1160L
Hogan, Linda	*The Woman Who Watches Over the World: A Native Memoir*	N/A
Kurlanksky, Mark	*World without Fish*	1230L
Laskin, David	*Braving the Elements*	N/A
Nerburn, Kent	*Chief Joseph & the Flight of the Nez Perce: The Untold Story of an American Tragedy*	N/A
Pollan, Michael	*The Omnivore's Dilemma*	930L
Pollan, Michael	*El dilema del omnivoro*	N/A
Santiago, Esmeralda	*When I Was Puerto Rican: A Memoir*	1020L
Santiago, Esmeralda	*Cuando era puertorriqueña*	N/A

Sherr, Lynn	*America the Beautiful: The Stirring True Story Behind Our Nation's Favorite Song*	1210L
Shetterly, Robert	*Americans Who Tell the Truth*	N/A
Silverstein, Ken	*The Radioactive Boy Scout: The True Frightening Story of a Boy and His Backyard Nuclear Reactor*	1300L
Stevens, William Kenneth	*Change in the Weather: People, Weather, and the Science of Climate Change*	N/A
Stewart, Brent S., Phillip J. Clapham, and James A. Powell	*National Audubon Society Guide to Marine Mammals of the World*	N/A
Westover, Tara	*Educated: A Memoir*	N/A

Unit 4 Independent Reading List: Praise, Mock, Mourn

Literature		
Author	Title	Lexile
Abdel-Fattah, Randa	*Does My Head Look Big in This?*	850L
Álvarez, Julia	*How the Garcia Girls Lost Their Accents*	950L
Anaya, Rudolfo	*Bless Me, Ultima*	840L
Anónimo	*Popol vuh*	N/A
Aristophanes	*The Birds*	NP
Bernier-Grand, Carmen T.	*Frida: ¡Viva la Vida! Long Live Life!*	750L
Choi, Sook Nyul	*Gathering of Pearls*	N/A
Hansberry, Lorraine	*A Raisin in the Sun*	NP
Kaczynski, Heather	*Dare Mighty Things*	N/A
Kaufman, Moisés	*The Laramie Project*	N/A
Kogawa, Joy	*Obasan*	990L
Mann, Abby	*Judgment at Nuremberg: A Play*	NP
García Márquez, Gabriel	*Crónica de una muerte anunciada*	1180L
Miller, Frank	*The Dark Knight*	NP
Morrison, Toni	*The Bluest Eye*	920L
Potok, Chaim	*The Chosen*	900L
Skármeta, Antonio	*El cartero de Neruda*	1270L
Smith, Zadie	*White Teeth*	960L
Strasser, Todd	*Price of Duty*	HL690L
Wein, Elizabeth	*Code Name Verity*	1020L
Whitaker, Alecia	*Wildflower*	830L

Nonfiction/Informational		
Author	**Title**	**Lexile**
Aronson, Marc and Patty Campbell (Editors)	*War Is . . .: Soldiers, Survivors, and Storytellers Talk about War*	N/A
Bagieu, Pénélope	*Brazen: Rebel Ladies Who Rocked the World*	GN770L
Brown, David O.	*Called to Rise: A Life in Faithful Service to the Community that Created Me*	N/A
Charleyboy, Lisa and Mary Beth Leatherdale (edited by)	*#NotYourPrincess: Voices of Native American Women*	N/A
Fleming, Melissa	*A Hope More Powerful than the Sea*	1040L
Haftlang, Zahed, Najah Aboud, and Meredith May	*I, Who Did Not Die*	N/A
Hakim, Joy	*The Story of Science: Aristotle Leads the Way*	950L
McKissack, Patricia C. and Fredrick L. McKissack	*Young, Black, and Determined: A Biography of Lorraine Hansberry*	1160L
Mlodinow, Leonard	*Euclid's Window: The Story of Geometry from Parallel Lines to Hyperspace*	N/A
Noah, Trevor	*Born a Crime: Stories from a South African Childhood*	HL770L
Prinstein, Mitchell J.	*Popular: The Power of Likability in a Status-Obsessed World*	N/A

Independent Reading Log

Directions: This log is a place to record your progress and thinking about your independent readin[g] during each unit. Add your log pages to your Reader/Writer Notebook or keep them as a separate place to record your reading insights.

Unit _____

Independent Reading Title _____

Author(s) _____ Text Type _____

Pages read: from _____ to _____

_____

_____

_____

_____

_____

Independent Reading Title _____

Author(s) _____ Text Type _____

Pages read: from _____ to _____

_____

_____

_____

_____

_____

_____

Independent Reading Title _____

Author(s) _____ Text Type _____

Pages read: from _____ to _____

_____

_____

_____

_____

_____

_____

_____

Unit _____

Independent Reading Title _____

Author(s) _____ Text Type _____

Pages read: from _____ to _____

_____
_____
_____
_____
_____
_____

Independent Reading Title _____

Author(s) _____ Text Type _____

Pages read: from _____ to _____

_____
_____
_____
_____
_____
_____

Independent Reading Title _____

Author(s) _____ Text Type _____

Pages read: from _____ to _____

_____
_____
_____
_____
_____
_____

Independent Reading Title _____

Author(s) _____ Text Type _____

Pages read: from _____ to _____

_____
_____
_____
_____
_____
_____

Learning Strategies

Reading Strategies

STRATEGY	DEFINITION	PURPOSE
Activating Prior Knowledge	Providing an opportunity for students to think about what they already know about a concept, place, person, culture, and so on, and share their knowledge with a wider audience	To prepare students to encounter new concepts, places, persons, cultures, and so on, prior to reading a text; an Anticipation Guide and a Quickwrite can be used to activate and assess prior knowledge
Chunking the Text	Breaking the text into smaller, manageable units of sense (e.g., words, sentences, paragraphs) by numbering, separating phrases, drawing boxes	To reduce the intimidation factor when encountering long words, sentences, or whole texts; to increase comprehension of difficult or challenging text
Close Reading	Accessing small chunks of text to read, reread, mark, and annotate key passages, word-for-word, sentence-by-sentence, and line-by-line	To develop comprehensive understanding by engaging in one or more focused readings of a text
Diffusing	Reading a passage, noting unfamiliar words, discovering meaning of unfamiliar words using context clues, dictionaries, and/or thesauruses, using context to distinguish between denotative and connotative meanings, and replacing unfamiliar words with familiar ones	To facilitate a close reading of text, the use of resources, an understanding of synonyms, and increased comprehension of text
Double-Entry Journal	Creating a two-column journal with a student-selected passage in one column and the student's response in the second column (e.g., asking questions of the text, forming personal responses, interpreting the text, reflecting on the process of making meaning of the text)	To assist in note-taking and organizing key textual elements and responses noted during reading in order to generate textual support that can be incorporated into a piece of writing at a later time
Graphic Organizer	Using a visual representation for the organization of information from the text	To facilitate increased comprehension and discussion
Guided Reading	Identifying and modeling a series of strategies to guide students through challenging text (e.g., making predictions, marking the text, skimming the text, diffusing vocabulary)	To model for students the use of multiple strategies to make meaning of challenging texts and help them learn to apply the strategies independently
KWHL Chart	Setting up discussion that allows students to activate prior knowledge by answering, "What do I **know**?"; sets a purpose by answering, "What do I **want** to know?"; helps preview a task by answering, "**How** will I learn it?"; and reflects on new knowledge by answering, "What have I **learned**?"	To organize thinking, access prior knowledge, and reflect on learning to increase comprehension and engagement
Marking the Text	Selecting text by highlighting, underlining, and/or annotating for specific components, such as main idea, imagery, literary devices, and so on	To focus reading for specific purposes, such as author's craft, and to organize information from selections; to facilitate reexamination of a text

STRATEGY	DEFINITION	PURPOSE
Metacognitive Markers	Responding to text with a system of cueing marks where students use a ? for questions about the text; a ! for reactions related to the text; an * for comments about the text; and an underline to signal key ideas	To track responses to texts and use those responses as a point of departure for talking or writing about texts
Note-taking	Making notes about a text to use in a written response	To remember key ideas and information, track connections made to the text, log questions and observations, and gather evidence to use later in writing assignments
OPTIC	Strategy for evaluating visual images. **O** (Overview): Write notes on what the visual appears to be about. **P** (Parts): Zoom in on the parts of the visual and describe any elements or details that seem important. **T** (Title): Highlight the words of the title of the visual (if one is available). **I** (Interrelationships): Use the title as the theory and the parts of the visual as clues to detect and specify how the elements of the graphic are related. **C** (Conclusion): Draw a conclusion about the visual as a whole. What does the visual mean? Summarize the message of the visual in one or two sentences.	To analyze graphic and visual images as forms of text
Predicting	Making guesses about the text by using the title and pictures and/or thinking ahead about events that may occur based on evidence in the text	To help students become actively involved, interested, and mentally prepared to understand ideas
Previewing	Examining a text's structure, features, layout, format, questions, directions, prior to reading	To gain familiarity with the text, make connections to the text, and extend prior knowledge to set a purpose for reading
QHT	Expanding prior knowledge of vocabulary words by marking words with a Q, H, or T (Q signals words students do not know; H signals words students have heard and might be able to identify; T signals words students know well enough to teach to their peers)	To allow students to build on their prior knowledge of words, to provide a forum for peer teaching and learning of new words, and to serve as a prereading exercise to aid in comprehension
Questioning the Text	Developing levels of questions about text; that is, literal, interpretive, and universal questions that prompt deeper thinking about a text before, during, or after reading	To engage more actively and independently with texts, read with greater purpose and focus, and ultimately answer questions to gain greater insight into the text; helps students to comprehend and interpret

STRATEGY	DEFINITION	PURPOSE
Paraphrasing	Restating in one's own words the essential information expressed in a text, whether it be narration, dialogue, or informational text, while maintaining the original text's meaning	To encourage and facilitate comprehension of challenging text
RAFT	Primarily used to generate new text, this strategy can also be used to analyze a text by examining the role of the speaker (R), the intended audience (A), the format of the text (F), and the topic of the text (T)	To initiate reader response; to facilitate an analysis of a text to gain focus prior to creating a new text
Rereading	Encountering the same text with more than one reading	To identify additional details; to clarify meaning and/or reinforce comprehension of texts
SIFT	Analyzing a fictional text by examining stylistic elements, especially symbol, imagery, and figures of speech in order to show how all work together to reveal tone and theme	To focus and facilitate an analysis of a fictional text by examining the title and text for symbolism, identifying images and sensory details, analyzing figurative language, and identifying how all these elements reveal tone and theme
Skimming/Scanning	Skimming by rapid or superficial reading of a text to form an overall impression or to obtain a general understanding of the material; scanning focuses on key words, phrases, or specific details and provides speedy recognition of information	To quickly form an overall impression prior to an in-depth study of a text; to answer specific questions or quickly locate targeted information or detail in a text
SMELL	Analyzing a persuasive speech or essay by asking five essential questions: • **S**ender-receiver relationship—What is the sender-receiver relationship? Who are the images and language meant to attract? Describe the speaker of the text. • **M**essage—What is the message? Summarize the statement made in the text. • **E**motional Strategies—What is the desired effect? • **L**ogical Strategies—What logic is operating? How does it (or its absence) affect the message? Consider the logic of the images as well as the words. • **L**anguage—What does the language of the text describe? How does it affect the meaning and effectiveness of the writing? Consider the language of the images as well as the words.	To analyze a persuasive speech or essay by focusing on five essential characteristics of the genre; analysis is related to rhetorical devices, logical fallacies, and how an author's use of language achieves specific purposes

STRATEGY	DEFINITION	PURPOSE
SOAPSTone	Analyzing text by discussing and identifying **S**peaker, **O**ccasion, **A**udience, **P**urpose, **S**ubject, and **Tone**	To facilitate the analysis of specific elements of nonfiction, literary, and informational texts, and show the relationship among the elements to an understanding of the whole
Summarizing	Giving a brief statement of the main points or essential information expressed in a text, whether it be narration, dialogue, or informational text	To facilitate comprehension and recall of a text
Think Aloud	Talking through a difficult passage or task by using a form of metacognition whereby the reader expresses how he/she has made sense of the text	To reflect on how readers make meaning of challenging texts and to facilitate discussion
TP-CASTT	Analyzing a poetic text by identifying and discussing **T**itle, **P**araphrase, **C**onnotation, **A**ttitude, **S**hift, **T**heme, and **T**itle again	To facilitate the analysis of specific elements of a literary text, especially poetry. To show how the elements work together to create meaning
Visualizing	Forming a picture (mentally and/or literally) while reading a text to deepen understanding	To increase reading comprehension, deepen understanding, and promote active engagement with text
Word Maps	Using a clearly defined graphic organizer such as concept circles or word webs to identify and reinforce word meanings	To provide a visual tool for identifying and remembering multiple aspects of words and word meanings
Word Sort	Organizing and sorting words into categories designated by the teacher or selected by the student and providing a written or oral justification for the classifications	To solidify understanding of word meanings by considering the multiple uses, meanings, and relationships of word parts, words, and groups of words

Writing Strategies

STRATEGY	DEFINITION	PURPOSE
Adding	Enhancing a text by finding areas to add facts, details, examples, and commentary; smoothing out transitions; and clarifying and strengthening ideas and assertions	To improve, refine, and clarify the writer's thoughts during drafting and/or revision
Brainstorming	Using a flexible but deliberate process of listing multiple ideas in a short period of time without excluding any idea from the preliminary list	To generate ideas, concepts, or key words that provide a focus and/or establish organization as part of the prewriting or revision process
Deleting	Enhancing a text by eliminating words, phrases, sentences, or ideas that inhibit clarity and cohesiveness	To improve, refine, and clarify the writer's thoughts during drafting and/or revision
Drafting	Composing a text in its initial form before developing it	To incorporate brainstormed or initial ideas into a written format
Freewriting	Writing freely without constraints in order to generate ideas and capture thinking	To generate ideas when planning a piece of writing, or to refine and clarify thoughts, spark new ideas, and/or generate content during drafting and/or revision
Generating Questions	Clarifying and developing ideas by asking questions of the draft. May be part of self-editing or peer editing	To clarify and develop ideas in a draft; used during drafting and as part of writer response
Graphic Organizer	Organizing ideas and information visually (e.g., Venn diagrams, flowcharts, cluster maps)	To provide a visual system for organizing multiple ideas, details, and/or textual support to be included in a piece of writing
Guided Writing	Modeling the writing that students are expected to produce by guiding students through the planning, generation of ideas, organization, drafting, revision, editing, and publication of texts before students are asked to perform the same process; coconstructing texts with students as part of guided writing	To demonstrate the writing process

Speaking and Listening Strategies

STRATEGY	DEFINITION	PURPOSE
Choral Reading	Reading text lines aloud in student groups and/or individually to present an interpretation	To develop fluency; differentiate between the reading of statements and questions; practice phrasing, pacing, and reading dialogue; show how a character's emotions are captured through vocal stress and intonation
Debate	Engaging in a structured argument to examine both sides of an issue	To provide students with an opportunity to collect and orally present evidence supporting the affirmative and negative arguments of a proposition or issue
Drama Games	Participating in creative dramatics (e.g., pantomime, tableau, role-playing) to reinforce an oral literacy skill or develop a deeper understanding of a concept	To engage students in the reading and presenting of text and to create meaning through a kinesthetic approach
Fishbowl (Inner/outer circles)	Discussing specific topics within groups; some students will form the inner circle and model appropriate discussion techniques while an outer circle of students listens to and evaluates the discussion process of the inner circle in order to respond effectively	To provide students with an opportunity to engage in a formal discussion and to experience roles both as participant and active listener; students also have the responsibility of supporting their opinions and responses using specific textual evidence
Note-taking	Creating a record of information while listening to a speaker or reading a text	To facilitate active listening or close reading; to record and organize ideas that assist in processing information
Oral Reading	Reading aloud one's own text or the texts of others (e.g., echo reading, choral reading, paired readings)	To share one's own work or the work of others; build fluency and increase confidence in presenting to a group
Rehearsal	Encouraging multiple practices of a piece of text prior to a performance	To provide students with an opportunity to clarify the meaning of a text prior to a performance as they refine the use of dramatic conventions (e.g., gestures, vocal interpretations, facial expressions)
Role-Playing	Assuming the role or persona of a character	To develop the voice, emotions, and mannerisms of a character to facilitate improved comprehension of a text
Socratic Seminar	Tying a focused discussion to an essential question, topic, or selected text in which students ask questions of each other; questions initiate a conversation that continues with a series of responses and additional questions	To help students formulate questions that address issues (in lieu of simply stating their opinions) to facilitate their own discussion and arrive at a new understanding; students also have the responsibility of supporting their opinions and responses using specific textual evidence

Collaborative Strategies

STRATEGY	DEFINITION	PURPOSE
Discussion Groups	Engaging in an interactive, small-group discussion, often with an assigned role; to consider a topic, text, or question	To gain new understanding of or insight into a text from multiple perspectives
Jigsaw	In groups, students read different texts or passages from a single text, then share and exchange information from their reading with another group. They then return to their original groups to share their new knowledge.	To summarize and present information to others in a way that facilitates an understanding of a text (or multiple texts) without having each student read the text in its entirety
Literature Circles	Groups of students read the same text to participate in a mutual reading experience; based on the objective(s) of the lesson, students take on a variety of roles throughout the reading experience; texts may be selected based on individual preferences or on the demands of the text.	To provide opportunities for students to interact with one another as they read, respond to, and interpret a common text
Think-Pair-Share	Pairing with a peer to share ideas before sharing ideas and discussion with a larger group	To construct meaning about a topic or question; to test thinking in relation to the ideas of others; to prepare for a discussion with a larger group

Graphic Organizer Directory

Contents

Active Listening Feedback

Presenter's name: _____

Content

What is the presenter's purpose? _____

What is the presenter's main point? _____

Do you agree with the presenter? Why or why not? _____

_____

_____

Form

Did the presenter use a clear, loud voice? ☐ yes ☐ no

Did the presenter make eye contact? ☐ yes ☐ no

One thing I really liked about the presentation:

_____

_____

_____

One question I still have:

_____

_____

_____

Other comments or notes:

Active Listening Notes

tle: _____

Who?

What?

Where?

When?

Why?

How?

Audience Notes and Feedback

Scoring Criteria	Notes/Feedback
Introduction/ Conclusion	
Timing	
Voice	
Eye Contact/ Gestures	
Use of Media, Visuals, Props	
Audience Engagement	

Cause and Effect

Title: _____

Cause: What happened?

Effect: An effect of this is

Cause: What happened?

Effect: An effect of this is

Cause: What happened?

Effect: An effect of this is

Cause: What happened?

Effect: An effect of this is

Character Map

Character name: _____

What does the character look like?

How does the character act and feel?

What do other characters say or think about the character?

Collaborative Dialogue

Topic: _____

Use the space below to record ideas.

"Wh-" Prompts
Who?   What?   Where?   When?   Why?

Speaker 1

Speaker 2

Conclusion Builder

Evidence

Evidence

Evidence

Based on this evidence, I can conclude

Conflict Map

Title: _____

What is the main conflict in this story?

What causes this conflict?

How is the conflict resolved?

What are some other ways the conflict could have been resolved?

Conversation for Quickwrite

1. Turn to a partner and restate the prompt in your own words.

2. Brainstorm key words to use in your quickwrite response.

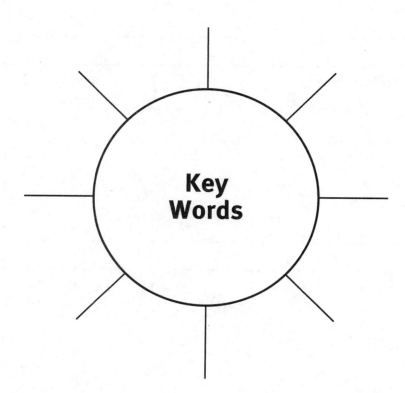

Key Words

3. Take turns explaining your ideas to your partner. Try using some of the key words you brainstormed.

4. On your own, write a response to the quickwrite.

Definition and Reflection

Academic Vocabulary Word
Definition in own words
Illustration (literal or symbolic)

My experiences with this concept:

- I haven't really thought about this concept.

_____

- I have only thought about this concept in English Language Arts class.

_____

- I have applied this concept in other classes.

_____

- I have applied this concept outside of school.

_____

My level of understanding:

- I am still trying to understand this concept.

_____

- I am familiar with this concept, but I am not comfortable applying it.

_____

- I am very comfortable with this concept and I know how to apply it.

_____

- I could teach this concept to another classmate.

_____

Discourse Starters

Questioning and Discussing a Text

One question I have is _____.

Could this mean _____?

Why do you think the author _____?

I understand _____, but I wonder _____.

I notice that _____.

I think this (word/sentence/paragraph) means _____.

I think _____ because the text says _____.

In paragraph _____, the author says _____.

According to the text, _____.

One way to interpret _____ is _____.

Summarizing

The main events that take place are _____

The major points of the text are _____

The main idea of _____ is _____

One central idea of this text is _____

Another central idea is _____

All in all, the message is _____

The author's main purpose is to _____

Basically, the author is saying that _____

Comparing and Contrasting

_____ and _____ are similar because _____.

_____ and _____ are similar in that they both _____.

_____ is _____. Similarly, _____ is _____.

One thing _____ and _____ have in common is _____.

_____ and _____ are different because _____.

_____ and _____ are different in that _____.

_____ is _____. On the other hand, _____ is _____.

One difference between _____ and _____ is _____.

Clarifying

I'm not sure I understand the instructions.

Could you repeat that please?

I have a question about _____

I am having trouble with _____

Will you explain that again?

Could you clarify _____?

Would you mind helping me with _____?

Which (page/paragraph/section) are we reading?

How do you spell/pronounce _____?

Discourse Starters

Agreeing and Disagreeing

I agree with the idea that _____ because _____.

I share your point of view because _____.

You made a good point when you said _____.

I agree with (a person) that _____.

Although I agree that _____, I also think _____.

I understand where you're coming from, but _____.

I disagree with the idea that _____ because _____.

I see it a different way because _____.

You have a point, but the evidence suggests _____.

Arguing and Persuading with Evidence

I believe that _____ because _____.

It is clear that _____ because _____.

One reason I think _____ is _____.

Based on evidence in the text, I think _____.

Evidence such as _____ suggests that _____.

An example to support my position is _____.

This is evident because _____.

What evidence supports the idea that _____?

Can you explain why you think _____?

Evaluating

This is effective because _____.

The evidence _____ is strong because _____.

This is convincing because _____.

I see why the author _____, but I think _____.

This is not very effective because _____.

The evidence _____ is weak because _____.

This would have been better if _____.

What do you think about the writer's choice to _____?

Why do you think _____ (is/isn't) effective?

Giving Feedback and Suggesting

The part where you _____ is strong because _____.

What impressed me the most is how you _____.

This is a good start. Maybe you should add _____.

I like how you _____, but I would try _____.

You might consider changing _____.

I would suggest revising _____ so that _____.

One suggestion would be to _____.

Why did you choose _____?

A better choice might be _____.

This would be clearer if _____.

Editor's Checklist

Over the course of the year with SpringBoard, customize this Editor's Checklist as your knowledge of language conventions grows. The three examples below show you how to write a good checklist item.

	Are all the sentences complete?
	Do the subject and verb of each sentence agree?
	Do all the sentences have correct punctuation?

Writer's Checklist

Ideas

Does your first paragraph hook the reader?
Is the purpose of your writing clear (to inform, to make an argument, etc.)?
Is the genre of writing appropriate for your purpose?
Is your main idea clear and easy to summarize?
Does your text contain details and information that support your main idea?
Are the ideas in the text well organized?
Do you connect your ideas by using transitions?
Do you use parallel structure to keep your ideas clear?
Does each paragraph have a conclusion that transitions to the next paragraph?
Does your writing end with a strong conclusion that restates the original purpose of the text?

Language

Do you keep a consistent point of view throughout?
Do you use the present tense when writing about a text?
Are any shifts in verb tense easy to follow and necessary?
Have you removed unnecessary or confusing words?
Do you use vivid verbs and descriptive adjectives when appropriate?
Do you use different styles of language (like figurative or sensory) when appropriate?
Do you use a variety of sentence types?
Do you vary the way you begin your sentences?
Did you split up run-on sentences?
Are your pronoun references clear?

Evaluating Online Sources

The URL
• What is its domain?
    • .com = a for-profit organization
    • .gov, .mil, .us (or other country code) = a government site
    • .edu = affiliated with an educational institution
    • .org = a nonprofit organization
• Is this URL someone's personal page?
• Do you recognize who is publishing this page?	

Sponsor: • Does the website give information about the organization or group that sponsors it? • Does it have a link (often called "About Us") that leads you to that information? • What do you learn?	
Timeliness: • When was the page last updated (usually this is posted at the top or bottom of the page)? • Is the topic something that changes frequently, like current events or technology?	
Purpose: • What is the purpose of the page? • What is its target audience? • Does it present information, opinion, or both? • Is it primarily objective or subjective? • How do you know?	
Author: • What credentials does the author have? • Is this person or group considered an authority on the topic?	
Links • Does the page provide links? • Do they work? • Are they helpful? • Are they objective or subjective?	

Fallacies 101

...d Baculum (Scare Tactics)	If you don't support the party's tax plan, you and your family will be reduced to poverty. Chairman of the Board: "All those opposed to my arguments for the opening of a new department, signify by saying, 'I resign.'"
...d hoc	Person 1: I should have gotten an A on that test. Person 2: You didn't study for that test at all. Person 1: That class is useless!
...d Hominem (Against the Man)/ ...enetic Fallacy	"My opponent, a vicious and evil person, should absolutely never be elected to office." The Volkswagen Beetle is an evil car because it was originally designed by Hitler's army.
...d Populum	You should turn to channel 6. It's the most watched channel this year. There is always a long line at that restaurant, so the food must be really good.
...ppeal To Pity	"Jonathan couldn't have cheated! He's such a nice boy and he tries so hard."
...rgument from Outrage	The airline cancelled my flight an hour before takeoff and wouldn't tell me why. This is an outrage! We should all boycott the company.
...ircular Reasoning	Emotional support animals should be allowed on airplanes, so the airline should change its policy. The policy should be changed because emotional support animals should be allowed on planes!
...ither/Or (False Dilemma)	We can either stop using cars or destroy Earth. We must drill now or we'll remain dependent on foreign oil suppliers.
...aulty Analogies	Buying into the stock market is the same as betting on a horse race.
...lasty Generalization	They hit two home runs in the first inning of the season. This team is going all the way to the World Series!
...lon-sequitur	I always see her with a book in her hands. She must hate watching TV.
...ost Hoc	I ate a turkey sandwich and now I feel tired, so the turkey must have made me tired.
...ed Herring	The new dress code banning t-shirts isn't fair. Students have the right to free speech just like anyone else.
...lippery Slope Fallacy	"If I don't study for the test, then I'm going to get a bad grade. If I get a bad grade on the test, I'll get a bad grade in the class, and I won't get into a good college. Getting into a good college is the most important part of getting a good job; so if I don't study for the test, I won't get a good job!"
...traw Man	People say that Mark Twain was a good author, but I disagree. If he was such a good author, why didn't he write using his own name?

Idea and Argument Evaluator

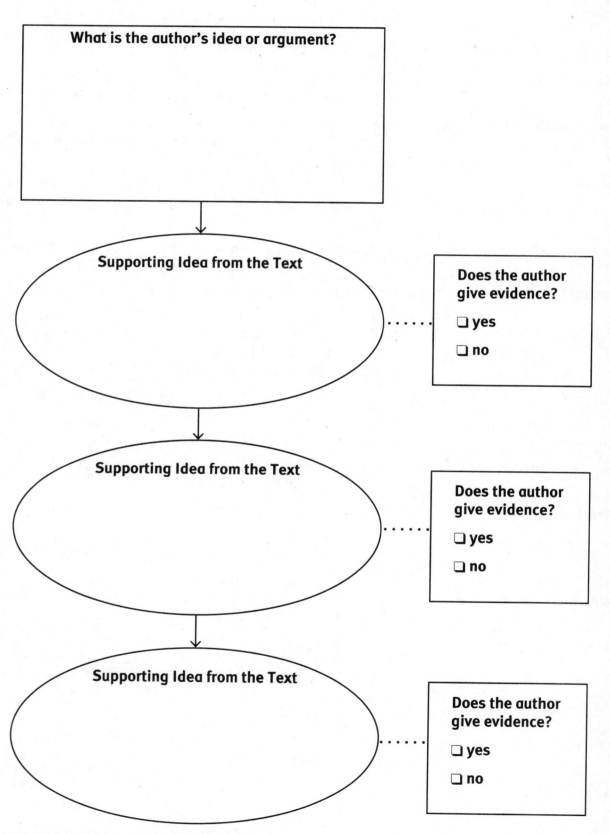

What is the author's idea or argument?

Supporting Idea from the Text

Does the author give evidence?

❏ yes

❏ no

Supporting Idea from the Text

Does the author give evidence?

❏ yes

❏ no

Supporting Idea from the Text

Does the author give evidence?

❏ yes

❏ no

Idea Connector

Directions: Write two simple sentences about the same topic. Next, write transition words around the Idea Connector. Then, choose an appropriate word to connect ideas in the two sentences. Write your combined sentence in the space below.

Sentence One

Sentence Two

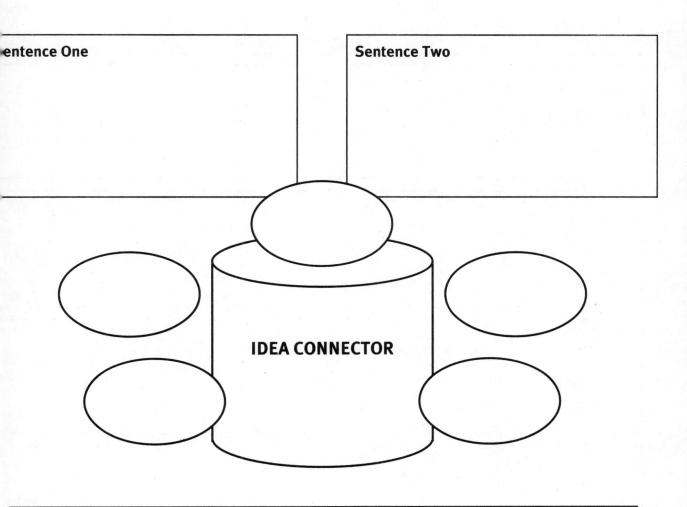

IDEA CONNECTOR

Combined Sentence

Key Idea and Details Chart

Title/Topic _____

Key Idea _____

_____

_____

Supporting detail 1 _____

_____

_____

Supporting detail 2 _____

_____

_____

Supporting detail 3 _____

_____

_____

Supporting detail 4 _____

_____

_____

Restate topic sentence: _____

_____

Concluding sentence: _____

_____

_____

Narrative Analysis and Writing

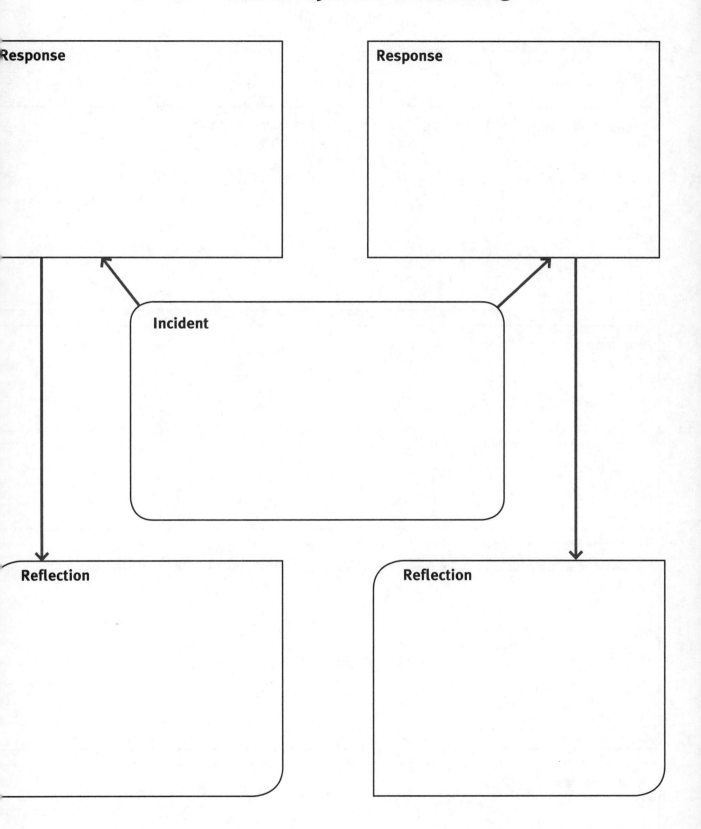

Response

Response

Incident

Reflection

Reflection

Notes for Reading Independently

Fiction

Title: _____

Author: _____

Something interesting I noticed:	A question I have:

Summary:

Illustration:

| | Connections to my life/other texts I've read: |

How challenging this text was:

Easy   1   2   3   4   5   6   7   8   9   10   *Challenging*

Notes for Reading Independently
Nonfiction

Title: _____

Author: _____

Main idea:

Facts I learned:

Summary:

Questions I still have:

Connections to my life/other texts I've read:

How challenging this text was:

Easy   1   2   3   4   5   6   7   8   9   10   *Challenging*

Opinion Builder

Reason

Reason

Based on these reasons, my opinion is

Reason

Reason

OPTIC

itle of Piece:	
rtist: _____	Type of artwork: _____

Overview	Look at the artwork for at least 10 seconds. Generate questions; e.g., What is the subject? What strikes you as interesting, odd, etc.? What is happening?
Parts	Look closely at the artwork, making note of important elements and details. Ask additional questions, such as: Who are the figures? What is the setting and time period? What symbols are present? What historical information would aid understanding of this piece?
Title	Consider what the title and any written elements of the text suggest about meaning. How does the title relate to what is portrayed?
Interrelationships	Look for connections between and among the title, caption, and the parts of the art. How are the different elements related?
Conclusion	Form a conclusion about the meaning/theme of the text. Remember the questions you asked when you first examined it. Be prepared to support your conclusions with evidence.

Paragraph Frame for Conclusions

Conclusion Words and Phrases

shows that

based on

suggests that

leads to

indicates that

influences

The _____ *(story, poem, play, passage, etc.)*
shows that *(helps us to conclude that)* _____
_____
_____

There are several reasons why. First, _____
_____
_____
_____
_____

A second reason is _____
_____
_____
_____
_____

Finally, _____
_____
_____
_____
_____

In conclusion, _____
_____
_____
_____
_____

Paragraph Frame for Sequencing

Sequence Words and Phrases

at the beginning

in the first place

as a result

later

eventually

in the end

lastly

In the _____ (story, poem, play, passage, etc.)

there are three important _____

(events, steps, directions, etc.)

First, _____

_____

_____

_____

Second, _____

_____

_____

_____

Third, _____

_____

_____

_____

Finally, _____

_____

_____

_____

Paraphrasing and Summarizing Map

What does the text say?	How can I say it in my own words?

How can I use my own words to summarize the text?

Peer Editing

Writer's name: _____

Did the writer answer the prompt? ☐ yes ☐ no

Did the writer use appropriate details or evidence to develop their writing? ☐ yes ☐ no

Is the writing organized in a way that makes sense? ☐ yes ☐ no

Did the writer use a variety of sentence types to make the writing more interesting? ☐ yes ☐ no

Are there any spelling or punctuation mistakes? ☐ yes ☐ no

Are there any grammar errors? ☐ yes ☐ no

Two things I really liked about the writer's story:

1. _____
_____
_____

2. _____
_____
_____

One thing I think the writer could do to improve the writing:

1. _____
_____
_____

Other comments or notes:

Persuasive/Argument Writing Map

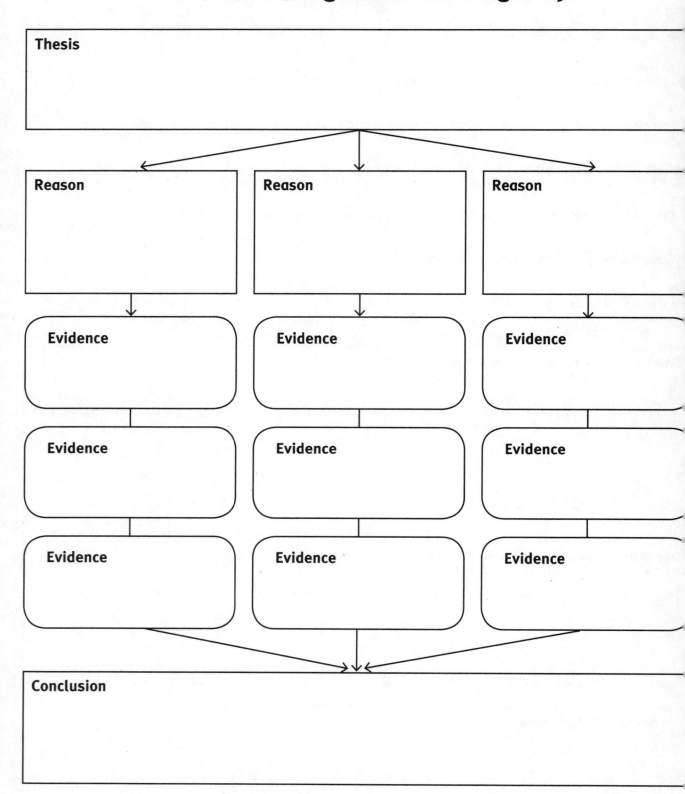

Thesis

Reason

Reason

Reason

Evidence

Evidence

Evidence

Evidence

Evidence

Evidence

Evidence

Evidence

Evidence

Conclusion

Presenting Scoring Guide

Scoring Criteria	Exemplary	Proficient	Emerging	Incomplete
Introduction / Conclusion	The presentation • provides a clear, engaging, and appropriate introduction to the topic or performance • provides a clear, engaging, and appropriate conclusion that closes, summarizes, draws connections to broader themes, or supports the ideas presented.	The presentation • provides a clear and appropriate introduction to the topic or performance • provides a clear and appropriate conclusion that closes, summarizes, draws connections to broader themes, or supports the ideas presented.	The presentation • provides an adequate introduction to the topic or performance • provides an adequate conclusion that closes, summarizes, draws connections to broader themes, or supports the ideas presented.	The presentation • does not provide an introduction to the topic or performance • does not provide a conclusion that closes, summarizes, draws connections to broader themes, or supports the ideas presented.
Timing	The presentation • thoroughly delivers its intended message within the allotted time • is thoughtfully and appropriately paced throughout.	The presentation • mostly delivers its intended message within the allotted time • is appropriately paced most of the time.	The presentation • delivers some of its intended message within the allotted time • is sometimes not paced appropriately.	The presentation • does not deliver its intended message within the allotted time • is not paced appropriately.
Voice (Volume, Enunciation, Rate)	The presentation • is delivered with adequate volume enabling audience members to fully comprehend what is said • is delivered with clear enunciation.	The presentation • is delivered with adequate volume enabling audience members to mostly comprehend what is said • is delivered with mostly clear enunciation.	The presentation • is delivered with somewhat adequate volume enabling audience members to comprehend some of what is said • is delivered with somewhat clear enunciation.	The presentation • is not delivered with adequate volume, so that audience members are unable to comprehend what is said • is delivered with unclear enunciation.
Eye Contact / Gestures	The presentation • is delivered with appropriate eye contact that helps engage audience members • makes use of natural gestures and/or body language to convey meaning.	The presentation • is delivered with some appropriate eye contact that helps engage audience members • makes use of gestures and/or body language to convey meaning.	The presentation • is delivered with occasional eye contact that sometimes engages audience members • makes some use of gestures and/or body language to convey meaning.	The presentation • is not delivered with eye contact to engage audience members • makes little or no use of gestures and/or body language to convey meaning.
Use of Media, Visuals, Props	The presentation • makes use of highly engaging visuals, multimedia, and/or props that enhance delivery.	The presentation • makes use of visuals, multimedia, and/or props that enhance delivery.	The presentation • makes use of some visuals, multimedia, and/or props that somewhat enhance delivery.	The presentation • makes use of few or no visuals, multimedia, and/or props that enhance delivery.
Audience Engagement	The presentation • includes thoughtful and appropriate interactions with and responses to audience members.	The presentation • includes appropriate interactions with and responses to audience members.	The presentation • includes a few interactions with and responses to audience members.	The presentation • does not include interactions with and responses to audience members.

RAFT

Role	Who or what are you as a writer?
Audience	As a writer, to whom are you writing?
Format	As a writer, what format would be appropriate for your audience (essay, letter, speech, poem, etc.)?
Topic	As a writer, what is the subject of your writing? What points do you want to make?

Roots and Affixes Brainstorm

Directions: Write the root or affix in the circle. Brainstorm or use a dictionary to find the meaning of the root or affix and add it to the circle. Then, find words that use that root or affix. Write one word in each box. Write a sentence for each word.

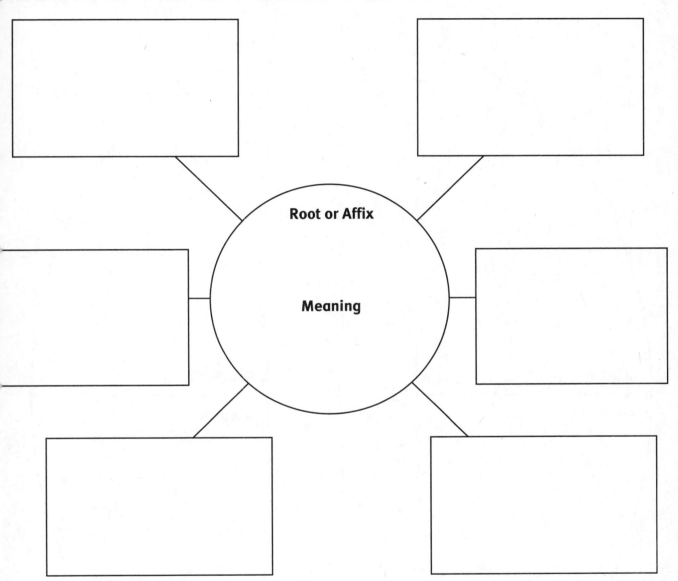

Root or Affix

Meaning

Round Table Discussion

Directions: Write the topic in the center box. One student begins by stating his or her ideas while the student to the left takes notes. Then the next student speaks while the student to his or her left takes notes, and so on.

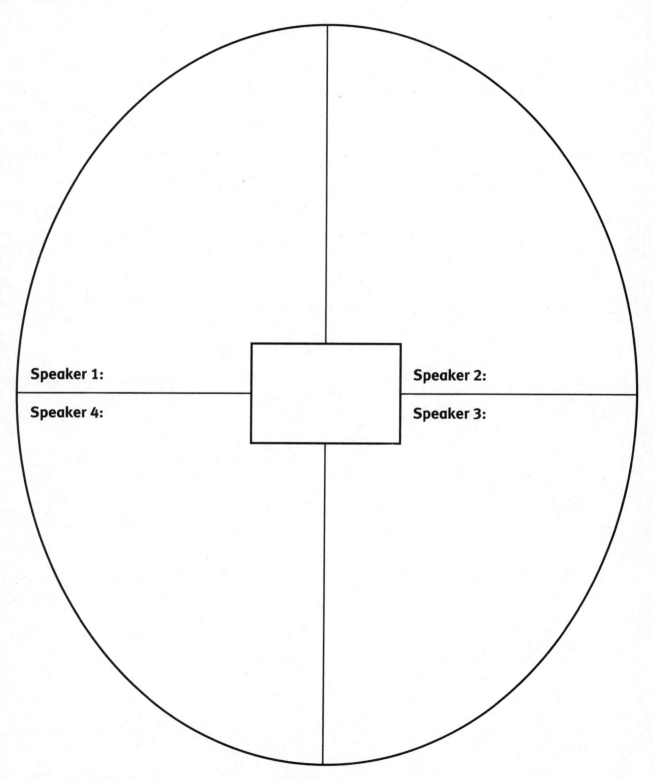

Speaker 1:

Speaker 2:

Speaker 4:

Speaker 3:

Sequence of Events Time Line

Title: _____

What happened first?		Next?

Beginning   Middle   End

Then?		Finally?

SMELL

Sender-Receiver Relationship—Who are the senders and receivers of the message, and what is their relationship (consider what different audiences the text may be addressing)?

Message—What is a literal summary of the content? What is the meaning/significance of this information?

Emotional Strategies—What emotional appeals (*pathos*) are included? What seems to be their desired effect?

Logical Strategies—What logical arguments/appeals (*logos*) are included? What is their effect?

Language—What specific language is used to support the message? How does it affect the text's effectiveness? Consider both images and actual words.

SOAPSTone

SOAPSTone	Analysis	Textual Support
Subject What does the reader know about the writer?		
Occasion What are the circumstances surrounding this text?		
Audience Who is the target audience?		
Purpose Why did the author write this text?		
Subject What is the topic?		
Tone What is the author's tone, or attitude?		

Text Structure Stairs

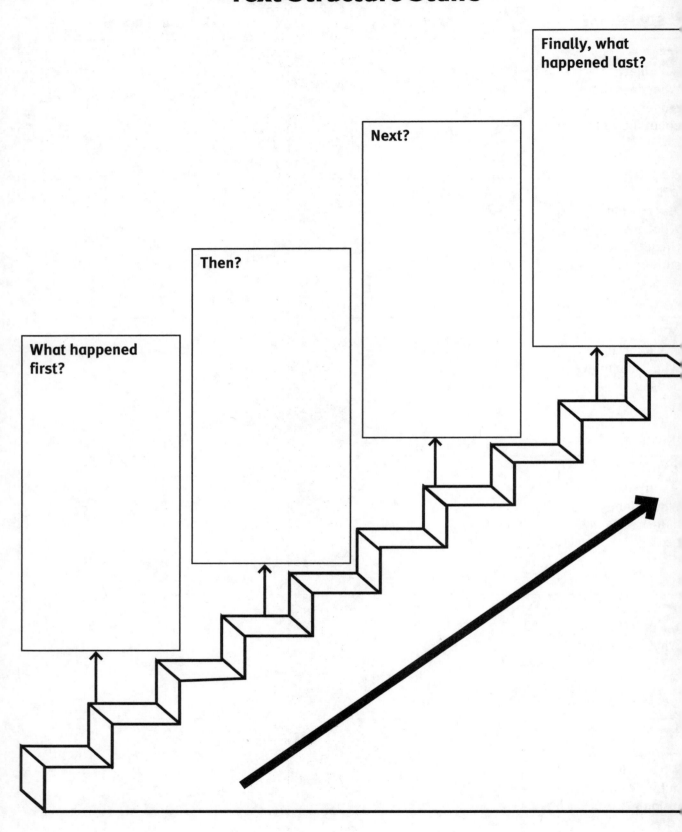

What happened first?

Then?

Next?

Finally, what happened last?

TP-CASTT Analysis

Poem Title:

Author:

Title: Make a Prediction. What do you think the title means before you read the poem?

Paraphrase: Translate the poem in your own words. What is the poem about? Rephrase difficult sections word for word.

Connotation: Look beyond the literal meaning of key words and images to their associations.

Attitude: What is the speaker's attitude? What is the author's attitude? How does the author feel about the speaker, about other characters, about the subject?

Shifts: Where do the shifts in tone, setting, voice, etc., occur? Look for time and place, keywords, punctuation, stanza divisions, changes in length or rhyme, and sentence structure. What is the purpose of each shift? How do they contribute to effect and meaning?

Title: Reexamine the title. What do you think it means now in the context of the poem?

Theme: Think of the literal and metaphorical layers of the poem. Then determine the overall theme. The theme must be written in a complete sentence.

TP-CASTT

Poem Title:

Author:

Title		
Paraphrase		
Connotation		
Attitude		
Shifts		
Title		
Theme		

Unknown Word Solver

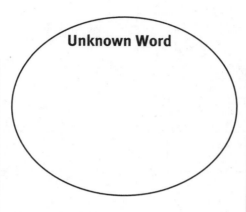

Unknown Word

Can you find any context clues? List them.

Do you recognize any word parts?

Prefix:

Root Word:

Suffix:

Do you know another meaning of this word that does not make sense in this context?

Does it look or sound like a word in another language?

What is the dictionary definition?

How can you define the word in your own words?

Venn Diagram for Writing a Comparison

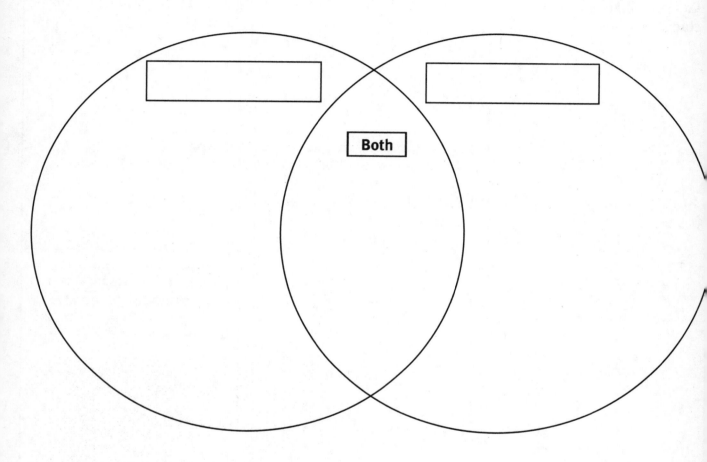

Both

They are similar in that _____

_____

_____

_____

_____

_____

_____

They are different in that _____

_____

_____

_____

_____

_____

_____

Verbal & Visual Word Association

Definition in Your Own Words	Important Elements

Academic Vocabulary Word

Visual Representation	Personal Association

Web Organizer

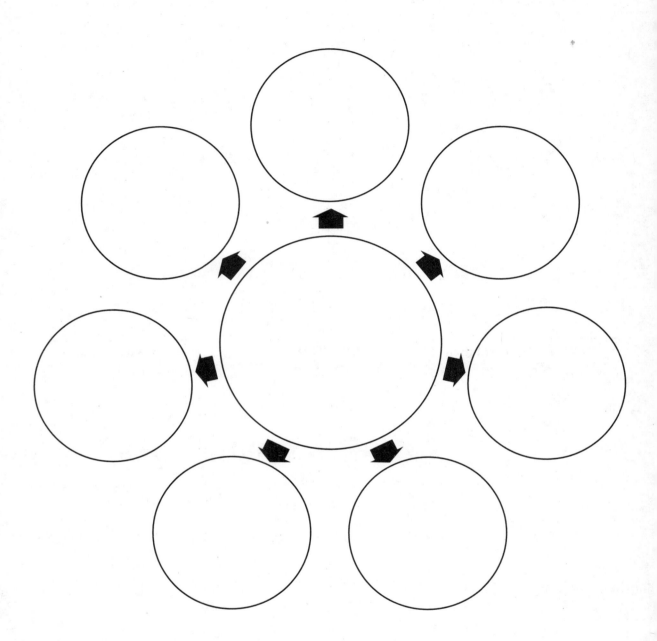

Word Choice Analyzer

Word or phrase from the text	Definition of word or phrase	How can I restate the definition in my own words?	What effect did the author produce by choosing these words?

Explain Your Analysis

The author uses the word or phrase _____ , which means

_____

Another way to say this is _____

_____

I think the author chose these words to _____

_____

_____

One way I can modify this sentence to add detail is to _____

_____

Word Map

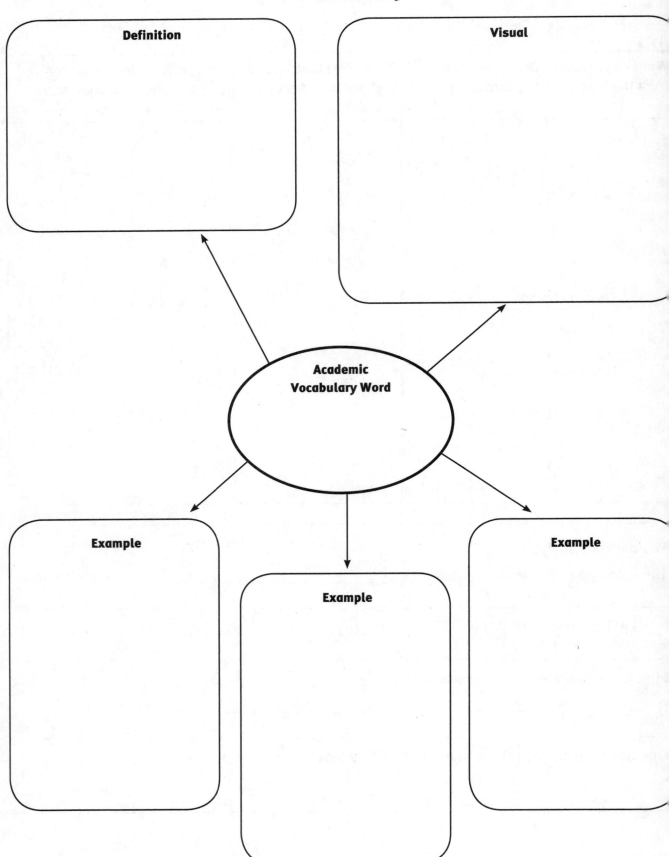

Definition

Visual

Academic Vocabulary Word

Example

Example

Example

...ive-voice verbs: verbs for which the subject performs the ...ion
...rbos en voz activa: forma verbal que indica que el sujeto ...liza la acción

...vertising techniques: specific methods used in print, ...phics, or videos to persuade people to buy a product or ...e a service
...nicas publicitarias: métodos específicos usados en ...presos, gráfica o videos para persuadir a las personas a ...mprar un producto o usar un servicio

...enda: a secret plan or motivation that causes someone to ...in a certain way
...enda: motivación o plan secreto que lleva a alguien a ...uar de determinado modo

...egory: a story in which the characters, objects, or actions ...e a meaning beyond the surface of the story
...goría: cuento en el que los personajes, objetos o acciones ...en un significado que va más allá de la superficie de la ...toria

...iteration: the repetition of initial consonant sounds in ...rds that are close together
...teración: repetición de sonidos consonánticos iniciales en ...abras cercanas

...usion: a reference made to a well-known person, event, or ...ce from history, music, art, or another literary work
...sión: referencia a una persona, evento o lugar muy ...ocidos de la historia, música, arte u otra obra literaria

...alogy: a comparison between two things for the purpose ...drawing conclusions on one based on its similarities to ...other
...logía: comparación entre dos cosas con el propósito de sacar ...clusiones sobre las semejanzas que una cosa tiene a otra

...aphora: the repetition of the same word or group of words ...he beginnings of two or more clauses or lines
...áfora: repetición de la misma palabra o grupo de palabras ...omienzo de una o más cláusulas o versos

...ecdotal evidence: evidence based on personal accounts of ...idents
...dencia anecdótica: evidencia basada en relatos ...sonales de los hechos

annotated bibliography: a list of sources used in research along with comments or summaries about each source
bibliografía anotada: lista de fuentes utilizadas en la investigación, junto con comentarios o resúmenes acerca de cada fuente

antagonist: the character who opposes or struggles against the main character
antagonista: personaje que se opone o lucha contra el personaje principal

aphorism: a short statement expressing an opinion or general truth
aforismo: afirmación corta que expresa una opinión o verdad general

appeals: the efforts to persuade an audience that a certain concept is true by directing statements toward reasoning or logic, character, or senses and emotions
llamados: serie de esfuerzos que alguien realiza con el fin de convencer a una audiencia de que determinado concepto es verdadero, persuadiéndola de ello mediante el uso del razonamiento o la lógica o bien apelando a su carácter, sentidos o emociones

Archetypal Criticism: criticism that deals with symbols and patterns that recur in the literature of widely diverse cultures
crítica de arquetipos: examinación de la literature basada en símbolos y diseño

archetypes: universal symbols—images, characters, motifs, or patterns—that recur in the myths, dreams, oral traditions, songs, literature, and other texts of peoples widely separated by time and place
arquetipos: símbolos universales—imágenes, personajes, motivos o patrones—reiterativos en los mitos, el arte y la literatura alrededor del mundo

archival footage: film footage taken from another, previously recorded, source
cortometraje de archivo: fragmento de película tomada de otra fuente grabada previamente

argument: a form of writing that presents a particular claim or idea and supports it with evidence
argumento: forma de redacción que presenta una opinión o idea particular y la apoya con evidencia

argumentation: the act or process of arguing that includes the *hook* (quotation, example, or idea that catches readers' attention), *claim* (the opinion or thesis statement), *support* (evidence in the form of facts, statistics, examples, anecdotes, or expert opinions), *concession* (the writer's admission that the other side of the argument has a valid point), *refutation* (a well-reasoned denial of an opponent's point, based on solid evidence), and *call to action* (a request of readers)

argumentación: la estructura de una argumentación incluye el *gancho* (cita, ejemplo o idea que capta la atención del lector), *afirmación* (declaración de opinión o tesis), *apoyo* (evidencia en forma de hechos, estadísticas, ejemplos, anécdotas u opiniones de expertos), *concesión* (admisión por parte del escritor de que la otra parte del debate tiene un punto válido), *refutación* (negación bien razonada de una opinión del oponente, basada en evidencia sólida) y *llamado a la acción* (petición inspirada de lectores)

argument by analogy: a comparison of two similar situations, implying that the outcome of one will resemble the outcome of the other

argumento por analogía: comparación de dos situaciones semejantes, infiriendo que el resultado de será parecido al resultado de la otra

artistic license: the practice of rewording of dialogue, alteration of language, or reordering of the plot of a text created by another artist

licencia artística: la costumbre de reformular un diálogo, aliteración de palabras, o arreglo de la trama de un texto creado por otro artista

aside: a short speech spoken by an actor directly to the audience and unheard by other actors on stage

aparte: alocución breve dicha por un actor directamente al público y que no escuchan los demás actores que están en el escenario

assonance: the repetition of similar vowel sounds in accented syllables, followed by different consonant sounds, in words that are close together

asonancia: repetición de sonidos vocálicos similares en sílabas acentuadas, seguida de diferentes sonidos consonánticos, en palabras que están cercanas

audience: the intended readers, listeners, or viewers of specific types of written, spoken, or visual texts

público: lectores objetivo, oyentes o espectadores de tipos específicos de textos escritos, hablados o visuales

audience analysis: determination of the characteristics and knowledge of the people who will read a work or hear a speech

análisis del público: determinar las características y conocimiento de las personas que leen una obra o escuchar un discurso

author's purpose: the specific reason or reasons for the writing; what the author hopes to accomplish

propósito del autor: razón específica para escribir; lo que autor espera lograr

autobiography: an account written by a person about his o her own life

autobiografía: narración de una vida escrita por el propio sujeto del relato

B

balanced sentence: a sentence that presents ideas of equal weight in similar grammatical forms to emphasize the similarity or difference between the ideas

oración balanceada: oración que representa ideas de igual peso en formas gramaticales similares para enfatizar la semejanza o diferencia entre las ideas

bias: an inclination or mental leaning for or against something; prevents impartial judgment

sesgo: inclinación o tendencia mental a favor o en contra algo, lo que impide una opinión imparcial

bibliography: a list of the sources used for research

bibliografía: lista de fuentes primarias en la preparación de un texto

biography: a description or account of events from a perso life, written by another person

biografía: descripción o narración de la vida de una perso o los sucesos importantes de su vida escritos por otra perso

blank verse: unrhymed verse

verso libre: verso que no tiene rima

block: to create the plan for how actors will position themselves on the stage in relation to one another, the audience, and the objects on the stage

ensayar: establecer un plan para determinar la posición qu los actores deberán ocupar en un escenario en relación a sí mismos, a la audiencia, al escenario y a los objetos del mism

blocking: in drama, the way actors position themselves in relation to one another, the audience, and the objects on the stage

bloqueo: en drama, el modo en que los actores se sitúan entre sí, con el público y los objetos en el escenario

book review: a formal assessment or examination of a bool

reseña de libro: evaluación o examinación formal de un libro

cacophonous: harsh and unpleasant sounding
cacofónico: sonidos molestos y desagradables

call to action: a restatement of the claim and what the writer wants the reader to do
llamado a la acción: repetición de la afirmación y lo que el escritor quiere que el lector responda

caricature: a visual or verbal representation in which characteristics or traits are exaggerated or distorted for emphasis
caricatura: representación visual o verbal en la que las características o rasgos se exageran o se distorsionan para dar énfasis

catalog poem: a poem that uses repetition and variation in the creation of a list, or catalog, of objects or desires, plans, or memories
lista en poema: poema que usa repetición y variación en la creación de una lista o catálogo, de objetos o deseos o planes o memorias

cause: an action, event, or situation that brings about a particular result
causa: acción, suceso o situación que produce un resultado particular

caveat: a cautionary detail to be thought through carefully when analyzing something
exhortación: advertencia o consejo a tener muy en cuenta a la hora de interpretar o analizar algo

censor: to examine materials for objectionable content
censurar: examinar materiales por contenido desagradable

censorship: the act of suppressing public speech or publication of materials deemed to be offensive by the censor
censura: acto de suprimir un discurso público o publicación de materiales considerados ofensivos por un censor

challenge: to oppose or refute a statement that has been made
poner en duda: oponerse a algo o refutar una declaración que alguien ha hecho

characterization: the methods a writer uses to develop characters
caracterización: métodos que usa un escritor para desarrollar personajes

characters: people, animals, or imaginary creatures that take part in the action of a story. A short story usually centers on a *main character* but may also contain one or more *minor characters*, who are not as complex, but whose thoughts, words, or actions move the plot along. A character who is *dynamic* changes in response to the events of the narrative; a character who is *static* remains the same throughout the narrative. A *round* character is fully developed—he or she shows a variety of traits; a *flat* character is one-dimensional, usually showing only one trait.
personajes: personas, animales o criaturas imaginarias que participan en la acción de un cuento. Un cuento corto normalmente se centra en un *personaje principal*, pero puede también contener uno o más *personajes secundarios*, que no son tan complejos, pero cuyos pensamientos, palabras o acciones hacen avanzar la trama. Un personaje que es *dinámico* cambia según los eventos del relato; un personaje que es *estático* permanece igual a lo largo del relato. Un personaje *complejo* está completamente desarrollado: muestra una diversidad de rasgos; un personaje *simple* es unidimensional, mostrando normalmente sólo un rasgo.

character foil: a character whose actions or thoughts are juxtaposed against those of a major character in order to highlight key attributes of the major character
antagonista: personaje cuyas acciones o pensamientos se yuxtaponen a los de un personaje principal con el fin de destacar atributos clave del personaje principal

character sketch: a brief description of a literary character
reseña del personaje: breve descripción de un personaje literario

chorus: in traditional or classic drama, a group of performers who speak as one and comment on the action of the play
coro: en el drama tradicional o clásico, grupo de actores que hablan al unísono y comentan la acción de la obra teatral

cinematic elements: the features of cinema—movies, film, video—that contribute to its form and structure: *angle* (the view from which the image is shot), *framing* (how a scene is structured), *lighting* (the type of lighting used to light a scene), *mise en scène* (the composition, setting, or staging of an image, or a scene in a film), and *sound* (the sound effects and music accompanying each scene)
elementos cinematográficos: las características del cine—películas, filmaciones, video—que contribuyen a darle forma y estructura: *angulación* (vista desde la cual se toma la imagen), *encuadre* (cómo se estructura una escena), iluminación (tipo de *iluminación* que se usa para una escena), y *montaje* (composición, ambiente o escenificación de una imagen o escena en una película), y *sonido* (efectos sonoros y música que acompañan cada escena)

cinematic techniques: the methods a director uses to communicate meaning and to evoke particular emotional responses from viewers

técnicas cinematográficas: métodos que emplea un director para comunicar un significado y evocar cierta respuesta emocional de los videntes

claim: a thesis statement describing the position the writer is taking on an issue

afirmación: declaración de opinión (o tesis) que asevera una idea o establece un debate hacia una posición específica

cliché: an overused expression or idea

cliché: expresión o idea que se usa en exceso

climax: the point at which the action reaches its peak; the point of greatest interest or suspense in a story; the turning point at which the outcome of a conflict is decided

clímax: punto en el que la acción alcanza su punto culminante; punto de mayor interés en un cuento; punto de inflexión en el que se decide el resultado del conflicto

coherence: the quality of unity or logical connection among ideas; the clear and orderly presentation of ideas in a paragraph or essay

coherencia: calidad de unidad o relación lógica entre las ideas; presentación clara y ordenada de las ideas en un párrafo o ensayo

commentary: the expression of opinions or explanations about an event or situation

comentario: expresión oral o escrita de opiniones o explicaciones sobre una situación, tema o suceso

commentary: explanations about the significance or importance of supporting details or examples in an analysis

comentario: explicaciones acerca de la importancia de los detalles que tienen apoyo o ejemplos en un análisis

complementary: combined in a way that enhances all elements combined

complementario: combinar dos o más elementos de una manera que mejora los dos

complex character: a character that has multiple or conflicting motivations

personaje complejo: personaje que tiene motivaciones multiples o conflictivas

complex sentence: a sentence containing one independent clause and one or more subordinate clauses

oración compleja: oración que contiene una cláusula independiente y una o más cláusulas subordinadas

complications: the events in a plot that develop a conflict; the complications move the plot forward in its rising action

complicaciones: sucesos de una trama que desarrollan el conflicto; las complicaciones hacen avanzar la trama en su acción ascendente

components: the parts or elements of a whole

componentes: partes o elementos que conforman un todo

compound sentence: a sentence containing two independent clauses

oración compuesta: oración que contiene dos cláusulas independientes

concession: an admission in an argument that the opposing side has valid points

concesión: admitir en un debate que el lado opositor tiene opiniones válidas

concluding statement: a statement that follows from and supports the claim made in an argument

declaración concluyente: declaración que sigue de la afirmación, o la apoya, en un argumento

conflict: a struggle or problem in a story. An *internal conflict* occurs when a character struggles between opposing needs or desires or emotions within his or her own mind. An *external conflict* occurs when a character struggles against an outside force. This force may be another character, a societal expectation, or something in the physical world.

conflicto: lucha o problema en un cuento. Un *conflicto interno* ocurre cuando un personaje lucha entre necesidades o deseos o emociones que se contraponen dentro de su mente. Un *conflicto externo* ocurre cuando un personaje lucha contra una fuerza externa. Esta fuerza puede ser otro personaje, una expectativa social o algo del mundo físico.

connotation: the associations and emotional overtones attached to a word beyond its literal definition, or denotation; a connotation may be positive, negative, or neutral

connotación: asociaciones y alusiones emocionales unidas a una palabra más allá de su definición literal o denotación; una connotación puede ser positiva, negativa, o neutra

consonance: the repetition of final consonant sounds in stressed syllables with different vowel sounds

consonancia: repetición de sonidos consonánticos finales en sílabas acentuadas con diferentes sonidos vocálicos

context: the circumstances or conditions in which something exists or takes place

contexto: circunstancias o condiciones en las que algo ocurre

conventions: standard features, practices, and forms associated with the way something is usually done

convenciones: prácticas y formas usuales asociadas con las costumbres de hacer algo

nterarguments: the arguments that can be made to
ose a viewpoint
traargumentos: argumentos que se presentan para
atir un punto de vista

nterclaim: a position taken by someone with an opposing
wpoint
trareclamación: posición que toma una persona con un
to de vista contrario

plet: two consecutive lines of verse with end rhyme; a
plet usually expresses a complete unit of thought
la: dos líneas de versos consecutivos con rima final; una
la normalmente expresa una unidad de pensamiento
pleta

dibility: the quality of being trusted or believed
dibilidad: calidad de ser confiable o creíble

ical lens: a particular identifiable perspective as in
der Response Criticism, Cultural Criticism, etc., through
ch a text can be analyzed and interpreted
crítico: punto de vista particular identificable como por
nplo Teoría de la recepción, Crítica sociocultural, etc., por
dio del que se puede analizar e interpretar un texto

tural conflict: a struggle that occurs when people with
erent cultural expectations or attitudes interact
flicto cultural: lucha que ocurre cuando interactúan
sonas con diferentes expectativas o actitudes culturales

tural Criticism: criticism that focuses on the elements
ulture and how they affect one's perceptions and
erstanding of texts
ica cultural: analizar un texto basándose en elementos
urales y como ellos afectan la percepción y lacomprensión
extos

ture: the shared set of arts, ideals, skills, institutions,
toms, attitude, values, and achievements that characterize
oup of people, and that are passed on or taught to
ceeding generations
tura: conjunto de artes, ideas, destrezas, instituciones,
umbres, actitud, valores y logros compartidos que
acterizan a un grupo de personas, y que se transfieren o
eñan a las generaciones siguientes

nulative (or loose) sentence: a sentence in which the
in clause comes first, followed by subordinate structures
lauses
ción acumulativa (o frases sueltas): oración cuya
usula principal viene primero, seguida de estructuras o
usulas subordinadas

D

deductive reasoning: a process of drawing a specific
conclusion from general information
razonamiento deductivo: proceso en que se usa información
general para sacar una conclusión específica

defend: to support a statement that has been made
defender: dar apoyo a una declaración que alguien ha hecho

denotation: the precise meaning of a word
denotación: significado literal de una palabra

detail: a specific fact, observation, or incident; any of the
small pieces or parts that make up something else
detalle: hecho, observación o incidente específico;
cualquiera de las pequeñas piezas o partes que constituyen
otra cosa

dialect: the distinctive language—including the sounds,
spelling, grammar, and diction—of a specific group or class
of people
dialecto: lenguaje distintivo, incluyendo sonidos, ortografía,
gramática y dicción, de un grupo o clase específico de
personas

dialogue: the words spoken by characters in a narrative or
film
diálogo: palabras que dicen los personajes en un relato o
película

dialogue tags: the phrases that attribute a quotation to the
speaker, for example, *she said* or *he bellowed*
marcas del diálogo: frases que atribuyen la cita de un
hablante, por ejemplo, *dijo ella* o *bramó él.*

diction: a writer's word choices, which often convey voice
and tone
dicción: selección de palabras por parte del escritor;
elemento estilístico que ayuda a transmitir voz y tono

diegetic sound: any sound that can logically be heard by
characters on screen
sonido diegético: sonidos lógicos que los personajes pueden
oír en una escena en la pantalla

direct characterization: specific information about a
character provided by the narrator or author
caracterización directa: información específica sobre un
personaje creada por un narrador o autor

discourse: the language or speech used in a particular
context or subject
discurso: lenguaje o habla usada en un contexto o tema en
particular

documentary or nonfiction film: a genre of filmmaking that provides a visual record of actual events using photographs, video footage, and interviews

documental o película de no-ficción: género cinematográfico que realiza un registro visual de sucesos basados en hechos por medio del uso de fotografías, registro en videos y entrevistas

dominant group: a more powerful group that may perceive another group as marginalized or subordinate

grupo dominante: un grupo más poderoso que puede percibir a otro grupo como maginado o subordinado

drama: a play written for stage, radio, film, or television, usually about a serious topic or situation

drama: obra teatral escrita para representar en un escenario, radio, cine o televisión, normalmente sobre un tema o situación seria

dramatic irony: a form of irony in which the reader or audience knows more about the circumstances or future events than the characters within the scene

ironía dramática: una forma de la ironía en que los lectores o el público sabe más sobre las circunstancias o sucesos futuros que los personajes en la escena

dramaturge: a member of an acting company who helps the director and actors make informed decisions about the performance by researching information relevant to the play and its context

dramaturgo: socio de una compañía teatral que ayuda al director y a los actores tomar decisiones informadas sobre la interpretación investigando información relevante a la obra teatral y su contexto

dynamic (or round) character: a character who evolves and grows in the story and has a complex personality

personaje dinámico: personaje complejo que evoluciona a lo largo de la trama literaria

E

editorial: an article in a newspaper or magazine expressing the opinion of its editor or publisher

editorial: artículo de periódico o revista, que expresa la opinión de su editor

effect: the result or influence of using a specific literary or cinematic device; a result produced by a cause

efecto: resultado o influencia de usar un recurso literario o cinematográfico específico; resultado o producto de una causa

elaborate: to expand on or add information or detail about a point and thus to develop the point more fully

elaborar: extender o agregar información o detalles sobre asunto, y asi desarrollar el asunto de manera más completa

empirical evidence: evidence based on experiences and direct observation through research

evidencia empírica: evidencia basada en experiencias y e observación directa por medio de la investigación

emulate: to imitate an original work or person
emular: imitar una obra original

enfranchisement: having the rights of citizenship, such as the right to vote

emancipación: tener los derechos de la ciudananía, tales como el derecho al voto

epigram: a short, witty saying
epigrama: dicho corto e ingenioso

epigraph: a phrase, quotation, or poem that is set at the beginning of a document or component

epígrafe: frase, cita, o poema que aparece al comienzo de documento o componente

epithet: a descriptive word or phrase used in place of or along with a name

epíteto: palabra o frase descriptiva usada en lugar de o jun con un nombre

ethos: (ethical appeal) a rhetorical appeal that focuses on character or qualifications of the speaker

ethos: (recurso ético) recurso retórico centrado en la ética en el carácter o capacidades del orador

euphonious: a harmonious or pleasing sound
eufónico: un sonido armonioso y agradable

evaluate: to make a judgment based on an analysis about value or worth of the information, idea, or object

evaluar: dar una opinión basándose en un análisis sobre el valor o mérito de la información, idea, u objeto

evidence: the information that supports a position in an argument; forms of evidence include facts, statistics (numerical facts), expert opinions, examples, and anecdote *see also* anecdotal, empirical, and logical evidence

evidencia: información que apoya o prueba una idea o afirmación; formas de evidencia incluyen hechos, estadístic (datos numéricos), opiniones de expertos, ejemplos y anécdotas; *ver también* evidencia anecdótica, empírica y lóg

exaggeration: a statement that represents something as larger, better, or worse than it really is

exageración: representar algo como más grande, mejor o peor que lo que realmente es

emplification: the act of defining by example by showing ecific, relevant examples that fit a writer's definition of a pic or concept

emplificación: definir por ejemplo mostrando ejemplos pecíficos y relevantes que se ajustan a la definición de un ma o concepto del escritor

planatory writing: a form of writing whose purpose is to plain, describe, or give information about a topic in order inform a reader

crito explicativo: forma de la escritura cuyo propósito explicar, describir o dar información sobre un tema para formar al lector

plicit theme: a theme that is clearly stated by the writer **ma explícito:** tema que está claramente establecido por el critor

position: events that give a reader background formation needed to understand a story (characters are troduced, the setting is described, and the conflict begins to fold)

posición: sucesos que dan al lector los antecedentes cesarios para comprender un cuento. Durante la posición, se presentan los personajes, se describe el biente y se comienza a revelar el conflicto.

tended metaphor: a comparison between two unlike ings that continues throughout a series of sentences in a ragraph or lines in a poem

táfora extendida: metáfora que se extiende por varios rsos o a través de un poema completo

ternal coherence: unity or logical connection between ragraphs with effective transitions and transitional devices

herencia externa: unidad o conexión lógica entre rrafos con transiciones efectivas y recursos transitionales

e rhymes: words that appear to rhyme because of identical elling patterns but do not actually rhyme, for example, *ugh* and *through*

lsas rimas: palabras, en inglés, que poseen una rminación idéntica y, por tanto, nos llevan erróneamente a nsar que riman, tales como *cough* y *through*

llacy: a false or misleading argument
lacia: argumento o poema falso o engañoso

lling action: the events in a play, story, or novel that follow e climax, or moment of greatest suspense, and lead to the solution

acción descendente: sucesos de una obra teatral, cuento o novela posteriores al clímax, o momento de mayor suspenso, y que conllevan a la resolución

faux pas: an embarrassing act or remark in a social situation (borrowed from French)
metedura de pata: comportamiento o comentario embarazoso en el marco de una situación social

Feminist Criticism: criticism that focuses on relationships between genders and examines a text based on the patterns of thought, behavior, values, enfranchisement, and power in relations between and within the sexes

crítica feminista: se enfoca en la relación entre los sexos y examina un texto basándose en el diseño de pensamiento, comportamiento, valores, emancipación, y poder en las relaciones entre los sexos

figurative: symbolic or emblematic; not literal
figurativo: simbólico o emblemático, no literal

figurative language: the use of words to describe one thing in terms of another
lenguaje figurativo: lenguaje imaginativo o figuras retóricas que no pretenden ser tomados literalmente; el lenguaje figurativo usa figuras literarias

film techniques: the methods a director uses to communicate meaning and to evoke particular emotional responses in viewers
técnicas cinematográficas: metodos que usa un director en la comunicación del significado y evocar una respuesta emocional específica en los videntes

fixed form: a form of poetry in which the length and pattern are determined by established usage of tradition, such as a sonnet
forma fija: forma de poesía en la que la longitud y el patrón están determinados por el uso de la tradición, como un soneto

flashback: an interruption or transition to a time before the current events in a narrative
flashback: interrupción en la secuencia de los sucesos para relatar sucesos ocurridos en el pasado

flat (or static) character: a character who is uncomplicated and stays the same without changing or growing during the story
personaje estático: personaje no complicado que permanence del mismo caracter y que no cambia a lo largo de una historia

folktale: a story without a known author that has been preserved through oral retellings

cuento folclórico: cuento sin autor conocido que se ha conservado por medio de relatos orales

footage: literally, a length of film; the expression is still used to refer to digital video clips

metraje: literalmente, la longitud de una película; la expresión aún se usa para referirse a video clips digitales

foreshadowing: the use of hints or clues in a narrative to suggest future action

presagio: uso de claves o pistas en un relato para sugerir una acción futura

form: the particular structure or organization of a work

forma: estructura o organización particular de una obra

found poem: a poem consisting of words, phrases, and/or lines that come directly from another text

poema encontrado: poema compuesto de palabras, frases o pasajes sacados directamente de otros textos

free verse: poetry without a fixed pattern of meter and rhyme

verso libre: poesía que no sigue ningún patrón, ritmo o rima regular

G

genre: a kind or style of literature or art, each with its own specific characteristics. For example, poetry, short story, and novel are literary genres. Painting and sculpture are artistic genres.

género: tipo o estilo de literatura o arte, cada uno con sus propias características específicas. Por ejemplo, la poesía, el cuento corto y la novela son géneros literarios. La pintura y la escultura son géneros artísticos.

genre conventions: the essential features and format that characterize a particular genre, or style of literature or art

convenciones genéricas: características básicas y el formato que caracterizan un género específico

graphic novel: a book-length narrative, or story, in the form of a comic strip rather than words

novela gráfica: narrativa o cuento del largo de un libro, en forma de tira cómica más que palabras

graphics: images or text used to provide information on screen

gráfica: imágenes o texto que se usa para dar información en pantalla

H

hamartia: a tragic hero's fatal flaw; an ingrained character trait that causes a hero to make decisions leading to his or h death or downfall

hamartia: error fatal de un héroe trágico; característica propia de un personaje que causa que un héroe tome decisiones que finalmente llevan a su muerte o caída

hero: the main character or protagonist of a play, with whom audiences become emotionally invested

héroe: personaje principal o protagonista de una obra teatra con el que el público se involucra emocionalmente

historical context: the circumstances or conditions in whic something takes place

contexto historico: circuntancias o condiciones en las cual algo sucede o pasa

Historical Criticism: criticism used to uncover meaning in literary text by examining the text in the context of the time period in which it was created

historicismo: método crítico que se usa para revelar el significado de un texto literario mediante el examen de dich texto en el contexto de la época en que fue escrito

hook: an opening in an argument or a piece of writing that grabs the reader's attention

gancho: cita, anécdota o ejemplo interesante al comienzo d un escrito, que capta la atención del lector

Horatian satire: satire that pokes fun at human foibles and folly with a witty, gentle, even indulgent tone

sátira de Horacio: sátira en que se burla de las debilidades y locuras con un tono suave, ingenioso, hasta indulgente

humor: the quality of being amusing

humor: calidad de ser divertido

hyperbole: exaggeration used to suggest strong emotion or create a comic effect

hipérbole: exageración que se usa para sugerir una emoció fuerte o crear un efecto cómico

I

iamb: a metrical foot that consists of an unstressed syllable followed by a stressed syllable

yambo: pie métrico que consta de una sílaba átona seguida de una sílaba acentuada

iambic pentameter: a rhythmic pattern of five feet (or units each consisting of one unstressed syllable followed by a stressed syllable

entámetro yámbico: patrón rítmico de cinco pies (o
unidades) de una sílaba átona seguida de una sílaba acentuada

image: a word or phrase that appeals to one of more of the
five senses and creates a picture
imagen: palabra o frase que apela a uno o más de los cinco
sentido y crea un cuadro

imagery: the verbal expression of sensory experience;
descriptive or figurative language used to create word
pictures; imagery is created by details that appeal to one or
more of the five senses
imaginería: lenguaje descriptivo o figurativo utilizado para
crear imágenes verbales; la imaginería es creada por detalles
que apelan a uno o más de los cinco sentidos

imperialism: a policy of extending the rule or influence
of a country over other countries or colonies; the political,
military, or economic domination of one country by another
imperialismo: política de extender el dominio o la influencia
de un país sobre otros países o colonias; dominio político;
militar o económico de un país sobre otro(s)

implied theme: a theme that is understood through the
writer's diction, language construction, and use of literary
devices
tema implícito: tema que se entiende a través de la dicción
del escritor, construcción lingüística y uso de recursos
literarios

indirect characterization: a narrator's or author's
development of a character through the character's
interactions with others, thoughts about circumstances, or
speaking his or her thoughts aloud
caracterización indirecta: el desarrollo de un personaje
según un narrador o autor por las interacciones del personaje
con otros, pensamientos sobre las circunstancias, o su
habilidad de enunciar sus pensamientos en voz alta

inductive reasoning: a process of looking at individual facts
to draw a general conclusion
razonamiento inductivo: proceso de observación de hechos
individuales para sacar una conclusión general

inference: a conclusion about ideas or information not
directly stated
inferencia: conclusión sobre las ideas o información no
presentadas directamente

interior monologue: a literary device in which a character's
internal emotions and thoughts are presented
monólogo interior: recurso literario en el que se presentan
las emociones internas y pensamientos de un personaje

interpretation: the act of making meaning from something,
such as a text
interpretación: acto de interpretar un significado de algo, tal
como un texto

internal coherence: unity or logical connection within
paragraphs
coherencia interna: unidad o conexión lógica entre párrafos

irony: a literary device that exploits readers' expectations;
irony occurs when what happens turns out to be quite
different from what was expected. *Dramatic irony* is a form of
irony in which the reader or audience knows more about the
circumstances or future events in a story than the characters
within it; *verbal irony* occurs when a speaker or narrator
says one thing while meaning the opposite; *situational irony*
occurs when an event contradicts the expectations of the
characters or the reader.
ironía: recurso literario que explota las expectativas de los
lectores; la ironía ocurre cuando lo que se espera resulta
ser bastante diferente de lo que realmente ocurre. La *ironía
dramática* es una forma de ironía en la que el lector o la
audiencia saben más acerca de las circunstancias o sucesos
futuros de un cuento que los personajes del mismo; la
ironía verbal ocurre cuando un orador o narrador dice
una cosa queriendo decir lo contrario; la *ironía situacional*
ocurre cuando un suceso contradice las expectativas de los
personajes o del lector.

J

justice: the quality of being reasonable and fair in the
administration of the law; the ideal of rightness or fairness
justicia: calidad de ser razonable e imparcial en la
administración de la ley; ideal de rectitud o equidad

Juvenalian satire: satire that denounces, sometimes harshly,
human vice and error in dignified and solemn tones
sátira de Juvenal: sátira de denuncia, a veces con aspereza,
los vicios y errores humanos con tonos dignos y solemnes

juxtaposition: the arrangement of two or more things for the
purpose of comparison
yuxtaposición: ordenamiento de dos o más cosas con el
objeto de compararlas

L

lede: an alternative spelling of lead; the opening of a news
article or a single sentence that describes the main point of
the article

entradilla: comienzo de una información periodística que resume lo más importante de ella

lining out: the process of creating line breaks to add shape and meaning in free verse poetry

llamada y respuesta: proceso de crear rupturas de lineas para dar forma y significado en la poesía del verso libre

literal: explicitly stated in a text; exact

literal: algo expresado de modo explícito y exacto en un texto

literal language: the exact meanings, or denotations, of words

lenguaje literal: los signficados y denotaciones exactos de las palabras

Literary Criticism: the formal practice of interpreting, evaluating, and explaining the meaning and significance of literary works

crítica literaria: práctica formal de interpretar, evaluar y explicar el significado y el valor de obras literarias

literary theory: a systematic study of literature using various methods to analyze texts

teoría literaria: intento de establecer principios para interpretar y evaluar textos literarios

logical evidence: evidence based on facts and a clear rationale

evidencia lógica: evidencia basada en hechos y una clara fundamentación

logical fallacy: a statement that is false because it is based on an error in reasoning

argumento falaz: afirmación de carácter falso por el hecho de estar basada en un error de razonamiento

logos: (logical appeal) a rhetorical appeal to reason or logic

logos: (apelación lógica) apelación retórica que usa la evidencia factual y la lógica para apelar al sentido de la razón

M

main idea: a statement (often one sentence) that summarizes the key details of a text

idea principal: declaración (con frecuencia una oración) que resume los detalles claves de un texto

marginalize: to relegate or confine a person to a lower or outer limit

marginar: relegar o confinar a una persona a un límite bajo o ajeno

Marxist Criticism: criticism that asserts that economics provides the foundation for all social, political, and ideological reality

crítica marxista: ver un text a través de la perspectiva en que la economía proporciona la fundación de toda realidad social, política, e ideológica

media: collectively refers to the organizations that communicate information to the public

medios de comunicación: colectivamente refiere a las organizaciones que comunican información al público

media channel: a method an organization uses to communicate, such as radio, television, website, newspaper, or magazine

canales mediaticos: método que usa una organización en la comunicación como radio, televisión, sitios de web, periódico, o revista

metacognition: the ability to know and be aware of one's own thought processes; self-reflection

metacognición: capacidad de conocer y estar consciente de los propios procesos del pensamiento; introspección

metaphor: a comparison between two unlike things in which one thing is spoken of as if it were another, for example, the moon was a crisp white cracker

metáfora: comparación entre dos cosas diferentes en la que se habla de una cosa como si fuera otra, por ejemplo, la luna era una galletita blanca crujiente

meter: a pattern of stressed and unstressed syllables in poetry

métrica: patrón de sílabas acentuadas y átonas en poesía

mise en scène: the composition, or setting, of a stage

puesta en escena: la composición o el lugar de un escenario

monologue: a dramatic speech delivered by a single character in a play

monólogo: discurso dramático que hace un solo personaje en una obra teatral

montage: a composite picture that is created by bringing together a number of images and arranging them to create a connected whole

montaje: cuadro compuesto que se crea al reunir un número de imágenes y que al organizarlas se crea un todo relacionado

mood: the atmosphere or predominant emotion in a literary work, the effect of the words on the audience

carácter: atmósfera o sentimiento general en una obra literaria

motif: a recurrent image, symbol, theme, character type, subject, or narrative detail that becomes a unifying element in an artistic work or text

motivo: imagen, símbolo, tema, tipo de personaje, tema o detalle narrativo recurrente que se convierte en un elemento unificador en una obra artística

tive: a character's reason for behaving in a certain way
tivación: razón esgrimida por un personaje para obrar de erminado modo

sical (or sound) device: the use of sound to convey and nforce the meaning or experience of poetry
ratos musicales: uso del sonido para transmitir y orzar el significado o experiencia de la poesía

th: a traditional story that explains the actions of gods or oes or the origins of the elements of nature
: cuento tradicional que explica las acciones de dioses o oes, o los orígenes de los elementos de la naturaleza

ration: the act of telling a story
ración: acto de contar un cuento

rative: a story about a series of events that includes racter development, plot structure, and theme; can be a rk of fiction or nonfiction
rativa: narración sobre una serie de sucesos que incluye el arrollo de personajes, estructora del argumento, y el tema; ede ser una obra de ficción o no ficción

rative arc: the story line of a text, including a beginning position), a middle (the *rising action*), a high point max), and an end (the *falling action* and *resolution*)
o narrativo: línea argumental de un texto, que consta de comienzo (*exposición*), una parte media (*acción creciente*), punto culminante (*clímax*) y un final (*acción decreciente* y olución*)

rrative pacing: the speed at which a narrative moves
mpás de la narrativa: la rapidez en que una narrativa pasa

rrator: the person telling the story
rrador: persona que cuenta una historia

n-diegetic sound: sound that cannot logically be heard by e characters on screen; examples include mood music and ce-overs
nido no diegético: voces y comentarios superpuestos; aidos que no provienen de la acción en pantalla.

t graf: an abbreviation of the expression *nutshell ragraph*; a statement that tells readers of a news article why ey should care about what happened
itome: texto introductorio que hace entender a los tores por qué debería importarles la noticia que se relata a ntinuación

O

objective: based on factual information
objetivo: basado en información de hechos

objective tone: a tone that is more clinical and that is not influenced by emotion
tono objetivo: tono que es mas aséptico y que no se deja influir por la emoción

objectivity: the representation of facts or ideas without injecting personal feelings or biases
objetividad: representación de los hechos o ideas sin agregar sentimientos o prejuicios personales

ode: a lyric poem expressing feelings or thoughts of a speaker, often celebrating a person, event, or thing
oda: poema lírico que expresa sentimientos o pensamientos de un orador, que frecuentemente celebra a una persona, suceso o cosa

omniscient narrator: a narrator who knows all and tells a story from the perspective of multiple characters
narrador omnisciente: narrador que conoce todo lo sucedido sobre un determinado acontecimiento y relata la historia desde la perspectiva de varios personajes

onomatopoeia: the occurrence of a word whose sound suggests its meaning
onomatopeya: palabras cuyo sonido sugiere su significado

oral interpretation: a planned oral reading that expresses the meaning of a written text
interpretación oral: lectura oral planeada que interpreta el signficado de un text escrito

oral tradition: the passing down of stories, tales, proverbs, and other culturally important ideas through oral retellings
tradición oral: traspaso de historias, cuentos, proverbios y otras historias de importancia cultural por medio de relatos orales

oxymoron: words that appear to contradict each other; for example, cold fire
oxímoron: palabras que parecen contradecirse mutuamente; por ejemplo, fuego frío

P

paradox: a statement that contains two seemingly incompatible points
paradoja: declaración que contiene dos asuntos aparentemente incompatibles

parallel structure (parallelism): refers to a grammatical or structural similarity between sentences or parts of a sentence, so that elements of equal importance are equally developed and similarly phrased for emphasis

estructura paralela (paralelismo): se refiere a una similitud gramatical o estructural entre oraciones o partes de una oración, de modo que los elementos de igual importancia se desarrollen por igual y se expresen de manera similar para dar énfasis

paraphrase: to briefly restate ideas from another source in one's own words

parafrasear: volver a presentar las ideas de otra fuente en nuestras propias palabras

parenthetical citations: used for citing sources directly in an essay

citas parentéticas: usadas en citas de fuentes primarias en un ensayo

parody: a literary or artistic work that imitates the characteristic style of an author or a work for comic effect or ridicule

parodia: obra literaria o artística que imita el estilo característico de un autor o una obra para dar un efecto cómico o ridículo

passive-voice verbs: verb form in which the subject receives the action; the passive voice consists of a form of the verb *be* plus a past participle of the verb

verbos en voz pasiva: forma verbal en la que el sujeto recibe la acción; la voz pasiva se forma con el verbo *ser* más el participio pasado de un verbo

pathos: (emotional appeal) a rhetorical appeal to the reader's or listener's senses or emotions

pathos: (apelación emocional) apelación retórica a los sentidos o emociones de los lectores u oyentes

patriarchal: having the male as head of the household and with authority over women and children

patriarcal: sociedad en que el varón es jefe del hogar en el cual mantiene autoridad sobre las mujeres y niños

perception: one person's interpretation of sensory or conceptual information

percepción: interpretación de una persona en cuanto a información sensorial o conceptual

periodic sentence: a sentence that makes sense only when the end of the sentence is reached, that is, when the main clause comes last

oración periódica: oración que tiene sentido sólo cuando se llega al final de la oración, es decir, cuando la cláusula principal viene al final

persona: the voice assumed by a writer to express ideas or beliefs that may not be his or her own

personaje: voz que asume un escritor para expresar ideas creencias que pueden no ser las propias

personification: a figure of speech that gives human quali to an animal, object, or idea

personificación: figura literaria que da características humanas a un animal, objeto o idea

perspective: a way of looking at the world or a mental concept about things or events, one that judges relationship within or among things or events

perspectiva: manera de visualizar el mundo o concepto mental de las cosas o sucesos, que juzga las relaciones dent o entre cosas o sucesos

persuasive argument: an argument that convinces reader to accept or believe a writer's perspective on a topic

argumento persuasivo: argumento que convence a los lectores a aceptar o creer en la perspectiva de un escritor acerca de un tema

photo essay: a collection of photographic images that reve the author's perspective on a subject

ensayo fotográfico: recolección de imágenes fotográficas que revelan la perspectiva del autor acerca de un tema

plagiarism: the unattributed use of another writer's words ideas

plagio: usar como propias las palabras o ideas de otro escri

plot: the sequence of related events that make up a story

trama: secuencia de sucesos relacionados que conforman cuento o novela

poetic structure: the organization of words, lines, and images as well as ideas

estructura poética: organización de las palabras, versos e imágenes, así como también de las ideas

poetry: language written in lines and stanzas

poesía: género literario que se concreta en un poema y est sujeto a medida o cadencia

point of view: the perspective from which a narrative is tol that is, first person, third-person limited, or third-person omniscient

punto de vista: perspectiva desde la cual se cuenta un relat es decir, primera persona, tercera persona limitada o tercer persona omnisciente

precept: a rule, instruction, or principle that guides a person's actions and/or moral behavior

precepto: regla, instrucción o principio que guía las accion de una persona y/o conducta moral de alguien

rimary footage: film footage shot by the filmmaker for the ›xt at hand
etraje principal: filmación hecha por el cineasta para el ›xto que tiene a mano

rimary source: an original document or image created by ›meone who experiences an event first hand
uente primaria: documento original que contiene ›formación de primera mano acerca de un tema

›rologue: the introduction or preface to a literary work
›rólogo: introducción o prefacio de una obra literaria

›rose: ordinary written or spoken language, using sentences ›nd paragraphs, without deliberate or regular meter or ›hyme; not poetry or song
›rosa: forma común del lenguaje escrito o hablado, usando ›raciones y párrafos, sin métrica o rima deliberada o regular; ›i poesía ni canción

›rosody: the pattern and rhythm of sounds in poetry, ›ncluding stress and intonation
›rosodia: rasgos fónicos de la métrica de la poesía, incluidos ›l énfasis y la entonación

›rotagonist: the central character in a work of literature, the ›ne who is involved in the main conflict in the plot
›rotagonista: personaje central de una obra literaria, el que ›articipa en el conflicto principal de la trama

›roverb: a short saying about a general truth
›roverbio: dicho corto sobre una verdad general

Q

qualify: to consider to what extent a statement is true or untrue (to what extent you agree or disagree)
calificar: consider hasta qué punto una declaración es verdadera o falsa

quatrain: a four-line stanza in a poem
cuarteta: en un poema, estrofa de cuatro versos

R

rationale: an explanation for a belief, statement, or behavior
fundamento: cimientos o bases en los que se apoya una creencia, afirmación o comportamiento

Reader Response Criticism: criticism that focuses on a reader's active engagement with a piece of print or nonprint text; shaped by the reader's own experiences, social ethics, moral values, and general views of the world

crítica de reacción del lector: análisis de un texto basado en las experiencias, ética social, valores, y percepciones generales del mundo

reasoning: the thinking or logic used to make a claim in an argument
razonamiento: pensamiento o lógica que se usa para hacer una afirmación en un argumento

rebuttal: a reason why a counterargument is wrong
refutación: razón por la cual un contraargumento es erróneo

refrain: a regularly repeated line or group of lines in a poem or song, usually at the end of a stanza
estribillo: verso o grupo de versos que se repiten con regularidad en un poema o canción, normalmente al final de una estrofa

refutation: the reasoning used to disprove an opposing point
refutación: razonamiento que se usa para rechazar una opinión contraria

reliability: the extent to which a source provides quality and trustworthy information
confiabilidad: grado en el que una fuente da información confiable y de buena calidad

renaissance: a rebirth or revival
renacimiento: un volver a nacer o una reanimación

repetition: the use of any element of language—a sound, a word, a phrase, a line, or a stanza—more than once
repetición: uso de cualquier elemento del lenguaje—un sonido, una palabra, una frase, un verso o una estrofa—más de una vez

resolution (denouement): the end of a text, in which the main conflict is finally resolved
resolución (desenlace): final de una obra teatral, cuento o novela, en el que el conflicto principal finalmente se resuelve

résumé: a document that outlines a person's skills, education, and work history
currículum vitae: documento que resume las destrezas, educación y experiencia laboral de una persona

retrospective: looking back to analyze the events in one's past
retrospectiva: mirar atrás en el tiempo para analizar los acontecimientos del pasado de una persona

revise: to rework or reorganize a piece of writing to improve its logic and flow after completing a first draft
revisar: rehacer o reorganizar un escrito para mejorar su lógica y fluidez tras haber terminado un primer borrador

rhetoric: the art of using words to persuade in writing or speaking

retórica: arte de usar las palabras para persuadir por escrito o de manera hablada

rhetorical appeals: emotional, ethical, and logical arguments used to persuade an audience to agree with the writer or speaker

recursos retóricos: uso de argumentos emocionales, éticos y lógicos para persuadir por escrito o de manera hablada

rhetorical context: the subject, purpose, audience, occasion, or situation in which writing or speaking occurs

contexto retórico: sujeto, propósito, audiencia, ocasión o situación en que ocurre el escrito

rhetorical devices: specific techniques used in writing or speaking to create a literary effect or enhance effectiveness

dispositivos retóricos: técnicas específicas que se usan al escribir o al hablar para crear un efecto literario o mejorar la efectividad

rhetorical question: a question that is asked for effect or one for which the answer is obvious

pregunta retórica: pregunta hecha para producir un efecto o cuya respuesta es obvia

rhetorical slanters: rhetorical devices used to present a subject in a biased way

sesgos retóricos: recursos retóricos que se usan para presentar un determinado asunto de un modo tendencioso

rhyme: the repetition of sounds at the ends of words
rima: repetición de sonidos al final de las palabras

rhyme scheme: a consistent pattern of rhyme throughout a poem

esquema de la rima: patrón consistente de una rima a lo largo de un poema

rhythm: the pattern of stressed and unstressed syllables in spoken or written language, especially in poetry

ritmo: patrón de sílabas acentuadas y no acentuadas en lenguaje hablado o escrito, especialmente en poesía

rising action: the movement of a plot toward a climax or moment of greatest excitement; the rising action is fueled by the characters' responses to the conflict

acción ascendente: movimiento de una trama hacia el clímax o momento de mayor emoción; la acción ascendente es impulsada por las reacciones de los personajes ante el conflicto

dynamic (or round) character: a character who evolves and grows in the story and has a complex personality

personaje dinámico: personaje que evoluciona y crece en la historia y que tiene una personalidad compleja

S

sarcasm: deliberate, often ironic ridicule
sarcasmo: burla deliberada, de carácter generalmente irónico

satire: a manner of writing that mocks social conventions, actions, or attitudes with wit and humor

sátira: manera de escribir en que se burla de convenciones sociales, acciones, o actitudes con ingenio y humor

scenario: an outline, a brief account, a script, or a synopsis of a proposed series of events

escenario: bosquejo, relato breve, libreto o sinopsis de una serie de sucesos propuestos

secondary audience: a group that may receive a message intended for a target audience

audiencia secundaria: grupo que puede recibir un mensaje orientado a una audiencia específica

secondary source: a discussion about or commentary on a primary source; the key feature of a secondary source is that it offers an interpretation of information gathered from primary sources

fuente secundaria: discusión o comentario acerca de una fuente primaria; la característica clave de una fuente secundaria es que ofrece una interpretación de la información recopilada en las fuentes primarias

sensory details: details that appeal to or evoke one or more of the five senses—sight, sound, smell, taste, and touch

detalles sensoriales: detalles que apelan o evocan uno o más de los cinco sentidos—vista, oído, gusto, olfato, y tacto

sensory images: images that appeal to the reader's senses—sight, sound, smell, taste, and touch

imágenes sensoriales: imágenes que apelan a los sentidos del lector—vista, oído, olfato, gusto, y tacto

sequence of events: the order in which things happen in a story

secuencia de eventos: orden en que los sucesos de una historia pasan:

setting: the time and place in which a story happens
ambiente: tiempo y lugar en el que ocurre un relato

simile: a comparison of two different things or ideas using the words *like* or *as*, for example, the moon was as white as milk

símil: comparación entre dos o más cosas o ideas diferentes usando las palabras *como* o *tan*, por ejemplo, la luna estaba tan blanca como la leche

uational irony: a form of irony that occurs when an event ntradicts the expectations of the characters or the reader
nía situacional: ocurre cuando un evento contradice las pectativas de los personajes o el lector

anters: rhetorical devices used to present the subject in a ased way
slayo: recursos retóricos para presentar el tema de odo sesgado

ogan: a short, catchy phrase used for advertising by a siness, club, or political party
logan: frase corta y tendenciosa que usa como publicidad ra un negocio, club o partido político

cial commentary: an expression of an opinion with the al of promoting change by appealing to a sense of justice
mentario social: expresión de una opinión con el objeto promover el cambio al apelar a un sentido de justicia

liloquy: a long speech delivered by an actor alone on the age; represents the character's internal thoughts
liloquio: discurso largo realizado por un actor sobre el cenario que representa sus pensamientos internos

nnet: a 14-line lyric poem, usually written in iambic ntameter and following a strict pattern of rhyme
neto: poema lírico de catorce versos, normalmente escrito un pentámetro yámbico y que sigue un patrón de rima tricto

und bite: a short excerpt from the recording of a speech piece of music which captures the essence of the longer cording
ña: corto fragmento de una grabación o de una pieza usical que capta la esencia de la grabación completa

eaker: the imaginary voice or persona of the writer or thor
ador: voz o persona imaginaria del escritor o autor

age directions: instructions written into the script of a ay that indicate stage actions, movements of performers, or oduction requirements
recciones escénicas: instrucciones escritas en un guión drama que indican acción, movimiento de actors, or quisitos de la producción

akeholder: a person motivated or affected by a course action
articipante: persona motivada o afectada por el curso de na acción

anza: a group of lines, usually similar in length and attern, that form a unit within a poem

estrofa: grupo de versos, normalmente similares en longitud y patrón, que forman una unidad dentro de un poema

static (or flat) character: a character who is uncomplicated and remains the same without changing or growing throughout a narrative
personaje estático: personaje que no cambia a lo largo de una narrativa

stereotype: an oversimplified, generalized conception, opinion, and/or image about particular groups of people
estereotipo: concepto generalizado, opinión y/o imagen demasiado simplificada acerca de grupos específicos de personas

stichomythia: in drama, the delivery of dialogue in a rapid, fast-paced manner, with actors speaking emotionally and leaving very little time between speakers
esticomitia: en el drama, es la rendición del diálogo de una manera rápida con actores que hablan con emoción, dejando espacio muy breve entre los hablantes

storyboard: a tool to show images and sequencing for the purpose of visualizing a film or a story
guión gráfico: método de mostrar imágenes y secuencias con el propósito de visualizar una película o historia

strategize: to plan the actions one will take to complete a task
estrategizar: planear las acciones de uno para complir una tarea

structure: the way a literary work is organized; the arrangement of the parts in a literary work
estructura: manera en que la obra literaria está organizada; disposición de las partes en una obra literaria

style: the distinctive way a writer uses language, characterized by elements of diction, syntax, imagery, organization, and so on
estilo: manera distintiva en que un escritor usa el lenguaje, caracterizada por elementos de dicción, sintaxis, lenguaje figurado, etc.

subculture: a smaller subsection of a culture, for example, within the culture of a high school may be many subcultures
subcultura: subsección más pequeña de una cultura, por ejemplo, dentro de la cultura de una escuela secundaria puede haber muchas subculturas

subjective: based on a person's point of view, opinions, values, or emotions
subjetivo: basado en el punto de vista, las opiniones, los valores o las emociones de alguien

subjective tone: a tone that is obviously influenced by the author's feelings or emotions

tono subjetivo: tono obviamente influído por los sentimientos o emociones del autor

subjectivity: judgment based on one's personal point of view, opinion, or values

subjetividad: en base en nuestro punto de vista, opinión o valores personales

subordinate: a person or group that is perceived as having a lower social or economic status

subordinado: persona o grupo percibido de ser de rango social o estado económico bajo

subplot: a secondary or side story that develops from and supports the main plot and usually involves minor characters

argumento secundario: una historia secundaria o periférica que apoya el argumento principal y que suele involucrar a personajes secundarios o menores

subtext: the underlying or implicit meaning in dialogue or the implied relationship between characters in a book, movie, play, or film; the subtext of a work is not explicitly stated

subtexto: significado subyacente o implícito en el diálogo o la relación implícita entre los personajes de un libro, película, u obra teatral. El subtexto de una obra no se establece de manera explícita.

survey: a method of collecting data from a group of people; it can be written, such as a print or online questionnaire, or oral, such as an in-person interview

encuesta: método para recolectar datos de un grupo de personas; puede ser escrita, como un impreso o cuestionario en línea, u oral, como en una entrevista personal

symbol: anything (object, animal, event, person, or place) that represents itself but also stands for something else on a figurative level

símbolo: cualquier cosa (objeto, animal, evento, persona o lugar) que se representa a sí misma, pero también representa otra cosa a nivel figurativo

symbolic: serving as a symbol; involving the use of symbols or symbolism

simbólico: que sirve como símbolo; que implica el uso de símbolos o simbolismo

synecdoche: a figure of speech in which a part is used to represent the whole or vice versa

sinécdoque: figura retórica en que una parte se usa para representar el todo, o vice-versa

syntax: the arrangement of words and the order of grammatical elements in a sentence; the way in which word are put together to make meaningful elements, such as phrases, clauses, and sentences

sintaxis: disposición de las palabras y orden de los element gramaticales en una oración; manera en que las palabras se juntan para formar elementos significativos como frases, cláusulas y oraciones

synthesis: the act of combining ideas from different source to create, express, or support a new idea

síntesis: acto de combinar ideas de diferentes fuentes para crear, expresar o apoyar una nueva idea

synthesize: to combine ideas from different sources to create, express, or support a new idea or claim

sintetizar: combinar ideas procedentes de distintas fuentes para crear, expresar o sustentar una nueva idea o afirmación

T

target audience: the intended group for which a work is designed to appeal or reach

público objetivo: grupo al que se pretende apelar o llegar con una obra

tenor: the intent, tone, or attitude conveyed by the words in a text

tenor: intención, tono o actitud transmitida por las palabras de un texto

textual evidence: the details, quotations, and examples fror a text that support the analysis or argument presented

evidencia textual: detalles, citas, y ejemplos de un texto qu apoyan el análisis o la argumentación presentada

theatrical elements: elements used by dramatists and directors to tell a story on stage. Elements include *costumes* (the clothing worn by actors to express their characters), *makeup* (cosmetics used to change actors' appearances and express their characters), *props* (objects used to help set the scene, advance a plot, and make a story realistic), *set* (the place where the action takes place, as suggested by objects, such as furniture, placed on a stage), and *acting choices* (gestures, movements, staging, and vocal techniques actors use to convey their characters and tell a story).

elementos teatrales: elementos utilizados por los dramaturgos y directores para contar una historia en el escenario. Los elementos incluyen *vestuario* (ropa que usan los actores para expresar sus personajes), *maquillaje* (cosméticos que se usan para cambiar la apariencia de los actores y expresar sus personajes), *elementos* (objetos que se usan para ayudar a montar la escena, avanzar la trama y crear una historia realista), *plató* (lugar donde tiene lugar la acción, según lo sugieren los objetos, como muebles, colocados sobre un escenario), y *opciones de actuación* (gestos, movimientos, representación y técnicas vocales que se usan para transmitir sus personajes y narrar una historia).

thematic statement: an interpretive statement articulating the central meaning or message of a text
oración temática: afirmación interpretativa que articula el significado o mensaje central de un texto

theme: a writer's central idea or main message; *see also* explicit theme, implied theme
tema: idea central o mensaje principal acerca de la vida de un escritor; *véase también* tema explícito, tema implícito

thesis: the main idea or point of an essay or article; in an argumentative essay the thesis is the writer's position on an issue
tesis: idea o punto principal de un ensayo o artículo; en un ensayo argumentativo, la tesis es la opinión del autor acerca de un tema

thumbnail sketch: a small drawing made to plan the composition of a more detailed or finished image that will be created later
boceto en miniatura: pequeño dibujo realizado para planificar la composición de una imagen más amplia o detallada que será posteriormente creada

tone: a writer's (or speaker's) attitude toward a subject, character, or audience
tono: actitud de un escritor u orador acerca de un tema

topic sentence: a sentence that states the main idea of a paragraph; in an essay, the topic sentence also makes a point that supports the thesis statement
oración principal: oración que establece la idea principal de un párrafo; en un ensayo, la oración principal también establece una proposición que apoya el enunciado de la tesis

tragedy: a dramatic play that tells the story of a character, usually of a noble class, who meets an untimely and unhappy death or downfall, often because of a specific character flaw or twist of fate

tragedia: obra teatral dramática que cuenta la historia de un personaje, normalmente de origen noble, que encuentra una muerte o caída imprevista o infeliz, con frecuencia debido a un defecto específico del personaje o una vuelta del destino

tragic hero: an archetypal hero based on the Greek concept of tragedy; the tragic hero has a flaw that makes him or her vulnerable to downfall or death
héroe trágico: héroe arquetípico basado en el concepto griego de la tragedia; el héroe trágico tiene un defecto que lo hace vulnerable a la caída o a la muerte

transcript: a written copy or record of a conversation that takes place between two or more people
transcripción: copia escrita de una conversación que sucede entre dos o más personas

U

unconventional: eccentric; unusual; original
no convencional: excéntrico; inusual; original

understatement: the representation of something as smaller or less significant than it really is; the opposite of exaggeration or hyperbole
subestimación: representación de algo como más pequeño o menos importante de lo que realmente es; lo opuesto a la exageración o hipérbole

V

valid: believable or truthful
válido: creíble o verídico

validity: the quality of truth or accuracy in a source
validez: calidad de verdad o precisión en una fuente

verbal irony: a form of irony that occurs when a speaker or narrator says one thing while meaning the opposite
ironía verbal: ocurre cuando un hablante o narrador dice una cosa mientras quiere decir lo opuesto

verbatim: in the exact words of a source
textualmente: palabras citadas exactamente como fueron expresadas

verify: to prove or confirm that something is true
verificar: probar o confirmar que algo es verdadero

vignette: a picture or visual or a brief descriptive literary piece
viñeta: ilustración o representación visual o pieza literaria descriptiva breve

visual delivery: the way a performer on stage interprets plot, character, and conflict through movement, gestures, and facial expressions

presentación visual: manera en que un actor en un escenario interpreta trama, carácter, y conflicto a través de movimiento, gestos, y expresiones de la cara

visual rhetoric: an argument or points made by visuals such as photographs or by other visual features of a text

retórica visual: argumentos o asuntos representados en visuales como fotos u otros rasgos visuales de un texto

visualize: to form a mental picture of something

visualizar: formarse una imagen mental de algo

vocal delivery: the way a performer on stage expresses the meaning of a text through volume, pitch, rate or speed of speech, pauses, pronunciation, and articulation

presentación vocal: manera en que se expresan las palabras en el escenario, por medio del volumen, tono, rapidez o velocidad del discurso, pausas, pronunciación y articulación

voice: a writer's (or speaker's) distinctive use of language to express ideas as well as his or her persona

voz: manera en que el escritor u orador usa las palabras y el tono para expresar ideas, así como también su personaje o personalidad

ndex of Skills

iterary Skills

Reading Skills

Writing Skills

Media Skills

Vocabulary Skills

Index of Authors and Titles

Credits

Image Credits

Va crwpitman/iStock; 1 Wiktor Szymanowicz/Barcroft Im/ arcroft Media/Getty Images; 6 That's Life used with the ermission of Mike Twohy and the Cartoonist Group. All ghts reserved.; 8 Marc Bryan-Brown/WireImage/Getty mages; 9 Inti St Clair / Getty Images; 17 Prisma Archivo/ lamy Photo; 18 Riekephotos/Shutterstock; 22 Erik Jacobs/ he New York Times; 23 Illustration by Paul Rogers; 38 esiree Navarro/WireImage/Getty Images; 46 Dinodia hotos/Alamy Stock Photo; 47 Sueddeutsche Zeitung Photo/ lamy Photo; 51 Glasshouse Images / Alamy Stock Photo; 53 ictureLux / The Hollywood Archive / Alamy Stock Photo; 7 Andrew Churchill/Dreamstime; 62 David Livingston/ etty Images; 67 vario images GmbH & Co.KG/Alamy tock Photo; 69 Thawat Tanhai/123rf; 71 John Halpern/ etty Images; 82 Courtesy of Kathleen Kingsbury; 92 urakkarademir/iStock; 100 De2marco/Dreamstime; 117 uanyu Han/Moment/Getty Images; 121 ZUMA Press, nc. / Alamy Stock Photo; 126 The Betrothed; Os Noivos, 947 (oil on linen), Portinari, Candido (1903-62) / Private ollection / Photo © Christie's Images / Bridgeman Images; 38 Okan Bulbul © The CollegeBoard; 145 Okan Bulbul 2019 The CollegeBoard; 155 olenaboldyreva/123rf; 166 DEUTSCH Jean-Claude / Getty Images; 167 Hamill Gallery, Boston MA; 169 Everett Collection Inc / Alamy Stock Photo; 69 Andyworks/iStock; 180 Jonathan Sherrill / Alamy tock Photo; 191 Venturelli/GC Images/Getty Images; 198 NASA Pictures / Alamy Stock Photo; 205 Simon Mendez 2019 The CollegeBoard; 218 Micheline Pelletier Decaux/ Contributor/Getty Images; 226 Agence Opale / Alamy Stock Photo; 228 Macduff Everton/Corbis/VCG/Getty Images; 234 Sueddeutsche Zeitung Photo / Alamy Stock Photo; 236 ITPhoto / Alamy Stock Photo; 233 Julieta Cervantes/ Brooklyn Youth Chorus; 238 Marek Uliasz/123rf; 245 Bettmann / Contributor/Getty Images; 266 Courtesy of Eula Biss; 270 n/a 272 The Print Collector / Alamy Stock Photo; 272 James Gillray / Library of Congress; 273 North Wind Picture Archives / Alamy Stock Photo; 276 Ronald Dumont/ Daily Express/Getty Images; 291 John Kelly / Alamy Stock Photo; 297 pablohart/iStock; 319 Peter Probst / Alamy Stock Photo; 321 Photo by Justin Hofman; 338 Courtesy of Natalie Hansford; 363 Princess Victoire of Saxe-Coburg-Gotha, 2012 oil on linen, painting: 96 x 72 inches (243.8 x 182.9 cm), framed: 106 3/8 x 82 inches (270.2 x 208.3 cm) © Kehinde Wiley, Photography: Jason Wyche, New York, Courtesy: Sean Kelly, New York; 367 © Carol Coffee Reposa; 372 The Picture Art Collection / Alamy Stock Photo; 371 kameshkova/iStock; 373 © Marcus Jackson; 378 The History Collection / Alamy Stock Photo; 380 Yulia She/Shutterstock; 385 Azoor Photo / Alamy Stock Photo; 385 benoitb/Getty Images; 386 Nataba/ iStock; 389 Petrarch, Scarpelli, Tancredi (1866-1937) / Private Collection / © Look and Learn / Bridgeman Images; 391 [Public domain], via Wikimedia Commons; 396 W.H. Auden, 1951 (photo) / Private Collection / Photo © Mark Gerson / Bridgeman Images; 399 Illustrations by Nathan Gelgud; 401 © Nina Subin; 405 Rita Dove, Charlottesville, Virginia, 1994 (b/w photo) / © Chris Felver / Bridgeman Images; 407 Rose-Marie Henriksson/Shutterstock; 411 Bettmann/Getty Images; 417 Fabrice Dall'Anese/Corbis/Getty Images; 427 Ulf Andersen/Hulton Archive/Getty Images; 429 Siesta, Nerva, 2001-02 (oil on board), Barden, Valerie (Contemporary Artist) / Private Collection / © Piers Feetham Gallery, London, UK / Bridgeman Images; 451 Picturenow/Universal Images Group/Getty Images; 455 Photo by Richard Termine; 463 Windmill Books / Contributor/Getty Images; 471 Lipnitzki/Roger Viollet/Getty Images; 486 Jack Vartoogian/ Archive Photos/Getty Images; 493 Antigone from 'Antigone' by Sophocles (oil on canvas), Stillman, Marie Spartali (1844-1927) / Simon Carter Gallery, Woodbridge, Suffolk, UK / Bridgeman Images; 506 Nicolas Economou/NurPhoto/Getty Images; 516 Jean-Marc ZAORSKI/Gamma-Rapho/Getty Images; 533 Photo by Dalia Khamissy

my name is Kaden I am Ke
I live with my mom
I am tall and brown hair
I like Pizza
I like to play hockey
I like gym

Tall athletic

it is ~~the~~ nice out
I did not like this year
I am going to play golf

Je m'appell Kaden Ja says ons
Je ve avec ma mom
Je sue grand
la Pizza
jouer au ochey
gem la shem
~~grand athletic~~ il grand athletic
il fait beau
I did not like this year
Je ~~g~~ joue au golf